KROPOTKIN

KROPOTKIN

The Politics of Community

Brian Morris

Kropotkin: The Politics of Community
Brian Morris
© Brian Morris 2004
This edition © 2018 PM Press

ISBN: 978–1–62963–505–7
Library of Congress Control Number: 2017964731

Cover by John Yates / www.stealworks.com
Interior design by briandesign

10 9 8 7 6 5 4 3 2 1

PM Press
PO Box 23912
Oakland, CA 94623
www.pmpress.org

Printed in the USA by the Employee Owners of Thomson-Shore in Dexter, Michigan.
www.thomsonshore.com

TO MY LIFELONG FRIENDS

PETER AND JOYCE SHARP

"Everything that needs to be said has already been said. But since no one was listening, everything must be said again."

Andre Gide (Ehrlich 1996)

"The crackpots, faddists, and terrorists have always given anarchism a bad name and they are still with us today."

Sam Dolgoff (Avrich 1995, 231)

CONTENTS

Part Three: Historical Studies

Part Four: Anarchism

PREFACE

I have been interested in the life and work of Peter Kropotkin ever since I read his "Appeal to the Young" more than half a century ago. But the writing of the present text, intended as a critical introduction to Kropotkin's social ecology and revolutionary anarchism, was specifically prompted by two concerns.

The first was personal, for in a review of my book *Ecology and Anarchism* (Images, 1996), which was a collection of various articles and reviews, Graham Purchase had chided me for not exploring the ideas of Kropotkin, although Kropotkin always hovered in the background of my writings. I thought I owed the anarchist-geographer some serious thought.

Second, toward the end of the last century, there were many books pouring off the academic press purporting to be about philosophers of ecology. These books not only completely ignored Kropotkin but even alluded to such iconic figures as Martin Heidegger, Jürgen Habermas, and Anthony Giddens, who were seminal scholars but were not, by any stretch of the imagination, ecological thinkers. But even when academic scholars seriously engaged with Kropotkin, they invariably depicted him as a crude positivist or as a Cartesian mechanistic philosopher. On the contrary, Kropotkin, drawing on the insights of Humboldt, Darwin, and his friend Élisée Reclus—as I explore in this book—was fundamentally an evolutionary naturalist. Apart from a few notable exceptions, academic scholars derided Kropotkin's anarchism, deeming it "unrealistic" and contrary to either common sense or human nature—one liberal political theorist even suggesting that Kropotkin lived in a "veritable fairyland."

In addition, what also troubled me as the twentieth century drew to a close was that even anarchists began to dismiss his writings as "historical baggage" that needed to be jettisoned or at least given a major overhaul. Embracing, often with unwarranted enthusiasm, such contemporary "fads" as neoprimitivism, Nietzschean aesthetics, misanthropic bourgeois individualism (as Kropotkin had earlier described it), and esoteric post-modernist theory—as expressed, for example, in the pages of *Freedom* or the *Green Anarchist*—many of these critics of Kropotkin arrogantly rejected his intellectual legacy as "obsolete."

In an earlier decade I had written a short introduction to the life and work of Mikhail Bakunin (Black Rose Books, 1993), defending his political integrity against his liberal and Marxist detractors, and I was similarly motivated to write the present book to defend and uphold both the importance and the contemporary relevance of Kropotkin's legacy. As with my other writings, I have tried to keep the text free of academic pretension and jargon and to write in a style that is lucid and readable, and thus of interest to scholars, students, and radical activists alike, as well as to the general reader.

During the last decade, however, in the wake of antiglobalization demonstrations and the rise of the Occupy movement in many major cities and the Democracy Project (in its various guises), there has been a resurgence of interest in the life and work of Kropotkin. He is no longer thought of as an intellectual crackpot, and we have thus seen a plethora of essays and books exploring various aspects of his legacy. Kropotkin's seminal role with regard to the "anarchist roots" of geography has been reaffirmed, particularly his status as a pioneer earth scientist and as one of the first scholars to explore the critical importance of climate change in the earth's history. It is significant that Kropotkin's portrait hangs in the library of the Royal Geographical Society in London.

Equally important, contemporary studies continue to reinforce the value of Kropotkin's political writings—specifically those on the social, historical, scientific, and philosophical basis of the anarchist movement. For in an important sense, Kropotkin's anarchism was ecological, social-ist, and libertarian, as the present book seeks to demonstrate. Kropotkin has even been interpreted as a major critic of "classical anarchism"—a rather banal and meaningless concept invented and propagated by liberal academics.

But what has been of particular significance since the present book first appeared (in 2004) has been the publication of Iain McKay's anthol-ogy of Kropotkin's political writings, *Direct Action Against Capital* (AK Press, 2014). For what the anthology amply demonstrates is that

Kropotkin was not a starry-eyed saint, completely lost in utopian dreams, but rather a practical thinker, actively involved in the economic and political struggles of the late nineteenth century. As a revolutionary anarchist Kropotkin was deeply opposed to capitalism and the state, as well as all forms of social oppression, while envisaging in concrete terms an alternative form of society based on mutual aid, voluntary associations, and communal self-management. But as a social ecologist, Kropotkin also envisaged reconciliation and a relation of mutual cooperation, between humans and the natural world, specifically other life forms. It is Kropotkin's vision of an ecological society based on "free communism," and his wider political and philosophical legacy, that this book aims to present.

Brian Morris
May 2017

LIST OF ABBREVIATIONS

The following abbreviations appear in citations throughout this book. They refer to works listed in the first section of the bibliography, "Kropotkin's Works in English."

AY: *Act for Yourselves*
CB: *The Conquest of Bread*
E: *Ethics: Origin and Development*
EE: *Evolution and Environment*
FFW: *Fields, Factories and Workshops*
FW: *Fugitive Writings*
GFR: *The Great French Revolution 1789–1793*
KRP: *Kropotkin's Revolutionary Pamphlet*
MA: *Mutual Aid: A Factor of Evolution*
MR: *Memoirs of a Revolutionist*
RFP: *In Russian and French Prisons*
RL: *Russian Literature: Ideals and Realities*
SW: *Selected Writings on Anarchism and Revolution*
WR: *Words of a Rebel*

MK refers to M. A. Miller's biography *Kropotkin*, and WA refers to *The Anarchist Prince*, a book by G. Woodcock and I. Avakumovic. Both are listed in the third section of the bibliography, "Books and Articles on Kropotkin."

INTRODUCTION

This book consists of a series of essays that offer reflections on the political philosophy and social ecology of the revolutionary anarchist Peter Kropotkin. It has no specific thesis other than to affirm the contemporary relevance of this much-neglected scholar and political activist. But the essays do aim, overall, to provide a critical introduction to Kropotkin's social anarchism and ecological thought.

A talented geographer, an explorer in his early youth, Kropotkin was one of the most seminal figures in the history of the anarchist movement and has long been considered one of its most important theoreticians. He has been described as a unique combination of the prophet and the scientist. Although Kropotkin made many important contributions to science, throughout much of his life he was a revolutionary socialist, devoting his time and energies to the anarchist cause. His friend Errico Malatesta affirmed that Kropotkin had without doubt contributed more than anyone to the development of anarchist theory. By his exemplary life, and by generating a "treasury of fertile ideas," Kropotkin undoubtedly stirred the imagination of his generation. Not without his faults, Kropotkin was gifted with a remarkable intelligence and a generous spirit, and thus, Malatesta concluded, he was one of the "shining lights" of the anarchist movement (Richards 1965, 268). Describing Kropotkin as "my great teacher," the redoubtable Emma Goldman likewise considered Kropotkin as the most outstanding exponent of anarchist communism, and wrote that he was recognized, by friend and foe alike, as "one of the greatest minds and most unique personalities of the nineteenth century" (1931, 1:168). Indeed, what is quite remarkable and consistent is that almost all of his contempo-

raries describe Kropotkin—his intellectual stature, demeanor, and personality—in the most glowing terms. He is described as kind, hospitable,
modest, warm, and affectionate, and as "brimming over with life" and with
an interest in everything and everybody. Bernard Shaw, the Fabian
socialist, no mean critic, famously recorded that Kropotkin "was amiable
to the point of saintliness, and with his red full beard and loveable expression might have been a shepherd from the delectable mountains" (WA,
225). But Kropotkin was a human being like the rest of us; he had his faults
and blind spots, he made mistakes, he had prejudices. Yet throughout his
long life, he held fast to the commitments that he made early in his life, and
thus remained a revolutionary socialist.

This introduction has two essential aims: to affirm the contemporary
relevance of Kropotkin and the social anarchist tradition he theorized and
defended, and to outline the content of the essays that together comprise
this study.

THE CONTEMPORARY RELEVANCE OF KROPOTKIN

The philosopher Richard Rorty has recently bewailed the fact that with the
"loss of faith" in both Marxism and liberal democracy, political theory has
turned increasingly toward philosophy. It has thus rejected both history and
utopian thinking. This, Rorty reflects, has been a gesture of despair. Such
political theory, of course, has long been around. It is particularly well
exemplified in the work of John Rawls (1971) and Robert Nozick (1974),
whose well-known texts hardly engage with the real world of politics and
history. Basing their theories on the concept of "natural rights," especially
the right to property, both these scholars essentially provide a purely normative defense of, respectively, the social democratic welfare state and the
"minimal state" of neoliberalism. In contrast, as a self-confessed follower
of Dewey, Rorty affirms that "historical narrative and utopian speculation
are the best sort of background for political deliberation" (1999, 234). This
is precisely what is unique and important about Kropotkin: he always
affirmed the "utopian social hope" that Rorty now rather belatedly wishes
to resurrect in this era of disillusion, when a "mood of apocalyptic despair"
is so all-pervasive. This despair, the combined result of both capitalist triumphalism and the subjective nihilism of postmodernism (actively promoted by Rorty himself!), is, of course, the luxury of a "pampered minority
in the North, especially bourgeois intellectuals." And such despair, as

Maria Mies and others have argued, only hinders people from arriving at a realistic assessment of the present crisis, and acting accordingly, particularly in envisaging an alternative to global capitalism (Mies and Bennholdt-Thomsen 1999, 7). Rorty, of course, is a typical liberal, whose own vision hardly extends beyond a defense of liberal capitalism and the American democratic state—both of which are in crisis and under challenge. Kropotkin never succumbed to "despair"—if anything, he erred to the opposite extreme and like many of his contemporaries evinced a rather naïve "optimism," fully expecting the imminent collapse of both capitalism and the modern state. But crucial to Kropotkin's political philosophy was not only that he expressed a utopian vision of a new form of society, one based on a decentralized confederation of free communities and voluntary associations, but also that he grounded his vision not in metaphysical speculations about "rights," but in a close historical and sociological study of social institutions and political forms. In many ways, as I shall explore in these essays, Kropotkin was way ahead of his time, and his social and political thought therefore still has a contemporary relevance. Peter Singer has suggested that the "left" needs a "new paradigm," a new approach to politics that develops a "spectrum of ideas about achieving a better society" (1995, 5). Many have seen Kropotkin, and the social anarchist tradition to which he belonged, as having a crucial part to play in the development of this new paradigm and in forging alternative social institutions to those of global capitalism (Ehrlich 1996; Macauley 1998; Bookchin 1999).

It is widely recognized by scholars across the political spectrum that the world is in a sorry mess and that there is a "global problematique," that both capitalism and the democratic nation-state are in "crisis." The "modern crisis" is reflected in four basic problems of unprecedented magnitude that now confront the world.

The *first* is an economic crisis, for under global capitalism there has been a growing concentration of economic power and the continuous expansion of economic inequalities. It is estimated that the four hundred richest people in the world have a combined wealth greater than the bottom 45 percent of the world's population—some 2.3 billion people. Over a billion people at the present time live on less than $400 per year (Singer 1999, 9). Not surprisingly, rampant poverty exists throughout the world, but particularly in Latin America and Africa. It is estimated that around 20 percent (one billion) of the world's population is suffering from absolute poverty; that is, these people are unable to obtain the basic conditions of human survival. Such poverty is not integral to the human condition, as some economists misleadingly contend, but is directly related to the "development" (i.e., the expansion of capitalism) advocated by neoliberalism. The impact of global capitalism has thus led to an increasing polarization of the rich and the poor and widespread poverty, particularly among rural women. This in turn has led to growing class, gender, ethnic, and religious conflict.

Second, there is the problem of the widespread existence of weapons of mass destruction (nuclear, chemical, biological) and the very high level of military spending that exists throughout the world. This is spent not only on weapons of mass destruction (which constitute only about 20 percent of global military spending) but on conventional weapons, research, and the militia. This stockpiling, however, can hardly be said to have kept the peace, for since the Second World War, there have been well over a hundred major wars in all parts of the world, killing millions of people. This state of affairs, and the aggression and insecurity that it engenders, is intrinsically linked to global capitalism.

Third, throughout the world one finds what has been described as a "dialectic of violence" reflected in the disintegration of local communities, the denial of human rights, widespread genocide, and political oppression by governments. Western governments, particularly the United States, have given full, even if covert, support to the most oppressive regimes and dictators—and still do, despite the rhetoric of "human rights." Chomsky's important writings on state-sponsored terrorism emphasized that military force was used not so much to bolster dictators as to keep the world open to the "fifth freedom"—the freedom to rob, to exploit and to dominate, and to undertake any course of action that ensures that the existing privileges enjoyed by U.S. capitalism are protected and advanced (1988, 1–7; Shiva 1998, 113). But equally important, many political writers, including many liberals, have emphasized that the impact of free-market capitalism, which has been a political project, has been socially devastating, not only leading to social inequalities and widespread poverty, but also to social chaos and political instability. The costs of neo-liberal capitalism has been one "of crime, incarceration, racial and ethnic conflict and family and community breakdown" (Gray 1998, 216).

Fourth, there is an "ecological crisis," reflected in the widespread pollution of the atmosphere, deforestation, increasing desertification, the creation of toxic wastelands, and a loss of species diversity. All this has led to the degradation of the environment generally and to a deterioration in the quality of life for many human communities. Indeed, some ecologists have argued that our environment is becoming ever less capable of sustaining the growing impact of our economic activities. But as Murray Bookchin (1999) has consistently argued, this "ecological crisis" is not simply due to over-population, or to technology per se, or to "anthropocentric" social attitudes, but rather is a direct result of an economic system that is intrinsically geared to expansion and profit.

All these four problems are intrinsically interlinked by what Paul Ekins describes as a "single, systematic problematique of great complexity" (1992, 13). Unlike other scholars, Ekins seems reluctant to give this "prob-lematique" a name; it is, of course, global capitalism that is the underlying cause of all four problems—the poverty and social inequality, the "military machine," the widespread repression and social disintegration, and the environmental crisis.

Yet as we move into the twenty-first century, the doyens of sociology and political theory in addressing these problems present us with a rather bleak future scenario. Hence the mood of despair that Rorty describes. We are therefore now at a point in history when the need for a new political vision is increasingly becoming an imperative—as many social anarchists have continually affirmed (Clark 1984; Ehrlich 1996; Biehl 1998). Yet all contemporary political projects—neoliberalism, social democracy, Marxism, and postmodernism (we can leave aside fascism and religious fun-damentalism)—are problematic, if not plain redundant. Neoliberalism, as advocated by the likes of Hayek, Ayn Rand, and Nozick, and by current cap-italist agencies like the World Bank and G.A.T.T. (General Agreement on Tariffs and Trade), is essentially a political project that portends only author-itarian government and laissez-faire capitalism—that is, more of the same—more economic inequality, more social disintegration, more poverty, more political repression, more ecological degradation. It is hardly to be won-dered then that liberal scholars are searching around for alternatives to neoliberalism. One well-known sociologist offers us a "third way" (between neoliberalism and Marxism). It is, however, a philosophy of despair. For Anthony Giddens argues that we need to orient ourselves to a world "where there are no alternatives to capitalism." Global capitalism seemingly rules the world, and all we can do, we are informed, is to argue about "how far, and in what ways capitalism should be governed and regulated" (1998, 43). On the other hand, liberal academics like John Gray have offered powerful critiques of global capitalism. Gray's study *False Dawn* (1998) is indeed one long polemic against the neoliberals—those "ranting evangelists" for global capitalism, as he describes them, and he emphasizes that the impact of global capitalism has been socially devastating. Gray details with some passion the impact of global capitalism—the "problematique" noted above—economic dislocation, increasing social inequalities, widespread poverty, social alienation, and political instability. He even speaks of the "incompatibility" of free-market capitalism with liberal democracy. Yet all that Gray can offer as a political alternative to global capitalism is a plurality of "capitalisms" and a new regime of "global governance." His politics thus differs little from that advocated by Giddens.

Other critics of global capitalism, like Bourdieu (1998) and Bauman (1999), who both present powerful critiques of the "new world *disorder*," seem equally bereft of any political vision. Bourdieu advocates neither the abolition of capitalism nor of the democratic state, but he simply bewails the fact that under neoliberal doctrines the state has regressed into a "repressive" policing agency and has abandoned its welfare functions.

For Bourdieu the state needs to be restored as the "guardian of public interest." As an old-fashioned state socialist Bourdieu thus concludes that alongside social movements and trade unions, a "special place" must be reserved for the state, or better still, a "supranational" or European state, capable of controlling the ill-effects of capitalism (1998, 104). He thus fails to recognize, like Giddens and Gray, that these new forms of "global governance" are precisely functional to the further development of global capitalism. Zygmunt Bauman, in contrast, affirms what Kropotkin had long ago argued, namely, that "individuals cannot be free unless they are free to institute a society which promotes and guards their freedom; unless they institute together an agency capable of achieving just that" (1999, 107). But the agency that Bauman has in mind is a "public space," an Agora or civil society, that seemingly mediates between the Ecclesia (the democratic state) and the Oikos (the economy, i.e., global capitalism). Thus, all these four contemporary scholars, whatever their differences as social democratic theorists, take for granted the present institutional framework, as defined by representative democracy and global capitalism.

Since the collapse of Soviet Communism, many Marxists, it seems, are undergoing an identity crisis. Marxist intellectuals like Robin Blackburn are beginning to take seriously the anarchist critique of Marx and the Bolsheviks, while at the same time searching around for some theory—other than anarchism—that might affirm their continuing radicalism. Abandoning orthodox Marxism, such intellectuals often end up embracing some form of social democracy. Blackburn seems to take his inspiration from the liberal economist Von Hayek, one of the gurus of Thatcherism (Blackburn 1991). Other Marxists have been moving in other directions to embrace a plethora of different guises—market socialism, identity politics, guild socialism, and even "post-Marxism," which entails the dissolution of social reality into discourses and the abandonment of class politics (see Wood 1986 for a critique of these latter-day Marxists). But however one interprets the concept of "dictatorship of the proletariat" or the role of a "revolutionary government," the classical conception of Marxism (and of Bolshevism and Maoism) is clearly obsolete as an alternative to global capitalism, given the tyranny exhibited by its "actually existing" forms (Cleaver 1996). Kropotkin, of course, along with many later anarchists (Rudolf Rocker, Emma Goldman, Voline, Gregory Petrovich Maximoff), long ago critiqued the Soviet Union and the form of authoritarian "state capitalism" (as they and Lenin described it) that was established by the Bolshevik regime.

Neoliberalism, social democracy, and Marxism have thus all failed the litmus test. Capitalism, as Marx and Engels graphically described it in *The Communist Manifesto* (1848), is of its very nature revolutionary. As a mode of production therefore it continually generates disruptions and dislocations in all areas of social life, an "everlasting uncertainty," sweeping away "ancient traditions." Capitalism then has always had a "cosmopolitan character," and the result of its impact is that—in the now-famous phrase—"all that is solid melts into air" (Marx and Engels 1968, 38). Thus the so-called postmodern condition—with its alienation, fragmentation, nihilism, cultural pastiche, relativistic theory, and "decentred subjectivity"—is not so much a new epoch but rather one of the cultural effects of global capitalism. But while Marx—along with Nietzsche and Kropotkin—saw this social condition as lamentable, as involving alienation and nihilism, as something to be overcome by a social transformation (Marx, Kropotkin) or the formation of a cultural elite *Ubermensch* ("over-man," Nietzsche)—surprise, surprise, we have in the last two decades seen the emergence of many "postmodern" intellectuals who seem to applaud or to wallow in this detached and disoriented condition. All the time, of course, continuing to enjoy a secure and easy life ensconced in some elite academy. Although some of these postmodern intellectuals have offered ultraradical critiques of "Power" or the "state apparatus" or an equally reified "hyperreality"— and thus the likes of Deleuze, Lyotard, Baudrillard, and Derrida have often misleadingly been described anarchists—one searches in vain among their opaque and obscurantist writings for any real social and political alternative to capitalism. Indeed, as Sadie Plant suggested, the nihilistic and relativistic theories of the postmodernists are unable to provide the meaning, purpose, or even a grasp of reality that all theories require if they are "to be put to any critical use in the understanding and transformation of experience" (1996, 170). No wonder the postmodernists have been described as neoconservatives. Indeed in their rejection of history, in reducing social reality to discourses, in their epistemic relativism, and in their seeming obsession with consumer capitalism, many have remarked that there seems to be an "unholy alliance" or an "exact fit" between such postmodern theorists and the capitalist triumphalism of the neoliberals. Postmodernism has in fact been described as a new Platonic idealism that has depoliticized both philosophy and the social sciences. It therefore offers little in the way of an alternative vision to global capitalism (for critiques of postmodernist politics from quite different perspectives, see Bookchin 1995, 172–204; Wood and Foster 1997; Mies and Bennholdt-Thomsen 1999, 198–201; on their sham scholarship and obscurantism, see Sokal and Bricmont 1999).

In this climate of "apocalyptic despair" and given the virtual absence of any credible alternative to neoliberalism, it behooves us, I think, to seriously reconsider the social and political writings of Kropotkin and the social anarchist tradition to which he belonged. Not simply as a "wreck" that needs to be salvaged, as suggested by David Miller (1984), nor as something that has to be rescued from the "historical dustbin" simply because it provides a corrective to all those who might "abuse" power and to remind us that noncoercive relationships are both possible and worthwhile. But rather as a viable and important political tradition in its own right, for Kropotkin's social anarchism offers, as John Clark rightly argued, the only viable alternative to democratic liberalism and Marxism, both of which, as we have noted, are now politically bankrupt. There is now a growing disillusionment with both liberal capitalism and state socialism, for these two world systems "no longer offer us a hopeful prospect of resolving the vast social and ecological crises that now confront humanity" (Clark 1984, 141). An alternative vision of society is therefore necessary, and the social and political writings of Kropotkin are an important and seminal contribution to this task of "re-enchanting" humanity as Bookchin (1995) describes this vision. These essays thus aim to provide a critical account of Kropotkin's anarchist philosophy, one that is evidently needed, for Kropotkin has been sadly neglected by academics. In the bookshops there are literally scores of texts on the political philosophies of, for example, Mill, Nietzsche, Heidegger, and Foucault, but apart from Graham Purchase's (1996) excellent primer, there is absolutely nothing on Kropotkin. This is somewhat surprising, given that Kropotkin's name continually crops up in many domains of scholarship, and anarchists have always attempted to keep his memory green and his writings in circulation, even though some bourgeois individualists and aesthetes, with some pretension, have described Kropotkin's writings as "obsolete."

As my main concern is expository, to offer the reader a critical account of Kropotkin's social and political theory, I have quoted liberally from Kropotkin's own writings, both to give the flavor of his work and to avoid any misunderstandings. As I have, inevitably, had to limit the scope of my study, I do not examine Kropotkin's scientific writings relating to geomorphology, his studies of Russian literature, and his numerous discussions of the revolutionary situation in Russia (on Kropotkin's importance as a geographer, see Keltie 1921, Breitbart 1981; on the revolution in Russia, see Kropotkin 1895, 1905; KRP, 252–59; SW, 135–58).

And in many of the essays I have also been unable to fully explore the many implications of Kropotkin's thought, for example, to include a more extensive discussion of the debates relating to alternatives to the prison system, sociobiology, poststructuralism, and the current enthusiasm for market socialism among many political theorists.

I have also tried to situate Kropotkin within the context of his own time—the late nineteenth century—and have thus not felt it necessary to continually berate Kropotkin for his lack of a gender perspective, or for his archaic language, or for his occasional positivistic enthusiasms, or for the fact that he naively thought a social revolution was imminent. I have tried to approach his work with an attitude of critical sympathy.

Of all political philosophies, anarchism has always had perhaps the worst press. It has been ignored, maligned, ridiculed, abused, misunderstood, and misrepresented by writers from all sides of the political spectrum—Marxists, liberals, democrats, and conservatives. Theodore Roosevelt, the American president, described anarchism as a "crime against the whole human race"—and it has been variously judged destructive, violent, and nihilistic. For some, anarchism is almost a synonym for terrorism and disorder, and anarchists themselves "muddled preachers of chaos" (Ritter 1980, 1). The Marxist historian Eric Hobsbawm thought of anarchism as a "tragic farce" belonging to a preindustrial era and to be little more than a "local problem" for the Bolsheviks (1973, 83). One Liberal scholar went further and considered Kropotkin's anarchism so contrary to common sense and "unrealistic" as to be unworthy of serious attention (Lancaster 1959, 261–63). The aim of this book is to suggest otherwise; to affirm that Kropotkin, and the social anarchism that he theorized and defended, is worth taking seriously.

The Contents of the Study

The study consists of four parts. In the first part, I outline Kropotkin's theory of social anarchism, which he himself described as anarchist communism. In chapter 1, I discuss Kropotkin's conception of a social revolution, for like many of his contemporaries, Kropotkin thought a revolution was imminent. Basing his ideas on what he felt had happened during the French Revolution (1789–1793), Kropotkin suggested that the coming revolution would be a popular insurrection and have two essential dimensions—a rejection of government and the expropriation by the peasants and all urban workers of all land, property, and instruments of production. He thus emphasized the need to strive for economic democracy and social justice and to activate a "spirit of revolt." Within the chapter I discuss Kropotkin's important critiques of capitalism (particularly private property and the wage system) and of government, both representative democracy and the "revolutionary government" of the Marxists that Kropotkin felt, with some prescience, would only lead to tyranny. Kropotkin argued that anarchism and communism combined two currents of thought—radical liberalism, which placed an emphasis on individual freedom and the negation of the state (anarchism), and libertarian socialism, which, stridently anticapitalist, opposed both private property and the wage system (communism).

Like many of his socialist contemporaries, including Marx, Kropotkin always expressed a deep interest in the Paris Commune, the revolutionary insurrection of 1871. Kropotkin's views on the Paris Commune are explored in chapter 2. While Marx thought of the Paris Commune as exemplifying a future "worker's state" and Bakunin considered it a form of anarchy, Kropotkin, in contrast, was far more skeptical. It was important for what it promised, Kropotkin argued, not for what it achieved, for the Paris commune retained both private property and representative government. Nevertheless it indicated for Kropotkin one of the most important social trends of the nineteenth century, the growing significance of free communes, voluntary associations, and mutual aid societies. Adopting the principle "from each according to his ability, to each according to his need," Kropotkin felt that social and individual needs could and should be organized and met through the local community and voluntary associations, not through the state or the market. I conclude the chapter with a discussion of Michael Taylor's (1982) defense of communitarian anarchism, which simply provides an update of Kropotkin's own theory of anarchist communism.

In chapter 3, I outline Kropotkin's own response to the various criticisms that have been leveled at anarchist communism and his seminal and rather neglected critique of the prison system. Kropotkin, in constructive fashion, tried to address all the familiar "objections" to anarchism—that it was simply a utopian dream fit only for saints, that coercive government was necessary to ensure social order and to prevent antisocial behavior, and that without compulsion nobody would bother to keep agreements or even work. Kropotkin took these criticisms seriously and tried to address them not metaphysically but in concrete terms. He was particularly anxious to make a distinction between coercive labor and creative work and to emphasize that social order could be maintained through the community rather than through state institutions. Kropotkin makes telling criticisms of both the concept of "law" and the prison system. He argued that punitive treatment does not act as a deterrent and so reduce crime, nor does it in any way serve to "reform" the prisoner. Kropotkin thus concludes that the whole system of prisons and coercive punishment should be abolished, believing that freedom, fraternity, and the practice of human solidarity is the only way of dealing, humanely, with antisocial behavior (for a recent discussion on the abolition of prisons, see James 1998, 96–107).

In the final two chapters of part 1, I deal with Kropotkin's practical suggestions on economic life and education. In chapter 4, I discuss Kropotkin's concrete proposals for the establishment of a viable social economy, one that implied the decentralization of industry, the production of food through intensive horticulture, and the need to combine, on a communal basis, agriculture and industrial workshops. Unlike his friend William Morris, Kropotkin was not hostile to technology per se and advocated the rational use of technology to ease the burden of overwork. I emphasize too that the kind of moral economy envisaged by Kropotkin opposed the factory system, the state ownership of land and capital and thus all "nationalization" or "collectivist" schemes, large-scale capitalist agriculture (which he felt depopulated the countryside and degraded the environment), as well as various forms of petty-commodity production advocated by many individualist anarchists. I conclude the chapter by briefly discussing the work of three contemporary scholars—Schumacher, Sale, and Bookchin—to indicate the enduring influence of Kropotkin's writings. Indeed, in a recent important text, Maria Mies advocates what she describes as a "subsistence perspective" that in all its essential features— an emphasis on self-provisioning and subsistence production, a decentralized regional economy, an advocacy of reciprocal exchange and direct democracy within the local community, and the repudiation of wage labor—simply echo Kropotkin's seminal ideas published a century ago (cf. Mies and Bennholdt-Thomsen 1999).

In chapter 5, I focus on Kropotkin's educational ideas, for although Kropotkin wrote little on education, he schematically outlined what he described as an "integral education." This implied a need to combine intellectual knowledge with manual skills, in order that every person could not only be involved in productive tasks but also live a full and diversified life. I note the important influence of Kropotkin on the "modern school" movement in the United States.

In part 2, I outline Kropotkin's metaphysics of nature and his social ethics. Richard De Haan has written that "there is no denying it, Kropotkin is hopelessly nineteenth century" (1965, 273), in that in his writings Kropotkin often expressed a rather positivistic outlook—reductionist, mechanistic, with allusions to the "laws of nature." But nevertheless Kropotkin was acutely aware that the advances in scientific knowledge that has occurred at the end of the nineteenth century, particularly evolutionary theory, had profoundly altered our conceptions of the universe, especially the place of human life within nature. As a basis for his political theory, Kropotkin therefore came to develop, in embryonic form, a new metaphysics of nature, which may be described as evolutionary holism. This new philosophy affirmed the importance of scientific materialism (as opposed to abstract metaphysics and religious mysticism) and a dialectical approach to the world. Although Kropotkin explicitly repudiated Hegelian dialectics, I suggest in chapter 6 that Kropotkin and Engels shared, in fact, a common philosophical outlook. I go on to outline the basic themes of this new evolutionary holism: an attempt to combine humanism and naturalism, an acknowledgement that evolutionary theory had completely undermined the Newtonian mechanistic conception of nature, and a recognition that there are several emergent levels of being, which implies the need for epistemological diversity in understanding the ontological unity of the world. I emphasize that Kropotkin's seminal ideas find a resonance in contemporary chaos theory and evolutionary biology. Kropotkin's evolutionary holism thus makes completely redundant the dichotomy—as expressed by Rorty (1999)—between an ultrarationalist Platonism (misleading conflated with the correspondence theory of truth) and the currently fashionable post-Nietzchean relativism and nihilism.

In the following chapter, I focus specifically on Kropotkin's biological writings and particularly his theory of mutual aid. After outlining the basic ideas that constitute Darwin's evolutionary paradigm—common descent, natural selection, speciation, and so on—I emphasize the important philosophical implications of this paradigm that undermined completely the mechanistic world-picture, along with its anthropocentrism, dualistic metaphysics, and essentialism. Wholeheartedly acknowledging Darwin's theory of evolution, Kropotkin's studies of mutual aid were motivated primarily by the need to counter the Hobbesian thesis of the "survival of the fittest." This thesis was being propagated in the nineteenth century by Spencer and Huxley, as well as being utilized as a justification of laissez-faire capitalism. Kropotkin attempted to demonstrate, through a wealth of biological data, that mutual aid and sociality was evident throughout the animal kingdom and was an important factor in evolution. I conclude chapter 7 by examining Kropotkin's neo-Lamarckian views on the "direct action" of the environment on living species and recent theories of symbiosis. But I emphasize that although Kropotkin stressed the continuity between natural ecology and social life, he rejected biological determinism and depicted the evolutionary process as implying spontaneity, potentiality, and openness, rather than natural law and a "pre-determined order" (Heller 1999, 125–29).

Kropotkin's ethical theory is largely a development of his studies of mutual aid, and chapter 8 is devoted to discussing Kropotkin's treatise on *Ethics*, which consists largely of a historical survey of various ethical theories. Kropotkin, in the study, puts a sustained emphasis on those moral philosophers who have been important in the development of a naturalistic approach to ethics. For Kropotkin the key figures are Epicurus, Francis Bacon, Benedict de Spinoza, Adam Smith, Herbert Spencer, and Charles Darwin. Kropotkin's own theory, which may be described as a form of ethical naturalism, stressed that the moral sentiment has its "origins" in the sociality and mutual aid that is inherent in the social life of animals, and that the "function" of morality is to sustain orderly social life. Kropotkin thus argues that morality has three essential elements—sociality (or sympathy), justice (or equity), and magnanimity, or morality proper. This third element, unique to humans, is manifested in the help or support that people give to others without thought or expectancy of reward. In the chapter, I discuss the telling criticisms that Kropotkin makes of alternative ethical theories—the idealist metaphysics of Plato, eudemonism (Epicurus), utilitarianism (Jeremy Bentham, John Stuart Mill), and the ethical rationalism of Kant. I conclude the chapter by responding to Kropotkin's many critics who have tended to dismiss his work on the grounds that Kropotkin committed the so-called naturalistic fallacy, deducing moral precepts from facts about the world. Drawing on the work of Warnock and Dennett, I defend Kropotkin's ethical naturalism.

Part 3 examines Kropotkin's historical studies—on tribal society, on the origins of the modern state and on radical aspects of the French Revolution. In chapter 9, I discuss Kropotkin's anthropological studies of tribal society, especially hunter-gatherers, and his determined effort to counter the Hobbesian view of such societies, which depicted tribal people as aggressive and isolated egoists, constantly engaged in warfare. From his own contacts with tribal people, and from a scholarly examination of the ethnographic record, Kropotkin argued that tribal peoples have a complex social life, a close intimacy with the natural world, high standards of morality, and social forms in which an ethic of generosity and sharing co-exists with an equal emphasis on individual autonomy. Tribal people thus expressed a form of anarchist communism. Kropotkin clearly recognized that "possessive individualism" was not a feature of tribal society but was rather a concomitant of industrial capitalism. This led Kropotkin to make a clear distinction between two forms of individualism: possessive or instrumental individualism and a form of individualism that Alan Ritter was later to describe as "communal individuality" (1980, 3). Kropotkin was thus not a libertarian but rather emphasized what he described as individualism, *pro sibi communisticum*, the mutual interdependence of individuality and community. I conclude the chapter with a discussion of Susan Brown's study *The Politics of Individualism* and respond to some of the misinterpretations of Kropotkin's anarchism that have been made by recent scholars. In an important sense, as William McKercher argues, Kropotkin belonged to the British Libertarian Socialist tradition that emphasized that the freedom of the individual was impossible without a community of equals (1989, 11). Although Kropotkin's portrayal of tribal society was sympathetic and has been confirmed by recent anthropological studies, Kropotkin never romanticized tribal life, nor did he advocate anarcho-primitivism, which has currently become rather fashionable in some urban contexts, especially by writers critical of what Mumford called the megamachine (Mumford 1970; D. Watson 1999).

Chapter 10 examines Kropotkin's theory of the modern state, its historical origins, and its role in the modern world. The "State" was always of crucial importance for anarchists like Kropotkin, for they challenged the Marxist theory that a future socialist society would be ushered in by a "worker's state," by a socialist party appropriating state power—"the dictatorship of the proletariat." It was important then for Kropotkin to understand what was the essential nature of the modern state. Kropotkin, of course, recognized that humans had lived in societies for thousands of years before the emergence of the state, and he recognized too that a crucial distinction needed to be made between the everyday social life of people and the state, something singularly lacking in writers like Fredy Perlman (1983). In his well-known "rant," Perlman seems to envisage nothing between hunter-gatherers living in an idyllic "state of nature" and the "Beast" (Leviathan)—a rubric under which he conflates civilization, the state, capitalism, modern technology, and even Western culture more generally. Perlman's linear conception of human history (an inversion of the "myth of progress"), his Eurocentrism and his Gnostic vision, thus completely denies the existence of human communities and the moral economy on which not only human life depends but upon which the "Beast" itself is parasitic and "colonizes" (Mies and Bennholdt-Thomson 1999). The only response to the "monster" Leviathan (specifically global capitalism and the state) that Perlman seems to offer is to rant, dance, write poetry, or to retreat alone, like the "mountain men" of old, into the so-called North American wilderness. Kropotkin's understanding of the rise of the modern bureaucratic state is much more nuanced, and though he repudiated both the state and capitalism, as well as certain modes of Western thought, Kropotkin never indulged in the Gnostic dismissal of "civilization" (literacy, metallurgy, artisan production, urban living, and agriculture)—as do contemporary "primitivists" (Zerzan 1994; D. Watson 1999).

Kropotkin saw the modern state as emerging around the sixteenth century, and he thought it, like all social phenomena, explicable in terms of a variety of different factors. These include: the concentration of power around such cities as Moscow, London, and Paris, which involved the coalescence of military power and economic wealth; the role of religion in sanctifying the power of the ruling dynasty; the reactivation of Roman Law and the development of an ideology relating to the "arts" of government; and the growing hegemony of the monarchy over the feudal lords and the "free cities" that had emerged from the tenth century onward. Kropotkin had, in fact, a particular interest in the medieval city, not because he advocated a city-state (as same of his critics misleadingly allege) but because he saw the city, with its guilds, voluntary associations, charters, and assemblies, as exhibiting patterns of social life that were independent of the territorial state. Kropotkin no more romanticized the medieval city than he did tribal society, but for Kropotkin both exhibited positive features and thus offered pointers to the development of a truly anarchist communist society. Kropotkin did not view human history as simply a history of progress: nor did he follow Christian eschatology, like Perlman, and view history as a "fall" from grace, from an Eden-like "golden age" of "pure anarchy" (hunter-gathering), and so interpret human history entirely in terms of the development of the "Beast"—the state, capitalism, and the megamachine. Kropotkin's approach was more nuanced and dialectical, for he saw the need to retain and build on what is best in human civilization, while eliminating the horrors associated with the "Beast." As with Bookchin, Kropotkin felt that there were two sides to the history of humanity—a legacy of domination (the "beast") and a legacy of freedom: "The legacy of freedom is the history of ever-expanding struggles for emancipation, while the legacy of domination is the chronicle of domination and all its brutalities" (Bookchin 1999, 278). These two have interacted and competed with each other in a truly dialectical fashion throughout history (KRP, 147; see Bookchin 1982).

To conclude the chapter, I discuss Kropotkin's views on nationalism and the role of national liberation movements.

In chapter 11, I explore recent critiques of classical anarchism offered by poststructuralist philosophers, who contend that anarchists like Kropotkin were blind to the more subtle forms of power and saw power only as negative and coercive. Kropotkin focused, it is suggested, narrowly on the state, and assumed that humans had a "benign essence" and failed to recognize that "power" is creative and productive. As much of the inspiration for this critique stems from Michel Foucault, I review, in the first part of this chapter, Foucault's theory of power. In essence, Foucault argued that at the end of the eighteenth century new modes of exercising power came into existence in Europe, techniques that he saw as fundamentally linked to the development of industrial capitalism. I discuss this new economy of power under a number of related concepts that Foucault himself employed—biopower, disciplinary power, pastoral power, and governmentality. I stress that Foucault saw a dialectical relationship existing between state power and these new techniques of governance and that their "productivity" refers to the fact that social control and regulation is achieved through noncoercive means, rather than they are positive in a normative sense. I emphasize that Foucault saw an intrinsic relationship between power and knowledge, and that "power" is seen by Foucault as forming a "network" that penetrates diverse aspects of the "social body"—sexuality, the body, economic life, the family, knowledge. I then go on to critique Foucault's rather totalizing theory of power, while at the same time clarifying the anarchist approach to power and authority. For Kropotkin recognized the intrusive nature of the modern state, and he was not simply anti-statist but challenged all forms of hierarchy and domination that curtailed the free development of the person—the existential individualism that Kropotkin advocated. I also suggest that Kropotkin was not an intellectual simpleton or utopian, who preached "unlimited freedom" or dreamed of a society where power had simply ceased to exist.

Chapter 12 is devoted to a discussion of Kropotkin's study of the French Revolution, Kropotkin's interest in the revolution being lifelong. Although his popular narrative of the revolution has tended to be ignored by academic historians, it is a pioneering study, for it outlines in some detail the important role that peasant insurrections, urban revolts, and the *enrages* (extremists) played in the French Revolution. The revolution itself Kropotkin interpreted as the combination of a current of revolutionary ideas held by the bourgeois radicals, which stemmed from the Enlightenment, and the revolutionary actions and continual revolts of the peasants and urban workers. Kropotkin emphasized that the French Revolution had three important outcomes: the return of the land to the peasantry, the abolition of feudalism and the undermining of the powers of the landed aristocracy, and an end to political absolutism. But for Kropotkin what was crucial about the revolution was the emergence of a popular movement and socialist ideas among the "sections" of the Paris Commune, a political movement that most clearly expressed the slogan of the revolution: liberty, equality, fraternity. Throughout the chapter I attempt to situate Kropotkin's work within contemporary debates on the French Revolution.

Part 4 is devoted to anarchism, both as a movement and as a political tradition. In chapter 13, I outline Kropotkin's history of the anarchist movement. For Kropotkin anarchism took two forms: on the one hand, it was inherent in social life itself and had coexisted with other social tendencies throughout history—being expressed in the writings of many scholars and in various social and religious movements that had resisted hierarchical power. On the other hand, anarchism was seen as a specific historical movement and political theory that had its origins at the end of the eighteenth century. It was William Godwin, Kropotkin felt, who had first stated in coherent form the basic principles of anarchism. But Kropotkin recognized also the important role played by Pierre-Joseph Proudhon and Mikhail Bakunin in the development of anarchism (libertarian socialism) within the European Labour movement, as this focused around the International Workingmen's Association. Kropotkin identified several forms of anarchism—the "mutualist" forms of individualist anarchism associated with Proudhon, Josiah Warren, and Benjamin Tucker; the "pure" or strident individualism that was advocated by Max Stirner and Friedrich Nietzsche; literary anarchism (expressed, for example, by Walt Whitman, Henrik Ibsen, and Kropotkin's friend Edward Carpenter); and the Christian pacifist anarchism associated with the followers of Leo Tolstoy. But the most prominent form of anarchism during the latter part of the nineteenth century was that advocated by Kropotkin himself—revolutionary socialism or anarchist communism. The identification of socialism with the "worship of authority" and nostalgic reaction—the veneration of the past and hierarchical values (John Ruskin, Henry Mayers Hyndman) or with centralized power and a planned economy (Henri de Saint-Simon, Vladimir Lenin, Adolf Hitler, Joseph Stalin)—seems to ignore completely the libertarian Socialist tradition that Kropotkin represented. No wonder some radical scholars want to dispense with the term "socialism," although they are bereft of any alternative project (G. Watson 1998; Cleaver 1996).

At the turn of the century, Kropotkin made telling criticism of the kind of individualism that was prophetically proclaimed by Stirner and Nietzsche. This kind of individualism, under the umbrella of "anarchy," has recently been reclaimed and reaffirmed by neoprimitivists, bourgeois aesthetes, and postmodernist theorists. But Stirner's anarchism was, for Kropotkin, rather limited, in that Stirner repudiated neither property nor the state in his sanctification of the unique "ego." Property, according to Stirner, "should not and cannot be abolished," for the ego is a "proprietor" and can lay claim to any object, creature, or person that the ego has power over. "I do not want the liberty of men, nor their equality; I want only *my* power over them, I want to make them my property, material for enjoyment" (1973, 318). Similarly with regard to the state: "I myself, decide over life and death of others, and not the state. Notions like theft and murder disappear before the sovereignty of the Ego" (Stirner quoted in Graur 1997, 49). Egoism, property, selfishness, power over others—these are important for Stirner, not love, community, mercy, gentleness, good nature, justice, or equity, for "no-one is a person to be respected," only an "object" for my use and enjoyment (Stirner 1973, 311). Unlike contemporary advocates of "anarchy," Kropotkin firmly repudiated this form of amoral individualism. Similarly with Nietzsche. Not by any stretch of the imagination was Nietzsche an anarchist. As forms of "decadence" or "nihilism," Nietzsche repudiated not only Christianity, but socialism, Buddhism, anarchism, dialectics, and all forms of morality as this is understood by ordinary mortals—sympathy toward others, kindness, love, nurturance, altruism, even the pity a woman may feel for a child. Morality, as Nietzsche defined it, was antilife. Expressing a rather ultra-Darwinian perspective, Nietzsche equated life with the "will to power," and the "drive to dominate," and thus sanctified the virtues associated with the aristocracy—nobility, courage, heroism, the experience of power, reverence for hierarchy, and tradition. As he put it, "Life itself is essentially appropriation, injury, overpowering of the strange and weaker, suppression, severity, imposition of one's own forms, exploitation . . . the intrinsic will to power is precisely the will to life" (1972, 175).

Taking Nietzsche at his word, as one critic puts it, one has to recognize that Nietzsche is not simply antisocialist but thoroughly reactionary (Landa 1999). Indeed, Nietzsche expressed in his writings what he often felt, a "contempt" for humanity (1968, 149). Even his apologists have to admit that Nietzsche's instincts were "profoundly undemocratic in almost every respect" (Chamberlain 1996, 41). But Nietzsche's alternative to democracy, the "rule of the rabble" as he described it, was not anarchism, which he considered decadent and degenerate (1968, 180), but rather autocracy and aristocratic rule. Not surprisingly, he praised the caste system in India, the Roman Empire, and the tsarist autocracy in Russia and considered democracy as the "decaying form" of the state (1968, 93). The very core of twentieth century intellectual life has been described as "decidedly Nietzschean" (Landa 1999, 4). But while many postmodernists have heralded Nietzsche as an important critic of modernity, Kropotkin tended to see this sad "wanderer" as almost the apotheosis of modernity and was highly critical of Nietzsche's advocacy of the "free spirit" and his "Dionysian aestheticism" if taken to extremes. Certainly Nietzsche's politics are almost the antithesis to those of Kropotkin.

In chapter 14, I examine Kropotkin's attitude toward terrorism and war. It has been the tendency of many scholars, and I specifically explore the writings of Max Nomad and Barbara Tuchman, to interpret the history of anarchism as having had a "dual nature"—consisting, on the one hand, of the activities of gentle scholars like Kropotkin, utopians completely out of touch with reality, and, on the other, of anarchist terrorists bent on mindless destruction and criminality. They then came to conclude that Kropotkin, for all his saintliness, was an advocate of terrorism. In the chapter, I attempt to show that this portrait of anarchism and Kropotkin is quite misleading and that although Kropotkin advocated a social revolution and the "spirit of revolt," he was never an enthusiast of "propaganda by the deed"—if by "deed" is meant individual acts of terrorism. But I suggest that Kropotkin's attitude to violence was ambivalent, and in the final sections of the chapter

I explore Kropotkin's attitude specifically to war and the reasons that led Kropotkin to abandon his anarchist principles and support the Allies at the outbreak of the First World War.

In the final chapter, I discuss Kropotkin's views on anarcho-syndicalism, a movement of revolutionary socialism that was particularly strong in France prior to the First World War. Kropotkin felt that this movement had its origins among the Bakunists in the First International. It shared with Kropotkin's own anarchist communism three essential tenets: a repudiation of individual terrorism, a critique and rejection of the parliamentary road to socialism, and the complete disavowal of the Marxist concept of the "dictatorship of the proletariat" by means of a revolutionary party. But Kropotkin was always skeptical of an overemphasis on trade unions, even though he supported the London dock strike of 1889 and the strategy of "direct action," for Kropotkin recognised the tendency of trade unions to be reformist in their aims—in colluding with the capitalist system—and authoritarian in their organization. Kropotkin therefore envisaged a social revolution as essentially involving an economic struggle and to entail a federation of syndicates (worker's unions), cooperative associations, and local communities—the free commune. But Kropotkin was equally skeptical of forming isolated communities or communist colonies, for experience had shown that these communities tended to be insular, were prone to becoming autocratic, or were modeled on the "patriarchal family," and thus denied members individual liberty, especially women. Liberty, equality, and solidarity, Kropotkin concluded, would not be a revolution if it maintained "slavery at home."

According to one critic, Kropotkin had wasted his life "on revolutionary dreams of an anarchistic paradise"—and thus ended his days cold, hungry, isolated, and forgotten in a remote village in Russia (Bunin 1951, 199–201). And this seems to be the verdict of many. He has indeed been shamefully neglected by academic scholars. Even the renowned liberal scholar (and apologist for capitalism) Isaiah Berlin hardly ever mentions Kropotkin in his voluminous essays on Russian and European political thinkers. This is no doubt due to the fact, as Camillo Berneri points out (1942), that Kropotkin was not a systemic thinker and tended to be overly optimistic—thus oversimplifying complex political issues—though Berneri was quick to admit that Kropotkin's writings contained important truths. But Kropotkin—like Berlin—wrote in a lucid style, and in academia there has always been a tendency to confuse profundity with obscurity. As Kropotkin's writings are easy to understand, it is thus assumed that he has nothing important to say—though this is very far from being the case, as I hope the essays in this book show. As he also never advocated a flight into the past, Kropotkin has not become an icon for those contemporary anarchists and ecological radicals who follow rather fashionable New Age preoccupations—like mysticism, pagan rituals, neoprimitivism, shamanism, and Zen Buddhism. As he was also highly critical of the bourgeois individualism of Stirner and Nietzsche (which is also rather fashionable these days), Kropotkin has been ignored, if not maligned as "obsolete" by the trendy postmodernist devotees of these two amoral egoists. Kropotkin, like Luigi Fabbri (1987), long ago critiqued this bourgeois influence within anarchism, which tended to reject organization, solidarity, and socialism, to even sanctify private property, and to offer paeans to the revelries of the ludic or aesthetic "free spirit." For some, drugs, sex, punk, terrorist acts, and antisocial behavior seem to be the acme of anarchy. Anyone suggesting, like Kropotkin, that amoral individualism may be a sick parody of anarchism is likely to be dismissed by neoromantic primitivists as "fascist" (see Bufe 1998 for a recent critique of the amoral egoism and mysticism that nowadays parades as "anarchy").

But it is also significant that Kropotkin, unlike Bakunin, never took an elitist view of revolutionary agency, one based on some secret society or "invisible dictatorship," even though he had been a member of the Chaikovsky Circle and thus was steeped in Russian populism. For Kropotkin any revolutionary transformation of capitalism had to be by means of a *popular* revolution. Nor did Kropotkin advocate what one ultra-Marxist (Neoist) has described as "swamp fever"—the embracing and glorification of political extremism and terrorism simply for its own sake, under the illusion that this makes one an authentic radical and anarchist (Blisset and Home 1999, 4). Kropotkin never harbored such illusions. What he consistently advocated was anarchist communism, and Kropotkin's ideas, as Max Nettlau wrote, were an extraordinary personal product, which reflected in the highest degree the "essence of his own being" (1996, 153).

Kropotkin was essentially an ecologist on the side of humanity and advocated an ethical naturalism that combined humanism and naturalism. He was a humanist in the best sense of the term, in that he stressed human agency and believed that humanity, while being a part of nature, has unique status arising out of its development of sociality. This implied an affirmation of the inherent unity of humankind, in that all humans share certain fundamental attributes, capacities, and moral values (cf. Malik 1996, 237). He thus thought that humans could trust their own reason as a guide to establishing ethical norms and should not rely on mystical revelation or any form of established authority. But because he advocated an evolutionary holism, emphasizing that humans were an intrinsic part of nature, Kropotkin also laid the conceptual foundations for a radical theory of social ecology. Indeed a recent essay was written specifically in the hope of restoring the importance of Kropotkin for critical social theory and to stress his importance for any future social ecology (Breitbart 1981, 139; Macauley 1998, 298).

In contrast to many other scholars, eager for fame and recognition, Kropotkin never set himself up as an intellectual guru, to surround himself with a lot of sycophantic devotees. But nevertheless, Kropotkin has had an extraordinary influence. He has indeed made an important impact on contemporary thought, in many different fields. He had an important influence on the animal ecologists Warder C. Allee and Ernest Thompson Seton; on the anthropologists Radcliffe-Brown and Ashley Montagu; on the advocates of urban ecology and the garden-city idea, such as a Patrick Geddes, Ebenezer Howard, and Lewis Mumford; on the communitarian politics of Leo Tolstoy, Mohandas Gandhi, and Paul Goodman; and, of course, he had an immense influence on several generations of anarchists. Errico Malatesta, Goldman, Rocker, and Nestor Makhno all attest to Kropotkin's deep influence on the orientation of their own anarchism. More recently, Kropotkin has a presence throughout the memoirs of, for example, the anarcho-syndicalist Sam Dolgoff (1986). But the writer who has most creatively explored and developed Kropotkin's seminal ideas, both on social ecology and on anarchist communism, is Murray Bookchin. In his excellent pioneering study *The Ecology of Freedom* (1982), Bookchin pays tribute to the influence of Kropotkin, who "is unique in his emphasis on the need for a reconciliation of humanity with nature, the role of mutual aid in natural social evolution, his hatred of hierarchy, and his vision of new techniques based on decentralization and human scale" ("Acknowledgments"). Bookchin explicitly regarded Kropotkin as "the real pioneer in the eco-anarchist tradition, as well as anarchist communism," and affirmed that his own work has the strongest affinities to Kropotkin's ecological holism and social anarchism (1999, 57–58). Like Kropotkin, Bookchin emphasizes that socialism is an integral part of anarchism, and Bookchin continues to offer salutary critiques of mystical ecology and spiritualism, technophobia, amoral egoism, and neoromantic primitivism (1999, 160–207). The suggestion that Bookchin does little more that than "update" or "filch" the theories of Geddes, Mumford, and Kropotkin (Purchase 1993, 35; Keulartz 1998, 93) is rather churlish and unfair to Bookchin, for it denies the original and creative synthesis that Bookchin has achieved in melding together ideas from many different sources, including those of Kropotkin, in the development of both ecological holism as a philosophy and social anarchism as a political theory. But Bookchin explicitly affirms his commitment to the kind of anarchism that Kropotkin had envisaged when he writes: "Anarchism's respect for artisanship, its commitment to mutual aid, its high regard for the natural world, and its emphasis on an ethical socialism are its virtues insofar as they seek to retain the richly articulated, co-operative, and self-expressive forms of human consociation scaled to human dimensions" (1996, 22).

In an era when corporate capitalism reigns triumphant, creating conditions that induce fear, social dislocation, economic insecurity, and political and ecological crises, and when there is a pervasive mood of "apocalyptic despair" among many intellectuals (and anarchists), there is surely a need to take seriously Kropotkin's vision of an alternative way of organizing social life. This book aims to present that vision.

PETER KROPOTKIN
A Biographical Note

Kropotkin was born in 1842 into the highest ranks of the Russian aristocracy, his princely forebears having been among the early rulers of Russia. It was joked that Kropotkin had more right to the throne of Russia than the czar, Alexander II, who was a German (Stepniak 1883, 94). At an early age he entered the Corps of Pages, a unique academy that combined the character of an elite military school with that of a court institution attached to the imperial household. Kropotkin often came into personal contact with the czar and graduated from the school with the highest distinction in 1862. To the consternation of everyone, especially his father, Kropotkin decided to join the newly formed mounted Cossack regiment of the Amur, in eastern Siberia. For a time the aide-de-coup to the governor of Transbaikalia, Kropotkin spent the next four years, though nominally on military service, traveling widely throughout the remote parts of Siberia and Manchuria. The geographical and ethnographic researches that he made on these expeditions formed the foundations of his later scientific writings.

Dismayed at the lack of any social reform, Kropotkin resigned from the army in 1867 and became secretary of the physical geography section of the Russian Geographical society, and he registered as a student at St. Petersburg University (he never completed his degree). The next five years of his life were almost exclusively devoted to scientific work. But in 1871 Kropotkin made a momentous decision. He was offered the post of secretary to the Russian Geographical Society and thus the opportunity to engage full-time in scientific research. However, after some reflection, Kropotkin declined: instead, he decided to devote himself to the liberation of the peasants and urban workers in Russia and to fight for social justice. Prompted by his friend Sergei Kravchinsky, better known as Stepniak, and his sister-in-law Sofia Lavrova, both of whom were already committed revolutionary socialists, Kropotkin decided to visit Switzerland, then the Mecca of radical activity.

Kropotkin's first journey to Western Europe in the spring of 1872 was a crucial event in his life, for in Switzerland he made contact with the Jura Federation, the Bakuninist faction of the International Workingmen's Association. Kropotkin was deeply impressed by the independence, integrity and devotion of the working people of the Jura mountains, and it was in Switzerland that he also first met such anarchists as Élisée Reclus and James Guillaume. These political contacts heralded Kropotkin's "conversion" to anarchism, and he returned to Russia with a large collection of socialist and anarchist literature. Kropotkin threw himself into the revolutionary struggle in Russia. He became a member of the influential populist group the Chaikovsky Circle. Kropotkin began lecturing and distributing radical and socialist propaganda among the peasants, as well as among the workers of St. Petersburg. But in Russia political repression was then at its height, and he was soon in trouble. In March 1874 he was arrested by police in St. Petersburg—having just given a lecture to the Russian Geographical Society on glacial formations!—and was imprisoned in the fortress of St. Peter and St. Paul. He was to spend two years in solitary confinement awaiting trial. His health steadily deteriorated, and he began to suffer from the dreaded scurvy. He was therefore moved to a prison attached to the military hospital in St. Petersburg, and it was from there, in June 1876, that Kropotkin made his dramatic escape. Making his way to England, Kropotkin was never to return to Russia until the revolution of 1917. He managed, however, through his geographical contacts in England, to obtain work as a scientific journalist, and he began writing essays and reviews on topics of scientific or geographical interest to various journals. Throughout his forty-one years of political exile, this was to be his main source of income. But Kropotkin did not stay long in England, and in January 1877 returned to Switzerland to become again a member of the Jura Federation. Between 1877 and 1882, Kropotkin traveled widely throughout Europe, attending anarchist conferences and making contact with many revolutionary socialists. At the end of 1878, Kropotkin met and married a young Polish Jew, Sophie Ananiev, who was a biology student. In his *Memoirs* Kropotkin does not mention his marriage and hardly refers to his wife, but the marriage seems to have been a happy one (Mannin 1964, 112).

In 1879, when the outlook for the Jura Federation looked bleak, Kropotkin, with the support of a few friends, launched a new anarchist paper, *Le Révolté*. He seems to have done most of the writing himself. His friend Élisée Reclus was later to collect the essays that Kropotkin had written for the paper and to publish them in Paris in 1885, under the title *Parole d'un Revolte*—the "Words of a Rebel." These essays give a succinct outline of the theory of anarchist communism, which Kropotkin came to espouse. He was later to become the main advocate of this form of anarchism. In March 1881, however, Alexander II was assassinated, and a few months later Kropotkin was expelled from Switzerland. He again settled in London, but both he and Sophie felt lonely in the city, and in October 1882 they moved to France. On leaving England, he recorded, they said to each other: "Better a French prison than this grave" (MR, 440–42).

Kropotkin only enjoyed a few months of freedom, for in December he was arrested and taken to Lyon. He was accused, along with many other anarchists, of belonging to an illegal organization—the International, even though the International had by then long ceased to exist as a viable organization. At the famous trial in Lyon, Kropotkin was found guilty and condemned to five years in prison. Kropotkin's second spell in prison lasted three years, and although as a political prisoner he was allowed a certain amount of freedom—to write articles and to cultivate a small garden—he nevertheless began to suffer from malaria and scurvy. He was finally released from Clairvaux prison in January 1886 and again made his way to London. He now found a lively socialist movement. It consisted, broadly speaking, of three groupings: the Social Democratic Federation, founded by Henry Hyndman; the breakaway Socialist League, associated with William Morris; and the Fabian Society. Associated with the likes of Bernard Shaw and Sydney and Beatrice Webb, the Fabians championed a form of parliamentary state socialism. Around March 1886 Kropotkin joined a small circle of anarchists known as the London Anarchist Group of Freedom. His aim was to distribute anarchist propaganda, and in October of that year the group became the Freedom Press and published the first issue of *Freedom*. It was a four-page sheet, mostly written by Kropotkin. *Freedom* and Freedom Press (which is now one of the main publishers of anarchist literature in Britain) are still flourishing after more than a hundred years. Kropotkin himself was to remain in close touch with *Freedom* for the next three decades (until 1914), and many of his early seminal articles on anarchism were published in the journal.

The remainder of Kropotkin's active life was devoted to the exposition and dissemination of anarchist ideas. He settled down in England, his last place of refuge, and established a pattern of life that combined manual labor—for Kropotkin and his wife were enthusiastic gardeners—political agitation, and the refined life of a scholar. He established close friendships and intellectual contacts with many important contemporary figures. These include Henry Bates, William Robertson Smith, Patrick Geddes, William Morris, and Keir Hardie. He traveled extensively in the 1890s; on his lecture tours, he never lost an opportunity to visit factories, coal mines, and workshops, and he always took a deep interest in agriculture. His home became an "open house" for a host of visitors—anarchist exiles like Malatesta and Rocker, as well as radical scholars and British Socialists. Kropotkin's outstanding intellectual abilities, his fluency in several languages, and his moral integrity were all affirmed by his contemporaries. And it was during his thirty years of exile in England that Kropotkin wrote a series of books on which his fame rests. These include *The Conquest of Bread* (1892), originally written as a series of articles for *La Revolté*, which gives an outline of his theory of anarchist communism as a utopian project; *Fields, Factories and Workshops* (1899) and *Mutual Aid* (1902)—both first published as a series of essays in *The Nineteenth Century*; *Memoirs of a Revolutionist* (1899), a graphic account of his early life; and *The Great French Revolution* (1909). All these books are written in a lucid and engaging style and have a simplicity and brevity of expression as well as a passion that is unusual in political and scientific texts. Kropotkin's books are thus inspiring and refreshingly free of the obscurantist jargon that these days masks as scholarship in the groves of academia, so his works reach out to a wide audience. Even so, all his serious writings are models of good scholarship. Equally important, Kropotkin was a sympathetic writer who could be critical of an individual scholar without indulging in misrepresentation and personal abuse. Kropotkin never wrote with rancor (Hewetson 1965, 70). In this text I have tried to emulate Kropotkin, and thus my essays on his social and political philosophy attempt to be scholarly, as well as lucid and readable.

At the outbreak of the First World War in 1914, Kropotkin, much to the surprise and consternation of his anarchist comrades, fervently supported the Allies. His prowar stand was seemingly motivated by Kropotkin's fear that "Prussian militarism" and German imperialism, if not opposed, would inevitably lead to reaction throughout Europe, and to the defeat of the revolutionary socialist movement, which Kropotkin strongly identified with France. His refusal to take an antimilitarist position led to Kropotkin's estrangement from most of his anarchist comrades, especially Malatesta, Goldman, and Rocker, with whom he had established deep friendships. But this "crisis" in his life was deepened by events in Russia. Kropotkin had never completely lost contact with his native Russia, and ever since 1897, when student demonstrations had been crushed with brutality and torture, Kropotkin had been writing letters and articles condemning the tsarist autocracy. After the 1905 revolution, Kropotkin wrote a series of articles and pamphlets on the impending Russian revolution, as well as played an active part, along with Alexander Shapiro and Marie Goldsmith, in a number of anarchist conferences. These were specifically devoted to linking the activities of Russian exiles with the revolutionary situation in Russia.

During the early years of the First World War Kropotkin, now living in Brighton, was not in good health and spent much of his time in a wheelchair. But although he kept up with his extensive correspondence and a few friends came to visit him, he became, because of his prowar stand, increasingly isolated from the main anarchist movement. Then, quite unexpectedly, in February 1917, there was a revolutionary insurrection in Russia, and Kropotkin's life was suddenly transformed. Although Kropotkin had long anticipated and dreaded the outbreak of the First World War, he was quite taken by surprise by the Russian revolution. Yet it was, in many ways, the kind of spontaneous revolution of working people that he had long envisaged and advocated. It also seemed that the moment had come for which he and many other Russian revolutionaries had long been struggling, namely, the downfall of the tsarist regime. It also enabled Kropotkin to realize the dream of his life, to return to his native Russia and to end his forty-year exile.

Kropotkin arrived in Petrograd in June 1917, and although it was two o'clock in the morning, a crowd of around sixty thousand people came to welcome him back to Russia. It seemed that through his writings Kropotkin had become something of a legendary figure. Kropotkin and Sophie took up residence in Moscow, but it was evident from the outset that politically Kropotkin cut a rather lonely figure. Most of the Russian anarchists kept aloof from him, feeling that Kropotkin, by supporting the war, had betrayed his own anarchist principles. He was out of favor too with the social revolutionaries and the Marxists (Bolsheviks), who generally dismissed him as an "old fool" or as "petty bourgeois." Evidently, Kropotkin made it clear that he still remained vehemently anti-Marxist. But he also adamantly refused to accept any position offered by the provisional government, under Kerensky. The only organization that Kropotkin became involved with in Moscow, it appears, was the Federation League. This was a group of scholars interested in sociological issues, who wished to promote federalism and decentralized politics. Unhappy living in Moscow, Kropotkin was also greatly perturbed at the increasing authoritarianism of the Bolshevik regime, which he described as a group of "robbers and gangsters" bent on looting and destruction (WA, 406). He and his wife, Sophie, therefore decided in June 1918 to move to the small village of Dmitrov, forty miles north of Moscow. Here Kropotkin spent the last three years of his life, virtually an "internal émigré" cut off from the political life of the capital. There he devoted his time to practical work with the local Dmitrov cooperative society and with writing his book on *Ethics*. The unfinished text was published posthumously in 1924.

In May 1919 Kropotkin had a meeting with Lenin, who evidently admired Kropotkin's book on the French Revolution and who may well have wanted to secure Kropotkin's goodwill and support in the difficult times through which the Bolsheviks were then passing. It was hardly a meeting of equals. Lenin was then at the height of his powers, the supreme ruler of the Soviet State; Kropotkin was old, frail, and hardly in a position to influence events in Russia. Kropotkin apparently talked about the importance of cooperatives, which Lenin thought "idle chatter"; Lenin talked about the need for a revolution that would necessarily involve a "red terror" under the Bolshevik Party. The two men clearly had different conceptions of a social revolution. Two years later, in February 1921, Kropotkin died, stricken with pneumonia. He was seventy-nine. Around a hundred thousand people attended his funeral. Many anarchists obtained temporary release from prison to be present. The funeral procession was five miles long, and the black banners of the anarchists carried the words: "Where there is authority there is no freedom." Victor Serge recorded that it was the last great demonstration against the Bolshevik tyranny (1963, 124; for biographical studies of Kropotkin, see Woodcock and Avakumovic 1950; M. A. Miller 1976; and Cahm 1989).

PART ONE
THE THEORY OF ANARCHIST COMMUNISM

1
THE COMING REVOLUTION
AND
ANARCHIST COMMUNISM

K ropotkin has been described as having the most well-developed and wide-ranging intellect ever to place itself at the service of anarchism (Shatz in CB, ix). And his career shows a remarkable degree of consistency, in that for almost half a century Kropotkin was the leading advocate of a particular brand of revolutionary socialism—anarchist communism.

Kropotkin presented his first major political statement at a congress of the Jura Federation in August 1878, attended by only eight delegates. In his address to the delegates Kropotkin advocated the negation of the nation-state, which he considered then to be in the process of disintegration, and its replacement by a free federation of communes and productive associations. This implied also a social revolution, a fundamental social change, during which, through "insurrectionary deeds," people would spontaneously expropriate land, capital, and the means of livelihood. In the following year, at the congress held at La Chaux-de-Fonds (October 1879), Kropotkin gave a similar address, titled "The Anarchist Idea from the Viewpoint of its Practical Realization." Martin Miller indicates three important points about this speech: that Kropotkin refused to advocate the formation of the anarchists into a political party and thus seek power through the state; that the coming social revolution was defined in terms of the collective expropriation of land, capital, and the means of production; and, finally, that Kropotkin still continued to use the Bakuninist term "collectivism" (MK, 142).

At the Jura congress of October 1880, also held at La Chaux-de-Fonds, Kropotkin abandoned the concept of "collectivism" (which he felt still implied a system of wage-labor) and advocated for the first time "anarchist communism." This entailed the free distribution of goods, the notion of an economic system based on the adage "from each according to his means, to each according to his needs." The congress thus affirmed the formation of anarchist communism as a distinctive form of socialism. For Kropotkin this was an "important stage" in the development of revolutionary socialism— although many of the delegates at the congress were hesitant about the term "communism," for in France it was intrinsically associated with monastic life.

Although Kropotkin played an important part in the development of anarchist communism and was later to become its chief exponent and advocate, he was not its originator. Already in 1876, François Dumertheray, who was later to help Kropotkin to establish the newspaper *Le Révolté*, published a little pamphlet in Geneva titled *Aux Travailleur Manuels Partisans de l'Action Politique*. This had advocated anarchist communism. The linkage between anarchism and communism indeed seems to have evolved spontaneously and independently among many of the "collectivist" followers of Bakunin in Italy, Spain, and Switzerland. People important in the development of anarchist communism, besides Kropotkin, include Élisée Reclus, Carlo Cafiero, Jean Grave, and Errico Malatesta (Cahm 1989, 51–64).

Kropotkin's early political writings on anarchist communism suggest a number of important themes that form the substance of his revolutionary politics. The first was the belief in the imminence of a social revolution that would entail the expropriation of land and property by working people and the subsequent demise of capitalism and the nation-state. Second, Kropotkin offered sustained critiques of all forms of government, including both representative democracy and the Marxist "dictatorship of the proletariat" by a revolutionary party, as well as of capitalism and the "wage system." This chapter will focus on these essential themes of Kropotkin's political credo.

Kropotkin's essay "An Appeal to the Young," first published in *Le Révolté* in August 1880, and subsequently republished many times as a pamphlet, is perhaps one of the most famous socialist tracts ever written. It has been described as "certainly one of the most moving exhortations of its kind," and it had a greater influence than any other of Kropotkin's pamphlets (WA, 177). In its appeal to the young to join the revolutionary struggle for social justice, the pamphlet certainly stirred the imagination of the teenage Victor Serge. For Serge recalled that the pamphlet "spoke to me at that time in a language of unprecedented clarity." Not only did it induce him to become a revolutionary socialist, but, he wrote, its message had remained close to his heart for the rest of his life (1963, 7–8).

Kropotkin's essay is a call to social revolution. It is addressed specifically to young people of the middle classes who are about to embark upon a professional career—as a doctor, scientist, lawyer, engineer, teacher, or artist. Kropotkin addresses them each in turn. To those wishing to become a doctor, he suggests that they look honestly at the social conditions of those who come to them for treatment and to ask themselves: What is it that I really need to prescribe? Not drugs. For what is needed is less the curing of sickness than its prevention. "To hell with drugs! Fresh air, proper feeding, less brutalising work: that is where we must start" (WR, 46).

To those contemplating becoming a scholar or scientist, he asks them to observe the fact that under the present capitalist system, science is carried out largely for the benefit of the privileged few and the owners of capital. Although the pursuit of scholarship may give the scientist immense personal satisfaction, it is more imperative, Kropotkin argues, to make science available to all humanity and to ensure that scientific findings are put to the common good.

To those who intend to practice law, Kropotkin asks them to critically examine what this vocation exactly entails—given the fact that law is always on the side of property and is frequently contrary to justice. You must realize, he writes, that "to remain the servant of written law is to find yourself each day in opposition to the law of conscience" (WR, 51).

With regard to the young engineer, teacher, and artist, Kropotkin likewise emphasizes that under the regime of private property and the wage system, a sad contradiction will always exist between their aspiration and ideals and the conditions that they find in the real world. Thus a mode of production geared to the benefit of all humanity, a broad humanitarian education for all, a setting where artists' talents serve the interests of the majority and not just the rich—all these are impossible under the present capitalist system. Thus the young student, Kropotkin writes, may well ask: "If the abstract science is a luxury and the practice of medicine a sham, if law is injustice and technical advances are instruments of exploitation; if education is defeated by the self interest of the educators, and if art, lacking a revolutionary ideal, can only degenerate, what is there left for me to do" (WR, 54).

And Kropotkin replies that the young people must go among the people, take their place alongside the socialists, and to work toward the complete transformation of society. Kropotkin concludes with this appeal: "All of you, sincere young people, men and women, peasant workers, clerks, soldiers, will understand your rights and come to us; you will come to work with your brothers in preparing the revolution which, abolishing every kind of slavery (will open) new horizons to all humanity, will finally succeed in establishing in human societies the true equality, the true liberty, work for all, and for all the enjoyment of the fruits of their labour, the full enjoyment of all their faculties" (WR, 62).

To struggle in the midst of the people for truth, justice, and equality, what could young people, Kropotkin writes, find more splendid, or more worthwhile (WR, 58).

This appeal echoes that of the Narodniks, and the motivation for the essay may well have stemmed from Kropotkin's own experiences in Russia and the movement of going "to the people"—as only the last section of the essay is addressed specifically to working-class youth.

Like many of his contemporaries, Kropotkin thought that a social revolution was imminent and that there were signs toward the end of the nineteenth century that both the centralized nation-state and the capitalist economic order were in decline. "It was an error which many others, including Kropotkin's leading Marxist opponents, made in those optimistic days," so write his biographers (WA, 307).

At the present time liberal scholars and postmodernist theorists give the impression that capitalism and the state are the only possible forms of social organization, and that no alternative is possible. History, we are informed, has come to an "end," and there has been an unholy alliance between the capitalist triumphalism of the neoliberals and the nihilistic pessimism of the postmodernists. The former glorify a rampant individualism, while the postmoderns, as neo-idealists, virtually eradicate human agency (Wood and Foster 1997). For Kropotkin, however, at the end of the nineteenth century, it was evident that "we are advancing rapidly towards revolution" (WR, 19), and one of his essays is in fact titled the "Inevitability of Revolution" (WR, 29–33).

Throughout human history, Kropotkin argued, there are periods or epochs when the inevitability of a great upheaval, or revolutionary cataclysm, shakes the very roots of society and "imposes itself on every area of our relationships" (WR, 29). One feels the inevitability of a revolution. Such he felt was happening in his own time. Capitalism was in crisis—with overproduction, high unemployment, widespread poverty, and rampant financial speculation—while the state was in the process of breakdown. The modern state, for Kropotkin, has the essential function of upholding and promoting a system of inequality; capitalism and the state were thus intrinsically and "symbiotically" linked. The state, he wrote, has "become the fortress of the rich against the exploited, of the employer against the proletarian," for the state is here "to protect exploitation, speculation and private property, it is itself the by-product of the rapine of the people" (WR, 27). But Kropotkin argued that states for historical reasons were in decline and showing signs of disintegration. "Having reached a high point in the eighteenth century, the old states of Europe have now entered into their decline; they are falling into decrepitude" (WR, 24).

Thus Kropotkin summed up the situation in Europe at the end of the nineteenth century as one involving economic chaos and the failure of capitalist production and the rapid breakdown of the state. Although Kropotkin's writings are full of apocalyptic imagery and almost imply a historical determinism, recent history, of course, has not borne out Kropotkin's premonitions—to the contrary, capitalism has now become global and penetrates almost every aspect of social life and the natural environment, and the nation-state, too, shows no signs of disappearing. Capitalism, in fact, with its logic of commodification, competition, and profit-maximization, now permeates the whole social fabric and continues to be supported and protected by the state in ways that Kropotkin suggested. "Today the state takes upon itself to meddle in all areas of our lives," wrote Kropotkin (WR, 25)—and this is still very much the case. It is of interest that while Michel Foucault critiques the "normalization," the "discipline," and the "biopower" of the modern state that are expressed in the "microphysics of power"—and in the process verily ablates social life and human agency in a "totalizing" vision of "power"— Giddens, in contrast, applauds and advocates the nation-state and its "civilizing" mission (Simons 1995; Giddens 1998, 48).

Kropotkin saw a deep contradiction between capitalism—based on exploitation and fraud—and the principles of morality and the sentiment of solidarity that was expressed in everyday social life. He thus saw international socialism with its emphasis on solidarity and equality—"land, capital and work shared by all"—and the suggestion of replacing the state by a federation of free communes, as both crucial in the "coming revolution." Kropotkin therefore concluded that Europe was proceeding down a steep slope toward a revolutionary outbreak, and that the "distinct character of the coming revolution will consist in international attempts at economic revolution, made by the people without waiting for the revolution to fall like manna from the heavens" (WR, 38).

Such a revolution, he suggested, essentially involved two things— awakening the "spirit of revolt," and the "expropriation" of land, capital, and the means of production by the working people.

As a close and perceptive student of the French Revolution, Kropotkin was always keen to draw lessons from the revolutionary upheavals that occurred in France between 1789 and 1793. The "causes" of this revolution, Kropotkin always recognized, were complex, multiple, and panoramic. It involved the bourgeoisie complaining at their loss of privileges and being hostile to the king; the peasants revolting against the salt tax and the feudal tithes; the urban workers reacting against their poverty and the general insecurity: the ridiculing of the establishment and the exposure of the vices of the court through popular broadsheets and popular songs. But most important for Kropotkin was the transformation of popular resentment and revolutionary ideas into social action—and the key here was the awakening of the *Spirit of Revolt* and the engendering of hope for the future. "Hope is born in men's hearts; let us remember that if exasperation often leads to riots, it is always hope, the hope of winning that makes the revolutions" (WR, 188).

The French Revolution, though it entailed the disorganization of the state by popular revolution, did not lead to a full social revolution. But it did, Kropotkin emphasizes, lead to two great achievements—the abolition of royal autocracy and the advent of bourgeois rule, and the abolition of serfdom and of feudal tenure in the countryside. (WR, 191; see chapter 12 below).

The coming revolution, Kropotkin felt, would follow the general pattern of the French Revolution in that it would be a popular revolution. But it would go a step further: it would not simply lead to a change of government but to the abolition of the state and its replacement by a federation of free communes (anarchism); it would also involve a complete transformation of property relations, that is, an end to capitalism and the wage system, and its replacement with a communist economic system based on free cooperation and mutual aid (socialism). In the initial stages of this social transformation, it was important to evoke the "spirit of revolt" among working people. Thus Kropotkin felt that every popular movement was a step toward a social revolution, for "It awakens the spirit of revolt, it makes men accustomed to seeing the established order (or rather the established disorder) as eminently unstable" (WR, 203).

Believing like many of his contemporaries that Western Europe was on the eve of a great revolution (Kropotkin was writing in the 1880s), Kropotkin placed great emphasis on *expropriation*—of land, capital, and the means of production by working people—as the key factor in the revolution. Expropriation, he wrote, "that is the guiding word of the coming revolution, without which it will fail in its historic mission." Such expropriation involved the return to the community, to the common people, "of everything that in the hands of anyone can be used to exploit others" (WR, 207–208). It entailed the expropriation, the repossession, of the factories, warehouses, and workshops; of the railways and the means of transportation; of the mansions and villas that then housed the rich and powerful; and of the land. Kropotkin affirmed that in relation to land, its cultivation was much better done when the peasants themselves owned the fields, orchards, and gardens—and this ruled out sharecropping, tenancy agreements, the private ownership of land, and the land "nationalization" schemes that were then being advocated by the partisans of Henry George. Kropotkin was also skeptical that the "agrarian problem" could be solved by small proprietorship and petty commodity production as was advocated by the followers of Proudhon. Those who sing the praises of "small property," he wrote, are half a century behind the times and ignore present-day realities. The future, according to Kropotkin, "does not belong to individual property, to the peasant penned in a fragment of land that barely sustains him. It belongs to communist cultivation" (WR, 215). Individual property he felt would be a hindrance to the development of agriculture, as well as a form of theft. For Kropotkin emphasized that cultural ideas and social products are in essence the result of the collective efforts of humanity: "We must understand without hesitation or reserve that all products, the whole of what man has accumulated and made use of, are due to the common work of all, and have only one owner humanity. We must see private property clearly for what it is in reality, a conscious or unconscious theft of the wealth of all people" (WR, 221).

Whereas liberals have thought of expropriation as a form of theft, for Kropotkin it was the other way around: private property was theft.

Throughout his writings Kropotkin stressed that all wealth and all knowledge are in essence a social product, part of an immense capital that humans have accumulated over the centuries. Humankind has amassed untold treasures, and this is expressed in landscape (the clearing of land, the draining of wetlands, the making of roads) and in the development of technology and industry. Equally, all scientific and cultural knowledge has been the collective creation of human civilization, for there is not even a thought or an invention that is not common property. Thus, "Every rood of soil we cultivate in Europe has been watered by the sweat of several generations of man," while thousands of writers, poets, and scholars have labored to increase human knowledge. Kropotkin therefore concludes that "Every discovery, every advance, each increase in the sum of human riches, owes its being to the physical and mental travail of the past and the present. . . . By what right then does anyone appropriate the least morsel of this immense whole and say—This is mine, not yours" (CB, 44–46).

But why then, Kropotkin asks, given this immense wealth inherited from the past, are so many people poor, and why is work such a painful drudgery for the majority of working people? And he replies that this is "because all that is necessary for production—the land, the mines, the highways, machinery, food, shelter, education, knowledge—all have been seized by the few in the course of that long story of robbery, enforced migration, and wars, of ignorance and oppression, which has been the life of the human race before it had learned to subdue the forces of nature" (CB, 43).

Expropriation of all property—factories, workshops, transport, land—by working people was therefore, for Kropotkin, the essence of the social revolution, and these would then be shared and utilized for the "common benefit." But the expropriation of land, and its management as common property, did not imply either authoritarian communism or mass production. "Does it follow that the social revolution should overthrow all the boundaries and hedges of private properties, demolish gardens and orchards, and drive the steam tractor over everything, so as to introduce the doubtful benefits of large-scale cultivation as certain authoritarian reformers imagine?" And Kropotkin replies: "This is precisely what, for our part, we want to avoid. We would take care not to touch the holding of the peasant who cultivates it himself with his children and without wage labour" (WR, 214).

Kropotkin emphasized that what was needed, and which he felt was imminent, was not a political revolution or even an armed struggle, but rather a social revolution, which involved the increasing expropriation of property (at the local level)—whether land, houses, or industrial machinery. But he emphasized that a key factor in the revolution would be agriculture and the need initially to provide everyone with the basic necessities of life, particularly bread.

Kropotkin, contrasting his own ideas with both authoritarian collectivism—the "worker's state"—and those who emphasized the retention of private property, described his own political theory as anarchist communism. He thus always stressed that the social revolution would "immediately take possession of the workshops, houses, granaries, and the whole social wealth"—including land—and that within each local community production and consumption would be cooperatively organized, so that the needs of all people could be adequately provided for (WR, 203).

Expropriation constituted, he noted, "the mother-idea" of the socialist, and socialism entailed an end to the wage system and the abolition of private property in land, housing, raw materials, and the instrument of production (WR, 180). Revolution for Kropotkin thus did not simply involve a change of rulers—"it is the seizing by the people of all social wealth" (WR, 175).

This also meant the demolition of all institutions that served to perpetuate economic and political enslavement, and the most crucial of these were governments. A social revolution thus did not simply mean a change of government: it involved both new forms of economic and social life and the overthrow of the state. All present governments, Kropotkin wrote, "should be abolished, so that freedom, equality and fraternity are no longer vain words and become living realities" (WR, 165). He elsewhere wrote that liberty, equality, and fraternity are "surely grand and glorious words" that we may inscribe on each banner, but they remain meaningless "when they are painted on prison walls" (AY, 63).

The notion of a "revolutionary government" Kropotkin considered to be a contradiction in terms, for "revolution" and "government" were incompatible concepts. "The one is always the negation of the other," he wrote, and apart from anarchy "there can be no revolution" (WR, 170). This is so whether the "revolutionary government" is elicited and entails universal suffrage (as with the Paris Commune of March 1871), or whether it implies the dictatorship of a revolutionary party. The very idea of a "dictatorship" Kropotkin considered to be the product of a "governmental fetish" and one that always led to the demise of the revolution. Nothing good, he wrote, "is made except by the free initiative of the people, and all power tends to kill it" (WR, 171). Kropotkin wrote these words in 1882. They have poignancy when one reflects on the outcome of the Russian Revolution after October 1917, when the country came under the "dictatorship" of the Bolshevik party. Kropotkin, in the article "On Revolutionary Government," quotes the words of the French conspiratorial revolutionary August Blanqui (1805–1881), who spent over thirty years of his life in prison: "Neither God nor Master" (WR, 173).

The "agrarian question" was always of vital concern to Kropotkin. Surveying the land situation in many countries of Western Europe, he noted the ubiquity of agrarian revolts against the landlords. In some regions, peasant uprisings and underground agitation were almost a permanent feature of the landscape. He noted, too, that throughout Europe, landed property is concentrated in a few hands. England, for example, he describes at the end of the nineteenth century as a land of fabulously rich landlords and a rural proletariat reduced to destitution. "Four-fifths of the arable land, some

23,976,000 hectares, are the property of 2,340 great landowners; 710 lords own a third of England . . . one earl owns a whole county" (WR, 109).

The wealth and power of the British landed aristocracy at the end of the nineteenth century, in which some seven thousand families owned four-fifths of the land of the British Isles, has been confirmed by many recent studies (see Cannadine 1990, 9). And far from being a model of rational agriculture, immense areas of England, he wrote, had been transformed into parkland in order that the rich aristocracy could stage their "monstrous hunts," or were devoted to the raising of beef cattle—to provide meat for the rich. This pattern of land ownership and land use has hardly changed in the last hundred years, although agriculture has become increasingly "industrial," and the infamous law of trespass still continues to deny the people of Britain free access to the countryside (Shoard 1997). Kropotkin felt that English landowners would inevitably resist any moves to end individual property in land, and therefore "to make its wishes prevail, the people of England will have to resort to force" (WR, 111).

The abolition of private property through the expropriation of land and other forms of productive capital and the "overthrow" of governments were the key ideas in Kropotkin's conception of a social revolution. Such a revolution he considered not only imminent but also imperative and that the "well-being of all" was not an idle dream but both possible and realizable. He summed up the social revolution with the words: "There must be expropriation. The well-being of all—the end; expropriation—the means" (CB, 55).

Anarchism, which Kropotkin described as the "no-government system of socialism"—for he saw communism and anarchy as interdependent—had two sources. It was the outcome of two currents of social thought—radical liberalism and socialism. In common with the most advanced representatives of liberal thought, political radicalism, anarchists maintain that the functions of the state must be reduced to a minimum—but they go further than the liberals and advocate the complete negation of the state. They thus believe the ultimate aim of the society is "the reduction of the functions of government to *nil*—that is, to a society without government, to anarchy." In common with the socialists, anarchists are stridently anticapitalist and repudiate the private ownership of land, capital, and machinery. But they take the socialist principle to its ultimate conclusion and advocate the complete negation of the wage-system and of private property (KRP, 46).

Kropotkin felt that anarchist communism was neither simply a utopian vision nor based on a priori metaphysical principles, but rather that it was inherent in the tendencies of modern society, and that it offered the best conditions for promoting the well-being of all people.

Embracing evolutionary theory and an advocate of historical sociology, Kropotkin suggested that sociological studies had indicated two tendencies—a tremendous increase in the powers of production and a growing recognition of the political rights of working people. Like Marx, Kropotkin acknowledged the profound changes that had taken place under industrial capitalism during the nineteenth century and that this had resulted in tremendous advances in scientific knowledge, in the social complexity of production, and in increased human wealth. But the outcome had not been the "well-being of all" or the greater happiness of humanity; to the contrary, through the "wage system" there had been an aggravation of class inequalities, and the owners of capital had accumulated unprecedented wealth, while the lot of most working people had been increasing poverty and insecurity. The chasm "Between the modern millionaire who squanders the produce of human labour in a gorgeous and vain luxury, and the pauper reduced to a miserable and insecure existence is thus growing wider and wider, so as to break the very unity of society" (KRP, 48). In the present era of capitalist triumphalism, with sociological gurus like Anthony Giddens informing us that "there are no alternatives to capitalism" (1998, 24), a rampant global capitalism is still producing the same extreme levels of social and economic inequality; a privileged few who are enjoying scandalous wealth coexisting with millions of people in the world who are starving or living in abject poverty or insecurity. Communism is either declared an "illusion" or misleadingly equated with the "state capitalism" of the Bolshevik regime in Russia.

But in the nineteenth century, there arose a social movement that offered an alternative to capitalism, challenging its hegemony; that movement was socialism.

Through socialism working people claimed a share of the riches they produced and a role in the management of production, and in the name of social justice declared that capitalism, along with its system of "wage-slavery," must be abolished. Kropotkin described socialism as *the* idea of the nineteenth century," and optimistically believed that neither coercion nor pseudo reforms could stop its growth (KRP, 49). He noted that the extension of political rights to the working classes did not entail introducing democratic ideas into the work place, and it is of interest that contemporary liberals like Giddens who stress the need for "deepening and widening democracy" never hint at introducing real "democracy" into business corporations or into the "global market place" (1998, 69–71). Democracy, as Chomsky put it, always stops at the factory gate.

But for Kropotkin "government" has to be submitted to the same criticism as "capital," and thus while most political radicals applaud universal suffrage and democracy, Kropotkin suggests that a deeper criticism is needed and that the inherent limitations of representative government must also be exposed. A critique of "Representative Government" was thus the subject of one of his earliest essays (1880; WR, 118–44).

To accomplish a political revolution that was both deep and lasting, Kropotkin firmly believed that there must also be an economic revolution—achieved through the expropriation of all forms of private property. Economic freedom, he wrote, is the only secure basis for political freedom (KRP, 49). Kropotkin was not an advocate of a democratic revolution and was always critical of the liberal state and of "representative" government. Faith in representative government he considered to be a widespread prejudice, one that he felt always needed to be repudiated. Putting one's faith in representative government—"government by proxy"—was, he wrote, particularly strong in France, even though the people had "elected" as president in 1848 an outright "brigand" in Louis Bonaparte. About twenty years later, in 1871, during the Paris Commune, the people of Paris began experimenting with new economic forms, but though repudiating the "empire" they continued to put their faith in representative government. The people, "hastened to apply once again, in the heart of the commune the representative system and to falsify its new idea by evolving the worm eaten heritage of the past. It abdicated its own initiative into the hands of an assembly of the people elected more or less at random" (WR, 121).

Although Kropotkin never equated representative government with the absolutist state, he nevertheless felt that the representative system retained all the prerogatives of absolute power while subordinating them to the more or less ideological fiction of popular sovereignty. In essence, representative government was the means whereby the bourgeoisie ensured their own political domination. The idea that representative or constitutional government had been instrumental in advancing human freedoms Kropotkin considered something of a myth, in that there was little correlation between civil liberties and the institution of parliament. All these liberties—the right to associate and to strike, the freedom of the press, the right to establish trade unions—had all been won by extraparliamentary agitation and had to be extorted from parliament by force. To attribute to parliaments, "What is due to general progress, to imagine that having a constitution is sufficient for the enjoyment of freedom, is to sin against the most elementary rules of historic judgement" (WR, 124).

The problems with government are the same, whether it is an absolutist state, a constitutional monarchy, or a republic, for all entail a denial of individual liberty. The "best way of being free is not to be represented, not to abandon affairs—all affairs—to providence or to elected ones, but to handle them ourselves" (WR, 122).

Kropotkin outlined what he thought were the main drawback of representative government, namely, "rather than protecting the poor against the rich, and the working class against the bourgeoisie, representative government has always done the opposite; it has always organized the defence of the privileges of the commercial and industrial capitalist classes as against both the landed aristocracy and the working classes. Representative government is thus largely a protection racket on behalf of the interests of the capitalist" (WR, 127). Like the old liberal Adam Smith, Kropotkin thus affirmed that representative government is for the security of property, and is, in reality, instituted for the defence of the rich against the poor, for those who have property against those who have none. Not severing politics from economics the classical liberals, as with Kropotkin, had a much more historical sense of what the state—representative government—is all about than it seems contemporary liberals like Morland (1997) and Giddens (1998) have. These scholars view the state as a neutral "referee" who simply maintains order, resolves disputes, and coordinates conflicting interests. Kropotkin, to the contrary, affirms that "parliamentary rule is capital rule" (AY, 41).

Thus, even more than the absolutist state, representative government will always seek to increase its powers by legislation and by "meddling with everything, all the time killing the initiative of the individual and the group to supplant them by law" (WR, 125). The very essence of representative government—the modern state—is "to legislate in every aspect of human activity, to meddle in the smallest details of the lives of its 'subjects'" (WR, 126). Kropotkin recognised, long before Foucault, that the modern state, as the "organ of capitalist domination," constituted a force that permeates all aspects of social life and regulates all aspects of society. For representative government has an inherent tendency to concentrate political power, either in the form of a personal autocracy, a Bonapartist dictatorship that takes on all the trappings of the "Royalist tradition," or in the form of a bureaucratic administration that is completely divorced from the control of ordinary people. "Bureaucracy carried to an extreme becomes the characteristic of representative government" (WR, 130).

Kropotkin therefore felt that representative government, in the form of the nation-state, rather than leading to a more peaceful world, had in fact accentuated conflict and wars, as the bourgeoisie attempted to establish dominion over markets by military means: "Never has there been so much extermination as under the representative system" (WR, 130).

Finally, as indicated above, representative government tends to undermine the power and initiative of individuals and their associations, for they are threatened, from cradle to the grave, by the threat of coercive power, and are rarely free from the state's laws and its "lofty surveillance" (WR, 125).

As an alternative to representative government Kropotkin does not advocate making each local commune a "state in miniature" (WR, 133); nor does he have any time for the "worker's state" of the Marxists. "To dream of a worker's state," he wrote, "governed by an elected assembly, is the most unhealthy of all dreams that our authoritarian education inspires." There is, he concludes, no such thing as a good parliament (WR, 137).

In exploring the history of the modern state (which we discuss more fully in chapter 10 below), Kropotkin's central argument is that the emerging bourgeoisie became the "apostle" of representative government, and that the "omnipotence" of this class was consolidated and legitimated through parliamentary rule. It was through the National Assembly that the French bourgeoisie consolidated its power and established powers that were way beyond the wildest dreams of earlier "absolutist" monarchs. This "Jacobin idea," Kropotkin wrote, is still the ideal of the bourgeoisie of all the European states, and "representative government is its arm." This form of government he saw as corresponding to the reign of the bourgeoisie (WR, 143).

But, as indicated, Kropotkin was equally critical of the idea of a socialist or worker's state, or, as we noted earlier, a "revolutionary government." The dangers of centralized government become particularly problematic when the powers of government become extended to include economic life. A government entrusted with the management of industry and trade, and with economic life more generally, would, Kropotkin argued, be worse than any kind of theocracy or dictatorship and become a permanent danger to liberty and peace. The "popular state" of the Marxists, he wrote, is "as great a danger to liberty as any form of autocracy if its government is entrusted with the management of all social organization including the production and distribution of wealth" (KRP, 50).

Leaving aside all metaphysical notions of the state, as to its divine or "social contract" derivation, Kropotkin emphasized the *recent* origins of the modern state and its intrinsic relationship with the rise of capitalism and class society. And the future, he suggests, lies not with the further concentration of power, or the extension of the state's functions, but rather, Kropotkin writes, the opposite: "in the direction of decentralization, both territorial and functional . . . it is the abandonment to the initiative of freely constituted groups of all those functions which are now considered as the functions of government" (KRP, 51).

Kropotkin saw a correspondence between the forms of political organization and the economy: "A society founded on serfdom is in keeping with absolute monarchy; a society based on the wage system and the exploitation of the masses by the capitalists finds its political expression in parliamentarianism (representative government)"—and both these states constitute forms of class-rule. But in a free society, where the distinction between the capitalist and the worker has disappeared, as people have regained possession of their common inheritance through expropriation, a new form of political organization is required. This for Kropotkin is a system of "no-government," a federation of free communes or voluntary forms of association (CB, 70; KRP, 52).

Anarchism for Kropotkin thus represented a synthesis of the two currents of thought that were characteristic of the nineteenth century—radical liberalism and socialism and a repudiation of both capitalism and government.

In his essay on the "commune" (1880; WR, 81–89) Kropotkin speaks of the social revolution as being the "liberation of the communes" from state control. By the term "commune," Kropotkin implies any group of people who share on the basis of equality a community of interests; as such it does not necessarily mean a territorial unit but rather is a generic name, "a synonym for the grouping of equals which knows neither frontiers or walls" (WR, 88). He is therefore anxious to distinguish the "commune" from both the city-state and the commune of the medieval period.

The early communes—and Kropotkin refers mainly to the city communes of the twelfth century in Europe—were largely riven by social inequalities and though declaring their independence of the landed aristocracy and the crown (state), such medieval communes, he writes, were essentially "citadels of rich merchants" (WR, 83). They tended to be isolated units and somewhat insular, as well as under the control of the merchants—the urban aristocracy—"a state within a state." The commune as Kropotkin envisaged it, however, was to be based on human solidarity and to be absolutely free to adopt all the institutions it wished. It must therefore break free of the state and become part of a free federation of communes, each commune related to others through a diversity of relations.

Kropotkin felt that the tendencies in modern society were conducive to the development of an anarchist society in which the socialization of wealth and integrated labor could be combined with the fullest possible freedom for the human individual (KRP, 54). This form of social organization, as depicted by anarchists, was in accordance, he wrote, with the philosophy of evolution, with its emphasis on the plasticity of organizations, the adaptability of living organisms, and the sociality and mutuality that were inherent in all forms of organic nature.

Throughout his writings, Kropotkin offers criticisms of the capitalist world economy—that "monstrous organization," as he describes it. He argued that through the institution of private property, the wealth of the community (land, railroads, coal mines, factories, housing) had all been appropriated by a "few"—the owners of capital, who used this wealth not for the benefit of the majority of people but in order to generate profit for themselves. Production "takes no care of the needs of the community; its only aim is to increase the profits of the capitalist" (KRP, 55). In addition, as capitalism is prone to periodic crises, unemployment is a constant feature of social life under capitalism.

Moreover, in order to find markets in Asia and Africa, European capitalists, backed by governments, not only reduce "third world" peasants to the status of colonial "serfs," but also continually cause conflict and warfare. All European nations, Kropotkin wrote, seem to follow a similar pattern in seeking colonial expansion, and thus wars continually break out for precedence in the market: "Wars for the possession of the East, wars for the empire of the sea, wars to impose duties on imports and to dictate conditions to neighbouring states; wars against those 'blacks' who revolt! The roar of the cannon never ceases in the world, whole races are massacred, the states of Europe spend a third of their budgets on armaments" (CB, 48).

While immense sums were being spent by European states for the sole purpose of controlling territories and markets abroad, the exploitation of working people was the norm at home, where the "wealth of the wealthy springs from the poverty of the poor" (CB, 77). Over the past hundred years the nature of the capitalist world economy, now a "global order," has hardly changed in its essential nature—still generating social inequalities and widespread poverty, penetrating more and more aspects of social life, and continuing to give rise to conflicts and wars throughout the world.

The injustices of the capitalist system, the emphasis it puts on profit and egoism, are thus seen by Kropotkin as having a deplorable effect on social morality—leading to hypocrisy, double standards, and sophistry (KRP, 56).

For Kropotkin then there was an inherent contradiction between private property (capitalism)—which he held responsible for the gross social inequalities, wars, poverty, nihilism, and the reduction of working life to drudgery—and the social well-being of all people. And the only answer to this was the creation of a social economy based on communist principles, whereby "the means of production and of satisfaction . . . of all needs of society, having been created by the common efforts of all, must be at the disposal of all" (KRP, 56).

Thus in order to abolish capitalist rule, Kropotkin argued that anarchists must repudiate the two institutions that form the basis of this rule, and which collectivists or state socialists (Marxists) seek to retain—representative government and the wages system. We have noted above Kropotkin's critique of representative government. In a well-known essay, he provides an equally important critique of the "wages system" (1888; CB, 175–89).

Kropotkin poses the question as to whether, with the abolition of private property and the possession in common of all the means of production, it would still be possible to maintain a wages system. He sympathetically considers the ideas of socialists like Robert Owen and Proudhon, who recommended the use of "labour cheques" as a mode of remuneration under a socialist system. He notes that Proudhon in this mutualist system tried to make capitalism less offensive, but he retained private property and instituted a system of economic remuneration that would be proportionate to the hours of labour spent by each person during production. Kropotkin discusses in detail the problematic nature of attempting to estimate the value of an hour's labor—how to calculate, for example, the relative worth of professional and unskilled work—and comes to the conclusion that there can be no exact measure of the use-value of human labor. Thus, "a society having taken possession of all social wealth, having boldly proclaimed the right of all to this wealth—whatever share they may have taken in producing it—will be compelled to abandon any system of wages, whether in currency or labour notes" (CB, 183).

In a similar vein he writes elsewhere: "Common possession of the necessaries for production implies the common enjoyment of the fruits of the common production; and we consider that an equitable organization of society can only arise when every wage system is abandoned, and when everybody, contributing for the common well-being to the full extent of his capacities, shall enjoy also from the common stock of society to the fullest possible extent of his needs" (KRP, 59).

Kropotkin thus argues that under anarchist communism not only the instruments of production will be owned and controlled by local communities but also the social wealth generated by society would be deemed common property and freely available to all. The economy would thus entail the principle "From each according to his ability, to each according to his needs." By this was meant the idea that all people should be free to engage in the essential work of the community, all economic relationships being regulated by voluntary contracts and associations, and that each person would receive from the common pool whatever he needed to satisfy his personal needs (WA, 322).

An anarchist communist society would therefore be one "that recognizes the absolute liberty of the individual, that does not admit of any authority, and makes use of no compulsion to drive people to work" (CB, 159).

It would be a "free" society, that is, a society free of coercive authority. Kropotkin could thus foresee a society "where the liberty of the individual will be limited by no laws, no bonds—by nothing else but his own social habits and the necessity, which everyone feels, of finding co-operation, support, and sympathy among his neighbours" (KRP, 63).

This would entail not increasing the powers of the state but rather having recourse to voluntary associations and to the free federation of all those branches or aspects of life that are now considered the domain of the state (KRP, 69).

Kropotkin's vision of anarchist communism therefore entailed two fundamental critiques and thus the repudiation of both the modern state—"representative government"—and of modern capitalism. It was, as he put it, a "revolt against capital and state." Representative government (liberal democracy) he felt had "accomplished its historical mission" (KRP, 68), and capitalism was clearly incapable of satisfying the needs of all. In his optimism, he felt that capitalism could not last much longer, and certainly, contrary to liberals like Berlin and Giddens, he was acutely aware of the fact that "it is futile to speak of liberty as long as economic slavery exists" (KRP, 124). Thus Kropotkin stressed the need for communism and continually affirmed that anarchism and communism complemented each other. He therefore concluded that anarchist communism "is the best basis for individual development and freedom; not that individualism which drives man to the war of each against all—this is the only one known up till now—but that which represents the full expansion of man's faculties, the superior development of what is original in him, the greatest fruitfulness of intelligence, feeling and will" (KRP, 141).

Although Kropotkin did not spell out in detail the kind of direct democracy that he envisaged would eventually replace representational government—or "liberal oligarchy," as Castoriadis describes it (1991, 221)—he clearly indicated that committees, voluntary associations, and local and regional assemblies would be needed to deal with issues of public interest. But these agencies would have no coercive authority nor would they enact "laws" (KRP, 68).

2
THE PARIS COMMUNE
AND FREE COMMUNISM

K ropotkin clearly felt, like many of his socialist contemporaries, that he was living on the "eve of great events," and that a social revolution was imminent. The political institutions in which people had put their trust in the early part of the nineteenth century were, he thought, increasingly being questioned, and that "faith in parliamentary rule, in suffrage, be it limited or universal, is disappearing" (AY, 20). The Paris Commune of 1871 had made a tremendous impact on Kropotkin and his socialist contemporaries, and it had generated intense theoretical debate on possible new forms of political organization. For Marxists this meant the "dictatorship of the proletariat," a "worker's state"; for the anarchists the complete abolition of governments and their replacement by a federation of free communes. Although Kropotkin was in no sense a historical determinist and always spoke in terms of social "tendencies" and recognized that all knowledge was "conditional," he nevertheless interpreted the emergence of the numerous forms of mutual aid societies and voluntary associations at the end of the nineteenth century as heralding the demise of the nation-state, which he felt had "served its time" (AY, 41). Such free associations, he thought, would supplant both the state and the capitalist economy, taking over many of their functions. Education, social order, leisure activities, health, as well as economic life could all be organized— and would come to be organized—through communes and voluntary associations. His reflections on the Paris Commune and on societies of "free cooperation" are therefore scattered throughout his writings.

The Paris Commune of 1871 has been described as one of the most important urban insurrections of the nineteenth century. It has long been

65

heralded as both an inspiration and a model for revolutionary socialists. In his well-known address "The Civil War in France," written only a few days after the defeat of the commune, Karl Marx wrote that the Paris Commune "will be for ever celebrated as the glorious harbinger of a new society" and that its martyrs will always be enshrined in the hearts of the working class (Marx and Engels 1968, 307). Twenty years later, Engels described the commune as exemplifying the "dictatorship of the proletariat" and wrote that the state, whether a democratic republic or a monarchy, was in reality "nothing but a machine for the oppression of one class by another." Writing almost as a quasi-anarchist, Engels depicted a time when people would be "able to throw the entire lumber of the state on the scrap heap." Engels was, of course, essentially referring to the French empire, for he applauds the commune—which was based on universal suffrage—as a "new and truly democratic" state (258).

The Paris Commune lasted only seventy-two days. It was formally installed in the Hotel de Ville on March 28, 1871. As an elected body, it took over the administration of Paris in opposition to both the German occupation and the national government under the unscrupulous Adolphe Thiers. Its membership consisted of around eighty delegates, about half of whom were manual workers or had been involved in revolutionary politics, most of them members of the International Workingmen's Association. Their politics had an anarchist tinge, for they were largely followers of Proudhon and his economic theory of mutualism. About a dozen members of the commune were Blanquists, advocates of a revolutionary party, although Blanqui himself was imprisoned on the eve of the commune and was not released from prison until 1879. The commune also included the veteran republican journalist Charles Delecluze, who died on the barricades, as well as the anarchists Louise Michel, Éliseé Reclus, and Gustav Courbet. After the bloody suppression of the commune at the end of May, Reclus and Courbet were both forced to flee to Switzerland, along with Benoit Malon. Also a member of the International, Malon later wrote a history of the commune, and in the following year (1872) graphically described to Kropotkin his experiences of the commune.

The Paris Commune came to an end after a week of bitter and bloody street fighting, many women participating both in the building of the barricades and in taking up arms on behalf of the revolution. "Barricades and street fighting, the traditional warfare of the urban insurgent, were simply the last resort of the Commune's struggle for revolutionary self-government" (Edwards 1973, 41).

Around twenty-five thousand communards were killed in the bloody week of May 22–28, against 877 government troops, and more than ten thousand communards were imprisoned. Many were deported to New Caledonia, a French colony in the Pacific. There many lived in huts for several years, under a most brutal prison regime. Louise Michel was not released from prison until 1880. More people were killed in the bloody suppression of the Paris Commune than during the terror of the French Revolution (Edwards 1971, 346).

Although the Paris Commune took a radical step of allowing trade unions and workers' cooperations to take over factories and made a number of important reforms, it never questioned the rights of private property. Nevertheless, the very existence of the commune aroused the fury and antipathy of the bourgeoisie throughout Europe. Thus, when the army of the French republic crushed the commune, its chief executive Thiers declared that: "the cause of justice, of order, of humanity, and of civilization has triumphed" and that order and security had been restored. But for socialists throughout Europe, both Marxists and anarchists, the Paris Commune became a source of inspiration and a symbol of hope for a better future, the sentiments well expressed by Marx. But it is evident that Marx saw state power—as an instrument of society rather than independent of it—as a necessary institution and that he interpreted the commune as a positive form of a "social republic," one involving the "self-government of the producers." It was, he wrote, "essentially a working-class government" (Marx and Engels 1968, 287–90). Marxists, therefore, have always been critical of the idea of rejecting the centralized nation-state and of its replacement by a federation of autonomous communities or soviets. They have advocated instead a "republic of labor" or the "dictatorship of the proletariat." Lenin interpreted this as implying the rule of a revolutionary (Bolshevik) party—a form of politics that is more akin to Blanquism—and it led Trotsky to be critical of the Paris Commune precisely because it lacked the central direction of such a revolutionary party (Edwards 1971, 359; for further important studies of the Paris Commune, see Jellinek 1937; Horne 1965; Bookchin 1998, 192–251).

Bakunin, who took a crucial part in the revolutionary uprisings at Lyon and Marseilles in September/October 1870, was to claim, in contrast to Marx, that the Paris Commune demonstrated the bankruptcy of state socialism. It was, "a bold, clearly formulated negation of the state," and though the majority of its members were Jacobins like Delecluze rather than socialists, nevertheless the Paris Commune was seen as inaugurating a new era. It initiated, Bakunin wrote, a social rather than a political revo-

lution. He concluded: "Contrary to the belief of the authoritarian communists that a social revolution must be decreed and organized either by a dictatorship or by a constituent assembly emerging from a political revolution,
our friends, the Paris Socialists, believed that revolution could neither be
made nor brought to its full development except by the spontaneous and
continuous action of the masses, the groups and associations of the people"
(quoted in Dolgoff 1973, 264–68).

The Paris Commune was always of central interest to Kropotkin. He
had met and engaged in long discussions with many of the communards—
particularly with Gustave Le Français, Louise Michel, Élisée Reclus,
Benoit Malon, and André Bastelica. In 1879 Kropotkin had established the
anarchist paper *Le Révolté*, and every March he wrote an anniversary
article celebrating the Paris Commune. The three for 1880, 1881, and 1882
were put together to form a single chapter of *Paroles d'un Révolté* ("Words
of a Rebel"), published in 1885 (Walter 1971, 11).

The revolution of 1871 was, for Kropotkin, above all a popular one,
made by the people themselves. "It sprang up spontaneously from within
the masses," he wrote, when on March 18, 1871, the people of Paris rose
against the despised government and proclaimed the city free and independent. The overthrow of central power, Kropotkin continued, took place
without the "usual scenes of a revolutionary uprising; on that day there
were neither volleys of shot nor floods of blood shed behind the barricades.
The rulers were eclipsed by an armed people going out into the streets; the
soldiers evacuated the city, the bureaucrats hastened towards Versailles,
taking with them everything they could carry. The government evaporated
like a pool of stagnant water in the spring breeze" (WR, 90).

In the years prior to the commune there emerged, Kropotkin suggested,
within the International Workingmen's Association two currents of political
thought—one advocating a people's state, the other anarchy, the free federation of worker's cooperatives. Kropotkin misleadingly thought of these
two conceptions in ethnic terms, the German Socialists supporting state
socialism, while the socialists of the "Latin race" (Spanish, French) advocating the complete abolition of the state. The socialist state, Kropotkin
suggested, was viewed by the majority of the French Socialists as the worst
of all tyrannies. But unlike Bakunin, Kropotkin did not feel that the Paris
Commune, in spite of its eminently popular character and the heroic struggles of the communards, was in fact a form of anarchy. The Commune of
1871 "could not be any more than a first sketch. Born at the end of the war,
surrounded by two armies ready to give a hand in crushing the people, it

dared not declare itself openly socialist, and proceeded neither to the expropriation of capital, nor to the organization of work, nor even to a general inventory of the city's resources. Nor did it break with the tradition of the State, of representative government, and (proclaim) the independence and free federation of communes" (WR, 93).

But Kropotkin felt that had the Paris Commune survived, then these "two revolutions" might well have occurred, driven by the force of events—Kropotkin, like other socialists at the time, sensing that a revolution was imminent. Thus, Kropotkin concluded that the Commune "gladdens our hearts not for what it achieved, but for what it has promised one day to achieve" (WR, 95). And for Kropotkin a social revolution implied the abolition of both government (state) and private property (capitalism), as well as of religious ideology. This entailed overcoming three "prejudices," sustained and advocated respectively by priests, proprietors, and rulers—god, property, and government (WR, 102).

Kropotkin suggested that there were two interrelated tendencies evident in the nineteenth century, one an ever-growing movement toward limiting the scope of government, the other a growing tendency toward free associations or "free communism." Overly optimistic, and at times somewhat prophetic in his utterances, Kropotkin tended to overemphasize the social significance of both these tendencies. Indeed, rather than seeing the demise of the nation-state and the replacement of capitalism by voluntary associations, the power and reach of these two institutions—the "big battalions" as Giddens describes states, business corporations, and the international agencies of capital (1994, 162)—have over the past hundred years continued to expand. "Capital" has become global and the modern "state" ever more powerful through disciplinary practices, biopower, and surveillance. But Kropotkin, nevertheless, was a perceptive observer of social life and graphically outlined the many forms of "free agreement" that emerged in the nineteenth century. These included many forms of association that were established without any intervention of central governments—railway networks, lifeboat associations, voluntary organizations like the Red Cross, trade unions, professional and scientific societies, and hospital associations (CB, 145–58). Hundreds of societies "are constituted everyday for the satisfaction of some of the infinitely varied needs of civilized man" (KRP, 66). Thus, he inferred that there was a general social trend in which the free association of individuals was supplanting government agencies in the performance of many social functions. He noted that many of these societies or associations made decisions at conferences through delegates, but that they did not institute "laws," only

"agreements" (KRP, 68). Kropotkin also emphasized that many public services—museums, libraries, parks, street lighting—were provided in the spirit
of communism and were focused on personal and social needs. These services put the needs of the individual *above* the valuation of the services that
the person may have rendered to society (KRP, 60).

But although Kropotkin emphasizes the power and intrusive nature of
the modern state, he also puts equal emphasis on the fact that much of
everyday social life and many social activities are independent of the state.
Like other anarchists, Kropotkin always made a clear distinction between
capitalism and government (state), and society, between what later Habermas
describes as "systems" and the human "life-world" (Outhwaite 1994, 86).
Every day, Kropotkin wrote, millions of social transactions are made without
the slightest interference of government (KRP, 64). Kropotkin's essential
conception of revolution was the replacement of state institutions based on
hierarchy and coercion with voluntary relationships, even though he tended
to see the state as an external, coercive institution. Gustav Landauer (1870–
1919), the German romantic socialist and anarchist who was greatly influenced by Kropotkin, put it well: "The state is a condition, a certain relationship among human beings, a mode of behaviour between men; we destroy it
by contracting other relationships, by behaving differently towards one
another . . . we are the state . . . until we have created institutions that form a
real community and society of men" (Lunn 1973, 226).

This, for Kropotkin, did not simply imply forming a "temporary autonomous zone" for free spirits within a rampant capitalism (Bey 1985),
but the creation of real social institutions based on voluntary cooperation
that would supplant both capitalism and the state.

In his study *Mutual Aid*, Kropotkin emphasized, and described in some
detail, the "mutual-aid tendency" that was still evident, and indeed, he
thought, expanding among European peoples. In spite of the fact that
throughout Europe, but especially in England and France, the common
lands of the village communities had been plundered, seized, or expropri-
ated by the landed aristocracy, communal institutions and habits of mutual
support still existed, Kropotkin argued, throughout many parts of France,
Germany, Spain, Switzerland, and the Scandinavian countries. He noted,
for example, that around two-thirds of the forests and alpine meadows of
Switzerland were still under communal control and that the village communities still maintained their customs and institutions of mutual aid (MA,
191–92). He noted, too, that wherever the peasants had been able to resist
the plunder of their lands, and to maintain a "spirit" of community, then

peasant associations had been formed, such as the Syndicats Agricoles in France, although such unions or syndicates had been forbidden by law in many European states until the end of the nineteenth century (MA, 196). Contrary to the opinion of the economists, Kropotkin maintained that communal ownership of land was in no way incompatible with intensive culture and agricultural improvement, for many peasant communities initiated the rotation of crops and agricultural improvements such as drainage and irrigation, without this entailing the privatization of land. With regard to African societies, Kropotkin affirms from the literature that in spite of tribal conflicts, the tyranny and oppression of local rulers, and the devastation caused by the Atlantic slave trade, local people continued to maintain a "certain civilization" and that mutual aid customs and institutions continued to thrive (MA, 203–206).

Equally important, Kropotkin emphasizes that outside the rural setting, mutual aid associations continued to flourish and expand throughout the nineteenth century, with the emergence, as we have noted, of varied forms of association—trade unions; friendly societies; trading guilds (in Russia, *artels*); the lifeboat association; various clubs that cater for leisure activities, such as alpine climbing and cycling; neighborhood associations; and scientific, literary, and education societies—all these exemplified for Kropotkin enduring social institutions of mutual aid and support (MA, 212–23). They also indicated the spontaneous initiatives of ordinary people, and, for Kropotkin, the fact that voluntary associations and local communes or municipalities could, and should, as earlier denoted, supplant state institutions and the market economy.

Kropotkin envisaged a society based on "free communism," a society without a state, where all essential social activities were controlled and organized through voluntary associations and a network of autonomous federated communes. Kropotkin was not politically naïve and recognized that no social life was possible without some forms of control and authority and that it was nonsensical to think of anarchy as implying the complete absence of power. What he envisaged was the creation of a society where power was dispersed, where "repression" was kept to a minimum, and where there were no institutionalized forms of hierarchy or coercive authority, implying that limits were put on the concentration of power—whether political, economic, or ideological. But Kropotkin clearly recognized that some social controls would be necessary in order to maintain social order. From his observation and studies of tribal and kin-based societies, Kropotkin recognized that social customs and economic interdependence spontaneously generated mechanisms for controlling violent and anti-social behavior in such societies. Like Tolstoy, he disavowed the use of coercion, or at least wanted to keep it to a minimum, suggesting that "society possesses a thousand other means of preventing anti-social acts" (KRP, 134). He suggested three main ways in which human societies dealt with antisocial behavior. The first is by repression, or by coercive means—which Kropotkin repudiates as both ineffective in the long term and contrary to human well-being: "Not only has a coercive system contributed and powerfully aided to create all the present economic, political and social evils, but it has given proof of its absolute impotence to raise the moral level of societies" (KRP, 137).

Second, there is the importance of moral teaching, but this was often ineffective, Kropotkin felt, given the influence of immoral teachings that stemmed from institutional religion. Christianity, he emphasized, was always in close alliance with state power.

Finally, there were the institutional controls on antisocial behavior, reflected in customary norms and the practice of mutual aid—a concept central to Kropotkin's social philosophy, which we discuss more fully below (see chapter 7).

But in contemporary Western society, face-to-face communication, mutual aid, and voluntary associations tend to be restricted, marginalized by the state:

> We live side by side without knowing one another. We come together at meetings on an election day: we listen to the lying or fanciful professions of faith in a candidate, and we return home. The state has the care of all questions of public interest; the state alone has the function of seeing that we do not harm the interests of our neighbour. . . .
>
> Our neighbour may die of hunger or murder his children—it is no business of ours; it is the business of the policeman. You hardly know one another, nothing unites you, everything tends to alienate you from one another. . . . (KRP, 140)

But throughout human history, tribal and peasant societies have developed various institutional forms and diffuse sanctions—ranging from simple expressions of disapproval to excommunication and ostracism—that have been utilized to counter antisocial acts. But given his general optimism, Kropotkin tended to think these diffuse sanctions, along with public opinion and formative habits, would tend, often unconsciously, to prevent antisocial behavior (KRP, 101). But as Graham Purchase insists, though overly optimistic, Kropotkin was not naïve; he thus recognized that in certain circumstances, often extreme sanctions would have to be applied to curb unwarranted behavior—in any human community (1996, 84).

In his study *Community, Anarchy and Liberty*, Michael Taylor (1982), although mentioning Kropotkin only once in the text, essentially offers a defense and a reaffirmation of anarchist communism (or communitarian anarchism). Using the concept of "public good," Taylor suggests that social order and the security of the person from robbery and violence—Kropotkin's antisocial acts—constitute public goods and that the provision of such goods can be achieved through three essential "methods": the state, the market, and the community. He offers succinct critiques of the liberal justification of the state, whether the "minimal" or welfare state, as well as of the more recent neoliberal (anarcho-capitalist) arguments for the provision of all public goods or services through the market (1982, 53–65). Taylor thus concludes—simply reaffirming what Kropotkin and many generations of social anarchists had long ago contended—that social order can be achieved most satisfactorily through the local community.

Although the concept of "community," like all general concepts, has an "open-texture," Taylor suggests that it has three "core" characteristics; namely, it implies shared beliefs and values by a group of people, social relationships that are direct and multiplex, and various forms of reciprocity, including mutual aid, cooperative associations, and other forms of sharing. But Taylor emphasizes also the importance of a sense of belonging and mutual affirmation, and drawing on contemporary anthropological studies, he outlines the many forms of social control and the various means of maintaining social order found in tribal and peasant societies, as well as in various intentional or utopian communities within the nation-state. These include: the threat of "self-help" retaliation; forms of reciprocity and food-sharing (that could be withdrawn); informal sanctions of approval and disapproval, including gossip, shaming, and ridicule; initiations and other forms of socialization; ostracism; and the threat of supernatural sanctions (1982, 65–91).

Taylor also emphasizes the fact that, for communities to be viable, economic inequalities and asymmetric power relations have to be contained and reduced to a minimum, for economic equality is viewed as an essential condition of community. He thus concludes that: "community makes possible the effective use of social controls which are an alternative to the concentrated force of the state" (1982, 140). He also repudiates the familiar liberal argument that community is inimical to liberty, although unwilling to concede that liberty is possible only in community. All this is consonant

and replicates Kropotkin's essential ideas outlined years before in numerous texts and pamphlets, none of which Taylor cites.

But Taylor implies that anarchy, and the use of informal methods of social
control, is only possible in "small and stable" communities, where there exists
a "coherent" worldview and people have a clear "sense of identity" (1982,
161). He thus seems highly skeptical of the possibility of anarchist communism on a wider scale, involving confederal relations between autonomous
communities, as Kropotkin envisaged. But contrary to liberal scholars, Taylor
clearly affirms the basic premises of communitarian anarchists like Kropotkin,
that liberty, equality, and community form a coherent set (1982, 166). But this,
of course, was the rallying cry of the French Revolution.

It is important to recognize that by "free communism" Kropotkin did
not imply a "city state," as he has often, quite misleadingly, been interpreted (Avrich 1988, 76; Black 1994, 32)—which is why he wrote little
about democracy or the Greek city-state, although he clearly envisaged
some form of direct democracy within the local community. Nor did
Kropotkin sanctify or give priority to the community over that of the individual—which is an equally misleading interpretation of Kropotkin's
thought (Keulartz 1998, 137).

As Kropotkin wrote:

> Anarchist communism maintains that most valuable of all conquests—indi-
> vidual liberty—and moreover extends it and gives it a solid basis—eco-
> nomic liberty—without which political liberty is delusive; it does not ask
> the individual who has rejected god the universal tyrant, god the king, and
> god the parliament, to give unto himself a god more terrible than any of the
> preceding—god the community, or to abdicate upon its altar this independ-
> ence, his will, his tastes, and to renew the vow of asceticism which he for-
> merly made before the crucified god. It says to him, on the contrary, "No
> society is free so long as the individual is not so." (1890, 14–15)

Quite ironically this quotation has been used by Black (1997, 32) to
defend the kind of Stirnerian individualism that Kropotkin repudiated, as
well as a critique of the "leftism" (i.e., socialism—"economic liberty") and
social anarchism that Kropotkin himself advocated throughout his life. This
kind of scholarship is quite shameful. What Kropotkin meant by "free communism" was the kind of society, based he felt on a confederation of free
communes and voluntary associations, that would allow the full development of what Alan Ritter was later to describe as "communal individuality"
(1980, 3)—not the amoral egoism of the Nietzschean free spirit.

3
OBJECTIONS TO ANARCHISM AND THE CRITIQUE OF PRISONS

In his writings Kropotkin always endeavored to address the various "objections" put forward against his theory of anarchist communism— that it is simply a utopian schema that might be viable if all humans were saints, but could not possibly work with respect to ordinary people; that without government or some form of coercive authority or "law," social chaos and disorder would inevitably ensue; that without compulsion nobody would bother to keep agreements or do any work; and, finally, that without state institutions (courts, police, prisons) antisocial tendencies would run amok, and in the words of Hobbes, there would be a "war of everyone against everyone," and thus life would be solitary, nasty, brutish, and short (1651, 100).

All these misleading interpretations of anarchism Kropotkin attempted to dispel.

The notion that it was a utopian vision relating to the future, and that as an ideal it was too beautiful and lofty for ordinary mortals, Kropotkin countered in two ways. First, he argued that this conception of a society based on anarchist principles was nothing new, and that throughout human history, there have been popular institutions and social movements that did not entail coercive forms of authority. Early tribal communities were "societies without government," and social life was organized through kinship (clan organization) and through the village community. Even in modern societies, Kropotkin argued, voluntary associations were important as a tendency and as a "latent force" within the society (KRP, 133).

Second, although Kropotkin never thought that one can simply "deduce" social ideas from the findings of the natural sciences (KRP, 115), he firmly believed that anarchist principles were based not on metaphysical speculations or on a utopian vision but rather on a socio-historical understanding of human social life, in all its aspects. He affirmed, as we shall explore, both evolutionary theory and the social sciences that were then emerging at the end of the nineteenth century. When we ask for the abolition of the state, "we are always told that we dream of a society composed of men better than they are in reality. But no; a thousand times, no. All we ask is that men should not be made worse than they are, by such institutions" (KRP, 134).

Kropotkin's anarchist communism was thus less a vision of a future utopia but rather an attempt to sustain and develop the kind of institutions based on sociality and free cooperation that already formed an essential part of all human societies, even the most tyrannical. It was to preserve and expand the precious "kernel" of social customs without which no human, or even animal society, could exist (KRP, 137).

As in common parlance the word "anarchy" is synonymous with disorder, there was the question also as to whether anarchy and the absence of "law" necessarily entail chaos and disorder. This equation of anarchy with disorder implies "First, that wherever there is no government, there is disorder; and it implies, moreover, that order, due to strong government and a strong police is always beneficial" (KRP, 62).

Both these suppositions Kropotkin felt were mistaken, for there is plenty of order in many branches of human social activity where the government, happily, does not intrude, and conversely, the kind of order found in many states, or that which was instituted by Thiers in suppressing the Paris Commune, are hardly estimable. Kropotkin wrote an important short essay specifically devoted to the issue of "Law and Authority" (1882, WR, 145–64), and we may outline some of its important themes.

We live at a time, Kropotkin suggests, when a great "fetish" has developed around the concept of "law." We are constantly being told to respect the "law," and so much emphasis has been put on this that it threatens to befog our intelligence completely. Servility toward the law has come to be considered a virtue, and the propagation of some new law is invariably seen as the remedy for all social problems. In contemporary society we no longer consider it possible to live otherwise than under the "regime of law." In fact, Kropotkin writes, for thousands of years those who govern us have continually repeated, in almost "mantra" fashion: Respect the law; obey authority (WR, 146). History books, the schools, political science, theology . . . all are aimed to inculcate in us the same prejudice—respect the law.

Since the advent of bourgeoisie rule, this "cult of law" has become firmly established. In the eighteenth century philosophers like Montesquieu, Voltaire, and Rousseau advocated equality before the law to counter the absolutist state, but along with the principle of representative government, the bourgeoisie of the nineteenth century had transformed the "law" into a "yoke," into an instrument of authority and oppression.

Kropotkin advocates repudiating this "fetish," challenging its corrupting influence. We need, he writes, not to "respect the law" but to revolt against it and to despise the law and all its attributes. We need to recognize that the "law" is a relatively modern phenomenon and that humans have lived for many centuries without any kind of written law. Since earliest times humans have regulated their lives through habits, local customs, and cultural usages. Among tribal communities, as well as among the peasants of Europe and Asia, mutual relations of the inhabitants are still regulated "not by the written law of the (state) legislators, but by old customs that are still generally accepted" (WR, 150). Such social practices are not established by state laws, nor are they based on religious precepts—they are anterior to all law and religion, and have their origins in the sociality of animal life: "The hospitality of primitive (i.e. clan-based) peoples, the respect for human life, the feeling for reciprocity, compassion for the weak, the courage to sacrifice oneself in the interests of others . . . all these qualities developed among mankind before there were any laws and independently of any religion, as they had developed among all the social animals" (WR, 151).

Kropotkin recognized that human nature was complex, and that alongside sociable feelings and solidarity, other passions and desires were only too evident and because of these passions other habits and customs had emerged. The latter include the desire to dominate others and to subjugate and impose one's will on other people. Such egoistic desires, in time, gave rise to priests and shamans who exploit people through religious ideology and to military chiefs and brigands who invade and pillage their neighbors. When class societies emerged, Kropotkin argued, "Law made its appearance, sanctified by the priest and having at its service the warrior's mace. It sought to stabilize the customs that were advantageous to the dominant group, and the military authority undertook to ensure obedience" (WR, 153).

The law therefore has what Kropotkin describes as a "double character" that it retains to this day—combining the principles of morality and solidarity that have developed through the common life of humans, with the orders and codes that are advantageous to the rulers, and that are needed to consolidate and consecrate class inequalities. No more than private capital, which was also born of fraud and violence and developed under the auspices of authority, "has the law any title to human respect" (WR, 153).

Kropotkin saw the development of legal codes as intrinsically linked with the bourgeoisie and with the rise of capitalism. Socialists—rather than the savants—have indicated how capitalism "was born of wars and pillage, of slavery and serfdom, of fraud and modern ways of exploitation. They have shown how it was nourished by the blood of the workers and how it has slowly conquered the entire world" (WR, 154).

Thus, most laws have only one aim: protecting private property (the wealth acquired through exploitation) and sanctioning new forms of exploitation as capital seizes on new areas of social life—telegraphs, electricity, railways, chemical industries. According to Kropotkin, all modern law has the same aim, namely, "to maintain the governmental machine that assures capital the exploitation and accumulation of all the wealth that is produced. Magistrates, police, armed forces, public institutions, finance—all serve the same God: Capital" (WR, 157).

Law has thus little to do with the protection of the individual; the essence of legal codes is the "protection of exploitation, directly by laws regarding property, and indirectly by sustaining the state" (WR, 158).

Kropotkin therefore suggests that modern laws could be considered under three categories.

The first are the laws whose essential purpose is the protection of private property and have no other purpose than that of upholding exploitation—"protecting the unjust appropriation of the work of humanity by certain monopolists (i.e. capitalists)" (WR, 160). Second, those laws that relate to the organization of the state, whether relating to taxes or custom duties, or to the state administration (bureaucracy, army, the police). These laws have no other purpose than to uphold and protect the government. Third, there are the laws that relate to the protection of persons and deal with so-called crimes. We are continually told of the benefits of the law and the salutary effects of punishment. But Kropotkin is adamant that these laws, and the harsh penalties that are meted out to offenders, have little impact on the rate of crime. For crimes are largely related to social and personal factors, not to the severity of punishments: "One fact has been clearly established: the severity of punishments in no way diminishes the number of crimes. You can hang, draw and quarter the murderers as much as you like, but the number of murders will not diminish" (WR, 162). Nor has the fear of punishment ever curtailed anyone from committing murder or theft. Even though modern penitentiaries are more corrupting than the dungeons of the medieval period, they neither serve to reduce crime, nor do they in any way "reform" the criminal.

Kropotkin thus concludes that guillotines and prisons must be abolished; that magistrates and police are unnecessary; and that all forms of law are useless and harmful. Freedom, fraternity, and the practice of human solidarity are the only effective means of countering the antisocial proclivities of the few among us who commit antisocial acts (WR, 164). We discuss below, in more detail, Kropotkin's important and pioneering essays on the prison system.

Because the Paris Commune had been violently suppressed in the name of restoring "order" and "authority," and because anarchy in ordinary speech had come to be used as a synonym for "disorder," Kropotkin wrote another short essay specifically on "Order" (WR, 76–80). He noted that terms like "anarchist," "sans-culottes" and "nihilist" had always been bestowed on people by the *enemies* of the popular revolution. And though the terms were meant to be derogatory, what they essentially conveyed was a "revolt" of the people and the "negation" of the existing order. Thus the word *nihilist*, for example, first popularized by Turgenev in his novel *Fathers and Sons*, was not entirely inappropriate, since it embraced an idea: "it expressed a negation of all the features of present-day civilization that are based on the oppression of one class by another; the negation of the existing economic system, the negation of governmentalism and power, of bourgeois politics, of routine science, of bourgeois morality, or art put at the service of the exploiters; of the . . . hypocrisy (of) present-day society" (WR, 77).

Likewise with the word "anarchist." Initially used as a term of abuse during the French Revolution (against the *enrages*), it was later adopted by Proudhon and used in a more positive sense. Kropotkin notes that many anarchist-communists within the First International initially avoided using the term "anarchist" (which they identified with the Proudhonists) and preferred to describe themselves as antistate socialists or as federalists. Kropotkin emphasizes that in its original Greek meaning *an-archy* signifies "no-power" and not "disorder," although this is how it is invariably used, even by philosophers. He quotes the English utilitarian philosopher Jeremy Bentham, who (in 1816) wrote: "The philosopher who wants to reform a bad law does not preach insurrection against it. . . . The character of the anarchist is quite different. He denies the existence of the law, he rejects its validity, he incites men to ignore it as a law and to rise up against its implementation."

Kropotkin stresses that the anarchist denies not only existing laws, but all forms of power and authority. The anarchist rebels, he wrote, "against power, authority, under whatever form it may appear" (WR, 78). Those postmodernists who interpret the so-called classical anarchists like Kropotkin as being narrowly "antistate" completely misunderstand the project of these early anarchists—who were opposed to all forms of power and coercive authority (May 1994).

In present-day society, Kropotkin asks, what do the terms "order" and "disorder" actually entail? "Order," he replies, means servitude, poverty, power in the hands of a corrupt minority; deprivation for nine-tenths of humanity; a woman selling herself to feed her children; wars . . . "order," finally, "is the drowning in blood of the Paris Commune."

In contrast, what is meant by "disorder"—the insurrection of peasants, the abolition of ancient slavery, and the struggles of all people against oppression and against an unjust and ignoble social order? Anarchy thus implies the negation of order, as well as the repudiation of law and authority (WR, 78–80).

The concept of "law" still holds a fascination for contemporary philosophers and political theorists, who—in Hobbesian fashion—see the only alternative to upholding state "law" to be chaos, brigandage, or tyranny. Examples are Ayn Rand and the liberal philosopher Bryan Magee. Rand, who thought of anarchy as a "naïve floating abstraction," suggested that the only alternative to organized government and free-market capitalism was the "chaos of gang warfare" (1964, 112). In his autobiography Magee also suggests that the "rule of law" is indispensable to civilized life and that "without law, everything becomes a matter of arbitrary power"—as if the only alternative to state power is banditry—but then admits that "law" may be cynically used as an "instrument of tyrannical government." All revolutions, he argues, are betrayed, and any revolution carried out in the name of civil liberties or to end tyranny inevitably ends in tyranny (Magee 1997, 31). But one can equally well argue that Napoleon, Stalin, and Hitler—the result of failed revolutions—were all "counter-revolutionary" and great advocates of "law" and "order."

Kropotkin also wrote extensively on the issue as to whether under anarchist communism (which involves no coercive authority) people will keep their agreements or even be inclined to work at all. He emphasized that there are two kinds of agreements—those that are freely entered upon by mutual agreement and those that are enforced agreement. Kropotkin argues that wage-labor is in essence a form of slavery imposed by force and that it is a mockery to call it a "free contract." Adam Smith, he suggests, was never guilty of such misrepresentation, and it is only the powers of the state that prevent working people from repudiating such "contracts" and taking possession of what has been appropriated by the few—the land and the means of production. He then affirms that no force is necessary if agreements or contracts are freely and mutually entered upon (KRP, 69). As for the notion that people will not work unless forced to do so, either by the threat of hunger or compulsion, Kropotkin reminds us that anti-abolitionists in America and the Russian nobility both expressed the same fears with respects to the emancipation of African slaves and serfs (whose emancipation they vehemently opposed), arguing that people would not work without some form of coercion. Of course, Kropotkin suggests, under the present economic system, in which the worker is compelled to work long hours for meager wages, under coercive management and in unhealthy working conditions, and with possible unemployment always threatening, work is a drudgery and often loathed. But economic life does not have to be organized this way, and Kropotkin makes a distinction between creative work and useless toil. The evidence of the political economists suggests that people produce most when they work in freedom, when they have a choice of occupation and don't have an overseer continually monitoring their activities, and when people see that work is conducive to their own and others' well-being.

Kropotkin emphasizes that manual work and the provision of the basic necessities of life—food, shelter, clothes, transport, heating, and lighting—are indispensable to human existence, but nevertheless he felt that the production of these necessities could be achieved by voluntary associations and in wholesome working conditions. A society that aims at the well-being of all, and at the possibility of all enjoying life to the full, will, he stressed, organize economic life through voluntary associations. Chattel slavery, serfdom, and wage-labor are all to be repudiated, not only because of their coercive nature but because they make all work a "drudgery." It is about time, he suggests, that we dispel the myth that "wage-labor" is the best incentive to productive work (CB, 163–66): "Overwork is repulsive to human nature—not work, overwork for supplying the few with luxury—not work for the well-being of all. Work is a physiological necessity, a necessity of spending accumulated bodily energy, a necessity which is health and life itself" (KRP, 71).

He agreed with Benjamin Franklin that four or five hours of useful work every day would be more than sufficient for supplying everyone with the basic necessities of life, and Kropotkin argued that there was no reason why a factory or workshop could not be as pleasant and healthy as a scientific laboratory. Although Kropotkin held traditional attitudes toward the family, he nevertheless stressed the emancipation of women: "To emancipate woman is to free her from the brutalizing toil of kitchen and washhouse; it is to organize your household in such a way as to enable her to rear her children, if she be so minded, while still retaining sufficient leisure to take her share of social life . . . liberty, equality, solidarity, would not be a revolution if it maintained slavery at home" (CB, 144).

The truly lazy person Kropotkin thought to be extremely rare, and as to the laziness of the great majority of workers, only philistine economists and philanthropists could utter such nonsense. Once work was no longer a drudgery and freely undertaken, then Kropotkin felt that idleness and malingering would disappear. When people are idle there is usually some reason. "Suppress the cause of idleness, and you may take it for granted that few individuals will really hate work, especially voluntary work, and that there will be no need to manipulate a code of laws on their account" (CB, 174).

Thus, Kropotkin concluded, under anarchist communism "work will become a pleasure and a relaxation in a society of equals" (CB, 139).

In a well-known essay, Bob Black (n.d.), with some pretension, calls for the abolition of work. "No-one should ever work," he writes. But as he defines work as "compulsory production" or "forced labour," his notion that "most brands of anarchism" have believed in work (in this sense) constitutes a wilful misrepresentation of an earlier generation of anarchists—though this assertion may bolster his own sense of originality and self-importance. As far as I am aware, no anarchist has ever advocated "forced labour," and critiques of "wage-slavery" under capitalism go back to the nineteenth century. Kropotkin certainly advocated the abolition of "work" as forced labor and as a drudgery. But like Tolstoy and his friend William Morris, Kropotkin affirmed that work was one of the basic conditions of human happiness—work, that is, that was voluntary, creative, productive, and pleasurable, and geared to the promotion of well-being.

But for all the value that Kropotkin placed upon work, he was clearly no advocate of Spartan austerity and was vehemently opposed to the state-imposed social engineering of the authoritarian communists—with its emphasis on obedience, rational planning, control, regimentation, and bureaucratic uniformity. Kropotkin was not only critical of the "phalanstery" (of the followers of Fourier) but also found Lenin's "state capitalism" equally unacceptable. Lenin's contention that: "unquestioning submission to a single will is absolutely necessary for the success of labour processes that are based on large-scale machine industry . . . today the revolution demands, in the interests of socialism, that the masses unquestioningly obey the single will of the leaders of the labour process" (Brinton 1970, 41).

This would have been absolutely anathema to Kropotkin.

For Kropotkin, not only was work to be based on free cooperation, but he considered that adequate leisure was no less vital for the development of the human personality. The essence of a social revolution was to provide bread for everyone: but humans are not beings "whose exclusive purpose in life is eating, drinking and providing shelter." For humans have a variety of other needs that have to be fulfilled. "After bread has been secured, leisure is the supreme aim" (CB, 124). And leisure takes into account many diverse interests: "Literature, science and art must be cultivated by free men. Only on this condition will they succeed in emancipating themselves from the yoke of the state, of capital, and of the bourgeois mediocrity which stifles them" (CB, 131).

Moreover, Kropotkin recognized the importance of privacy in human life and wrote: "Isolation, alternating with time spent in society, is the normal desire of human nature" (CB, 140). Prison, phalansteries, monasteries . . . all are seen as restrictive in that they encumber the human spirit.

The final objection to anarchism is that without state power, antisocial behavior would be rampant, and some form of government is therefore necessary to punish those who break the laws of society. We noted earlier some of Kropotkin's reflections on this issue, and to conclude this chapter, we may briefly discuss his critique of the prison system and his thoughts on the control of antisocial behavior.

Kropotkin, of course, had first-hand experiences with the prisons of both Russia and France. As a young military officer in Siberia, aged only twenty (1862), Kropotkin was appointed secretary of a committee with the task of reporting on the reform of prisoners. Kropotkin took the project seriously: he read and studied books and reports on the subject of prisons, traveled widely, and met and discussed the issues with a considerable number of people. He visited a number of prisons, as well as the labor camps of political exiles who were working as convicts in the most awful conditions, in the silver and gold mines of Transbaikal. The conclusion that Kropotkin came to was that the prisons and labor camps were a disgrace to humanity and that a new system of penal organization was imperative. "I must confess," he wrote later, "that at that time I still believed that prisons could be reformatories, and that the privation of liberty is compatible with moral amelioration . . . but I was only twenty years old" (RFP, 18).

A decade later, arrested for his involvement with a group of Russian populists, the Chaikovsky Circle, Kropotkin was to spend two years of solitary confinement in the infamous fortress of St. Peter and St. Paul in St. Petersburg, awaiting trial. On entering this dark, damp, and dismal dungeon, he later recalled, he often thought of Bakunin, who had spent six years imprisoned in the fortress. Although allowed to write up his geographical studies, Kropotkin suffered much from the isolation and, as the cell was extremely damp, began to suffer from rheumatism. He was later transferred to the newly opened House of Detention in St. Petersburg, which was then considered a model prison. But as he suffered from scurvy and his health deteriorated he was again transferred, in May 1876, to a small prison attached to the military hospital. It was from here that Kropotkin made his famous and dramatic escape from prison. This escape is graphically described in his *Memoirs* (MR, 365–75). He was also later to give a vivid description of the conditions in the St. Peter and St. Paul Fortress, noting the horrors of solitary confinement, the ill treatment meted out to prisoners for the slightest misdemeanor, the problems with scurvy and tuberculosis due to the unhealthy and harsh prison conditions, and the fact that there was a very high level of suicide and insanity. Out of one hundred and ninety prisoners in the fortress, Kropotkin records, "nine went mad, eleven attempted suicide" (RFP, 103).

After some five years of anarchist activities in Switzerland and France, Kropotkin was again arrested in December 1882, accused of belonging to an illegal political organization, the International Workingmen's Association. Found guilty, Kropotkin was sentenced to five years in prison. After a couple of months in the Lyon prison, Kropotkin was moved, along with twenty-two other prisoners, to the central prison at Clairvaux. Kropotkin spent three years in French prisons, being released in January 1886. As a political prisoner, conditions in the prison were not unduly harsh, as Kropotkin was allowed to write and study and to cultivate a small garden within the prison, but he still continued to suffer from scurvy and rheumatism. But his sojourn in Clairvaux gave Kropotkin the opportunity to study at first hand the prison conditions experienced by the fourteen hundred common-law prisoners who were also incarcerated at Clairvaux. Kropotkin was later to describe in detail his experiences in "In French Prisons," noting that although the common-law prisoners were subject to a regime of compulsory labor, absolute silence, and unnecessary punishments, the conditions in French prisons were much less brutal and more humane than those in Russia and Germany (RFP, 257–98).

Given these first-hand experiences of prison life, Kropotkin was able to reflect on the moral influence of prisons on prisoners and whether or not prisons are necessary. The first thing that struck Kropotkin is that prisons do not in fact reform prisoners or deter crime. All that we know about prisons affirms that the "supposed double influence of prisons—the deterring and the moralizing—exist only in the imagination of lawyers" (RFP, 305). This is because once a man has been in prison, he will inevitably return—and the statistics prove it. Nearly one-half of all people condemned by the French courts, Kropotkin wrote, are regularly released prisoners; he thus records that nearly one-half of those tried for murder, and around 75 percent of those tried for burglary, are recidivists. It is also important to note, Kropotkin suggests, that the offense for which a man returns to prison is always more serious than his first. "If, before, it was petty thieving, he returns now for some daring burglary, if he was imprisoned for the first time for some act of violence, often he will return as a murderer" (KRP, 221).

Kropotkin thus concludes that whatever prison scheme is instituted, even if it involves the seclusion of the prisoners or severe restrictions on conversation, nevertheless prisons remain "nurseries of criminal education." Some of the most terrible acts of brutal murder, he suggests, have been hatched in prison (RFP, 308–309).

What is also apparent, Kropotkin argues, is that no matter how cruel and oppressive a system of punishment may be—even if it involves the death penalty—the number of murders and other crimes remains relatively constant. Harsh punishments in no way act as a deterrent.

The main reason why prisons do not reform prisoners is that prison life "kills all the qualities in a man which make him best adapted to community life" (KRP, 221). Most important of these is that prison deprives a man of his liberty, and without liberty no person can improve his moral dispositions—in fact, prisons do the opposite, they "demoralize" the inmates. For a start, few prisoners recognize the justice of the system and tend to feel that the real criminals are outside the prison and go unpunished. Then all communications and social contacts with the outside world are severed, thus breaking the most important relationships—and influences—that a prisoner has with his kin and society. But crucial for Kropotkin in the process of "demoralization" is that of forced labor. Everyone knows, he writes, the ill effects of laziness, and the moralizing influence of labor. But he contends "there is labor and labor." There is free labor, which raises a man and makes him feel a part of the universal life of the world. And there is forced labor, that of the slave, which degrades humanity and is done only for fear of punishment. Such is prison labor. It demoralizes the prisoners, for nothing is more revolting than being compelled to work, especially work that is tedious and has no intrinsic value or meaning (RFP, 314–15; KRP, 223).

Equally significant for Kropotkin is that prisons are institutions that depersonalize the inmates, for "prisons are made for degrading all those who enter them, for killing the many last feelings of self-respect." For prisoners are treated as a thing, they are given a number, marched in file, and if a prisoner succumbs to the most human of all desires and talks to a comrade, he will commit a breach of discipline and be punished. Human feelings are not allowed in prison (RFP, 328–30; cf. Goffman 1961 on total institutions). For Kropotkin, the most terrible condemnation of the whole penal system is this emphasis in regimentation, order, and discipline, and thus the suppression of individual liberty and autonomy (KRP, 225).

But Kropotkin recognized that "men are men" and that you cannot give immense power and authority to the prison guards without corrupting them—for people will inevitably abuse power. The outcome is an institution consisting of two opposed groups—as to the "league of prisoners there is opposed a league of jailers" (KRP, 227).

Kropotkin thus concludes that prisons essentially function to systematically kill in the inmates "every feeling of self-respect, dignity, compassion and love" while favoring and encouraging the growth of opposite feelings (RFP, 334). What they do not do is improve or reform the prisoner. Kropotkin admits that some reforms of the prison system could be made. Prisoners could be allowed to freely converse with one another and be given more satisfying work and better wages, or could even learn a trade. His main conclusion, however, is that prisons cannot be improved, and thus the best thing that can be done is to abolish—or rather demolish—the whole prison system. For prisons do not act as a deterrent: all that they do is to make the prisoners less adapted to society by degrading their intellectual and moral faculties.

But how is one to deal with those people who commit antisocial acts, who break the law—Kropotkin meaning by law the basic principles of morality that humans everywhere acknowledge? Kropotkin's essential answer is that, like diseases, crimes are best prevented rather than cured. This means understanding the causes of crime or antisocial behavior. Kropotkin suggests that there are three basic causes at work in producing such behavior—environmental, biological, and social causes.

With regard to environmental or physical causes, these relate to the statistical evidence that suggests that the number of murders committed each year in Europe can be roughly predicted and that climatic and geographical factors seem to influence crime rates. Thus acts of violence seem to predominate in summer, while crimes against property take place mainly in the winter, Kropotkin citing the work of the Italian criminologist Enrico Ferri (KRP, 229).

The second cause of crime relates to "inherited capacities" or physiology and their influence on human behavior. The most prominent scholar to advance this theory of crime was Cesare Lombroso, who believed criminals to be "atavistic types," and thus maintained that the majority of prison inmates had some mental defect and that it was easy to recognize the physical attributes of the "born criminal." Although Kropotkin does not deny that defects in bodily structure—"cerebral diseases"—may lead, in some cases, to brutal murders, he qualifies such biological determinism in three ways. First, he argues that not all persons who suffer from a "mental disease" do in fact commit antisocial acts, still fewer become assassins. Second, he suggests that all people, on reflective analysis, may become aware that on certain occasions they may be prone to commit antisocial acts. That they do not do so is because social and educational factors, as well as hereditary factors, influence human behavior. Third, Kropotkin emphasizes that society has no right to exterminate those who have diseased brains—on this issue he differed significantly from the elitist Nietzsche, who thought invalids a "parasite" on society, "degenerates" whose life ought to be suppressed (Nietzsche 1968, 88). But Kropotkin recognized that afflictions of the mind are "incipient" in all of us and stressed the importance of social circumstances and social upbringing in limiting antisocial or criminal acts.

Kropotkin therefore highlighted the social causes of crime as the main causes of "antisocial deeds." He emphasized that the moral and material filth to be found in the overcrowded cities of Europe at the end of the nineteenth century, where a large proportion of the population lived in poverty, a "hand-to-mouth" existence, and many children were homeless, was certainly not conducive to social well-being. It was hardly surprising, then, Kropotkin reflects, that "our big cities chiefly supply prisons with inmates." But even more surprising, he suggests, is the fact that so few working people take to violence and crime and the depths of social sentiments and warm friendliness that are to be found in even the worst neighborhoods (RFP, 363).

Kropotkin also emphasizes that two-thirds of the acts condemned as crimes were principally acts against property, and that in advocating the abolition of prisons and a more fraternal attitude to prisoners, he was not suggesting the substitution of mental hospitals for prisons. "It is not insane asylums," he wrote, "that must be built instead of prisons"—such an idea was abhorrent to him, for the asylum is always a prison, and a physician's prison "would be much worse than our present jails" (KRP, 233). Kropotkin balked at the idea of putting prisons under the control of peda-gogists and medical men. What most of those sent to prison needed was fra-ternal help from those around them, and he affirmed that human fraternity and liberty were the only correctives needed to counter antisocial behavior. As society as a whole is responsible for every antisocial act committed, then what is needed is a mode of social life that will engender social well-being and limit or check antisocial feelings.

"Fraternal treatment to check the development of anti-social feelings which grow up in some of us—not imprisonment—is the only means that we are authorized in applying, and can apply," Kropotkin wrote. This is not utopian. What is utopian is to fancy that harsh punishments can check the growth of antisocial feelings or the level of crime (RFP, 353).

Kropotkin recognized, of course, that in every society, no matter how well organized, some people will commit antisocial deeds, but he still affirmed that the only practical corrective was still fraternal treatment and moral support. During his time, Kropotkin believed, "we live too isolated. Private property has led us to an egoistic individualism in all our mutual relations. We know one another only slightly; our points of contact are too rare. But we have seen in history examples of a communal life which is more intimately bound together—the 'composite family' in China, the agrarian communes, for example. These people really know one another. By force of circumstances they must aid one another materially and morally" (KRP, 233).

What was needed then was to create *new* forms of social solidarity. "Let us organize our society so as to assure to everybody the possibility of regular work for the benefit of the commonwealth—and that means of course the thorough transformation of the present relations between work and capital; let us assure to every child a sound education and instruction, both in manual labour and science, so as to permit him to acquire . . . the knowledge and habits of earnest work—and we shall be in no more need of dungeons and jails, of judges and hangmen" (RFP, 365–66).

In summary, Kropotkin concludes: "Society itself is responsible for the anti-social deeds perpetrated in its midst, and that no punishment, no prisons and no hangmen can diminish the numbers of such deeds; nothing short of a re-organization of society itself" (KRP, 71).

4
AGRARIAN SOCIALISM

A narchists have often been dismissed by Marxists as utopian dreamers or as simply advocates of petty-commodity production. It is plainly evident that Kropotkin cannot be accused of either of these failings. As a geographer he was throughout his life interested in practical issues, on how humans could best produce their basic livelihood, and made practical suggestion along these lines. He emphasized that we must "act for ourselves" and that the emancipation of working people must be the task of the working people themselves (AY, 32). Liberty and social justice could be attained through neither the state nor through the "dictator-ship" of a revolutionary or "vanguard" party. Equally, he put an emphasis on "local action" and considered the idea that the coming revolution would follow "one single programme" all over Europe to be a fallacy (AY, 44). He advocated the expropriation, not the retention, of private property and stressed that the three basic necessities of human life (which he always emphasized)—food, clothing, and dwellings—must all be communal. Under anarchist communism, production would be communal—though Kropotkin never denied the freedom of individuals to engage in individual production if they so desired. The management of local affairs would also be communal, organized through voluntary associations; and, finally, the products of labor were to be communal, to be shared according to indi-vidual needs. Kropotkin thus repudiated the state ownership of land and capital and all "nationalization" schemes; he was equally against private property (petty-bourgeois capitalism) and any form of "wage system" as advocated by Proudhon and many individualist anarchists.

Because Kropotkin was a practical idealist emphasizing the importance of local action, and because he felt it was the first and imperative duty of

89

any popular movement to leave nobody without food, shelter, and clothing, Kropotkin always stressed the importance of agriculture, particularly self-sufficiency in agriculture (AY, 62). Advocating self-sufficiency in agriculture almost a century before John Seymour (whose popular books made an important impact in the 1970s), Kropotkin, however, always put an emphasis on agrarian communes rather than on family households and on linking agriculture with industry.

One of the criticisms that Kropotkin made of capitalism was that it not only involved the exploitation of the urban proletariat and colonial peoples, but that it also led to the depopulation of the countryside through industrial farming practices (CB, 182). Geared also to the generation of profits, it inevitably neglected the needs of the community as a whole. Thus what he felt was imperative was a social economy, based on voluntary cooperation, which aimed to produce "The greatest amount of goods necessary for the well-being of all, with the least possible waste of human energy" (CB, 119).

This could never be the aim of a private owner of land, still less that of a capitalist entrepreneur. With intensive agriculture, however, organized on a cooperative basis, the essential needs of the people could, Kropotkin felt, easily be procured, and, as earlier noted, he estimated that nobody need work more than four or five hours a day (CB, 123). This would leave ample time free for leisure activities—which Kropotkin felt essential for human well-being. Like the early Marx, Kropotkin envisaged everybody combining manual work, whether in husbandry or industry, with intellectual and artistic work. Kropotkin with his wife, Sophie, cultivated throughout his life a vegetable plot, and he is so able to write of "the poetry of work in the fields," if this work is voluntary and under the control of the producer. Work did not have to be drudgery; there were joys in creative work, and Kropotkin saw no reason why everyone, and not just the idle rich, should not enjoy comfort and leisure (CB, 135). The phalanstery of the Fourierists, an industry managed by a state or party bureaucracy, domestic slavery, huge "Bonanza" capitalist farms—all were anathema to Kropotkin. He is equally critical of the division of labor, which as a productive technique had been lauded by Adam Smith and other political economists. For Kropotkin this essentially meant "labelling and stamping men for life," overspecialization and the destruction of fulfilling and creative work. The ideal of industrial agriculture is to do away with people—agricultural work—entirely (CB, 199). Thus Kropotkin advocates the "decentralisation of industry" and the bringing together of workshops, factories, and agricultural production, both within the city and in the countryside.

In his essay on "Agriculture" (CB, 210–29), Kropotkin repudiates two of the underlying principles of economic science, namely, that people are always and only motivated by self-interest or profit and that scarcity is the lot of humanity, so that there will always be insufficient goods to satisfy everyone. Kropotkin argues to the contrary; that with the judicial use of scientific knowledge and machinery, and by means of intensive agriculture, especially market-gardening, people will easily be able to produce enough agriculture produce to feed everyone adequately. Although he acknowledges the productivity of large-scale, extensive agriculture on the American prairies, he also highlights its problems—soil exhaustion, its "military" organization, and the fact that it depopulates the landscape. With intensive agriculture, however, put into practice by a local commune, a limited space may be well cultivated—and improved by manures and concentrated work. Kropotkin was fond of quoting the peasant adage that "the soil is worth what the man is worth."

By intensive agriculture—market gardening, intensive field cultivation, irrigated meadows, greenhouse culture, as well as kitchen gardens—Kropotkin argues that not only could labor be greatly reduced—to a few hours each day—but high yields of a variety of cereals, vegetables, fruit, and other crops could easily be produced. This emphasis on agricultural self-sufficiency did not in the least imply, for Kropotkin, an end to economic exchange, but he did recognize that such improvements would entail a social revolution. But to free the peasant cultivator from the three "vultures"—the state, landlord, and banker—was, he felt, imperative, and Kropotkin saw agrarian socialism which provided everyone with their basic livelihood as more than a "fancy dream" (CB, 210–17).

Kropotkin's basic ideas on economic life were published in a series of articles in the *Nineteenth Century* (1888–90), which were later collected as the well-known book *Fields, Factories and Workshops* (1899). Colin Ward described the book as "one of those great prophetic works of the nineteenth century whose hour is yet to come" (FFW, ii). The book reiterates many of the ideas that Kropotkin was expressing at the same time in articles in the anarchist journal *Le Révolté*. These too were published earlier in book form (1892), but *Fields, Factories and Workshops* additionally incorporates a wealth of detailed information, both ethnographic and statistical, on economic life in Europe at the end of the nineteenth century.

The book is essentially in four parts and argues four essential themes.

The first is that there is a growing tendency toward the decentralization of industry, away from large-scale monopoly production. Critical of the idea that each nation had to have its own economic or trade speciality, Kropotkin suggested that there was a growing tendency for industrial production to become dispersed, for the economy of each nation and territory to diversify, and the unit of production to become decentralized. Thus, "Industries of all kinds decentralise and are scattered all over the globe; and everywhere a variety, an integrated variety of trades grows, instead of specialisation. Such are the prominent features of the times we live in" (FFW, 38).

Kropotkin recognized, as the sociologist Immanuel Wallerstein was later to explore, that historically there had been shifts in the center of gravity of commercial enterprise. Since the rise of capitalism in Europe, around the time of the Renaissance, economic hegemony had thus shifted from Italy and Spain to Holland and finally to Britain during the nineteenth century. But for Kropotkin the decentralization of industry was an altogether different process, and he thought it excluded the very possibility of future economic hegemony. The history of the past century has proved otherwise, with the United States becoming an hegenomic power after the Second World War and powerful multinational corporations—rather than small-scale industry—becoming a dominant factor in economic life.

Second, in his discussion of the "possibilities of agriculture," Kropotkin argued that all countries, including Britain, could and should become self-sufficient in agriculture. Focusing on Britain, Kropotkin challenges the idea that Britain is so overpopulated that it cannot produce enough food— the population of Britain at the end of the nineteenth century standing at around forty-six million people. He challenges also the idea that there is any necessary advantage in Britain being primarily an exporter of manufactured goods—even though at the time Britain imported around 60 percent of its food requirements. Kropotkin also challenges the Malthusian notion that population will always outstrip food supply, and thus there will always be scarcity, that there will always be an insufficient supply of the necessities of life (FFW, 78). Much of the problem of British agriculture, according to Kropotkin, stemmed from the fact that there is a high concentration of land ownership, much of the land being in the hands of large landowners; that the land is used as a commodity for the generation of profit rather than for the needs of the majority; and that large areas of land are devoted to game reserves for elite sportsmen as "deer forests" or pheasant-shooting areas. The landscape of Britain, he suggested, had been "starved of human labour," for Kropotkin emphasized that humans were an intrinsic part of nature and that soils could actually be improved in terms of productivity by human activity. He pleads that there are no infertile soils and that the most fertile soils are not those of the Russian steppes or the prairies of North America but rather are to be found where there has been intensive human activity over the centuries—"in the peat bogs of Ireland, on the sand dunes of Northern France, on the craggy mountains of the Rhine"—where soils have been made by human work (FFW, 54).

Kropotkin based his ideas on agricultural self-sufficiency to a large extent on his own observations derived from his travels throughout Europe. Colin Ward remarks that Kropotkin never seems to have been without his notebook, and certainly Kropotkin had a much more intimate knowledge of agricultural practices than most economists, many of whom had never ventured out of the Academia, or the reading room, of the British Museum. Such self-sufficiency could be achieved, he felt, by an intensive and diversified agricultural system and by integrating industry and agriculture. He details in his book the nature and possibilities of the various form of intensive culture that we earlier noted: fruit orchards, market-gardening (such as flourished around Paris, in many parts of southern England, and in the Channel Islands), irrigated meadows, the growing of fruit and vegetables in greenhouses (once the preserve of the rich), and the development of intensive forms of agriculture.

Kropotkin continually emphasizes that soils are *made*, that practical knowledge is essential, that microclimates can be improved as well as the soil, that new varieties can be selected, and that, as in Asian communities, plants can be treated on an individual basis. He continually makes a plea for an end to capitalist agriculture and for the development of small holdings, integrated into a communal system. It is clearly evident that Kropotkin is seeking to develop an integrated farming culture that avoids the two extremes; between, on the one hand, the small culture of the French peasant or maraicher (market gardener), which retains private property and petty commodity production; and, on the other hand, the large, extensive farms of capitalist agriculture, worked in military fashion by "labour battalions," which tends to remove people from the land completely, exhausts the soil, and is a form of "robbery culture" (FFW, 104). Kropotkin clearly felt that, though not spelled out in detail, "associated labour," "common tenancy," and the practice of intensive agriculture were the most reasonable forms of economic life. Together these would make the best use of the land, enable local communities and regions to be self-sufficient in the basic necessities of life, and reduce the amount of labor devoted to basic production. Kropotkin recognized that many market gardeners worked long hours with little time for leisure activities, but he nevertheless felt that on a communal basis such intensive agriculture would enable people to produce more with less labor and that there would be ample time to enjoy the many pleasures of human life (FFW, 67).

This leads to the *third* important theme of Kropotkin's book, detailed in the chapters on "small industries and industrial villages." This is the need to integrate industry with agriculture—but on a small scale. Kropotkin does not advocate the kind of industrial agriculture that has developed under capitalism in recent decades. What he does suggest is the need to combine agriculture, workshops and factories in an integrated social economy that is centered on meeting basic human needs and also gives people time to engage in leisure pursuits.

The main purpose of a social economy was the "economy of energy required for the satisfaction of human needs" (FFW, 17). This meant combining agriculture and industry, which during the nineteenth century had been totally estranged. Kropotkin emphasized the viability of small industries and argued that the efficiency of large-scale production had less to do with the technological limitations of small workshops than with the nature of production under capitalism—which involved the control of markets and the production of cheap and shoddy goods. The notion that small-scale industry and workshops were doomed to disappear, and that there was a growing "concentration of capital"—accepted by both political economists and Marxists, Kropotkin questioned and sought to demonstrate that at the end of the nineteenth century, small industries and workshops were still an important factor in the industrial life of Europe. But though advocating small industries and workshops—he notes that watch-making in Switzerland and cutlery manufacture in Sheffield were both centered on small workshops—Kropotkin is not against the application of science to industry and agriculture, nor does he deny that factories may be necessary for the manufacture of certain products. Oceanic steamers, he wrote, cannot be made in the village workshop (FFW, 153). He emphasizes too the need for labor-saving technology and saw no reason why "the small car should not be of more general use than it is now"—though he could hardly foresee the problematic nature of a transport system focused almost exclusively on the private car (FFW, 152). But Kropotkin recognised only too clearly that the "Leviathan" factory under capitalism was a "curse" exploiting men, women, and children; reducing work to monotonous toil under unhealthy working conditions; regimented, controlled, and involving long hours with little remuneration. There is nothing "natural" or inevitable about "capitalist centralisation," Kropotkin wrote, and it needs to be replaced by a social economy based on small industries and workshops (with the workers themselves the "real managers of industries") that are closely interlinked with agricultural production. Thus, the future economy would combine small-scale industry with intensive agricultural productivity by means of small holdings—and this was not only Kropotkin's ideal, but it was the expression, he thought, of growing tendencies with European society.

But this combination of agriculture and industry at the social and economic level needed to be complemented, Kropotkin felt, at the level of the individual. At the time he wrote it was very common for working people to alternate between agricultural work and industry. Russian peasants, for example, might spend much of the year in Moscow or St. Petersburg engaged in industrial work, to return each summer to their native villages to help in the harvesting of crops. Similarly, throughout Europe working people during the summer months often migrated to the countryside to engage in agricultural work—hay-making, helping with the harvest, hop or fruit picking. And Kropotkin firmly believed that it was essential for humans to combine in their working lives both intellectual and manual work. Critical, like the early Marx, of the economic division of labor, which confined working people to monotonous jobs for long hours all year round, Kropotkin called for a social economy in which people would productively engage in a variety of different tasks, both intellectual and manual. And he advocated an integral system of education to allow the development in each individual of a wide range of talents and capacities. This was the *fourth* theme of Kropotkin's study, the advocacy of working conditions and a system of education that combines intellectual and manual work. His basic ideas are summed up with his suggestion that a future society

> must find the best means of combining agriculture with manufacture—the work in the field with a decentralised industry and it will have to provide for "integrated education," which education alone, by teaching both science and handicraft from earliest childhood, can give to society the men and women it really needs. Each nation—her own agriculturist and manufacturer; each individual working in the field and in some industrial art; each individual combining scientific knowledge with the knowledge of a handicraft—such is, we affirm, the present tendency of civilised nations. (FFW, 27)

The evolution of social life in Western Europe has certainly not developed along the lines that Kropotkin envisaged, and many have dismissed his ideas as utopian and impractical. Kropotkin certainly had an optimistic temperament, and even Malatesta questioned the viability of his analysis of agricultural production, focused as it was on a few cultivators and the most gifted agronomists and market gardeners in limited areas. As always, Malatesta wrote, "Kropotkin saw things as he would have wished them to be and as we all hope they will be one day; he considered as existing or immediately realisable that which must be won through long and bitter struggle" (quoted in Richards 1965, 266).

But faced with contemporary realities and the acute problems associated with industrial farming—that "Soviet-American fetish" as James Scott describes it (1998, 196)—Kropotkin's vision has a relevance and is suggestive of a more viable and sustainable future, both on social and ecological grounds. The problems of industrial agriculture are well known and have been detailed in numerous studies. Indeed, Scott, in a chapter on "Taming Nature," gives a very good critique of the state-sponsored, "high modernist" agriculture under so-called democratic capitalism, geared as it is, as Kropotkin continually emphasized, to production and profit. Scott explores in detail its ecological and social costs, as the emphasis is put, in its myopic vision, on monocropping, mechanization, genetic uniformity, and its intensive use of fertilizers and pesticides. The main problem of industrial agriculture can be summed up as follows: the treating of land simply as a commodity and as a factor of production; extensive rural depopulation and rural dislocation; widespread degradation of the environment with the loss of wildlife and wildlife habitats; increasing health risks, both to farm workers and to the general public through poisons and contaminated food; the abuse of farm animals through "factory" production methods; and the undermining of subsistence farming and local economies throughout the "Third World"— Asia, Latin America, and Africa (Clunies-Ross and Hildyard 1992).

Kropotkin, like many of his socialist contemporaries at the end of the nineteenth century, had a rather uncritical attitude to modern science. He was also unconcerned with population issues, and according to Colin Ward, had a rather "mechanistic nineteenth century attitude to land" (FFW, 116)—although given the pantheistic sentiments expressed in his memoirs, this statement needs some qualification. Nevertheless, Kropotkin put great faith in science and in labor-saving technology to improve agriculture and small-scale industries. But Kropotkin's vision of a social economy that was based on small industries and rural workshops and on a labor-intensive, diversified form of agriculture is a far cry from the industrial agriculture that now dominates the rural landscape. As a geographer, Kropotkin would no doubt have sympathized with present concerns regarding overpopulation—given the finite nature of the earth's resources and energy—and would certainly have repudiated the unholy alliance between capitalism and science.

Kropotkin's *Fields, Factories and Workshops* is a prophetic work that has not only had a deep influence on generations of scholars and activists since it was first published in 1899, but its basic ideas still resonate in much current radical thinking and have a continuing relevance. Colin Ward has emphasized Kropotkin's widespread influence and the celebration of his work in many different quarters. Kropotkin had particular influence on many social reformers who advocated garden-city experiments and decentralized planning—Ebenezer Howard, Patrick Geddes, and Lewis Mumford. Geddes, of course, was a close friend and associate of Kropotkin and shared with Kropotkin a similar philosophy of life—an ecological vision that embraced biology, history, and sociology, an emphasis on the cooperative activities of all organisms, and a distrust of all forms of large-scale organization—although Kropotkin put no emphasis at all on "planning" that implies a continuing state presence (on Geddes, see Mumford 1956, 99–114).

Lewis Mumford (1895–1990) was a disciple of both Kropotkin and Geddes, whose work and inspiration he continually evoked and affirmed, although he was an original radical scholar in his own right, and his works on urban life have become classics. Although not an anarchist, Mumford was deeply influenced by Kropotkin, and Kropotkin's presence is evident in almost all his writings, for Kropotkin's *Fields, Factories and Workshops*—along with Geddes's *Cities in Evolution* (1968) and Ebenezer Howard's *Garden Cities of Tomorrow* (1965)—made a deep impact on Mumford. Describing Kropotkin's study as a "remarkable" book, Mumford in his seminal study *The City in History* wrote of Kropotkin:

> Almost half a century in advance of contemporary economic and technical opinion, he had grasped the fact that the flexibility and adaptability of electric communication and electric power, along with the possibilities of intensive, biodynamic farming had laid the foundations for a more decentralised development in small units, responsive to direct human contact, and enjoying both urban and rural advantages . . . with the small unit as a basis, he saw the opportunity for a more responsible and responsive local life, with greater scope for the human agents who were neglected and frustrated by mass organisation. (1961, 585–86; on Mumford's life, see Miller 1989)

But Colin Ward emphasizes Kropotkin's influence not only on Geddes and Mumford but on a host of anarchists, reformers, and advocates of intensive horticulture, small holdings, and agrarian communes—Tolstoy, Gandhi, Buber, Makhno, and Paul Goodman. The libertarian communist Goodman called for a revitalization of self-governing communities to counter the increasingly centralized and militarist United States government and in a celebration of Kropotkin's book, remarked that "The ways that Kropotkin suggested, how men can at once begin to live better, are still the ways; the evils he attacked are mostly still the evils; the popular misconceptions of the relations of machinery and social planning" (Goodman 1948).

He admitted that his well-known book *Communitas* (1947), written in collaboration with his architect brother Percival, hardly contained one important proposition that was not taken from Kropotkin's book *Fields, Factories and Workshops* (Goodman 1948).

Kropotkin's influence and basic ideas, though not always acknowledged, are reflected in many contemporary currents of social thought, and three are worth briefly discussing—the advocacy of intermediate technology by E. F. Schumacher, the bioregionalism of Kirkpatrick Sale, and the radical agriculture proposed by the social ecologist Murray Bookchin.

Although by no means an anarchist text, E. F. Schumacher's study *Small is Beautiful* (1974) has become something of a classic, and his writings have not only had an important influence on the Green Party but in the development of the intermediate technology movement that has responded to his call for a "technology with a human face." Many of his suggestions for an alternative future are important and echo the concerns of Kropotkin and other anarchist communists: his advocacy of appropriate or intermediate technology and the economics of permanence; his criticism of nuclear power and orthodox economic theory; and his suggestive insights on the links between industrial capitalism and positivist philosophy with its anthropocentric "man against nature" ethos. His wider views on agriculture also reflect Kropotkin's essential concerns, given its need to fulfil three tasks: (1) to keep humans in touch with living nature, of which they are an intrinsic part; (2) to humanize and ennoble the wider habitat; (3) and to bring forth the foodstuffs and other materials for human existence (Schumacher 1974, 93).

And Schumacher's essay on "Peace and Permanence" certainly reflects the influence of Gandhi and more indirectly that of Kropotkin. But Schumacher's politics are essentially liberal, for what he advocates is a balance between management and workers, whereby public (state) ownership is utilized to sustain and preserve "non-economic values" (his phrase) debased by capitalism. Many of Schumacher's ideas have been expressed long ago by Kropotkin and anarchist writers. Yet he does not—like Kropotkin—follow the logic of his argument and advocate the dismantling of the private enterprise system (capitalism) and the state. For nowhere does he suggest that we should put an end to the system that fosters nuclear weaponry, that creates pollution, that "ravishes nature," and "mutilates man" (his phrases). Misleadingly equating philosophical materialism with the ideology of capitalism, Schumacher rather pleads merely for the re-assertion of orthodox religious values to counterbalance the detrimental effects of the capitalist system. The advocacy of intermediate technology, small-scale operations, and giving humans ample room for creativity (all worthy objectives) is set within a Keynesian mixed economy and a plea for spiritual values—"seek ye first the kingdom of God." This is a far cry from Kropotkin's anarchist communism.

Kirkpatrick Sale describes himself as a disciple of Lewis Mumford and E. F. Schumacher—and his book *Dwellers in the Land* (1985) is dedicated to Schumacher. But although he hardly ever mentions Kropotkin, Sales's writings in essence simply reaffirm Kropotkin's own vision, in his plea for a "return to land" and in his call for self-sufficiency, human-scale technology, mutualism, and a decentralized form of politics. Sale's study *Dwellers in the Land*, subtitled "The Bioregional Vision," presents a commitment not to the pristine wilderness, as with the deep ecologists, but to a regional consciousness in which humans and nature (in all its diversity) are intrinsically interlinked. Like Kropotkin, the book expressly situates humans in the natural world, and Sale gives priority neither to nature (biocentrism) nor to humans (anthropocentrism) but to their interrelationship—an ecocentric approach. He gives a good, even if brief, discussion of the present ecological crisis—the problems of industrial agriculture, the depletion of fossil foods, deforestation, the adverse climate changes, urbanization, and pollution. Yet though recognizing the critical nature of this crisis, and the enormous cultural transformation that is needed to escape global disaster, Sale refuses to side with the voices of doom. Instead, he advocates the need for a new philosophy, a new ecological worldview to replace the moribund industrial-scientific perspective. But he turns neither to systems theory nor to religious mysticism but argues for what he refers to as a bioregional vision or paradigm. What we must learn to become, Sale suggests, are "dwellers in the land," to understand ourselves as participants in and not masters over the natural world—the biotic community or place in which we obtain our livelihood. And in understanding our place in the world, Sale feels that we must learn from these "two great teachers"—from "living nature" and the accumulated wisdom and history of humankind (1985, 46). However, it was not Schumacher who first suggested this but the libertarian socialists Kropotkin and William Morris long ago.

Sale thus argues that humans' potential and well-being are best developed in small communities and bioregions rather than under nation-states and that the economy of these communities and bioregions should be based on stability, conservation, and self-sufficiency, agricultural systems being designed to cause the minimum amount of environmental disruption. The need is to create a healthy, mature ecosystem where sources of energy are immediate and renewable, the level of resource use sustainable, and waste materials are returned to the earth without any environmental damage. Sale stresses that the self-sufficiency (but not isolation) of a bioregion should be an important aim, in that it tends for economic stability, precludes vassalage to national bureaucracies and transnational corporations, and fosters a more developed sense of community. Such an economy must be based on mutual aid and not on mechanisms of the market, and Sale argues that the latter, based as it is on competition, exploitation, and individual profit, must be phased out. Sales cites Schumacher as his support—although Schumacher never really questioned the market economy.

In such a bioregion, the "wealth of nature is the wealth of all," and Sale is against the private ownership of land, advocating only usufruct rights. With regards to politics, Sale suggests a perspective that is essentially close to anarchism—an emphasis on decentralization, bioregional diversity, and shared decision-making.

Sale sees his "bioregional vision" as a realistic vision, one that is practical, grounded in historical researches, and rooted in American values. These values include: a belief in local control and a distrust in arbitrary power, whether exerted by governments or corporations; a stress of self-reliance and community—power; decentralizatism and an appreciation for the rich potential of individualism; and a concern for the natural world. Such prototypical American, or at least Jeffersonian, values Sale sees as a source of his own bioregional vision.

Although in recent years Sale has come to describe himself as an advocate of "tribal anarcho-communism," it is of interest that Sale distances himself from the anarchist tradition, and apart from Bookchin, Sale makes hardly any mention at all of anarchists, whether individualist anarchists like Warren and Tucker or anarchist communists like Reclus, Berkman, and Kropotkin. Yet all the basic themes of his "bioregional vision"—an ecological worldview, a decentralized and participatory form of politics to replace the nation state, an economy based on mutual aid and cooperation rather than on the competitive market, an emphasis on community and economic self-sufficiency, a stress on small-scale industry, and finally, an affirmation of individual liberty—all these of course simply echo what Kropotkin was advocating around a century ago.

Murray Bookchin, in contrast to Schumacher and Kirkpatrick Sale, explicitly links his advocacy of radical agriculture to the perspective of such libertarian socialists as Fourier, Kropotkin, and William Morris. In his pioneering essay on "radical agriculture" (1976), Bookchin draws a sharp contrast between modern agricultural practices, which envision food production as a business enterprise operated solely for the generation of profit, and which in its "denatured" outlook hardly differs from any other branch of capitalist industry, and both the early forms of agriculture and the radical approach to agriculture that he advocates. This radical approach seeks to transcend the prevailing instrumentalist approach that views food production as simply a human technique, opposed to natural "resources." Bookchin indeed writes of modern capitalist agriculture as being inherently "anti-ecological." In contrast, this radical approach "is literally ecological in the strict sense that the land is viewed as oikos—a home. Land is neither a resource nor a 'tool,' but the oikos of myriad kinds of bacteria, fungi, insects, earthworms and small mammals. If hunting leaves this oikos essentially undisturbed agriculture by contrast affects it profoundly, and makes humanity an integral part of it" (1976, 7).

Like Marx and Wendell Berry—as well as Kropotkin—Bookchin suggests that humans do not simply live in an "environment" that surrounds them and is separate, but rather that humans and the natural landscape "create one another, depend on one another, are literally a part of one another" (Berry 1977, 22). Bookchin, like Kropotkin, therefore emphasizes that humans are an intrinsic part of the natural world, not above it as "master" or "lord" as in the mechanistic philosophy of the seventeenth century. But this is not to deny the uniqueness of human consciousness in its scope and insight, "but uniqueness is no warrant for domination and exploitation." He thus advocates a truly ecological outlook that sees the biotic world as a holistic unity of which humanity is a part, and which thus implies a radical agriculture that "seeks to restore humanity's sense of community; first, by giving full recognition to the soil as an ecosystem, a biotic community; and second, by viewing agriculture as the activity of a natural human community, a rural society and culture" (1976, 8).

Such a radical agriculture, which incorporates a balanced ecotechnology, Bookchin sees as essentially libertarian in its emphasis on community and mutualism, and this perspective, he acknowledges, derives from the writings of William Morris and Kropotkin (1976, 11).

The spirit of Kropotkin thus finds a resonance in much contemporary literature—in the writings of Schumacher and Sale with regard to intermediate "human-scale" technology and bioregionalism, in the radical agriculture of Bookchin, as well as in the essays on organic farming advocated by Wendell Berry. One of Berry's essays is indeed titled "Where Cities and Farms Come Together"—one of Kropotkin's essential themes.

5
INTEGRAL EDUCATION

In emphasizing the need for every person to live a full and diversified life, one that combined both intellectual and manual work, Kropotkin also suggested that this should be complemented by an educational program that combined the teaching of science with that of handicraft. His most extended discussion of his "integral education" is to be found in the final chapter of *Fields, Factories and Workshops* (1899), titled "Brain Work and Manual Work." (The original article was published in 1890.)

But the concept of "integral education" was not unique to Kropotkin: it was an intrinsic part of a libertarian approach to education that went back to the Utopian socialist Charles Fourier (1772–1837)—that "bizarre genius," as Proudhon described him. The term "integral education" was in fact first coined by Fourier in 1822 (See Beecher and Bienvenu 1972, 257–64). The development and the shifts in meaning of the concept of "integral education" and its links with libertarian education have been thoughtfully explored by Michael Smith (1983). His study outlines the libertarian education of not only Fourier but of such key figures as Proudhon, Paul Robin, Jean Grave, Sebastian Faure, and Francisco Ferrer. Some of the key themes associated with their libertarian and integral education, which were implicitly acknowledged by Kropotkin, were the following:

Schools and forms of education must be based on libertarian principles, and thus there was a repudiation of compulsion, regimentation, and coercive discipline. Although children's progress may be monitored, formal examinations were rejected. Education was thus conceived as emancipatory—from church dogma, the narrow confines the capitalist production, and state control. It was acknowledged that children should be involved from their earliest years in political activity, essentially through democratic participation in the running of the school (Smith 1989, 221).

There was also a disavowal of religious education, which at the end of the nineteenth century dominated the school system throughout Europe, the Christian churches having a high degree of control over all aspects of education. The libertarians like Robin and Ferrer emphasized that education should be secular and humanist and affirmed the ideals of rationalism and the scientific spirit. Science was seen by these early anarchists as essentially liberatory and as providing an alternative worldview to that of religion.

An emphasis was thus placed on co-education and on equality between the sexes, co-education—contrary to the church teachings—being seen as an important factor in the emancipation of women. In this regard, Proudhon, in contrast to other anarchists, had very regressive views, many of his theories being rather sexist and "backward-looking" (Smith 1983, 27).

There was an equal emphasis on the all-around development of the human personality—and thus education was to involve not only books and the intellect (as in grammar schools) but also the emotions, practical skills, physical activity, and social and moral training. There was a particular emphasis on the dignity of labor. The full development of the individual personality was thus to be physical as well as mental, emotional as well as cognitive, and social as well as personal. Education was thus to be both comprehensive and integral. This entailed bridging the gap between the school and work and integrating wider life experiences into education. Although libertarian education and anarchism have often been interpreted as "anti-intellectual" in that an emphasis was put on practical activities and working with the hands, this is somewhat misleading. None of the early anarchists repudiated science and the intellect; what they emphasized was "integral education." As Bakunin put it: "everyone shall work and everyone shall be educated . . . it follows that it is to the interest of both labour and science that there be no workers nor scientists but only men" (Maximoff 1953, 328–29).

Education was therefore conceived as a continuing process, and thus schools were to be centers of education and open to people of all ages. The school was thus envisaged as a "popular university," a center also for adult education. These settings were seen as particularly important in the "self-education" of the workings classes, and anarcho-syndicalists like Grave and Faure were instrumental in the founding of libertarian schools in France (Smith 1983, 18–50).

Kropotkin had imbibed and was an advocate of all these general principles of libertarian education. He was, in fact, a close friend and associate of both Robin and Grave, who, unlike Kropotkin, were both experienced teachers and conversant in educational matters. Paul Robin (1837–1912) had collaborated with the communard Ferdinand Buisson in the writing of the *Dictionaire de Pedogogie* and from 1880 until 1894 was in charge of an orphanage-school at Cempuis in the Department of Seine. It was an attempt to establish a genuinely libertarian school—until Robin was dismissed from his post under pressure from the local church, part of the reaction against anarchists after the outbreak of terrorist activity in France between 1892 and 1894. Robin in fact had drafted a paper on "integral education," which was adopted as policy at the Third Congress of the International Workingmen's Association, held in Brussels in 1868.

Jean Grave (1854–1939), an anarchist-communist like Kropotkin, was editor of the anarchist periodicals *Le Révolté* and *La Révolté* (1884–1894) and *Les Temps Nouveaux* (1895–1914). From about the middle of the 1890s, Grave was engaged in a sustained campaign to promote libertarian ideas in education, and he played a leading role in the formation of the League for Libertarian Education (Smith 1983, 39). Both Robin and Grave thus had strong interests in educational theory and both had an important influence on other anarchists at the turn of the century. Thus, the views expressed by Kropotkin on education in *Fields, Factories and Workshops* were not so much his own as a reflection of the general theories on libertarian education that had long been expressed by continental anarchists such as Robin and Grave. What, however, was of interest about Kropotkin's contribution, as Smith writes, is that he set out for the very first time in British educational circles a distinctively anarchist position (1989, 217).

In *Fields, Factories and Workshops*, Kropotkin noted that with the increasing division of labor during the nineteenth century, a great gulf had come to separate intellectual from manual work and that manual work and handicraft had increasingly come to be despised and devalued. Men of science despise manual labor and "have raised the contempt of manual labour to the height of a theory" (FFW, 170). But this he felt was a relatively new phenomenon, for all earlier scholars—Galileo, Newton, Leibnitz, and Linnaeus—had involved themselves in practical work and industry. Galileo made his own telescopes, Leibnitz was always inventing machines, and Linnaeus obtained his knowledge of plants while working as a practical gardener. Handicraft and industry was thus not an obstacle to abstract reasoning—it rather favored it.

But given this increasing specialization, and the growing divorce between intellectual science and manual labor (handicraft), there had arisen a great "outcry" throughout Europe—as well as in Russia and the United States—for "technical education." But Kropotkin was rather skeptical of this movement for technical education, believing it would perpetuate the current division between intellectual and manual work. He thus made a clear distinction between *technical* education, advocated by contemporary educationalists and the *integral* education that he felt would lead to the dissolution of the divide between "brain work and manual work." This placed Kropotkin squarely in the tradition of libertarian education that stemmed from Godwin and Fourier.

Kropotkin therefore described the need to combine science and industry: "We maintain that in the interests of both science and industry, as well as of society as a whole, every human being without distinction of birth, ought to receive such an education as would enable him or her, to combine a thorough knowledge of science with a thorough knowledge of handicraft. We fully recognise the necessity of specialisation of knowledge, but we maintain that specialisation must follow general education, and that general education must be given in science and handicraft alike" (FFW, 172).

This entailed not a technical education but an integral or comprehensive education. Kropotkin was, however, very critical of the system of education that prevailed at the end of the nineteenth century. Schools were often a kind of army barrack or "small prison"; children were taught a "mass of rubbish." Subjects such as mathematics were taught by memory and rote; and both science and mathematics taught in "purely abstract fashion," divorced from the child's own experiences. "Superficiality, parrot-like repetition, slavishness, and inertia of mind, he wrote, are the results of our method of education"— for it tends to kill independence of thought and does not teach children *how* to learn (FFW, 176). Kropotkin thus emphasized the need to combine science and intellectual pursuits with industry and practical activities, and whether it involved science, handicraft, or art, the chief aim of the school should not be to make a specialist but rather to teach the young person the elements of knowledge and the good methods of work with regard to a range of subjects, as well as to promote, or even inspire, their social skills so that they feel "at unison with the rest of humanity" (FFW, 178).

Kropotkin recognized, of course, that people had different capacities and inclinations and that not everyone would necessarily enjoy the pursuit of scientific work. Some people may take pleasure in science, some in handicraft, some in the arts—and others in the various pursuits related to the production of wealth. But education, he felt, should be integrated, and every person—whether scientist, sociologist, or surgeon by inclination—would profit if they spent part of their lives in the workshop or engaged in farming activities. He particularly felt that the separation of handicraft and science led to the "decay" of both, and he stressed that in many instances practical inventions, rather than involving the application of scientific knowledge, often created new branches of science. An invention or a discovery had been made (like that of gunpowder); science then comes in to interpret it (FFW, 184).

As a scientist Kropotkin clearly felt that theory arises out of practice, not vice versa, and that a science too divorced from practice inevitably becomes sterile. He thus stressed the importance of practical knowledge: "Those men—the Watts and the Stephensons—knew something which the savants do not know—they knew the use of their hands; their surroundings stimulated their inventive powers. . . . They had breathed the atmosphere of the workshop and the building yards" (FFW, 183). It was not good for scientists and intellectuals to remain "strangers to the world" (FFW, 185).

Like many of his socialist contemporaries, Kropotkin placed a great deal of faith in the capacity of education to change society and hoped both to give working people a grounding in scientific knowledge and to give professional scientists direct experience of manual work—whether at the blaze of the iron furnace, at the lathe in an engineering workshop, or with the tillers of soil in the fields (FFW, 185). In fact, this anarchist communist vision aimed to eradicate not only all class divisions but the deep dichotomy that existed between manual and intellectual labor. "Integrated education" was one of the means of dissolving this dichotomy, for Kropotkin firmly believed that the well-being of humanity was best promoted "When a variety of agricultural, industrial and intellectual pursuits are combined in each community; and that man shows his best when he is in a position to apply his usually varied capacities to several pursuits in the farm, the workshop, the factory, the study or the studio, instead of being riveted for life to one of these pursuits" (FFW, 18). Integral education was consonant with these wider aims.

Michael Smith has suggested that what Kropotkin was essentially propounding was a comprehensive core curriculum that related to all children and that aimed at equality and sought to equip the individual child with a general culture that was comprehensive, secular, up-to-date, relevant practically, and yet genuinely engaged with contemporary science (1983, 56). It was in this sense an integral education that aimed at the development of the whole person.

It is evident that, like other progressive educationalists such as Dewey, Kropotkin firmly believed in "learning by doing" and stressed the importance of beginning with the child's own concrete experiences. But Kropotkin's discussion of integral education was at a very general level, for he had little direct experience of teaching himself—apart from his lecturing. He certainly lacked the practical experience of Robin, Tolstoy, Faure, and Ferrer, all of whom had founded libertarian schools and written extensively on education. Kropotkin's own account of education therefore contains little detail on what would constitute the actual practices of a libertarian school that was devoted to "integral education." Given that his article on education was initially addressed to a liberal public, Michael Smith has suggested that his writings on education lack any real emancipatory thrust: "There is typically a passion for liberation through education in anarchist educators which one does not find in Kropotkin's article" (1989, 224).

Although Kropotkin placed a great emphasis on education, it is evident that he did not conceive of education and schooling as the primary means of achieving a social revolution. He would not have agreed with Tolstoy that "only by education, free education, can we ever manage to rid ourselves of the existing horrible order of things and to replace it with a rational organisation" (Avrich 1980, 5), for Kropotkin had a much broader conception of what a social revolution entailed. Many anarchists of his own generation had indeed pinned their hopes on education as a means of initiating a new social order, and as Avrich writes, no other social movement has assigned education a more prominent place in its writings and activities than did anarchism. Kropotkin shared these aspirations and in 1898 had signed, along with Tolstoy and Louise Michel, Jean Grave's International Manifesto on "Integral Instruction," published in the anarchist journal *Les Temps Nouveaux*. But Smith's suggestion that Kropotkin's writings on education are "a wise blend of common sense and current theory: but it is not distinctively anarchist. The impression one gets is that the innovative scientist, not the committed anarchist, is speaking" (1989, 228), is somewhat misleading. For, as Smith himself emphasizes, Kropotkin's views on education largely followed those of his anarchist contemporaries and close colleagues—Robin, Grave, Faure—and these are essentially libertarian. Kropotkin simply did not equate education with social revolution.

But although Kropotkin's own writings on education are limited, his personality and his more general writings had a profound influence on later libertarian educationalists, particularly those associated with the Ferrer Association and the Modern School movement in the United States. This movement was founded in 1910, to mark the death of the Spanish educator, freethinker, and anarchist, Francisco Ferrer y Guardia, who was executed in October 1909 after a mock trial, for allegedly fomenting popular insurrection. This history of the Ferrer Association and the Modern School movement has been admirably portrayed by Paul Avrich. Its foundation took place under the aegis of the anarchist movement, and its leading figures included many well-known anarchists and freethinkers—Emma Goldman, Harry Kelly, Alexander Berkman, Leonard Abbott, Joseph Cohen, and Will Durant, who was later to achieve fame as the author of *The Story of Philosophy*, a best-seller that sold more than three million copies. Durant had visited Kropotkin in Brighton in the summer in 1912 and was deeply impressed by Kropotkin, whom he described as both a philosopher and a saint. He found Kropotkin a gentle old man "whom I learned to love even while he was scolding me for lecturing too much about sex." Kropotkin had known Ferrer personally and supported his educational work, and he urged Durant to follow in his footsteps (Durant 1923, 89–90; Avrich 1980, 95).

Avrich describes Kropotkin as the "chief ideological mentor" of the Modern School movement, for his writings and personality profoundly influenced a whole generation of American anarchists, anarcho-syndicalists, and radical freethinkers. Alexander Berkman described Kropotkin as "my teacher and inspiration," while Emma Goldman saw in him the father of modern anarchism whose personality "towered high above most of his contemporaries by virtue of his humanity and faith in the masses" (Goldman 1931, 2:509).

Avrich describes Kropotkin's influence as follows: "His vision of a free society appealed to those who were repelled by an increasingly centralised and conformist world. His emphasis on the natural and spontaneous, his criticisms of arid ideological dogma, his distrust of bureaucracy and standardization, his faith in voluntary co-operation and mutual aid, attracted an untold number of radicals and reformers" (1980, 135).

Kropotkin was thus one of the most influential and most widely read anarchist writers in America, and he had a particularly pervasive influence on the radical educationalists associated with the Modern School movement.

PART TWO
ECOLOGY AND
SOCIAL ETHICS

6
MODERN SCIENCE
AND ANARCHISM

It is fashionable these days to dismiss Kropotkin as a crude positivist and an ardent follower of Auguste Comte, simply because Kropotkin repudiated religious and metaphysical explanations of natural phenomena and supported the development of social science. He has even, along with Darwin, been interpreted—quite falsely—as an advocate of mechanistic science. It is clear, however, that Kropotkin was much more sensitive to, and au fait with, the profound implications—both social and philosophical—that had been wrought by evolutionary theory and other advances in scientific knowledge of the end of nineteenth century than are many contemporary philosophers. For such philosophers give the impression that nothing of intellectual importance happened between 1650 and 1950, when they came on the scene to critique the Cartesian metaphysics and mechanistic philosophy, along with its anthropocentrism, abstract individualism, and dualistic paradigm.

Kropotkin was acutely aware that not only had scientific conceptions of the universe profoundly changed over the centuries but also that in the late nineteenth century another "profound modification" was taking place in how scientists interpreted the facts of the universe (KRP, 115).

At the time of the Greeks, and during the medieval period in Europe, humans thought that the earth was placed at the center of the universe, and humans conceived of themselves as the "superior being" on the planet, the "elected" of the creator. But an "immense change" in our conception of the world took place in Europe in the sixteenth century, with the rise of mechanistic science, "when it was demonstrated that far from being the centre of the universe, the earth was only a grain of sand in the solar system. . . .

113

How small man appeared in comparison to this immensity without limits, how ridiculous his pretensions!" (KRP, 116). This transformation in cosmogony had a profound effect on the philosophy of the period, and modern science could be dated from the sixteenth century. But, Kropotkin suggests, "a change much more profound and with far wider reaching results is being effected at the present time in the whole of the sciences, and anarchism is but one of many manifestations of this evolution" (KRP, 116).

Thus, Kropotkin felt that at the end of the nineteenth century profound changes were occurring within the whole of the natural sciences and that the mechanistic conception of the universe was fast "disappearing" and was being replaced by an evolutionary, holistic worldview. Thus in astronomy, after earlier having fixed their attention on the sun and larger planets, scientists were beginning to study the universe in terms of the content of infinite space, and even universal gravitation was being questioned, to be seen as the result of all the disordered and incoherent movements of infinitely small atoms. "Thus the centre, the origin of force, formerly transferred from the earth to the sun, now turns out to be scattered and disseminated. It is everywhere and nowhere" (KRP, 117).

This new conception implied a new metaphysics. "The idea of force governing the world, pre-established law, pre-conceived harmony, disappears, to make room for the harmony that Fourier had caught a glimpse of; the one which results from the disorderly and incoherent movements of numberless hosts of matter, each of which goes its own way and all of which hold each in equilibrium" (KRP, 118).

Entities like magnetism, heat, and electricity therefore disappear, to be reinterpreted in terms of the vibrations and movements of "infinitely small atoms." The new research thus "accustoms man to conceive the life of the universe as a never-ending series of transformations of energy: mechanical energy may become converted into sound, light, electricity; and conversely, each of these forms of energy may be converted into others" (E, 3).

Thus, for Kropotkin, there can be no universal order: pattern, organization, and stability were not the products of a simple and unitary mechanism, still less an attribute of the divinity, but rather they spontaneously emerged. Order was scattered and disseminated, everywhere and nowhere, but nonetheless real.

With the emergence of evolutionary theory and the development of the microscope, profound changes were also taking place within the science of biology. The notion of a species and its attributes was thus being replaced by a theory that emphasized the variations of the individual organism and its adaptation to the surrounding environment, Kropotkin always emphasizing a rather Lamarckian theory of evolution, through the inheritance of acquired characteristics. Thus, researches into physiology had revealed, Kropotkin suggests, that individuals are not a simple unity, but are constituted of organs and cells that have a life of their own. "The individual is quite a world of federations, a whole universe in himself" (KRP, 119).

But more than this: "in each microscopic cell he discovers today a world of autonomous organisms, each of which lives its own life . . . in short, each individual is a cosmos of organs, each organ is a cosmos of cells, each cell is a cosmos of infinitely small ones" (KRP, 119).

This applies equally to humans, who until recently, he wrote, had been spoken of as an "entire being, one and indivisible," a unitary subject that was consonant with religious traditions, with their concept of the soul. But modern psychology now see the human subject as composite and as constituted by a "multitude of separate faculties, autonomous tendencies, equal among themselves performing their functions independently" (KRP, 119)—a conception that has been affirmed by recent evolutionary psychology (Barkow, Cosmides, Tooby 1992).

These new researches in the realm of the natural sciences had led, Kropotkin believed, to a "profound modification" in our conception of the universe. Kropotkin clearly eschewed a narrow empiricist outlook, for he recognized that what had fundamentally changed was not the facts per se but our "way of looking" at the facts. And he recognized too that the new metaphysics of nature completely undermined such notions as "natural law" or a preconceived "harmony in nature." What used to be called "natural law," he wrote, is "nothing but a certain relation among phenomena" and each "law" has only a temporary character of causality. Given the importance of chance in nature—a volcanic eruption, lighting—there is nothing preconceived in what we call the harmony in nature, Kropotkin suggests. "Harmony . . . appears as a temporary adjustment established among all forces acting upon a given spot—a provisory adaptation. And that adjustment will only last under one condition; that of being continually modified; of representing every moment the resultant of all conflicting actions" (KRP, 121).

Kropotkin was thus clearly advocating, in embryonic form, an ecological worldview very different from the earlier mechanistic conception of the universe and a metaphysics of nature that was a form of evolutionary holism. Kropotkin's basic ideas therefore find a resonance in contemporary chaos theory and in recent studies in biology that we discuss below.

But Kropotkin felt that not only had great strides been made in the natural sciences, particularly in the realm of biology, but an analogous transformation was occurring in the social sciences. Along with the "new philosophy," a different conception of society was also emerging, and this new conception was being expressed, Kropotkin thought, by the political tradition of anarchism.

"Anarchism, therefore, appears as a constituent part of the new philosophy, and that is why anarchists come into contact on so many points with the greatest thinkers and poets of the present day" (KRP, 123). This new conception of society, of a society free from the domination by minority groups—whether priests, capitalists, or state bureaucrats—Kropotkin describes as follows: "It seeks the most complete development of individuality combined with the highest development of voluntary association in all its aspects, in all possible degrees, for all imaginable aims; ever changing, ever-modified associations which carry in themselves the elements of their durability and constantly assume new forms which answer best to the multiple aspirations of all" (KRP, 123–24).

Kropotkin therefore did not envisage a future anarchist communist society as being static, homogenous, or as reflecting some preconceived harmony; it was one that rather reflected a dynamic equilibrium. Diversity and conflict were intrinsic to social life, and those working toward the establishment of a free society must understand "that variety, conflict even, is life and that uniformity is death" (KRP, 143). And Kropotkin recognized, too, that although social life evolves in ways that are analogous to organic evolution, this does not imply a linear progression. Like the anthropologist Franz Boas, Kropotkin accepted biological evolution, and affirmed the principle of social evolution but this was seen in historic terms, not as orthogenetic or linear. As he wrote: "Humanity is not a rolling ball, nor even a marching column." It is rather a whole that evolves simultaneously, as does organic life, in a multitude of different ways, creating a diversity of different forms (KRP, 142).

Later in *Ethics* he wrote that "we certainly must abandon the idea of representing human history as an uninterrupted chain of development from the prehistoric stone-age to the present time. The development of human societies is not continuous" (E, 17).

Like Cornelius Castoriadis (1975), Kropotkin recognized that social life was essentially a creative process and would have agreed with Whitehead that entities in the world (both organic and social) are processes that express a "creative advance into novelty" (1929, 28).

Kropotkin therefore argued that anarchism, as a political philosophy and movement, should embrace a materialist philosophy of nature and base itself on modern science. He emphasized that anarchism was a social movement born among the people. It was, in essence, a practical response to actual social conditions and that anarchists, in criticizing existing institutions, envisaged an "ideal" future society. Anarchism as a social movement thus did not come out of the universities nor from the philosopher's study. But it was important, Kropotkin suggested, for anarchism to situate itself within the various currents of philosophical thought—and Kropotkin firmly argued that anarchism must "place" itself within the emerging philosophy of scientific materialism. "Scientific—not in the sense of adopting an incomprehensible terminology, or by clinging to ancient metaphysics, but in the sense of finding a basis for its principles in the natural sciences of the time, and of becoming one of their departments" (KRP, 156).

This implied attempting to understand both natural and social phenomena in terms of "mechanical explanations"—not in terms of spiritual concepts or metaphysical notions. Kropotkin thus rejected Cartesian philosophy—with its anthropocentrism, mechanistic paradigm, and dualistic ontology. He also rejected Hegelian philosophy—its objective idealism, teleology, and obscurantist terminology—as well as all spiritual and religious metaphysics that explain phenomena and events in terms of spirits, witches, deities, or the divinity. Anarchism as a philosophy or worldview is therefore based, according to Kropotkin:

> Upon a mechanical explanation of all phenomena, embracing the whole of nature—that is, including in it the life of human societies and their economic, political and moral problems. Its method of investigation is that of the exact Natural Sciences, and, if it pretends to be scientific, every conclusion it comes to must be verified by the method by which every scientific conclusion must be verified. It aims to construct a synthetic philosophy comprehending in one generalisation all the phenomena of nature—and therefore also the life of societies. (KRP, 150)

Kropotkin, following the radical implications of Darwin's theory of evolution, therefore rejected any metaphysical dualism between humans (and their social life) and nature—for Kropotkin continually emphasized that humans are a part of nature. But unlike Bakunin and Marx, Kropotkin was highly critical of Hegelian philosophy. As a naturalist and geographer, Kropotkin failed to be convinced that the mental and social life of humans developed in accordance with certain "in-dwelling laws of the spirit" and repudiated all metaphysical and teleological explanations of the world—in terms of a "universal spirit, or a creative force in nature, the incarnation of the Idea, Nature's goal, the Aim of existence"—or of humanity conceived as some spiritual essence. We need, he believed, to sweep away these Hegelian metaphysical concepts—while trying to discern any embryonic or useful generalization that they many contain. Kropotkin was equally critical of anthropomorphic conceptions—the notion that nature was a being endowed with human attributes (KRP, 152).

As a naturalist Kropotkin was skeptical of the "dialectical method" associated with Hegel, which had been espoused with great enthusiasm by the Marxists, especially Engels. For Kropotkin, this "method" was reminiscent of medieval scholasticism and was something long since passed. But when one reads both Engels and Kropotkin and their excitement regarding the new metaphysics of nature that had been heralded by Darwin's evolutionary theory and by the new advances in the natural sciences at the end of the nineteenth century, it is clear that there was no great gulf between them. Even so, they differed radically in terms of their politics. Engels, it may be recalled, was a consistent state socialist, an advocate of a centralized "worker's state" and always poured scorn on anarchism (Marx, Engels, Lenin 1972).

Engels conceived of dialectical thought (as Kropotkin conceived his own philosophy) as entailing a materialist conception of nature (and history) that was directly based on the scientific development that had occurred at the end of the nineteenth century. Both saw this new conception of nature, or "mode of thought," as directly opposed to what they described as "metaphysics"—whether in terms of Hegelian idealism or the static Newtonian conception of the universe that Engels referred to as "mechanical materialism." For Engels, "dialectics" essentially implied three principles—an emphasis on process or change, a conception of totality or holism, and a stress on contradiction. We may briefly outline these three principles in turn.

Engels, like Kropotkin, has often been portrayed as a crude positivist or as a mechanical materialist. This is, I think, extremely unfair to Engels (and Kropotkin). Such criticisms are often disguised criticisms of scientific rationality itself in favor of some form of religious mysticism or aim to uphold—even after Darwin—a radical neo-Kantian dualism between humanity and nature. But Engels (again like Kropotkin) was perceptive of the scientific revolution that had occurred at the end of the nineteenth century, which had completely transformed our understanding of nature. These developments, above all, proved that "nature also has its history in time." Thus the first principle of dialectics is the view, expressed long ago by Heraclitus and the Stoics, that all things in the universe are in a process of change. Thus nature is historical at every level, and no phenomenon of nature simply exists—it has a history; it comes into being, it endures, changes, and develops; and finally it ceases to exist. Aspects of nature may appear to be fixed or stable or in static equilibrium, but nothing is really permanently so.

It is clear from his study *Anti-Duhring* (1894) that Engels not only denied that social life could be understood in a mechanistic fashion but, as we have noted, strongly emphasized that contemporary developments in physics, chemistry, and biology had completely undermined the mechanistic philosophy of the Enlightenment. A "new outlook on nature," he sensed, like Kropotkin, was in the process of development. With regard to this first principle. Engels notes that a naive but intrinsically correct conception of the world had first been formulated by Heraclitus: "everything is and is not, for everything is FLUID, is constantly changing, constantly coming into being and passing away" (1969, 30).

Thus the great merit of Hegel's philosophy, Engels wrote, was that "for the first time the whole world, natural, historical, intellectual, is represented as a process, i.e., as in constant motion, change, transformation, development" (1969, 34).

But he specifically criticized Hegel for his idealism and for not conceding to nature "any development in time"—for Hegel was not an evolutionary thinker (Morris 1987, 9–10).

The first principle in Engels's understanding of dialectics is then the idea that both the natural world and social life are in a constant state of flux and that modern science has made the "immutable" concepts of nature held by Newton, Linnaeus, and Hegel redundant. Kropotkin would have wholeheartedly affirmed this conception of nature, and it is of interest that the process philosopher Alfred North Whitehead, who also advocated a form of evolutionary holism and an ecological perspective, explicitly, like Kropotkin, repudiated Hegelian "dialectics."

The second principle in Engels's understanding of dialectics emphasised the notion of totality. This is the idea that all the seemingly disparate elements of which the world is constituted are interconnected and that no phenomenon (whether natural or social) can be fully understood in isolation, but rather must be seen as part of a totality. This principle entailed an evolutionary form of holism and a conception of nature that was neither cosmological nor mechanistic but ecological (Morris 1981). As Engels put it: dialectics is the "science of inter-connections," in contrast to metaphysics (1940, 26). Dialectics, he wrote, "comprehends things and their representations in their essential connection," and Engels emphasized the importance of Darwin's theory that had dealt a critical blow at the "metaphysical conception" of nature, in showing that all organic beings—plants, animals, and humans—are the products of a process of evolution and thus interconnected (1969, 33). Like Kropotkin, Engels emphasizes that humans are an intrinsic part of nature, and though Noske has alleged that Engels along with Marx emphasized that humans could "transcend" nature and that they advocated the "domination" of nature (1997, 75–78), this is quite misleading. For Engels not only drew attention to ecological problems like deforestation, but he ridiculed the idea that humans could "transcend" or "dominate" nature: "At every step we are reminded that we by no means rule over nature a conqueror over a foreign people, like someone standing outside nature—but that we, with flesh, blood and brain, belong to nature, and exist in its midst" (1940, 292). Engels therefore called for a "comprehensive view of the inter-connections in nature by means of the facts provided by empirical natural science itself." The emphasis on totality is by its very nature opposed to any form of reductionism, of explaining the whole by means of the parts; nor, it must be stressed, does it abolish the role and autonomy of the part (the individual) in favor of the whole—the totality.

But it may be noted that in emphasizing, like Kropotkin, the close interaction between humanity and nature, Engels stressed both a naturalistic conception of history—nature influencing human life—and the fact that humanity reacts on nature, "changing it and creating new conditions of existence for himself." In words that echo those of Kropotkin, he wrote: "There is damned little left of 'nature' as it was in Germany at the time when the Germanic people immigrated into it" (1940, 172).

It would seem that on the issue of "totality" Engels and Kropotkin shared a similar vision, for both affirmed an evolutionary holism and an ecological perspective.

The third principle of dialectics is expressed by Engels in terms of the notion of contradiction, or the "unity of opposites." Ordinary, common-sense understanding, traditional logic, and metaphysical philosophy (Descartes) tend to imply, Engels suggests, thinking in terms of "absolutely irreconcilable antitheses . . . a thing either exists or does not exist; a thing cannot at the same time be itself and something else. Positive and negative absolutely exclude one another." This kind of thinking Hegel referred to as understanding (*ver-*

stand), thinking in terms of dualistic oppositions. Dialectical thinking (*vernunft*), in contrast, Engels writes, avoids this kind of abstract, restricted mode of thought, lost, as it is, in "insoluble contradictions."

"In the contemplation of individual things, it forgets the connection between them; in the contemplation of their existence, it forgets the beginning and end of that existence, of their repose, it forgets their motion" (1969, 31–32).

Every organic thing is at every moment the same and not the same; every moment it assimilates matter from without, while at the same time getting rid of waste materials. Engels thus suggests the need to understand things and processes in terms of what he describes as the "laws of dialectics," and these he conceives as providing a dynamic of change. He therefore suggests that certain oppositions—chance/necessity, quantity/quality, identity/difference, individual/society—mutually interpenetrate and are best conceived as a "unity of opposites" or as the "inter-penetration of opposites." He further argues that a characteristic typical of processes of change is the "negation of the negation"—the development of a new synthesis that negates, preserves, and transcends (*aufheben*) the elements of the contradiction. Engels therefore made a clear distinction between two philosophical tendencies: "The metaphysical with fixed categories, the dialectical (especially associated with Aristotle and Hegel) with fluid categories" (1940, 153), and he concluded that "modern materialism is essentially dialectic" (1969, 36).

John Rees sums up the general form of the dialectic with the words: "it is an internally contradictory totality in a constant process of change" (1998, 7; for useful discussions of Engels and dialectics, see McGarr 1994, Sayers 1996).

Although Kropotkin emphasized the importance of conflict (as well as cooperation) it is none too clear whether or not he would have affirmed the third principle of Engels's dialectics. Nevertheless in an important sense he was a dialectical thinker, even though he explicitly repudiated Hegelian-Marxist dialectics. But he was adamant that: "In anarchism there is no room for those, pseudo-scientific laws with which the German metaphysicians of the first twenty years of the nineteenth century had to content themselves. Anarchism does not recognise any method other than the natural-scientific. Its object is to form a scientific concept of the universe embracing the whole of nature and including man" (KRP, 192).

Anarchism thus has its roots in naturalism and in natural-scientific methods. He emphasized that the remarkable discoveries of the nineteenth century in all fields of science were made "Not by the dialectic method, but by the natural-scientific method, the method of induction and deduction. And since man is a part of nature, and since the life of his "spirit," personal as well as social, is just as much a phenomenon of nature as is the growth of a flower or the evolution of social life amongst the ants and bees, there is no cause for suddenly changing our method of investigation when we pass from the flower to man, or from a settlement of beavers to a human town" (KRP, 152).

Although, as with Darwin, Kropotkin emphasized that he was following "the true Baconian method" of induction, it is clear that both men realized that scientific knowledge was more than a mere collection of facts and essentially involved questioning, hypotheses, and verification (refutation). Darwin was "first and foremost a naturalist" and so was Kropotkin (Mayr 1991, 9–10). Both men adopted what was more or less a hypothetico-deductive approach, but both also had a passion for gathering empirical data to ground their theories, and Kropotkin continually emphasized that unlike the "truths" of religious "believers," scientific knowledge was never more than a succession of "approximations" on the road to discovery (E, 10). And although Kropotkin affirms the unity of the sciences, his approach was holistic and ecological, not reductionist, and his ethical naturalism repudiated the rigid positivistic dichotomy between facts and values. He was therefore extremely critical of the neo-Darwinist "philistines" who interpreted social inequalities in terms of a "law of nature," and he emphasized that every scientific investigation only bears fruit if it has a definite aim and proposes significant questions (KRP, 153).

Kropotkin's conception of scientific naturalism, and the holistic philosophy of nature that he embraced, is very graphically expressed in his *Memoirs*. His own philosophical outlook was formed very early in life, for, as Heiner Becker has suggested, Kropotkin's thought had an essential coherence and unity, and he "conceived a theory—one might even say with justification a vision—quite early in his career, and he systematically devoted almost the whole of his life to elaborating and illustrating it" (1989, 225).

This vision or philosophy was neither religious nor a crude form of mechanistic materialism but rather one, drawing on the writings of the Stoics, Goethe, Humboldt, and Darwin (all of whom he admired) that can be described as ecological—a social ecology. This ecological vision emerged early in life. He describes his early experiences as follows: "The infinite immensity of the universe, the greatness of nature, its poetry, its ever throbbing life, impressed me more and more; and that never ceasing life and its harmonies gave me the ecstasy of admiration which the young soul thirsts for, while my favorite poets supplied me with an expression of that awakening of mankind and faith in its progress" (MR, 97).

Poetry and science, music and chemistry, for Kropotkin, went "hand-in-hand," and he continues: "The never-ceasing life of the universe, which I conceive as *life* and evolution, became for me an inexhaustive source of higher poetical thought, and gradually the sense of man's one-ness with nature, both animate and inanimate—became the philosophy of my life" (MR, 117).

Although Kropotkin was always a great advocate of modern science, such pantheistic sentiments, echoing those of Goethe, make it quite mis-leading to interpret Kropotkin as if he were a Cartesian dualist or a "mech-anistic" philosopher of the seventeenth century, still less a crude Comtean positivist. Kropotkin's "integrative" philosophy affirms not a form of posi-tivism but a "poetry of nature." It was thus quite understandable that he should be critical of scholastic education, the school being modeled on that of the medieval monastery (MR, 125), and come to stress the importance of "integral education" and the teaching of the natural sciences—physics, astronomy, botany, and zoology. What was needed, he felt, was an integra-tive natural philosophy along the lines suggested by Alexander Humboldt in his *Cosmos*. "The philosophy and poetry of nature, the methods of all the exact sciences, and the inspired conception of the life of nature must [be a] part of education," Kropotkin wrote (MR, 89).

The new naturalistic philosophy of nature that Kropotkin felt was emerging at the end of the nineteenth century and that he expressed in embryonic form has more recently been affirmed and developed by several scholars, and it has been described under various headings: as an "ecolog-ical world view" (Sale), "dialectical naturalism" (Bookchin), or "holism" (Bohm). Some recent texts on the philosophy of biology have, however, been particularly important in outlining the basic premises of this new meta-physics of nature, and the following common themes are noteworthy.

The new philosophy of nature attempts to combine *humanism*, the emphasis on human agency and the recognition that human social life and culture constitute a relatively autonomous realm of being, and *naturalism*, the recognition that humans are an intrinsic part of nature. It thus attempts to avoid the two extremes: that of idealism, which postulates a radical separa-tion of humanity and nature, or denies the reality of an external world (exem-plified by neo-Kantian philosophy, hermeneutics, and postmodernism), and a reductive form of materialism (expressed, in particular, by the genetic determinism of the ultra-Darwinists and sociobiologists). Evolutionary holism emphasises that humanity and nature are dialectically interrelated.

It thus acknowledges the critical importance of the theory of *evolution*, which completely undermined the Newtonian picture of the world as a mechanism. Thus, the world is envisaged as one of perpetual change, a process in which new forms of life are continually created, expressing life's inherent tendency to create novelty. This evolutionary perspective is not only an "antidote to our cosmic arrogance," as Stephen Jay Gould expresses it (1980, 14), but renders untenable the equation of evolution with any scheme of linear progression. Evolutionary theory suggests that the past is the key to the present and that emergent life results from a combination of chance and necessity that composes the evolutionary process: "Necessity given by the physical and chemical properties of the universe, and chance, contingency, by the radical indeterminacy of living (and social) processes" (Rose 1997, 15).

It recognizes that the world, although having an ontological unity, comprises several *emergent levels of being*—inorganic matter (atoms, molecules), cells, organisms, psyche, social life, ecosystems, and the biosphere. These different levels are relatively autonomous and distinct, but they are also united, for there is continuity as well as difference between them. Thus, although biological phenomena emerge from merely physical and chemical, that is, nonbiological conditions, they do so by purely *natural* processes, and contemporary biology repudiates any recourse to vitalism or to quasi-spiritual explanations (mysticism). The distinction between the different levels is one of scale and complexity, for the higher levels reflect more complex forms of matter. "Matter takes on a more organised form in a fish than in the water through which it swims. . . . Physiological principles are not applicable to stones and planets" (Rose 1997, 92). But the whole and the part are not reducible to each other: the higher levels of organization do not determine the parts, nor is the whole simply a collection of its constituents, for the whole is in fact these parts unified, organized, and acting together. Equally the new philosophy of nature rejects any form of reductionism, for example, of social life to the human individual, of the organism to its constituent parts (cells, genes).

Different disciplines therefore relate to the different levels of the organization of matter, and thus, although there is an ontological unity, to interpret the world we need different forms of understanding. As Steven Rose puts it, "we need *epistemological diversity* in order to understand the ontological unity of our world" (1997, 296; my italics). This means that we recognize that causes are always multiple and can be described at many different levels and in terms of several languages.

The world is not "fragmentary" but a "whole," and its underlying reality has to be seen in terms of a "universal flux of events and processes." The existent "things" or forms that constitute the ordered world of experience are not, however, imposed from without (either by God, culture, or the transcendental ego) but emerge spontaneously and reflect "an ordered and structured inner movement that is essential to what things are." This order is described by David Bohm as "implicate" (1980, 9–12). Organisms—which are the fundamental units of life—are therefore not simply complex, molecular machines, but integrated entities with the capacity of active self-maintenance, and are centers of autonomous action and creativity. Thus, *autopoiesis*, self-making (*auto*, self; *poiesis*, making), is seen as the major organizing principle of all living systems from the single cell to the biosphere. This means that organisms have agency and are not simply passive in relation to their environment; the relationship between the organism and its environment is therefore interdependent and dialectical. The organism, as Rose graphically puts it, is both the weaver (being) and the pattern that it weaves (becoming) (Rose 1997, 171). The process of morphogenesis, which is grounded in the inherent properties of the physical world, is thus seen by many contemporary biologists as a crucial aspect of the evolutionary process (Goodwin 1994).

Evolutionary holism offers a new ethical paradigm that transcends both anthropocentrism—the view that humans are above or outside of nature and that the natural world simply has an instrumental value for humans (St. Augustine expressed this view succinctly long before Descartes)—and biocentrism (or mystical holism). This is the view that as humans are simply a part of nature, they should "obey" the "laws of nature" and orient their lives in conformity with the world—conceived as an "organism" or as a cosmic unity. Many biologists have, in fact, repudiated the concept of "holism," given its association with the mystical forms of holism that reflect earlier, premodern conceptions of nature as a cosmological system. They have therefore advocated neither "atomism" nor "holism" but dialectics (Lewontin 1991, 15). But the new philosophy advocates an evolutionary holism that is ecological and ecocentric and very different from the earlier cosmological conceptions of nature.

Finally, the new philosophy of evolutionary holism affirms a dialectical approach to nature, as a way of thinking about the world. The dialectic, as such, explains nothing, proves nothing, and causes nothing to happen. It is rather a mode of thought (outlined above) that takes us beyond ordinary common-sense understanding, formal logic, and the kind of metaphysics that was expressed by Cartesian and empiricist philosophy. As Ollman succinctly expresses it: "Dialectics restructures our thinking about reality by replacing the common sense notion of 'thing,' as something that *has* a history and *has* external connections with other things, with notions of 'process' which *contains* its history . . . and 'relation' which *contains* as part of what it is its ties with other relations" (1993, 11).

Such are the main ideas that constitute what Kropotkin described as the "new philosophy," an evolutionary holism that he expressed in embryonic form, in spite of his dislike for "dialectics."

In a recent, rather superficial critique of radical ecology, Jozef Keulartz (1998), besides completely misrepresenting both Kropotkin and anarchism on a number of different issues, interprets holism as implying the thesis that the "whole determines the part—e.g., that the individual is at the mercy of social systems and historical forces" and thus that it is the individual's duty to submit to "historical necessity"—as another philosopher puts it (Bunge 1994, 30). This represents, on Keulartz's part, a complete misunderstanding of evolutionary holism—as reflected in the writings of Kropotkin, Whitehead, Mumford, and Bookchin. Then, equally fallaciously, Keulartz makes the "banal affirmation" that there is a simple and direct "passage from ontology to politics" (Castoriadis 1991, 125) and declares that eco-anarchists (to the extent that they advocate a holistic perspective) are supportive of "totalitarian politics." The whole analysis in superficial and misguided and indicates the poverty of the kind of Habermasian neo-Kantian philosophy that Keulartz supports as "post-naturalism."

A much more engaged and sympathetic assessment of Kropotkin's metaphysics of nature is offered by Graham Purchase, who recognizes and emphasizes that many of Kropotkin's seminal ideas find a resonance in contemporary chaos theory and evolutionary biology. Kropotkin, he writes, like other anarchists, had always been fascinated by the complexity of spontaneous natural order and that this concept of complex self-regulation lies at the heart of modern conceptions of natural processes. For Kropotkin, "Self organisation was a fundamental principle of life which was observable throughout nature, from the simple organisation of the individual cell to the infinitely more complex organisation of the biosphere or universe" (KRP, 118–19; Purchase 1996, 138).

But order and stability for Kropotkin were not the products of a simple or unitary mechanism, but rather were diffuse and dissipated and emerged spontaneously as a process. Moreover, such vibrant self-organization is dependent not only on critical levels of complexity but also on the ability of the organism "to live in a balance between complex dynamical order and total disorder (Purchase 1996, 130). For Kropotkin, spontaneity and relative instability were among the hallmarks of a living system, for the universe was in a continual state of flux. "Nature could never be conceived or represented as a static and unchangeable order." Kropotkin therefore never committed himself "to the religion of the super-organicism or a naive holistic outlook in which nature is regarded as a seamless and unbroken wholeness or unity . . . nor does Kropotkin idealise nature, for in nature areas of sustained inter-connectedness and symbiosis are typically counterposed by areas of 'reaction,' 'conflict' and 'opposition'" (Purchase 1996, 137).

Purchase therefore rightly concludes that Kropotkin was suggesting in embryonic form an evolutionary holistic perspective that is consistent with recent developments in chaos theory and the emerging sciences dealing with the laws of self-organization and complexity (Kauffman 1995).

7
MUTUAL AID
A Factor in Evolution

U
nlike many of his contemporaries, and even some important naturalists like Louis Agassiz and Jean-Henri Fabre, Kropotkin was an
avid supporter of Darwin's theory of evolution. He not only wholeheartedly accepted Charles Darwin's (1809–1882) basic ideas, but he also
recognized that evolutionary biology, along with other advances in the natural sciences that had occurred at the end of the nineteenth century, had
completely undermined the metaphysics of nature that was associated with
the Enlightenment.

In many ways, Kropotkin, like Marx, stood firmly in the tradition of the
Enlightenment, and he affirmed many of its basic principles. These include
an affirmation of reason, which culminated during the French Revolution in
the bizarre worship of the goddess Reason; a stress on the importance of free
inquiry and secularism; an advocacy of scientific materialism and the repudiation of mythology, mysticism, and religious dogma as modes of understanding the world; a respect for craftsmanship and an enthusiasm for
industry, coupled with a belief in human progress through the application of
science and technology; an emphasis on individual liberty and equality and
the promotion of a cosmopolitan outlook; and finally, a repudiation not only
of sacred texts but of the past, of the classical literature of antiquity, as a
source of authority—hence inaugurating the so-called epoch of "modernity."

Although Enlightenment thought had a certain coherence—reflected in
the writings of Diderot, Voltaire, Hume, Rousseau, Adam Smith, Bentham,
Kant, and Herder—it was by no means monolithic and was in fact complex
and ridden with inner tensions and ambiguities. The identification of the
Enlightenment with a blind faith in progress or with a naive rationalism is

facile in extreme. Equally problematic is the tendency of postmodernist scholars to blame the ills of the twentieth century on the Enlightenment philosophers—ignoring completely the realities of capitalism and fascist ideology. This is about as misleading and ahistoric as blaming Jesus for the Catholic Inquisition (for useful sympathetic studies of the Enlightenment, though not uncritical, see Gay 1969; Porter 1990; Callinicos 1999, 10–38).

It has long been recognized that the Enlightenment thinkers left an "ambiguous legacy," and Kropotkin approached this legacy with a certain critical engagement. He did not reject this legacy wholesale and thus embrace an extreme form of romanticism—with its idealistic metaphysics, its repudiation of science and reason, its negation of universal truths, its subjective individualism, its reactionary politics, and its obsession with hermeneutics (myth, symbol, rhetoric). These are only too evident in the neoromanticism of contemporary "postmodernism," especially among the fashionable acolytes of Nietzsche and Heidegger.

But equally, Kropotkin was not uncritical of Enlightenment thought, and he broke completely with the philosophes in a number of ways—in terms of ethical theory (rejecting both Kant's moral philosophy and utilitarianism), in terms of political theory, and most importantly, in terms of the Enlightenment metaphysics of nature.

The revolutionary slogans of the French Revolution, "liberty, equality, and fraternity," are of course only intelligible against the background of the philosophes' writings—particularly Rousseau—but Kropotkin sought not to discredit these slogans in defense of hierarchy and bourgeois individualism, but to develop ways in which these ideals could become a living, social reality. He thus came to repudiate not only capitalism and the market economy (lauded by Adam Smith) but the entire democratic politics of the philosophes. But equally significant, Kropotkin recognized that evolutionary theory and advances in the natural sciences had completely undermined the mechanistic philosophy of the Enlightenment. He thus came to acknowledge the "new philosophy"—evolutionary holism. For Kropotkin the key figures in the emergence of this new metaphysics of nature were Goethe, Humboldt, and Darwin. All three men, like Kropotkin, were enthusiastic naturalists—in the widest sense. But Kropotkin's own writings indicate a particularly strong allegiance to Darwin's ideas—and the integrity and importance of Darwin's evolutionary theory he always acknowledged, and at times fervently defended.

Darwin's "dangerous idea," as Daniel Dennett (1995) describes it, namely, the theory of evolution by common descent through natural selection, has been the subject of a plethora of studies. But Darwin's basic ideas are perhaps best introduced through the lucid writings of the philosopher-naturalist, Ernst Mayr. This scholar's history of biology (1982) in fact indicates only too well, by comparison, how shallow and schematic are Foucault's historiography and his theory of "epistemes" (1970; see Morris 1991, 434). Darwin's originality and importance, Mayr suggests, consist of bringing together and integrating into an evolutionary paradigm five basic ideas:

1. *Evolution*—The theory of evolution, as such, suggests that the world is neither constant nor perpetually cycling—as in Nietzsche's theory of eternal recurrence—nor is it divinely created: but it is rather steadily changing, such that organisms are transformed in time. The evidence for evolution, Mayr writes, is now so overwhelming, that it has become as self-evident as the fact that the earth rotates around the sun (1997, 178).

2. *Common Descent*—This is the theory that all living organisms are descended from a common ancestor, and that all groups of organisms—bacteria, fungi, plants, animals—ultimately go back to a single origin of life on earth. Every organism, whether as an individual or as a species, is thus the product of a long history, a history that dates back more than two billion years. As Lynn Margulis put it: "we evolved from a long line of progenitors, ultimately from the first bacteria" (1998, 4).

3. *Multiplication of species*—This is the idea that through a process of speciation there arises an increasing and astonishingly prolific diversity of organic life—a species being defined as a population of organisms that form a "reproductive community." Mayr writes: "Modern biologists are almost unanimously agreed that there are real discontinuities in organic nature, which delimit natural entities that are designated as species" (1988, 331). The species, therefore, is one of the basic units of biology, and the diversity of organic life is the product of evolution. It is estimated that there are now on earth around thirty million species of animals, half a million species of plant, and one hundred thousand species of fungi.

4. *Gradualism*—Evolutionary change takes place through the *gradual* change of populations over time, rather than involving the sudden origin of new species (but cf. Gould 1984, 259, on the theory of punctuated equilibrium).

5. *Natural selection*—This is the theory that evolutionary change comes about through a two-step process—the abundant production of genetic variation in every generation and the selection by means of differential survival and reproduction of those individual organisms that are adapted to the changing environmental conditions (1997, 177–89). Like Darwin, Mayr emphasizes that natural selection operates not at the level of

the gene (or group) but at the level of the phenotype—the individual organism (1991, 87–88).

Mayr thus defines evolution as "changes in the diversity and adaptation of populations of living organisms" and suggests that "living systems evolve in order to meet the challenge of the environment" (1976, 1–17).

Mayr was of the opinion that Darwin's evolutionary theory was in many ways completely alien to the Western philosophical tradition (from Plato to the Enlightenment) and thus constitutes an intellectual revolution that was far more fundamental and far-reaching than is usually recognized—though Kropotkin always acknowledged the fundamental revolution in thought that Darwin's theory had initiated. Indeed Mayr affirms that Darwin's was perhaps "the most fundamental of all intellectual revolutions in the history of mankind" (1976, 277).

Mayr highlighted other important dimensions to the Darwinian revolution.

Darwin not only completely refuted the idea that the earth and its diversity of life was the result of divine creation, but he also undermined the belief in *cosmic teleology*, the idea that nature has a final goal or purpose. This does not deny the fact that the development or behavior of individual organisms is purposive (teleonomic), only that the world itself is not a teleological process. It thus does not have a predetermined end or purpose, leading to "higher" or more "perfect" modes of life. Humans cannot therefore be seen as the "pinnacle" of the evolutionary process (Mayr 1988, 38–43).

Darwin also conclusively demonstrated that humans are not some divine creature set apart from the rest of nature but are an intrinsic part of it and that they have evolved from earlier apelike ancestors. This idea completely undermined the *anthropocentrism*, not only of Christian doctrine but also of Cartesian metaphysics. Mayr notes that the chemical and chromosomal similarity between humans and African apes is so great that "it is puzzling why they are so relatively different in morphology and brain development (1991, 24–25). As Darwin wrote in his notebook, some twenty-one years before he published *The Origin of Species* (1859), "Man in his arrogance thinks himself a great work worthy the interposition of a deity. More humble and I think truer to consider him created from animals" (1987, 300).

This is an aspect of Darwin's theory that Gould has consistently emphasized in suggesting that Darwin's evolutionary perspective is an important "antidote" to the cosmic arrogance of humans (1980, 13–14).

Darwin thus completely undermined, long before Heidegger and poststructuralists came upon the scene, the philosophy of *essentialism*, which, stemming from Plato, is deeply entrenched in the Western philosophical tradition as well as being anchored in ordinary language. This form of "topological" thinking suggests that organic forms or species have an underlying essence (idea) that are fixed and real and distinct from the observable flux of life. Darwin introduced a new way of thinking that Mayr describes as "population thinking," which recognizes and stresses the uniqueness of everything in the organic world. What then is important is not only the type (species), but the individual. The realization of the uniqueness and individuality of every living organism was, according to Mayr, perhaps the most revolutionary aspect of Darwin's thought (Mayr 1976, 27–28; 1982, 487).

Darwin was an uncompromising philosophical materialist, and "first and foremost a naturalist," and he proposed a theory of evolutionary holism that transcended the rival theories of *vitalism* and *mechanism*, both of which still have their adherents. Mayr suggests that Darwin's theory implies an emergent theory of holism and organicism that acknowledges the physicality of the world but repudiates any form of reductionism. Such a theory acknowledges that there is nothing in the processes, functions, and activities of living organisms that conflicts with, or is outside of, any of the laws of physics and chemistry. In this sense biologists are thorough-going materialists, and reject any recourse to spiritual or immaterial forces in explaining natural phenomena. But this theory recognizes, too, that in any structured system, new properties and capacities emerge at higher levels of integration, and these cannot be explained solely through a knowledge of the lower-level constituents. Thus, living beings are more than a collection of molecules, and Darwin's organicism opposes all reductionist forms of explanation. Biological concepts such as predation, territory, hibernation, and display can therefore never be reduced to chemistry or physics without losing entirely their essential meaning. Mayr therefore suggests the importance of a holistic-organismic approach to biology. (Mayr 1982, 64–71; 1997, 16–20).

Such in outline are the main tenets of Darwin's theory of evolution that Kropotkin wholeheartedly affirmed.

What was important about Darwin, and this Kropotkin (along with Mayr) clearly recognized and affirmed, was that he initiated a new ecological worldview: in introducing the idea that humans are not the special products of God's creation but evolved according to principles that operate throughout the natural world; in stressing the intrinsic organic (not spiritual) link between humans and nature; in undermining completely—long before quantum physics, feminist philosophy, and deep ecology—the mechanistic world picture, along with its dualisms, its cosmic teleology, and its essentialism; in emphasizing the crucial importance of openness, chance, probability, and the subjective agency and individualism of all organisms in the evolutionary process; and in suggesting a way of understanding that was both historical and naturalistic. In thus conceiving the world not as a machine but as a historical process, as an open system, Darwin completely undermined the positivistic conception of causality, along with its "determinism." Thus, any event or phenomena can only be explained in terms of a multiplicity of causes, relating to factors on many different—emergent—levels of being. As Mayr emphasized, Darwin's theory completely undermined the physicist conception of law and entailed a "complete rejection of Cartesian-Newtonian determinism" (1991, 49). All this is completely lost in Barbara Noske's recent study (1997), although the importance and the revolutionary implications of Darwin's' evolutionary theory was emphasized by Kropotkin over a hundred years ago and has been admirably portrayed in the more recent writings of Mayr (summarized above) and Stephen Jay Gould (1980, 1984).

Although Kropotkin fully endorsed Darwin's theory of evolution, he was particularly concerned at the end of the nineteenth century with the fact that this theory was continually being used to justify both the European domination of the rest of the world and the predominance of laissez-faire capitalism. It was Herbert Spencer (1820–1903) who first coined the phrase "the survival of the fittest," and Darwin took this to be a synonym for what he called "natural selection." Darwin emphasized that the "struggle for existence" was intrinsic to organic life: "as more individuals are produced than can possibly survive, there must in every case be a struggle for existence, either one individual with another of the same species, or with individuals of distinct species, or with the physical conditions of life" (1951, 63–65).

Darwin recognized that this was the doctrine of Malthus.

But at the end of the century, the concepts "survival of the fittest" and the "struggle for existence" had become slogans both to portray the animal world (and tribal societies) in Hobbesian fashion—as "nasty, brutish and short"—and to justify laissez-faire capitalism. The slogans were interpreted as ethical principles to sanction "cut-throat" economic competition, social inequalities, and a rampant individualism. Both Rockefeller and Carnegie invoked the Darwinian principle of "survival of the fittest" to justify the concentration of wealth, industrial and commercial, in the hands of a few, and the competitive ethos of capitalism (Hofstadter 1944, 45). But what particularly troubled Kropotkin was that Darwin's evolutionary theory was not only being narrowly interpreted by the capitalists but also by leading scholars such as Herbert Spencer and Thomas Huxley, both of whom were important advocates of evolutionary theory. In 1888 Huxley (1825–1895), well known as "Darwin's bulldog," published in the widely read magazine *The Nineteenth Century* what Kropotkin called his "struggle for existence" manifesto. It was titled "The Struggle for Existence in Human Society." In this essay Huxley portrayed both the animal world and the earliest clan period of humankind in a rather Hobbesian fashion. He suggested that from the point of view of the moralist, the animal world is on about the same level "as a gladiator's show." Only the strongest, the swiftest, and the most cunning live to fight another day.

The same applied to tribal society: "Among primitive men, the weakest and stupidest went to the wall, while the toughest and shrewdest, those who are best fitted to cope with their circumstances, but not the best in any other sense, survived. Life was a continual free fight, and beyond the united and temporary relations of the family, the Hobbesian war of each of us against all was the normal state of existence" (Huxley quoted in MA, 23).

This led Huxley to postulate a fundamental discontinuity between pre-human nature and "ethical man," and he followed Hobbes in affirming that members of tribal societies lived in a "state of nature"—lacking any morality or sociality. He essentially, as Kropotkin wrote, "denied the presence of any moral principle in the life of nature"—though he later came to realize the presence of the ethical principle in the social life of animals (E, 13). In his *Memoirs* Kropotkin referred to Huxley's article as "atrocious" and a misrepresentation of the facts of nature (MR, 499).

But Kropotkin was equally critical of Spencer's overemphasis on the "struggle of existence," especially his Hobbesian view of tribal life and his failure to recognize that members of clan-based societies were social beings. Remaining true to Hobbes, Kropotkin wrote, Spencer considers tribal communities as "loose aggregations of individuals who are strangers to one another, continually fighting and quarrelling" (E, 46; cf. Spencer 1885, 1:459–60).

It was in response to the writings of Huxley and Spencer that Kropotkin wrote an important series of articles on mutual aid, aiming to counter the overemphasis that had been placed on the "struggle for existence" by both these scholars. The five articles appeared in *The Nineteenth Century* (1890–1896) and were subsequently published as the book *Mutual Aid: A Factor of Evolution* (1902). The anthropologist Ashley Montagu has described this work as "one of the world's great books." It is, perhaps, Kropotkin's most popular work, and as a classic reply to the school of the "survival of the fittest," the book has an enduring significance. It is worth noting that Kropotkin was greatly encouraged to publish his theories by the editor of *The Nineteenth Century*, James Knowles, as well as by the well-known naturalist Henry W. Bates, who was then Secretary of the Royal Geographical Society.

Although the "struggle for existence" and the competition for food and life within each species had become an article of faith among most Darwinists—Huxley and Spencer were the foremost representatives of this tendency—Kropotkin from his earliest years had misgivings about this interpretation of nature. During his early travels in Eastern Siberia and Manchuria, two aspects of animal life, he wrote, impressed him most. The first was that life in this terrain did indeed involve a struggle for existence, with inclement weather conditions and the periodic wholesale destruction of life through natural agencies. He thus realized at a very early date the importance of the "natural checks" to animal populations that occurred in the northern regions of Eurasia. Second, on his journeys Kropotkin failed to observe the bitter struggle for existence among animals of the same species—which was considered by most Darwinists as the main factor of evolution. He vividly recalled the impressions gained when he explored the Vitim regions in the company of talented zoologist and friend Ivan Polyakoff.

> We were both under the fresh impression of the *Origin of Species*, but we vainly looked for the keen competition between the animals of the same species which the reading of Darwin's work had prepared us to expect. . . . We saw plenty of adaptations for struggling . . . against the adverse circumstances of climate, or against various enemies, and Polyakoff wrote many a good page upon the mutual dependency of carnivores, ruminants, and rodents in their geographical distribution; we witnessed numerous of facts of mutual support, especially during the migrations of birds and ruminants; but even in the Amur and Usuri regions, where animal life swarms in abundance, facts of real competition and struggle between higher animals of the same species came very seldom under my notice, though I eagerly searched for them. (MA, 26–27)

Kropotkin's misgivings were later confirmed when he read a lecture by a well-known Russian zoologist, Karl Fedorovich Kessler, who was the rector of the University of St. Petersburg. Addressing a congress of Russian naturalists in January 1880, a few months before his death, Kessler had emphasized that mutual aid, rather than the pitiless struggle for existence, was a crucial factor in the lives of animals, particularly of the higher mammals. Kropotkin quotes extracts from Kessler's address published in the *Memoirs of the St. Petersburg Society of Naturalists* (11, no. 1: 124–27): "I obviously do not deny the struggle for existence but I maintain that the progressive development of the animal kingdom, and especially of mankind, is favoured much more by mutual support than by mutual struggle. I am inclined to think that in the evolution of the organic world—in the progressive modification of organic beings—mutual support among individuals plays a much more important part than their mutual struggle" (MA, 26).

Kropotkin noted that in contrast to the naturalists of Western Europe, the Russian followers of Darwin, like Kessler, had all tended to emphasize the importance of mutual aid and to downplay the narrow Malthusian conception of competition and the perpetual struggle for existence.

But in emphasizing the importance of mutual aid as a factor in evolution and in countering the perspectives of Huxley (and the political economists), who conceived the animal world as a world of Hobbesian struggle —nature "red in tooth and claw," as Tennyson famously expressed it ("In Memoriam," line 60)—Kropotkin had no intention of advocating the opposite view. He thus did not espouse the romantic view of Rousseau, "who saw nothing in nature but love, peace and harmony destroyed by the accession of man" (MA, 23). Anybody taking a walk in the forest, or even consulting the works of the great naturalists, like Audubon, could not fail to notice, Kropotkin wrote, the important part taken by social life in the life of animals; but it would also prevent them from seeing in nature "nothing but harmony and peace." Rousseau, Kropotkin concluded, "had committed the error of excluding the beak and claw fight from his thoughts; and Huxley committed the opposite error" (MA, 24)—in pessimistically accepting the Hobbesian view that struggle, competition, the war of each against all, is a "law of nature."

In advocating and illustrating the importance of mutual aid among animals, and in challenging Huxley's one-sided interpretation, Kropotkin never intended to imply that mutual aid was the *only* factor in evolution. As he wrote: his book was on mutual aid viewed as *one* of the factors of evolution, "not on *all* factors of evolution and their respective values." He would be the last, he noted, to underrate the part which the self-assertion of the individual had played in the evolution of humankind (MA, 18). Thus, Kropotkin came to conclude that "sociability is as much a law of nature as mutual struggle," and that those animals that acquire habits of mutual aid are undoubtedly the "fittest"—in terms of the struggle for existence. "We may safely say that mutual aid is as much a law of animal life as mutual struggle, but that, as a factor of evolution, it most probably has a far greater importance in as much as it favours the development of such habits and characters as insure the maintenance and further development of the species" (MA, 24).

Kropotkin recognized, of course, that in emphasizing the importance of mutual aid and sociality in the life of animals, he was not saying anything new or original. The idea, as he put it, was "in the air," particularly among Russian naturalists. But to counter the one-sided Hobbesian view of nature that was being expressed by Huxley and Spencer, Kropotkin devoted the whole of *Mutual Aid* to presenting a wealth of empirical data to substantiate his thesis, namely, the importance of mutual aid in both the life of animals and in human societies throughout history.

Developments in the fields of biology, ecology, history, and anthropology over the past hundred years have inevitably made some of Kropotkin's work rather dated, and perhaps questionable; but as Ashley Montagu and Purchase (1996) note, both his data and his discussion stands up remarkably well in the light of recent scientific knowledge.

The first two chapters of *Mutual Aid* are devoted to illustrating the importance of social life and cooperation among animals, ranging from insects to the larger mammals. For his empirical evidence Kropotkin draws not only on his own observations and experiences in Siberia but also on the work of numerous biologists, naturalists, and travelers who were writing at the end of the nineteenth century. Of particular importance to Kropotkin were such studies as Pierre Huber, *Les Fourmis Indigènes* (1861); Alfred Espinas, *Les Sociétés Animales* (1877); Georges Romanes, *Animal Intelligence* (1882); W. H. Hudson, *Naturalist in La Plata* (1892); and the *Journals* of Audubon.

In presenting the "abundance of facts" regarding mutual aid, Kropotkin begins with the life of the invertebrates. He recognized that knowledge of invertebrates at that period was rather scant, but details of the life of ants, bees, termites, and burying beetles had advanced tremendously toward the end of the century, largely through the exemplary studies of the likes of Forel, Huber, Fabre, and Lubbock. Kropotkin emphasizes that there is a good deal of evidence to suggest that these insects display sociability, cooperative behavior, and mutual aid and that far from being automatons they display intelligence and individual initiative that Kropotkin saw as intrinsic to social existence:

> The ants and termites have renounced the "Hobbesian war" and they are
> the better for it. Their wonderful nests, their buildings, superior in relative

size to those of man; their paved roads . . . and granaries; their corn-fields, harvesting and "malting" of grain; their rational methods of nursing their eggs and larvae; and of building special nests for rearing aphids whom Linnaeus so picturesquely described as "the cows of the ants"; and, finally, their courage, pluck and superior intelligence—all these are the natural outcome of mutual aid which they practice at every stage of their busy and laborious life. (MA, 30)

Although this extract indicates a degree of anthropomorphic thinking, Kropotkin, like Whitehead, evidently felt that all organic beings expressed at least a modicum of intelligence (consciousness) and individual agency and that these traits were intrinsically linked to sociality. He continues, "That mode of life also necessarily resulted in the development of another essential feature in the life of ants; the immense development of individual initiative which, in turn, evidently led the development of that higher and varied intelligence which cannot but strike the human observer" (MA, 30).

Thus, for Kropotkin, mutual aid and individual initiative are two factors infinitely more important than mutual struggle in the evolution of the animal kingdom.

With regard to bird life, Kropotkin indicates, with a wealth of illustration, that mutual aid and cooperative behavior plays a crucial role in the life of many birds—the hunting associations of birds of prey (such as the kite and bald eagle), the collective behavior during migration, the giving of alarm signals, mutual support during nesting and breeding, or in warding off predators and establishing common security. "Life in society," and "sociability," is a ubiquitous feature, Kropotkin contends, of bird life.

Mutual aid is equally evident among mammals, and given the fact that most species of mammals are to some degree sociable beings, Kropotkin writes that "association and mutual aid are the rule with mammals" (MA, 48).

He details the various forms of sociality among the ruminants—Kropotkin noting that the prairies and steppes of both North America and Eurasia were, prior to the invasion and settlement of Europeans, once densely populated with herds of buffalo, deer, and burrowing rodents (such as the souslik and prairie dog), all of which were social mammals, and indicated well-developed practices of mutual aid and cooperation. Kropotkin argues that even among predators, such as jackals, wolves, hyenas, coyotes, and wild dogs, social habits are the norm, evident in cooperative hunting, group associations, and mutual support. With respect to the majority of mammals, sociality and mutual support is then their chief instrument in the struggle for life, and humans tend to be their main enemy (MA, 53). Kropotkin notes that among primates and elephants, sympathy and mutual attachment are highly developed; that they often post sentries in order to protect the interests of the group; and that they become quite unhappy when solitary.

Kropotkin therefore concludes that sociability "pervades all nature" and is a distinctive feature of all animal life—and that this sociability has been fully observed and recorded by many of the best naturalists—Audubon, Darwin, Hudson. Cooperative associations, sociability, and mutualism are then not only evident among animals but lie at "the very origin of evolution in the animal kingdom." "Society" was thus not created by humans—it is prior to the origin of humanity; and sociality is expressed in all the many domains of animal existence—migration, breeding, feeding, and mutual defense. It also "Takes higher forms, guaranteeing more independence to the individual without depriving it of the benefits of social life . . . sociability—that is, the need of the animal of associating with its like—the love of society for society's sake, combined with the 'joy of life' only now begins to receive due attention from the zoologists" (MA, 58).

Kropotkin therefore concludes that sociability is of utmost importance in the struggle for life, that intelligence is an eminently social faculty, and that language, imitation, and accumulated experience as well as individual initiative and agency are intrinsically linked to the development of social life and intelligence. Kropotkin also emphasized the fact that many external factors—adverse climatic conditions, migration, disease, predators—were often important as "natural checks" on overpopulation, thus mitigating competition and the struggle for existence between members of the same species. But the idea that Kropotkin thought the "struggle for existence" was an "illusion" (Bowler 1992, 333) is quite misleading. Kropotkin never doubted the reality of the "struggle for existence" in the life of organic beings. "No naturalist will doubt that the idea of a struggle for life carried on through organic nature is the great generalisation of our century. Life *is* struggle: and in that struggle the fittest survive" (MA, 65).

No one will deny, he wrote, that there is a struggle against adverse circumstances and a certain amount of real competition between members of the same species with regard to food, safety, shelter, and the possibility of leaving offspring (MA, 63). What he questioned was the "over-emphasis" by Huxley and Spencer on the struggle for existence between individuals—on competition, predation, on the "war of each against all" (Hobbes)—and the corresponding disavowal of mutual aid and sociability. As Kropotkin concluded, the fittest are the most sociable animals, and sociability appears as the chief factor of evolution (MA, 61): "In the great struggle for life which every animal species carries on against the hostile agencies of climate, surroundings, and natural enemies, big and small, those species which most consistently carry out the principle of mutual support, have the best chance to survive, while others die out" (E, 43).

In such phrases Kropotkin sometimes implies that mutual aid is often of benefit to the group or population, or to the species—an idea foreign to classical Darwinian theory, which sees the individual organism (and not the group or species) as the "unit" of selection (Mayr 1997, 200–203). But as Stephen Jay Gould points out, Kropotkin also (and often) recognized "that selection for mutual aid directly benefits each individual in its own struggle for personal success" (1992, 338).

What Kropotkin's writings on animal life clearly indicate, however, is that he followed Darwin in rejecting anthropocentrism and in suggesting that the difference between humans and animals (even invertebrates) was a matter of degree, not of kind. Kropotkin's basic ideas were very clearly expressed in the writings of his friend, the artist-naturalist Ernest Thompson Seton (1860–1946), whom Kropotkin had first met in 1897 through their mutual friend James Mavor. Seton had written "we and the beasts are kin. Man has nothing that the animals have not at least a vestige of, and animals have nothing than man does not in some degree share" (1898, 12). This expressed Kropotkin's essential thought, for no one, he felt, who believed in evolution could doubt that the human mind, as well as the human body, had its origin in the animals. Thus Kropotkin (like Seton) acknowledged the subjectivity, sociality, conscious agency, moral reasoning, and the complex forms of communication that were evident among nonhuman animals. It is easy to accuse Kropotkin (and Seton) of anthropomorphism, of humanizing animals, of imposing human social analysis on organic life, and of writing a lot of "twaddle." But the studies of Seton, and, more recently, those of Jane Goodall (1986) and Cynthia Moss (1988), have tended to confirm, through detailed empirical observations, Kropotkin's essential thoughts on animal life.

Yet although Kropotkin put an important emphasis on mutual aid and on "individual initiative" in the evolutionary process, he also stressed "the direct influence of the surroundings for producing variation in a definite direction" (E, 45). Although, like Darwin, Kropotkin repudiated the vitalism and teleology—the "tendency to progression"—inherent in Jean-Baptiste Lamarck's (1744–1829) theory of evolution, Kropotkin nevertheless always supported the idea that the "main factor of all evolution is the direct action of surroundings" and that "natural selection" was merely a useful auxiliary

(EE, 156–57). In this Kropotkin always felt that he was defending the integrity of Darwin's own theory of evolution, against the neo-Darwinism of August Weismann (1834–1914), for Weismann placed a strong emphasis on "natural selection" as the key mechanism (i.e., process) in evolution and categorically repudiated the theory of the inheritance of acquired characteristics that stemmed from Lamarck. Mayr refers to Weismann as "one of the towering figures in the history of evolutionary biology" (1991, 111).

Kropotkin argued that Darwin's theory of evolution, as expressed in his published writings and correspondence, changed over time, and he indicated and emphasized the three different aspects that the struggle for life may take in nature. Initially Darwin put an emphasis on the struggle for existence between the *individual* members of the same species and on the importance of natural selection (as a working hypothesis). As Darwin had a "paternal predilection" for this hypothesis he tended to initially downplay the "direct action" of the surrounding environment upon living beings (EE, 121). He then came, Kropotkin suggests, to place less and less value on the struggle of one organism with another of the same species and to recognize more the significance of mutual aid and cooperation and the *associated* struggle of groups of individuals against the environment. Finally, Darwin came to recognize the influence of the surrounding environment upon organic forms, and during the last twenty-five years (Kropotkin was writing in 1910), the consensus of opinion had come out strongly in favor of this third aspect, namely, the "direct action of [the] environment, which lays much less stress on [the] struggle for life as a species-producing agency than is required by the theory of natural selection" (EE, 118).

In a series of articles published between 1910 and 1915, Kropotkin came to strongly argue, and to illustrate, the theory of the inheritance of acquired characteristics, and thus to support the neo-Lamarckian tendency that was evident around the turn of the century. He rightly argued that Darwin and most of his contemporaries—Spencer, Huxley, Haeckel—never doubted the inheritance of acquired characteristics whenever they substantially affect the "inner structure" of a plant or an animal (EE, 185). He thus came to contest Weismann's emphasis on natural selection which he described as both "anti-Darwinian" and as reflecting an "anti-Lamarckian prejudice." Kropotkin recognized, of course, that rats that had their tails amputated did not give birth to tailless offspring, and he noted too that the actual processes of heredity were then virtually unknown and were thus open to much speculation (EE, 191). But nevertheless Kropotkin emphasized that a good number of empirical studies since Darwin wrote his *Origin of Species* had established beyond doubt that the inner structures and outward forms of plants and animals had been produced by the "direct action of the environment" and that the hereditary transmission of the so-called acquired characteristics in plants and animals had been proved by direct experiment (EE, 152). This did not deny the intervention of natural selection; this was viewed by Kropotkin as an "auxilliary" process (EE, 142). Kropotkin quotes a letter from Darwin to the celebrated geographer Moritz Wagner (1813–1887), suggesting that Darwin had come to recognize that he had given insufficient weight to the "direct action of the environment" in his earlier studies (EE, 134).

Although it is easy to criticize Kropotkin for his neo-Lamarckian views, specifically in defending the theory of the "inheritance of acquired characteristics" as against Weismann's critique, it has to be remembered that most biologists at the end of the nineteenth century, including Darwin himself, as well as Engels, Haeckel, Wagner, and Huxley, all accepted the validity of this theory. As Mayr wrote, the theory of acquired characteristics, espoused by Lamarck and affirmed by Kropotkin and others, seemed formerly so consistent with known facts that it would be churlish to criticize anyone for holding such a theory, which has since been shown to be wrong (1982, 12). Not until after the emergence of genetics and the "evolutionary synthesis" of the late 1930s—associated with the work of J. B. S. Haldane, Julian Huxley, Theodosius Dobzhansky, and Ernst Mayr—did the theory of the inheritance of acquired characteristics finally lose ground. As Mayr put it, the path of science is never straight. The majority of contemporary biologists therefore agree with Mayr that the Lamarkian theory is untenable, for the newly acquired characteristics of the phenotype (organism) cannot be transmitted to the next generation (1997, 187; Rose, 1997, 179). But although this may be true of the "higher" animals, recent studies in microbiology have indicated that cytoplasmic inheritance may well be evident.

According to Margulis, "Both endocytobiology and symbiogenesis are simultaneously neo-Lamarckian and Darwinian evolutionary ideas. Mitochondria, plastids, and other organelles began as bacteria; thus acquired characteristics . . . are inherited." Like Kropotkin, she affirms that Darwin himself was a Lamarckian, and even anticipated symbiogenesis, in recognizing that every living creature is a "microcosm" (1997, 305).

Kropotkin's study *Mutual Aid*, given its purpose in countering Huxley's portrayal of animal life as inherently competitive and antisocial, is inevitably polemical, extravagant, and one-sided. Of this Kropotkin was acutely aware. He realized only too well from his own travels and experiences, and from his wide reading (of field naturalists as diverse as Pallas, Audubon, Brehm, and Darwin), that the theory of evolution was an "immense" subject and that the evolution of organic life could only be understood in terms of a multitude of factors. Paying tribute to Darwin's synthesis of biological knowledge, Kropotkin notes that these factors include the variability and geographical distribution of organisms, natural selection, the effects of isolation, hybridism, sexual selection, the evolution of instincts, as well as mutual aid and the immensely vast problem of heredity (EE, 122–23). He admits that in the book *Mutual Aid* animals and humans are represented in it under too favorable an aspect: "that their sociable qualities are insisted upon, while their anti-social and self-asserting instincts are hardly touched upon" (MA, 18). But he felt that this was unavoidable given the fact that the Hobbesian view had become an "article of faith" among many biologists, and the "harsh, pitiless struggle for life" among both animals and humans had become the accepted norm. It was therefore necessary to indicate the overwhelming importance that sociable habits play in nature and in the evolution of both animal species and human beings. For while Kropotkin acknowledged that sociality, intelligence, and individual initiative and agency were present in all organic beings, he recognized too that these were subject to development and that they varied enormously in degree as between different species. Needless to say, there are still many neo-Darwinist scholars and sociologists around who appear not to have heard of Kropotkin and who still portray the natural world, specifically animal life, as "red in tooth and claw." For example, Daniel Dennett explicitly affirms the Hobbesian thesis of Huxley: "Hobbes was right: life in the state of nature *is* nasty, brutish and short, for virtually all nonhuman species. If 'doing what comes naturally' meant doing what virtually all other animal species do, it would be hazardous to the health and well being of us all." Animals—including chimpanzees—"are the true denizens of Hobbes' state of nature, much more nasty and brutish than many would like us to believe" (1995, 478–81).

The subjective agency, sociability, and the moral aspects of animal life are ignored by Dennett, just as he completely fails to acknowledge the nasty and brutish things that humans have done to one another over the centuries—especially since the rise of the modern state. But believing that those animals that practice mutual aid were more "fit" than those that were constantly at war with each other, Kropotkin extolled the importance of sociality and cooperation for human life: "Don't compete! Competition is always injurious to the species, and you have plenty of resources to avoid it! That is the *tendency* in nature, not always realised in full, but always present. That is watchword that comes to us from the bush, the forest, the river, the ocean. Therefore combine—practice mutual aid!" (MA, 73).

In his valuable introduction to Kropotkin's life and thought, Graham Purchase emphasizes the many insightful things that Kropotkin has to say about the role of sociability and cooperation in nature. He highlights several important themes.

First, although mutual aid certainly carries an important "survival" function, it may not necessarily entail survival per se, for Kropotkin always spoke in terms of evolutionary "tendencies," and a tendency does not imply necessity or determinism. Nor is pure chance involved. Purchase quotes Dobzhansky on this issue: "Evolution is neither necessary in the sense of being predestined, nor is it a matter of chance or accident. It is governed by natural selection, in which ingredients of chance and anti-chance are blended in a way which makes the dichotomy meaningless and which renders evolution to be a creative process" (quoted in Midgley 1985, 81).

Like Dobzhansky, Kropotkin affirmed that "nothing in biology makes sense except in the light of evolution" (Mayr 1997, 178); like Whitehead, Kropotkin held that nature is a process and that the whole spectacle of evolution is a "creative advance of nature . . . into novelty" (1920, 178).

Purchase also emphasized that Kropotkin makes a clear distinction between the survival (or evolutionary) function of mutual aid and the related concepts of sociability or association—or "society for society's sake." According to Kropotkin, "It is extremely difficult to say what brings animals together—the needs of mutual protection, or simply the pleasure of feeling surrounded by their congeners . . . in several species, such as rats, marmots, hares, etc. . . . sociable life is maintained notwithstanding the quarrelsome or otherwise egoistic inclinations of the isolated individual. Thus it is not imposed, as in the case with ants and bees, by the very physiological structure of the individuals" (MA, 52, 58).

In recent years, there has been a profusion of studies on human cooperative practices and on altruism by neo-Darwinists and sociobiologists that have attempted to explain such behavior in terms of the function for the individual, or rather the genes, the organism being considered merely their "carrier." The triumph of molecular biology had indeed led many biologists to feel that all biological functions, as well as all forms of social behavior such as mutualism and altruism, can be explained in terms of molecular structures. Critiques of this "ultra-Darwinism," as Rose describes it, have been recently and cogently voiced by a number of scholars. They have indicated its many limitations—its mechanistic "Cartesian" conception of life; its reductive epistemology; its adaptationist paradigm; its genocentric approach, with its emphasis on competition and the "selfish gene" (rather than on the role that the organism and mutual aid play in the evolutionary process); and the tendency not to recognize the importance of morphogenesis and symbiosis as evolutionary factors (Goodwin 1994; Capra 1997; Rose 1997). Purchase merely notes that by emphasising nonfunctional sociability when criticizing modern sociobiology, "it is possible to show how reductionist and absurd such gene-psychology is in explaining complex social interaction." Most social activities, whether of animals or humans, have to be understood from an evolutionary holistic perspective and cannot be interpreted as simply "a function of gene survival" (1996, 49).

Midgley, in fact, suggests that sociobiology (E. O. Wilson, Dawkins) is nothing but crude Hobbesian psychological egoism, only with the bizarre substitution of the gene (personified and given agency) for the self-preservation of the individual organism (1985, 125).

Purchase highlights the importance of Kropotkin's idea that intelligence is developed from and to some degree dependent upon social cooperation, for, as Kropotkin put it, intelligence is an "eminently social faculty." Thus, Purchase concludes that if sociability and co-operation are inherent in human nature, and do not have to be imposed on humans by some system of authority, then "social anarchism is biologically no less plausible than that of state capitalism" (1996, 50).

The role and extent of mutualism and symbiosis within and between species has become much more evident in recent years, and numerous studies have been written on these topics. Kropotkin was mainly concerned with cooperation within animal species rather than between them, and, as we have noted, he gave numerous examples of mutual aid among animals—cooperative hunting, individuals defending the group against predators, the giving of alarm signals, and so on. With some flourish, he even proclaimed that the ants and termites "have renounced the Hobbesian war," and they are the better for it! (MA, 30). But like many other Russian naturalists, Kropotkin never mentions the term "symbiosis," and his emphasis is on the social life of specific animals, not on cooperation between species. In fact, he acknowledged that between species there is often "an immense amount of warfare and extermination going on" (MA, 24)—although "warfare" is a somewhat unfortunate term to describe predation and interspecific conflict. Moreover, Kropotkin made only the briefest mention of microorganisms, although he acknowledged that "We must be prepared to learn someday, from the students of microscopical pond-life facts of unconscious mutual support, even from the life of micro-organisms" (MA, 27; see Todes 1989; Sapp 1994, 23).

Lynn Margulis's criticism of Kropotkin's work, namely, that it accentuated "the confounding of mutual aid with symbiosis" (1997, 300), is therefore entirely misplaced and unfair to the naturalist. For apart from mentioning the mutualism between ants and aphids, Kropotkin nowhere in his writings discussed "symbiosis," at least in the sense of implying a close and direct physical contact between organisms of different species.

The concept of "symbiosis" was first used by the German mycologist Anton de Bary (1831–1888) in an address titled "The Phenomena of Symbiosis" given at a meeting of naturalists and physicians in 1878. He defined it as "the living together of unlike named organisms" (Sapp 1994, 7). Examples of symbiosis are: lichens (a mutualistic association of fungi and algae), the nitrogen-fixing bacteria in the root nodules of legumes, and the mycorrhizal fungi associated with many trees and orchids. Even Herodotus had noted the mutualism that existed between the Nile crocodile and a species of plover that took parasites from inside the reptile's mouth and yet was never harmed. Espinas, in his study of animal societies, which Kropotkin greatly admired, included many examples of mutualistic association between different animal species, for example, tick-birds and the rhinoceros, ants and aphids, and mixed flocks of birds (Sapp 1994, 18–20). But in the first decade of the twentieth century, the Russian biologist Konstantin Merezhkovsky (1855–1921) argued in a series of papers that the chloroplasts (the structures containing chlorophyll within a plant cell) were symbiotic microorganisms and that the nucleus and cytoplasm also emerged from a symbiosis of two distinct organisms. In 1910, he proposed the term *symbiogenesis* to describe the formation of a new organism by the combination or association of two independent microbes that had entered into symbiosis (Sapp 1994, 51). Since that time, it has increasingly come to be recognized that symbiosis is a fundamental aspect of all organic life and that symbiogenesis is a major source of evolutionary novelty. That symbiosis could lead to evolutionary change and to the formation of new forms of life was initially inferred from the association of algae and fungi in the formation of lichen, but in a number of important studies, Lynn Margulis has argued that symbiogenesis has played a crucial role in the emergence and development of all the major groups of organisms—the protoctista (slime molds, algae, ciliates, protozoa), fungi, plants, and animals (Margulis and Sagan 1986). From the origin of life some 3.5 billion years ago, Margulis has thus emphasized the symbiogenetic origin, in sequence, of all the major life-forms. All life on the earth today is therefore the progeny of some ancient bacterium: "Symbiosis is not a marginal or rare phenomenon. It is natural and common. We abide in a symbiotic world" (1998, 9).

Symbiogenesis is, therefore, now considered, along with morphogenesis (the idea that the laws of complexity spontaneously generate much of the order evident in the natural world), as a principle avenue of evolution of all organisms. Competition, then, is not the only driving force of evolution: mutualism and symbiosis are "an equally universal feature of the biological realm" (Goodwin 1994, 166). In similar fashion, Steven Rose believes that symbiogenesis "provides an important alternative perspective to the ruthlessly individualistic competitive metaphor which underlies the ultra-Darwinist" worldview (1997, 269)—the Hobbesian view that Kropotkin long ago critiqued.

Finally, we may quote from another recent study of holistic biology, which also in substance confirms Kropotkin's essential thesis: "Life is much less a competitive struggle for survival than a triumph of co-operation and creativity. Indeed, since the creation of the first nucleated cells, evolution has proceeded through ever more intricate arrangements of co-operation and co-evolution" (Capra 1997, 238).

Writing at the end of the nineteenth century, Kropotkin was not able to provide anything like a full analysis of symbiotic evolution—the concept of symbiogenesis did not even emerge until 1910—but he did offer some insightful reflections and recognized that each cell was itself a "cosmos" (KRP, 119). Thus it is important to recognize that Kropotkin was a pioneer environmentalist (along with his friend Élisée Reclus) and "one of the earliest and most able exponents of symbiotic evolution," a scholar who certainly deserves much greater recognition than he has hitherto been accorded" (Purchase 1996, 50).

It is quite ironic how many recent sociobiologists can write texts on the evolution of cooperation (e.g., Axelrod 1984) without even mentioning Kropotkin. In a lecture celebrating the centenary of the Rationalist Press Association (1999), Helena Cronin discussed human nature from an evolutionary perspective. She challenged the notion, put out by economists and rational choice theorists, that humans were intrinsically aggressive, competitive, and egoistic, and that nature was "red in tooth and claw." Instead, she emphasized that humans were social beings—cooperative, compassionate, with an innate sense of fairness, and were actively engaged in mutual aid and reciprocal altruism. Her talk was titled "Natural Born Coop-erators." She seemed to think that these were "new" ideas recently discov-ered by neo-Darwinian scholars and evolutionary psychologists. Eager to emphasize her own originality, she thus completely forgot to mention that Kropotkin had advanced these same ideas a hundred years ago.

In common with the majority of Russian naturalists and biologists of his day—but unlike Tolstoy—Kropotkin wholeheartedly embraced Darwin's theory of evolution. He was indeed, like many of his Russian contemporaries, a genuine admirer of Darwin. But like many Russian zoologists—such as Kessler, whose ideas he early embraced—Kropotkin was highly critical, as we have noted, of the overemphasis that British scholars had placed on the "struggle for existence." In an exemplary study of Russian evolutionary thought and the "mutual aid" school to which Kropotkin belonged, Daniel Todes (1988, 1989) has lucidly described the widespread reaction of Russian scholars to the Malthusian dimension of Darwin's evolutionary theory. Kropotkin exemplified this reaction, and it had several aspects.

Kropotkin sought initially not to repudiate the concept of "struggle for existence" entirely but to clarify its meaning and to suggest that it had var-ious components—as Darwin himself acknowledged in the quotation cited earlier. Thus, although Kropotkin came to acknowledge the importance of intraspecific and interspecific competition and conflict, he tended to shift the emphasis toward the struggle of the organism against the environment.

Kropotkin also emphasized the fact that the physio-geographical con-ditions of the Russian setting, as he had personally observed them in eastern Siberia and Manchuria, did not resonate at all with the Malthusian perception of overpopulation and the subsequent competition for limited resources. As Kropotkin expressed in a letter dated August 15, 1909, to the anarchist and biologist Marie Goldsmith, "Russian zoologists investigated enormous continental regions in the temperate zone, where the struggle of the species against natural conditions . . . is more obvious; while Wallace and Darwin primarily studied the coastal zones of tropical lands, where over-crowding is more noticeable. In the continental regions that we visited there is a paucity of animal population; over-crowding is possible there, but only temporarily" (quoted in Todes 1993, 368).

The Malthusian doctrine of overpopulation and competition was thus foreign to the Russian experience.

But essentially, Kropotkin, like other Russian naturalists, was critical of the Hobbesian interpretation of nature on ideological grounds, seeing it as a reflection and justification for bourgeois political economy (laissez-faire capitalism) and a soulless individualism. The biologist N. I. Danilev-sky indeed saw Darwinism in 1885 as part of a British cultural tradition, which contrasted sharply with Slavic "collectivism" in its preoccupation with competition. Like Marx, Danilevsky saw a close correspondence between Darwin's theory of natural selection and both the Hobbesian theory of politics and the economic theories of Malthus and Adam Smith (Gould 1983, 58–59; Todes 1993, 362).

It was this ideological and cultural bias that Kropotkin challenged, emphasizing the fact that the preoccupation with overpopulation, competition, and the intraspecific struggle for existence reflected a distorted and socially insidious conception of nature. This Hobbesian image of nature, it may be noted, is still evident in the writings of many contemporary ultra-Darwinists (Dawkins, E. O. Wilson, and Dennett), as Midgley and others have critically discussed.

It was a reading of Todes's seminal article on Kropotkin and Russian evolutionary thought that led the well-known biologist Stephen Jay Gould to completely change his opinion about Kropotkin. He confessed that he had always viewed Kropotkin as "daftly idiosyncratic," a "kooky" intellectual, well-meaning, idealistic, but one of the "soft and wooly thinkers who let hope and sentimentality" get in the way of analysis, and a unwillingness to accept nature as she is, "warts and all." He was, Gould admits, "a man of strange politics and unworkable ideals" (1992, 331). A reading of Todes's article and Kropotkin's own *Mutual Aid* led Gould to realize that Kropotkin was not an isolated thinker, but part of a much broader current of thought, and that Kropotkin's basic argument was essentially correct. Thus, he came to the conclusion that "Kropotkin was no crackpot." But like T. H. Huxley, Gould still maintains a "picket fence" between humans and animal life and argues that nature (or at least our understanding of the natural world) offers no basis or guidance at all for our moral values—except, perhaps, as an indicator of what to avoid in human society (1992, 327–29).

8
ETHICAL NATURALISM

That fine historian of anarchism, Paul Avrich suggested that Kropotkin, for all his scientific gifts, was essentially a moral philosopher—a moralist "whose techniques of scientific investigation served to buttress his ethical teachings." For what dominates all of Kropotkin's writings is an ethical vision—the vision of a new society that is based on mutual support and voluntary cooperation, not on coercive authority, hierarchy, and exploitation. In fact, Kropotkin was rather unique among scholars in combining a deep love of science with an equally passionate interest in ethical issues, and these interests are concurrent throughout his life. But he was no armchair scholar, even though age and physical infirmities severely curtailed his political activities in the last two decades of his life. Kropotkin was always a devoted anarchist militant, as well as a moralist (Avrich 1988, 71–73).

One of Kropotkin's earliest pamphlets, in fact, was on the issue of "Anarchist Morality" (1892), an essay prompted by some anarchist comrades who took the socialist adage "To each according to his need" as implying the freedom to help themselves to goods from a store run by a fellow anarchist. Kropotkin was appealed to and he subsequently wrote the pamphlet in response (KRP, 79). His writings on ethics, in essence, are an expansion and development of his theory of "mutual aid," and shortly after the publication of his classic work, Kropotkin wrote two articles specifically on moral issues. Titled "The Ethical Need of the Present Day" and "The Morality of Nature," these were published in *The Nineteenth Century* (1904–1905) and were later revised and incorporated into his study *Ethics: Origin and Development*. Kropotkin devoted the last years of his life to the

151

writing of this text, which remained unfinished at his death. It was published posthumously in 1922, edited by his friend Nicholas Lebedev (E, ix–xvi).

Kropotkin's book on *Ethics* essentially consists of a historical survey of various ethical theories, a sustained focus being put on what Kropotkin described as a naturalistic or realistic approach to ethics—represented by a number of key thinkers whom Kropotkin clearly felt were of importance in the development of a "realistic basis" for ethics—Epicurus, Bacon, Hobbes, Spinoza, Adam Smith, Comte, Proudhon, Darwin.

As in his earlier studies, Kropotkin was keen to emphasize at the beginning of his study the important advances in scientific knowledge that had been made at the end of nineteenth century. These new vistas opened up by science had, he felt, both a practical and a philosophical significance. On the one hand, through science, the productive capacity of human labor had reached a point where the means of satisfying basic human needs—food, clothing, shelter—were in excess of the needs themselves. Thus, Kropotkin argued, like Marx, that with modern technology, "Well being can be secured for all, without placing on anyone the burden of oppressive, degrading toil, and humanity can at last rebuild its entire social life on the basis of justice" (E, 2).

On the other hand, modern scientific research had completely undermined traditional religious belief and metaphysical conceptions of the universe and the place of humanity in nature and thus heralded a new philosophy of nature, which for Kropotkin was both "poetical and inspiring." As he wrote: "The traditional views about the position of man in the universe, the origin of life, and the nature of reason were entirely upset by the rapid development of biology, the appearance of the theory of evolution and the progress made in the study of human and animal psychology" (E, 1).

Modern science for Kropotkin had thus achieved a double aim: "On the one side it has given to man a very valuable lesson in modesty. It has taught him to consider himself as but an infinitesimally small particle of the universe. It has driven him out of his narrow egotistical seclusion, and has dissipated the self-conceit under which he considered himself the centre of the universe and the object of the special attention of the creator." But at the same time modern science had provided humanity with great potential for progress "if it skillfully utilizes the unlimited energies of Nature" (E, 4).

But for Kropotkin there was one branch of knowledge that had failed to engage with the new scientific researches, particularly in biology and anthropology, and that was ethics, the study of the fundamental principles of morality. What he felt was therefore needed was a new ethics based on naturalistic principles—Kropotkin using the term "naturalism" to indicate a form of ethics that was free of superstition, religious dogma, and metaphysical abstractions.

If contemplation of the universe and a close acquaintance with the natural world were able to inspire great naturalists and poets in the nineteenth century (Goethe, Shelley, Byron), then, Kropotkin asked, why should not a deeper penetration into the "life of man and his destinies" not also inspire the poet—and also be relevant to ethical theory? "If the study of nature has yielded the elements of a philosophy, which embraces the life of the cosmos, the evolution of living beings, the laws of physical activity, and the development of society, it must also be able to give us the rational origin and the sources of moral feelings" (E, 5).

Kropotkin's study was therefore concerned not with treating morality as some autonomous realm, completely independent of the material world and social life (as in Kantian metaphysics), but with an attempt to delineate the origins or "sources" of moral sentiments and the role or "function" that morality plays in human social life. He was not therefore concerned with semantics, with the *meaning* of moral concepts, issues that fascinate contemporary philosophers, leading them to emphasize what is clearly self-evident, namely that moral judgments are prescriptive, giving rise to ethical theory or prescriptivism (Hare 1952; Raphael 1994, 29); Kropotkin was more interested in exploring the origin of moral sentiments and the part they played in social life.

Kropotkin's own ethical theory focused around three key concepts that he considered to be the basic "elements" of morality. Rooted in human nature, these elements formed an "organic" unity—sociality (or mutual aid), justice (or equity), and morality per se. The third element he felt unique to humans, and it was expressed through altruism and self-sacrifice—although Kropotkin disliked both terms and preferred such concepts as "beneficence" and "magnanimity"—the offering of help or support to others without thought or expectancy of reward (E, 319).

Like many other scholars, Kropotkin felt that human life, indeed life itself, expressed a certain duality, a "double tendency" as he put it. This was not simply a metaphysical assertion but was based on the study of nature and on an understanding of human history. This "double tendency" consisted, on the one hand, of a tendency toward the greater development of sociality and mutual aid, and on the other, a consequent increase in the intensity of life and individuality—with the potential increase in human happiness and freedom. "Without the continual growth of sociality, and consequently of the intensity and variety of sensations, life is impossible, therein lies it essence" (E, 20).

This led Kropotkin to suggest that within the human psyche there existed two sets of opposed feelings, one relating to struggle, independence, and self-preservation, the other relating to mutual sympathy and social unity: "In one set are the feelings which induce man to subdue other men in order to utilize them for his individual ends, while those in the other set induce human beings to unite for attaining common ends by common effort" (E, 22).

These two tendencies or instincts, the self-preservation instinct, reflected in a "hodge-podge of instincts and feelings" (hatred, the passion for domination, greed, self-assertion, egoism) and the social instinct, reflected in mutual aid, are discussed by Kropotkin throughout the text. Both form an essential component of his ethical theory. But Kropotkin's key idea is to suggest that there is a need in ethical theory to discover, not a compromise, but a dialectical "synthesis" between these two sets of feelings—which were described by such nineteenth-century scholars as Comte and Spencer as altruism and egoism. Thus the "purpose" or aim of ethics, or of "empirical morality" (as opposed to a morality sanctioned by religion or based on a transcendental [idealist] metaphysics), was, according to Kropotkin, to create an atmosphere in society that would be most conducive both "to the welfare of all and the fullest happiness of every separate being" (E, 26). Such an ethic must not fetter in any way, he argued, individual initiative or the development of individuality. The welfare of all, for Kropotkin, was not to be at the expense of the individual but rather "would become a groundwork for the fullest development of the personality" (E, 28). The emphasis on altruism and social welfare must not, then, in any way oblate personal energies, initiative, or freedom. Equally, Kropotkin was against any form of individualism or egoism, as expressed by Stirner and Nietzsche, that led to a repudiation of morality, or implied a sterile amoralism.

In advocating a naturalistic approach to ethics—and in this Kropotkin felt he was simply following a long tradition that culminated in Darwin's evolutionary approach to ethics—Kropotkin argued that moral sentiments had their "source" in the sociality or mutual aid that he felt pervaded the animal kingdom. He reacted against Huxley's contention, expressed in his famous article, "Evolution and Ethics" (1893), that there was an absolute dichotomy between the "cosmic process" (the evolution of life) and the "ethical process" (the moral life of humanity). According to Huxley, the whole of nature, red in tooth and claw, was a negation of moral principles, and thus an understanding of evolutionary processes and of nature gave us no reason why "what we call good is preferable to what we call evil." In fact, Huxley contended that the "cosmic process" was the antithesis, even the "enemy," of morality. Kropotkin felt that this dualistic approach was unhelpful. He asked the simple question: what are the "roots" or "origin" of the "moral law" that clearly plays such an important role in human life? Surely it is not outside of nature, and thus of divine origin?

Kropotkin thought the issue straightforward, for in essence he argued there were but two principal schools of ethical theory—those who insisted our moral concepts are of divine origin and thus connect ethics intrinsically with religion, and those who adopt a naturalistic approach, seeking to free ethics from the sanction of religion and to create a realistic ethics. Kropotkin affirms the second approach and argues that "the moral conceptions of man are merely the further developments of the moral habits of mutual aid, which are so generally inherent in social animals that they may be called a law of nature" (E, 282–86). The sociality or mutual aid that is characteristic of the social animals contain, Kropotkin argued, in "embryonic form" the moral sentiments that later play such a crucial role in human life.

In the chapter "The Moral Principle in Nature," Kropotkin discusses in detail Darwin's theory of ethics, for Darwin's evolutionary naturalism form the basis and the inspiration of Kropotkin's own ethical theory (E, 32–48). For Darwin the moral sense was not seen as some "wondrous" gift of unknown origin, as it was for Kant, but rather as deriving from the social instincts that were inherent in mammalian life. Quoting Darwin, Kropotkin contends that the true source of all moral feelings is found "in the social instincts which lead the animal to take pleasure in the society of its fellows, to feel a certain amount of sympathy with them, and to perform various services for them" (Darwin 1909, 150; E, 33). Thus Kropotkin followed Darwin in recognizing that the "intellectual faculties of animals differ from those of man in degree but not in their essence" (E, 35), and in strongly affirming that the social instincts—sociality, mutual aid—form the basis "for the further development of moral feelings" (E, 45). Mutual aid is therefore seen by Kropotkin—following, he felt, Darwin's seminal insights—as being a predominant fact of nature, and a key factor in the evolutionary process, as well as being "more permanently at work in the social animals than even the purely egotistical instinct of direct self-preservation" (E, 15). In his study *Mutual Aid*, Kropotkin provided ample illustration of mutual sympathy and mutual support with respect to a wide range of animal species. And it was such mutual aid (or sociality) that indicated "the natural origin not only of the rudiments of ethics but also of the higher ethical feelings" (E, 16). Thus Kropotkin concluded, with Darwin, that the social instinct is "the common source out of which all morality originates" (E, 37). It was the origin not only of feelings of benevolence and sympathy, which implied the identification of the individual with the group, which was the "starting point" of all ethical theory, but also of justice (or equity) and of self-sacrifice, which for Kropotkin, were the two other important elements of morality.

As an evolutionary naturalist, Kropotkin took it for granted that moral concepts were extremely varied and continually developing; he certainly had a much better understanding of anthropology than many of his philosophical critics. But he was critical of moral relativism and the idea that morality is "nothing but a set of conventional customs" (E, 34). Kropotkin recognized, of course, that the social life of tribal peoples was complex and culturally diverse, each clan or tribe having its own "very complicated ethics," that is, its own system of morality (E, 73). Yet he put a fundamental emphasis on humanity, and on the fact that we are, first of all, human beings, with intrinsic capacities and powers. Kropotkin recognized, like Darwin, that humans, like all other species, have a nature, qualities that define us as a unique organism and that this nature was a product of an evolutionary process (Buss 1999, 47). All social and psychological theories imply its existence, although many contemporary scholars fail to specify what they imply when they write of the "individual" or the "subject" and tend to suggest that humans are simply the "effect" of discourses or culture. But according to Erich Fromm, "Man is not a blank sheet of paper on which culture can write its text: he is an entity charged with energy and structured in specific ways" (1949, 23). This is also Kropotkin's essential standpoint. This did not imply that human nature and human subjectivity expressed or were manifest of some unchanging "essence." Indeed, the conflation, by postmodernist scholars, of human "nature" as expressed by evolutionary theorists like Kropotkin, with the metaphysics of Plato and his concept of "essence" (Eidos) is quite fallacious. For Kropotkin, as for contemporary evolutionists like Singer and Dennett, humans are characterized not by some external, supranatural Platonic essence (benign or otherwise) but by an evolving human nature that exhibits increasing levels of both sociality and individuality. Kropotkin therefore argued that the moral sentiment was derived from the social instinct, or mutual aid, which was deeply ingrained in all social animals, including humans. As he succinctly put it: "The source of morality lies in a sociality inherent in all the higher animals, and so much more in man" (E, 78). But he also argued that this sociality was accompanied, and became increasingly developed within the human species, by a sense of equity or justice, which for Kropotkin also formed one of the basic elements of morality. But morality itself finds its most developed or "true" expression in acts of self-sacrifice or altruism—or "magnanimity," which is reflected in "those moments when man gives to others his powers and at times his life, without thought of what he will obtain in return" (E, 246). Mutual aid, justice, and morality form a developing series that for Kropotkin are "rooted" in human psychology (E, 31). Morality, as such, though it is found in "rudimentary" or "embryonic" form among social animals, is for Kropotkin unique to humans. "Moral tendencies are observed among social animals, but morality as the joint product of instinct, feeling, and reason, exists only in man. It developed gradually, it is developing now, and will continue to grow" (E, 252).

Morality, for Kropotkin, springs on the one hand from the deep-seated instinct for sociality, which is inherent in humans and is expressed in the sympathy we offer to others, and, on the other hand, it derives from the conception of justice (or equity) inherent in our reason (E, 146).

Kropotkin's historical survey of various moral teachings, which I shall review below only in summary fashion, is critical, balanced, and eminently readable. It puts a key emphasis on those scholars who have contributed to the development of a naturalistic approach to ethics. The moral philosopher Alasdair MacIntyre covered roughly the same ground half a century later in his *A Short History of Ethics* (1967). But MacIntyre's study lacks any anthropological perspective and not only fails to mention Kropotkin, but even more surprisingly, fails also to mention Darwin. In a more recent controversial reevaluation of moral philosophy—in which Aristotle, Kant, and Nietzsche have pride of place—MacIntyre (1985) continues to ignore Darwin, as if evolutionary theory had no relevance at all for ethics. Kropotkin, of course, thought otherwise.

Kropotkin begins his survey by examining the moral conceptions of "primitive" (i.e., clan-based or tribal) peoples (E, 62–83). Contrary to the views of Hobbes and Spencer, Kropotkin emphasizes that tribal people have orderly and complex forms of social life, in which food-sharing, reciprocity, communal activities, and various forms of mutual aid are of central importance. Each tribal community has its own system of morality, and moral and customary rules take various forms—some are related to subsistence activities, others deal with social issues, while there is an important group of regulations that have a purely sacred or religious character and are thus seen as "obligatory." Kropotkin emphasizes that among tribal people the individual strongly identifies with the clan or tribal community and that a "code of custom" is an important moral force: "Custom, i.e., the habit of living according to establishment traditions, the fear of change, and inertia of thought, plays . . . the principal role in the preservation of the established rules of social life" (E, 85). Thus among tribal people, Kropotkin suggests, one finds expressed the fundamental rule of all social life, namely, "do not unto others what you do not wish to have done unto you" (E, 76), as well as a strong emphasis on the need for equality and fairness in relationships and disputes. Justice, in the sense of equity, is thus an intrinsic part of tribal morality (E, 74).

Besides the "code of custom," Kropotkin emphasized that rules of conduct (morality) was also given religious sanction, in being placed under the protection of the ancestral spirits or various "deified powers." This was equally true of Greek culture. But in outlining the moral teachings of ancient Greece (E, 84–113) Kropotkin put the focus not on Greek religion and culture but rather on the various philosophical traditions. Toward Plato, Kropotkin expresses little sympathy. He regarded Plato as having introduced into ethics an idealist interpretation of morality. Instead of showing how the principles of morality emerge from the life of nature itself, from the sociality of humans and from the nature of human intelligence, Plato "sought the foundations of morality outside of the universe, in the "idea," which underlies the structure of cosmic life" (E, 91). Conceptions of the good and justice are therefore explained by Plato in terms of the "idea," relating to an abstract realm that is beyond the limits of human knowledge and experience. Plato's mode of thinking was metaphysical rather empirical, Kropotkin suggests, and it was Plato who, in philosophical terms, introduced the fundamental idea of "the extra-human and extra-natural origin of morality" (E, 93). This idea was concordant with both mysticism and Christianity and has remained, Kropotkin contended, a constituent part of Western philosophy ever since.

Kropotkin is more sympathetic toward Aristotle, for Aristotle repudiated Plato's "two-world" theory and sought an exploration of moral concepts in the actual life of humans, "in their striving for happiness and what is useful to them—and in human reason" (E, 97). But for Kropotkin it was the followers of Epicurus and the Stoics who were most important in the development of naturalistic ethics, for they taught, like Aristotle, that "Owing to his reason and owing to this social mode of life, man naturally develops and strengthens his moral tendencies, which are useful for the maintenance of the sociality essential to him" (E, 114). For Epicurus, the fundamental trait of humanity, or of any living creature, is the search for pleasure or happiness, and according to Kropotkin, it was Epicurus who developed a consistent theory of eudemonism, the moral teaching that is based on the striving for happiness. He quotes Epicurus: "The aim of life toward which all living beings are unconsciously striving is happiness" (E, 103). This did not imply simply the pursuit of sensual pleasure but happiness in the widest sense, or mental tranquility, "the happy life in its entirety" (E, 105). Kropotkin discusses the importance of friendship for the Epicureans and their repudiation of conventional religion.

With the Stoics, in contrast, the aim of life was the cultivation of virtue and thus consisted "in a life that is in accord with nature, and through developing reason, and the knowledge of the life of the universe" (E, 109). Kropotkin noted that the Stoics did not seek the origin of the moral sentiments in any supernatural power, but they asserted that nature itself contained inherent moral laws, and that these laws preached the gospel of universal brotherhood (E, 110–11). He also noted that Cicero, who was strongly influenced by the Stoics, considered justice as one of the foundations of morality. Throughout his text Kropotkin maintains that the ideas of Epicurus and the Stoics have resonance and a continuing influence on the history of ethics—in particular, with regard to naturalistic tendency, expressed by Bacon, Spinoza, Comte, and Darwin (E, 110). But Kropotkin felt that there were two serious limitations in the ethical perspectives of the Greek philosophers, specifically those of Aristotle and Epicurus. The first is that while attributing great importance to reason, this reason was narrowly focused and thus limited in its scope—for it aimed only on the "evaluation of various acts and modes of life with the purpose of determining which of them are a road to man's happiness" (E, 143). Second, given the fact that both men lived in a society based on slavery, neither Aristotle nor Epicurus developed a consistent theory of justice, or at least acknowledged that justice consisted of equity among humans (E, 145).

Toward the ethical teaching of Christianity and Buddhism, Kropotkin is sympathetic and not unduly hostile, given his opposition to all forms of organized religion and the fact that he wished to established an ethical naturalism based on human reason not faith. The teachings of the Buddha he affirms. The founder of Buddhism "taught contempt for wealth and power, love for all men, friends and enemies alike; he taught sympathy for all living things, he preached kindness, and recognized the equality of all classes" (E, 17). Likewise with the founder of Christianity, for Jesus was not a priest, nor an intellectual, but simply a moral teacher. Like the Buddha, he thus spent his life not in the temple or the academy, but among the poor. He was a preacher who railed against the abuses and injustices of his own society. Equality and the forgiveness of injuries were the two fundamental features of his teachings. Unfortunately, both Christianity and Buddhism, as they developed into institutional religions, took on all the vices of government, which, for Kropotkin, "constituted a flagrant deviation from the will of the two founders of religion" (E, 119). Christianity, in fact, became the state religion of the Roman Empire, and, as well as supporting slavery, provided ideological support for the rise of the modern state (E, 122–27).

But Kropotkin emphasizes that all the basic moral rules associated with Christianity and Buddhism—equality, fraternity, sympathy for others, "love thy neighbour as thyself," compassion, mutual aid—were characteristic features of tribal and pagan society and were evident in human society long before the origin of these two world religions (E, 122–25).

Like many of his contemporaries, Kropotkin thought of the medieval period in Europe, from the collapse of the Roman Empire to the Renaissance, as a period of intellectual sterility—a "dark age." But with the decline of feudalism, the increase in mercantile trade, the rise of popular religious movements (such as the Anabaptists), and the emergence of "free cities" in the late medieval period, a "spirit of freedom" emerged, which gave birth to a revival of knowledge, art, and the freedom of thought (rationalism). This "tremendous upheaval" in social life that occurred in Europe between the twelfth and sixteenth centuries was, Kropotkin suggested, of particular importance in giving rise to the development of rationalistic ethics (E, 132–39). This renaissance of rationalist philosophy, which drew particularly on the writings of Epicurus and the Stoics, was for Kropotkin of fundamental importance in establishing a naturalistic approach to morality. The key figures in this renaissance for Kropotkin were Bacon, Hobbes, Spinoza, Locke, and the Enlightenment philosophers, particularly Hume and Adam Smith.

Kropotkin always expressed an admiration for Bacon as the "great founder of inductive science" and for first clearly formulating the notion that within the human psyche there exist two contrasting appetites or instincts—one related to self-preservation, the other relating the individual to some greater whole, a social instinct (E, 44). Aristotle, with his emphasis on empirical knowledge, was indeed seen by Kropotkin as a "forerunner" of Bacon's philosophy, while Darwin, in turn, was viewed as opening up a new path for science that was initially indicated by Bacon. The English empiricist was thus a pivotal figure in Kropotkin's interpretation.

Toward Thomas Hobbes, however, Kropotkin was far more critical. Although Hobbes definitely renounced religion and supported and encouraged a naturalistic approach to philosophy and politics, Kropotkin deplored many aspects of his philosophy. These were: a very inadequate understanding of tribal life, and given Hobbes's overemphasis on egosim, a rather contemptuous attitude toward humanity in general. Indeed, Kropotkin was adamant that "the entire ethical system of Hobbes is based on [a] superficial representation of human nature" (E, 150). But what most concerned Kropotkin was the conflation by Hobbes, in his classic study *Leviathan* (1652), of sociality and morality with the coercive state and its laws. For Kropotkin, law and morality were distinct concepts, and he contended that the law merely utilized the "social feelings of man, to slip in, among the moral principles he accepts, various mandates useful to an exploiting minority" (KRP, 94).

Spinoza, like Hobbes, also denied the extranatural origin of morality. But in contrast to Hobbes, Spinoza created, Kropotkin argued, a truly ethical teaching, permeated by a deep moral feeling. Spinoza built his ethics on a eudemonistic basis, that is, on the striving for human happiness, and it was, Kropotkin wrote, thoroughly scientific. "It knows no metaphysical subtleties, nor revelations from above. Its conclusions are derived from the knowledge of man, and of nature in general" (E, 158–61). All that was lacking in Spinoza was a truly social perspective, for in building his ethics on egoism (like Hobbes), he completely ignored the "social propensities of man" (E, 161).

Kropotkin's account gives excellent critical summaries of a whole range of philosophers associated with the Enlightenment—Locke, Voltaire, Holbach, Diderot, Hume, and Adam Smith. But the key figure among these, for Kropotkin, is Adam Smith, whose study *The Theory of Moral Sentiments* (1759) clearly made a deep impression on the anarchist. What was important about Smith was that he firmly rejected the supernatural origin of morality and thus came to explain it on a purely natural basis—as an inherent quality of human nature, based on the feeling of sympathy. Hume also ascribed a special importance to sympathy, but Hume saw morality as determined not by reason but rather by some "internal sense or feeling"— hence, he initiated the emotive theory of ethics. But with Smith, sympathy was a feeling inherent in humanity as a social being, and it developed from social life; it could not therefore be derived simply from reasoning about the utility of social acts. Kropotkin followed Smith in being somewhat skeptical of the basic Enlightenment view of ethics, namely, that the highest moral law consisted in following pleasure and avoiding pain (E, 189). Almost all the Enlightenment thinkers ascribed to this view of ethics, which in essence suggested that humans always strive after happiness and in their very nature attempt to avoid suffering and seek pleasure. As Locke had earlier expressed it: "Things then, are good or evil only in reference to pleasure and pain. That we call good, which is apt to cause or increase pleasure, or diminish pain in us" (E, 165). This idea was later to become the basis of utilitarianism, the ethical theory associated with Bentham and John Stuart Mill. In the search for happiness, humans are guided by reason, and, according to the Encyclopedists, "all men have equal rights to happiness" (E, 191).

Kropotkin's response to this was to suggest that identifying the good (morality) with utility did not solve the problem as to the origins of morality: "To say that man always strives for happiness and for the greatest possible freedom from evil, is merely to utter the forever obvious, superficial truth, expressed even in proverbs. And indeed, it has often been remarked that if the moral life led man to unhappiness, all morality would have long ago vanished from the world."

Utilitarian ethics is therefore not so much wrong as limited, for morality is more than the mere "prudent weighing of pleasures" (E, 144).

Kropotkin also emphasized that the mere seeking after pleasure might be negative as well as positive and could lead to the most "vicious" acts. As Fromm was later to write, "there are people who enjoy submission and not freedom, who derive pleasure from hate and not from love, from exploitation and not from productive work" (1949, 15).

Kropotkin thus came to emphasize that our moral conceptions are the product of both our feelings and our reason and have developed naturally in the life of human societies (E, 199). The only problem with Adam Smith's theory, Kropotkin argued, was that he failed to recognize that sympathy and the feeling of solidarity was not unique to humans but also existed among social animals (E, 208; KRP, 95).

Immanuel Kant, in Kropotkin's estimation, stood at the juncture between metaphysical philosophy of an earlier period and the scientific philosophy of the nineteenth century. Critical of the empirical theories of the Enlightenment, particularly utilitarianism, Kant attempted to establish a rationalist theory of ethics. As Kropotkin put it, Kant "intended to discover the fundamental laws of morality not through the study of human nature and through observation of life and the actions of men, but through abstract theory." Kant therefore stood opposed to the kind of ethical naturalism that Kropotkin was attempting to establish. Reflecting on the basis of morality, Kant came to the conclusion that it was derived from our sense of duty, which he viewed as inherent in human reason. For Kant, duty, or the moral law, has the character of "categorical imperative," and its obligatory nature is related to three basic axioms that Kropotkin outlines. First, moral duty is inherent in human nature, and this implies a moral agent who is free and rational. Second, moral conduct implies treating other humans as ends in themselves, never as means. This entails an ethic of "respect for persons." And third, moral actions should be undertaken as if a person was legislating for all humankind. As Kant wrote: "Act as if the maxim of thy action were to become by thy will a universal law of nature" (E, 215–16).

In stressing the importance of reason, in emphasizing the fact that a sense of moral duty is inherent in humans, and in insisting that morality cannot be based simply on considerations of happiness or utility, Kant's ethical theory, Kropotkin admits, has an indisputable "elevating character" (E, 216). But Kant's ethical theory, Kropotkin argued, leaves us in complete ignorance with respect to the principal problem of ethics, namely, the "origin" of our inherent moral sense. Why should humans obey the moral law—the "categorical imperative"? And what is the source of this sense of duty—this "mysterious command" (E, 39; KRP, 82)? Kropotkin laments the fact that Kant denied the importance, indeed the very existence of sympathy and sociality, which had been emphasized by Hume and Adam Smith, and concluded that Kant was quite "unable to answer the fundamental question of ethics"—which is why Kant often tended to imply that morality had a divine origin. But in treating morality as an autonomous realm, completely separate from the natural world and social life, Kant, according to Kropotkin, never developed any consistent theory of justice or social equality. Kropotkin therefore came to the conclusion that Kant's teaching contributed almost nothing to the further development of ethics and in fact retarded its development in Germany (E, 219–24). This is contrary to the views of many contemporary scholars for whom Kantian ethics still has a perennial fascination and interest, the advocacy of "post-naturalism" usually implying a return to Kantian metaphysics.

In his discussion of ethical teachings during the nineteenth century, Kropotkin emphasizes the crucial significance of three distinct currents of thought—positivism, socialism, and evolutionary theory. And he highlights the importance, with regard to the development of ethical theory, of four scholars in particular (leaving aside Darwin), namely, Comte, Proudhon, Spencer, and Guyau. None of these thinkers is considered by contemporary scholars to be important moral philosophers, and they have now largely been forgotten. Philosophers seem more impressed by the esoteric and rather narrow ethical theories of Kant, Moore, and Hare (cf. MacIntyre 1967; Raphael 1994).

What was common to all these four scholars was that they attempted, like Darwin, to build ethics on a purely scientific (i.e., empirical) basis—as opposed to theological and metaphysical interpretations of morality. They thus aimed to free morality from all mystical or divine revelations and to base moral conceptions on general facts about the natural world, in particular about human sociality and history. This did not imply equating facts about the world with moral precepts but recognizing that it was the sociality of humans that formed the basis of moral sentiments. Thus, although these scholars recognized that both egoism and altruism were important in human life, all put an emphasis on the sociality of humans and saw morality as essentially a "reconciliation of these two opposing sentiments." Thus, social life in essence consists of a synthesis between the moral tendencies based on a sense of duty (Kant) and those that originate in the principle of the greatest happiness and utility (the utilitarianism of Bentham and Mill) (E, 241). These scholars therefore recognized and affirmed the egoistic striving of the individual for personal happiness (i.e., the utilitarian element in morality)—but they also stressed the crucial importance of the feeling for sociality, mutual sympathy, and reason in the development of morality (E, 253). These scholars, in brief, Kropotkin suggests, attempt to base—not reduce—moral concepts on the "concrete facts of life." The moral philosophy of Proudhon was of particular significance to Kropotkin in that it emphasized the crucial importance of equity or justice as a fundamental principle of all morality (E, 270).

Basing his ideas on the writings Comte, Proudhon, Spencer, Darwin, and Guyau, whose theories he attempts to synthesize, Kropotkin therefore concludes that morality essentially has a "three-fold" nature. The primary source of morality is sociality or mutual aid, which may be observed even among social animals, but which finds its highest development in humans. A sense of sympathy is thus seen as inherent in the human personality. Second, a sense of justice also forms a basic principle of moral sentiments. Justice, Kropotkin argued, was the recognition of equity and the striving of humans for equality (E, 278): "The basis of all morality lies in the feeling of sociality, inherent in the entire animal world, and in the conceptions of equity, which constitutes one of the fundamental primary judgements of human reason" (E, 312).

He emphasized of course that conceptions of justice were of a historical nature and continually changing (E, 279).

Finally, besides sociality and justice, there was a third crucial element to ethics, and that was the principle of magnanimity, which was unique to humans, and which could be considered morality proper. Morality consisted in living for others and was exemplified in the impulse of a person who plunges into a river to save another person from drowning, without any thought of personal safety or reward (E, 245). Such altruism, for Kropotkin, did not in any way imply a denial of human agency, but he was insistent that humans possess an "inherent feeling" that leads them to identify with others (E, 261). He also affirmed its varied and changing nature. "This feeling of social sympathy which develops gradually with the increasing complexity of social life, becomes more and more varied, rational and free in its manifestations. In man the feeling of social sympathy becomes the source of morality" (E, 280).

This, in a nutshell, is Kropotkin's theory of the "origins" of morality. As to the purpose or "function" of morality, Kropotkin suggests that it provides some of the basic principles without which humans could hardly exist as social beings, but then, "it appeals to something superior to that; to love, courage, fraternity, self-respect, accord with one's ideal. It tells man that if he desires to have a life in which all his forces, physical, intellectual, emotional, may find a full exercise, he must once and for ever abandon the idea that such a life is attainable on the path of disregard for others" (E, 25).

Kropotkin, of course, always emphasized the importance of reason in the development of what might be described as an "ecological" ethic, and he recognized too that there were no fixed rules of conduct and that an individual must weigh for themselves the value of different ethical arguments (Padovan 1999, 489). "Look at Nature": "Study human history," he loudly proclaimed, but then he noted that "true ethics does not trace a stiff line of conduct, because it is the individual himself who must weigh the relative value of the different motives affecting him" (E, 25; for Kropotkin's ethics, see Marshall 1992, 320–22; Padovan 1999).

Yet although Kropotkin advanced an ecological ethic, and always denied that there was any "gulf" between humans and animal life, he never expressed in his writings any concern for conservation issues. Unlike his friend Élisée Reclus, Kropotkin never discussed in any detail the "devastation" of the landscape, the deforestation and irreparable loss of the larger mammals, and the general degradation of the countryside caused by the "bourgeois exploiters of the land." He thus never formulated an ethic that would embrace the earth itself (Reclus 1995; FW, 126; Amster 1998).

Herbert Read, who was an informed literary critic as well as an anarchist, reflecting on Kropotkin's *Ethics*, suggested that "No better history of ethics has ever been written" (WA, 420). Yet Kropotkin's study of ethics has either been completely ignored or curtly dismissed by moral philosophers and historians of anarchism. Peter Marshall, for example, repudiates Kropotkin's attempt to deduce an objective ethics from a philosophy of nature suggesting that "By drawing moral conclusions from observations of natural phenomena, he committed the 'naturalistic fallacy' that is to say, he unjustifiably inferred an 'ought' from an 'is,' a statement of how things should be from a statement of how things are" (1992, 337).

Marshall affirms, in contrast, that human values are human creations—which is something that Kropotkin would hardly have disputed. In similar fashion, George Crowder critiques ethical naturalism as implying a conflation—a "confusion"—of the descriptive and the normative and suggests that it implies an "attachment to eternal and universal values independent of history and culture" (1992, 354). Kropotkin's whole approach implied nothing of the kind. It is doubtful if he was so naïve as to confuse empirical facts with moral values, and he always emphasized that moral values are *not* eternal and "independent" of human social life and history any more than human society and culture are independent from the natural world. Crowder also contends that Kropotkin was a positivist, although in fact, the ethical theory of positivists (Hume, Moore, Ayer) implied an *opposition* to ethical naturalism and the affirmation of a radical dualism between moral values and empirical knowledge, the "ought" and the "is." In fact, the notion of a "naturalistic fallacy" stems from Hume and G. E. Moore, who both seem to insist that it is a fallacy to deduce values from facts. Moore, of course, who focused entirely on the meaning of the "good," argued that it can never be *defined* in terms of natural properties. The "good" (including moral values) is therefore nonnatural and indefinable. It could only be experienced by a kind of moral intuition. By Moore's criteria, not only is utilitarianism a form of naturalism but also those theological theories that define moral concepts in terms of the will of God. Indeed, as Daniel Dennett suggests, you could hardly find a better example of the naturalistic fallacy than the practice of justifying an ethical precept, an "ought," by citing as your "is" what the Bible says (1995, 476). MacIntyre suggested that Moore's book *Principia*

Ethica (1903), contained more unwarranted assertions than any other single book on moral philosophy (1967, 250). Moore's ethical theory, intuitionism, is, to say the least, rather vacuous as a guide to the ethical life. Hume's account of the supposed "fallacy" of deducing values from facts is more ambiguous, for although he clearly stressed the importance of distinguishing descriptive (empirical) from normative statements (moral or political values), Hume did not advocate a rigid separation, only that when these are empirically linked, "reasons should be given." In Hume's own philosophy, in which the concept of sympathy is crucial, the transition from the is to the ought is often made (MacIntyre 1967, 173–74; Rachels 1990, 67).

It is of interest that although Peter Singer affirms the fallacy of deducing values from facts, and suggests that the gap between facts and values is "unbridgeable," he himself explicitly adopts a utilitarian approach to ethics and suggests that we can "base" policies (i.e., moral and political precepts) on similarities we identify between humans and nonhuman animals—which would suggest a form of ethical naturalism (1999, 17). What he repudiates, of course, is any direct or simple reading of moral or political premises from evolutionary theory and cites the use made of Darwinian theory to justify laissez-faire capitalism (1999, 11). Kropotkin had made these same criticisms a century earlier. Indeed, Singer's advocacy of left-wing politics based on Darwinian evolutionary theory and his stress on the importance of ethical life simply echo Kropotkin's own concerns. Almost all the basic features that Singer identifies in a manifesto for a "Darwinian left"—acknowledge that there is such a thing a human nature, promote institutions that foster cooperation rather than competition, recognize that the way we exploit nonhumans animals is a legacy of a pre-Darwinian past that exaggerated the "gulf" between humans and animals, and stand up for the traditional values of social justice, in being on the side of the weak, poor, and oppressed (1999, 61–62)—all these were explicitly recognized and advocated by Kropotkin a century ago. What Kropotkin perhaps would not have accepted was Singer's strident assertion, following Moore, that we have to reject *any* inference from what is "natural" to what is "right." Is it possible to justify or advocate any moral precept without any reference to the empirical world? What is important, surely, is not the inference per se, but how it is rationally justified. If, for example, traffic is approaching, it is perfectly valid to say to a child, "you ought not to cross the road now," as this advice is thoroughly rational (Raphael 1994, 32). To suggest that there can be no *logical* link from the state of the traffic to the moral imperative may be valid, but to deny any linkage is trivial and scholastic.

But what are the alternatives to the ethical naturalism that Kropotkin advocated—one that was informed by an ecological perspective and an integrative approach to the sciences? The alternative ethical theories are, of course, many and varied, and all still have their adherents—utilitarianism, emotivism, theological approaches to ethics, Kantian rationalism, and its offspring, prescriptivism. Many of these theories Kropotkin critiqued, and all essentially imply a rather etoliated form of "naturalism," but one that separates morality radically from social life and evolutionary process and overemphasizes the "autonomy of ethics." The moral relativism and the absurd and esoteric doctrines of the followers of Nietzsche currently in fashion are even more unhelpful and have had, according to one well-known liberal philosopher, an insidious effect on ethical theory (Warnock 1998, 115–17).

But although Crowder suggests that the dominant outlook of moral philosophers—the "weight of opinion"—is against ethical naturalism (1992, 354), in fact forms of ethical naturalism are still advocated by many contemporary scholars, who, without even mentioning Kropotkin, essentially affirm the anarchists' basic ideas (see for example, Wright 1994; Wilson 1998). I will therefore conclude by briefly mentioning two important but very different scholars who have sustained such a perspective.

Morality, for Mary Warnock, is "thinking of others" and involves displaying sympathy, kindness, compassion, and generosity. It is something eminently social, and, like Kropotkin, she believes "it is the imaginative conception of the needs and wishes of others besides oneself, the sense of them as important, to which we have given the name sympathy which is the source of ethics" (1998, 88). Although at times she tends to conflate state laws with morality, Warnock nevertheless gives morality priority over rights (laws), stresses the importance of justice, and stridently critiques Moore's thesis regarding the absolute autonomy of ethics. Like MacIntyre, she has little regard for the "guru of the Bloomsbury group," or for the triviality of linguistic philosophy as it was applied to ethics, and poses the question: what other "grounds" for morality "could there possibly be except the nature of things and especially the nature of human beings who alone have a use for the concepts of morality" (1998, 77). In reply she affirms the stance of Aristotle, who, in all his philosophy, began with the phenomena—what we know about the world we live in and what we have to say about it. Thus for Warnock, "Ethics or morality derives from certain incontrovertible *FACTS* about human beings . . . and among these is the fact that humans have a certain awareness of their own position in the world" (1998, 107).

She agrees then with Kropotkin both as to the "sources" of morality and as to its contents: "Besides love, responsibility, human beings are linked to one another much more widely by sympathy, an imaginative understanding of other members of their species, based on what they have in common. . . . For each one to take on the needs, wishes, desires of others and make them into his goal is the beginning of the ethical" (1998, 86).

With this Kropotkin would have heartedly concurred.

In his study of evolution and the meanings of life, Daniel Dennett suggests that Moore's "naturalistic fallacy" is itself a fallacy and, like Warnock, asks the simple question: if "ought" cannot be derived from "is," just what *can* "ought" be derived from? Is morality entirely "autonomous" from our understanding of the world, and from empirical knowledge? Does it float "untethered to facts from any other discipline or tradition?" (1995, 467) Are moral precepts solely derived, as Marshall and Crowder seem to imply, from some mysterious moral intuition inherent in the human psyche? Dennett's answer is the following: "From what can 'ought' be derived? The most compelling answer is this: ethics must be somehow based on an appreciation of human nature—on a sense of what a human being is or might be. . . . If *that* is naturalism then naturalism is no fallacy. No one could seriously deny that ethics is responsive to such facts about human nature."

People may well disagree about where to look for the most telling facts about human nature and even about the facts themselves. In contrast to Kropotkin, Dennett seems to have a rather Hobbesian view of the world and lacks Kropotkin's sociological perspective. Mutualism is thus only briefly discussed—Dennett makes no mention of Kropotkin—and there is little discussion on the social origins of morality. Nevertheless, Dennett rightly concludes that "The fallacy is not naturalism but, rather, any simple-minded attempt to rush from facts to values" (1995, 458).

Like Aristotle and Spinoza, Kropotkin affirmed a naturalistic approach to ethics and emphasized the importance of the ethical life. He attempted to resolve the conflict between individual self-interest and the welfare of all by creating an ethical theory that was focused around three basic moral concepts—sociality, justice, and magnanimity. He saw such an ethic, which may be described as "evolutionary" or "ecological," as a prerequisite to the creation of an anarchist-communist society and as an alternative to the dominant ethic of capitalism, which sanctioned self-interest, avarice, profit, and a disregard for others. He insisted that "greed and envy are not engrained forever in the character of human beings," as Singer writes (1993,

5), but that there were alternative ways of living. It was a mistake, too, Kropotkin argued, to view nature simply as a struggle for existence, in which those who concern themselves about their own food, safety, and sexual satisfaction are bound to survive at the expense of others. "This is not what biology and evolutionary theory tells us"—for it ignores the crucial importance of mutual aid. So affirms Singer (1993, 102) without even mentioning Kropotkin, who wrote extensively on this very issue a century ago. The anarchist also crucially affirmed the importance of reason, not only in avoiding a narrow subjectivism, but also the amoralism and moral relativism that was fashionable at the end of the nineteenth century. But Kropotkin never saw moral principles as conveying absolute truths, only as "guides" to help us to live an ethical life. Kropotkin summed up the whole question of morality by quoting these lines from Guyau: "We are not enough for ourselves: we have more fears that our own suffering claim, more capacity for joy than our own existence can justify" (KRP, 109).

(For an important study of the evolutionary approach to ethics, besides those of Wilson and Dennett, see Rachels 1990, who as an academic philosopher discusses Kant, Aquinas, and Moore but has no mention of Kropotkin, who actually made one of the few attempts at drawing out the moral implications of Darwin's thought, the subject of Rachels's book.)

PART THREE
HISTORICAL
STUDIES

9
TRIBAL LIFE
AND ANARCHISM

In the metaphysics that Kropotkin embraced, that of evolutionary holism, reality is conceived as rational and orderly, although always undergoing constant change. Like Whitehead, Kropotkin repudiated Hegelian dialectics, but he nevertheless perceived the world as in a state of continuous change and conflict, as well as operating in accordance with certain discernible laws. He shared with Marx a great debt to both the logic and content of the eighteenth-century French Enlightenment (MK, 182), but as we have explored, he rejected entirely its metaphysics of nature. He thus repudiated the anthropocentrism and essentialism of Enlightenment thought—this long before the obscurantist musings of Heidegger and Deleuze on the same subject—as well as its radical dualisms (humanity/nature, mind/body, individual/society) and its mechanistic world picture. But in embracing evolutionary theory, Kropotkin not only rejected the Enlightenment's philosophy of nature but also it's social theory. He was, in particular, strongly opposed to the views of such philosophers as Hobbes, Locke, and Rousseau, all "contract theorists" who tended to view humans in a "state of nature"—that is, human society before the emergence of the state—as essentially asocial, atomistic beings. Hobbes especially considered the human person as a self-directing machine, a possessive individual who was aggressive, competitive, acquisitive, antisocial, and power-seeking, ever engaged in a restless desire for power. Life in the "state of nature," that is, tribal society, was thus uncivilized—lacking culture, art, sociality, and morality. It exhibited a "war of every one against every one." As Hobbes graphically expressed it, in the oft-quoted phrase, in the state of nature there is continual fear and conflict, and the "life of man" is "solitary, poor, nasty, brutish and short" (1651, 10; McPherson 1962, 19–29).

173

Although acknowledging the social nature of the individual, Locke and the political economists tended to reaffirm this liberal conception of the individual as a "possessive" individual, the competitive owner of private property, both in terms of real property and in terms of owning "property in the person" (Brown 1973, 3).

Kropotkin rejected entirely the Hobbesian view of social life along with the possessive individualism of liberal social theory. For Kropotkin, as for Aristotle and Marx, humans were intrinsically social animals: indeed, as we have seen, sociality and mutual aid were held by Kropotkin to be intrinsic to animal life itself and thus, as Martin Miller puts it, the primordial existence of humans was lived within a social context, not in isolated hostility. Humans without society had simply never existed; neither had absolute freedom—in the sense of license to do anything.

According to Kropotkin, these were merely myths propagated by the likes of Hobbes to justify the nation-state and its form of governance. Humans had always existed in society, in the sense of a community of people bound together for common purposes—as anthropologists have demonstrated (MK, 184).

As the Hobbesian view of society was still being expressed by scholars like Huxley and Spencer at the end of the nineteenth century, Kropotkin in his writings felt it important to defend the integrity of tribal society. He thus attempted to indicate that clan-based societies do not live in a perpetual state of fear, natural lust, and hostility (as Hobbes postulated) but are characterized by social institutions based on mutual aid and reciprocity and by explicit moral principles.

In *Mutual Aid*, Kropotkin devoted separate chapters to outlining the social life of what he described—following the terminology of Lewis Morgan and other early anthropologists—as "savages" (hunter-gatherers) and "barbarians" (agricultural peoples living in settled villages). Believing firmly in the "idea of unity in nature" and that there was no "gulf" or "abyss" (as Heidegger contended) between humans and animals, Kropotkin stressed that humans were no exception to the general principles of sociability and mutual aid that he felt played a crucial role on the evolution of animal life. Humans, therefore, were also "subject to the great principles of mutual aid which grants the best chances of survival to those who best support each other in the struggle for life" (MA, 102). All humans, throughout history and without exception, thus live in societies, and Kropotkin felt that the "social instinct" was deeply rooted in human psychology "man did not create society; society existed before man" (FW, 162). He even suggested that "social life—that is, we, not I—is the normal form of life. It is life itself" (E, 60). Such sociability and mutual aid was expressed in many different ways—for mutual defence, in collective hunting and the sharing of food, in the rearing of children or "simply for enjoying life in common" (MA, 74).

Kropotkin acknowledged that human history was complex and diverse and that it could not be interpreted in terms of a linear evolution, for the evolution of humanity "has not the character of one unbroken series." Human "civilization" emerged in specific regions, only later to become extinct and to begin anew elsewhere (MA, 104): "We certainly must abandon the idea of representing human history as an uninterrupted chain of development from the pre-historic stone-age to the present time. The development of human societies was not continuous" (E, 17).

But he nevertheless felt that there were common patterns of social organization evident among early human societies—which were inde-pendent of both climate and race—and that the same process of evolution had been going on among humankind with "a wonderful similarity" (MA, 127). It was represented by two distinct phases: an earlier phase of hunter-gathering when "clan organization" and "tribal solidarity" were the primary forms of organization; and a later phase that emerged with the development of agricultural and pastoralism. In this later stage or era, the patriarchal "family" emerged as a distinct social unit, and the "village community" became the chief means of "barbarian" people in their struggle against a hostile environment (MA, 113).

Drawing on his own experiences among the Tungus and other native peoples of Siberia, and on the few anthropological studies that were avail-able at the end of the nineteenth century, Kropotkin sought to emphasize that the Hobbesian view of "primitive man," as depicted by Spencer and Huxley, one of "perpetual warfare," bore very little relation to the realities of tribal life. For studies of the "Bushmen" and Hottentot (the Khoisan people) of southern Africa, the Dayaks of Borneo, the aboriginal people of Australia, the natives of Papua New Guinea, and the Aleuts of North Alaska (as recorded by the Russian scholar Ivan Venyaminov) all indicated the importance of mutual aid and social solidarity among tribal communities. Kropotkin indicated, with ethnographic data drawn from numerous sources, the complexity in the organization of their marriage rules, the fact that the band or clan and not the family was of crucial importance in their social life and that "unbridled individualism" was a characteristic of modern societies rather than tribal life (MA, 80–82). The emphasis among these tribal communities, as recorded by sympathetic observers, was on the sharing of food and goods, on the importance of generosity, on equality among clan members, and on sociability. Kropotkin notes the high standard of morality among such people as the Aleuts and Eskimo (Inuit), and he describes their social life as one based on "communism" and tribal solidarity. Archaeological and historical data on early European peoples indicated similar patterns of social organization and a similar cultural ethos.

Kropotkin writes particularly perceptively of the unwritten encyclopedic knowledge of the natural world possessed by tribal peoples and of the close relationship that existed between humans and animals among such peoples, as well as among the early ancestors of Europeans (development studies, it is worth noting, have only recently become aware of the existence of such indigenous knowledge). "Primitive" humans, he wrote, "lived in close intimacy with the animals," some of them probably sharing their shelter. "Not more than about one hundred and fifty years ago the natives of Siberia and America astonished our naturalists by their thorough knowledge of the habits of the most retiring beasts and birds; but primitive man stood in still closer relations to the animals and knew them still better . . . our primitive ancestors *lived with the animals, in midst of them*" (E, 50; Kropotkin's italics).

Animal psychology was thus the first psychology studied by humans, and early humans were fully cognizant of the social behavior of wild animals.

Among tribal peoples then, Kropotkin suggested, a close intimacy existed between humans and animals. They had a deep knowledge of the habits and ecology of animals, which was expressed in proverbs and sayings; they considered animals, as social beings, to be considerably wiser than themselves, for they had observed that all animals were in continual communication.

"Warning each other by means of hardly perceptible signs or sounds, informing one another about all sorts of events" (E, 54). Thus, generally speaking, for the tribal person, "animals are mysterious enigmatic beings, possessed of a wide knowledge of the things of nature" (E, 57). Kropotkin noted the deep reverence that tribal people often expressed toward specific animals and the "totemic" (kin) relations that existed between clan members and certain animal species. When hunting, therefore, a man was bound to respect certain rules of propriety toward the animals and had to perform certain expiatory rituals after the hunt. When he journeyed in Siberia, Kropotkin "often noticed the care with which my Tungus or Mongol guide would take not to kill any animal uselessly. The fact is that every life is respected by a savage, or rather was, before he came into contact with

Europeans" (E, 59). Kropotkin notes that tribal people, far from expressing contempt for human life, hated murder and bloodshed, and to spill blood, whether of a human or an animal, was a "grave matter"—one that needed atonement. Although he was incorrect in suggesting that murder among hunter-gatherers like the Inuit was unknown—he obtained his data from a Russian missionary (MA, 91; FW, 163)—Kropotkin's observations on tribal life were succinct and generally valid and substantive.

The conception of the person as an "isolated" being, the "abstract" or "possessive" individual, was, Kropotkin held, a late product of human civilization, for among tribal people, especially early hunter-gatherers, there was a close identification of the individual with his or her "clan" or "tribe." Kropotkin indeed thought that in such social contexts, there was very little development or self-assertion of the "personality" or the "individual" as such. People had a "sociocentric" (rather than an egocentric) conception of the person, which did not of course imply a lack of individuality or subjective agency. An "isolated" life seemed "strange" to people in clan-based societies, and anyone living a solitary life was more than likely to be considered a sorcerer or associated with evil powers (E, 60).

In recognizing—unlike most of his contemporaries—the close intimacy that pertained between humans and animals, and the social and cultural complexity of tribal life, Kropotkin's essential observations have been more than confirmed by recent anthropological research (for perceptive studies of human/animal relationship among tribal people, see, for example, Ingold 1980; Nelson 1983; Brown 1992).

Kropotkin has often been accused of looking with "undue nostalgia" towards the past, and as portraying tribal life as more idyllic than it actually was through an "optimistic misinterpretation" of tribal practices and social forms (cf. FW, 158). But it has to be remembered that Kropotkin was attempting to counter the Hobbesian portrayal of tribal life by his contemporaries, and he did not in fact ignore the violence and murder that was evident in tribal society, nor the power that was often possessed by the shamans. He noted, for example, that solidarity often did not extend beyond the clan or tribe and that "quarrels arose between people of different clans and tribes which could end in violence or even murder" (FW, 163).

But Kropotkin's understanding of social life was sensitive, and given the state of anthropological knowledge at the end of the nineteenth century, extremely perceptive. Thus, he wrote about the Bushmen, the Khoisan foragers of southern Africa, as follows: "But still we know that when the Europeans came, the Bushmen lived in small tribes (or clans), sometimes federated together; that they used to hunt in common, and divided the spoil without quarrelling; that they never abandoned their wounded, and displayed strong affection to their comrades" (MA, 83).

In an important article on the Bushmen, Alan Barnard (1993)—himself a recognized authority on the Khoisan people—emphasizes Kropotkin's insightful grasp of the essentials of Khoisan foraging culture. For in recognizing the importance of food-sharing and reciprocity, the egalitarian ethos and the communal ownership of land, Kropotkin accurately depicted the social characteristics of what Barnard describes as their "foraging ethos." He also notes Kropotkin's intuitive understanding of Khoisan culture: "the existence of 'sharing' practices among the Khoekhoe and 'reciprocity' among the Bushmen should cause us to rethink our notions of what constitutes a typical hunting and herding society, and indeed to consider the notion of a pan-Khoisan constellation of economic institutions. Kropotkin grasped this, and expressed this view accurately in his very brief discussion of mutual aid among the Bushman and Khoekoe" (1993, 35).

Barnard concluded that Kropotkin's descriptions of societies that he considered "communist" might still serve as models of ethnographic generalization, if not charters for political action. But then Kropotkin in *Mutual Aid* was seeking a better understanding of the social life of tribal people, not advocating a return to a hunter-gathering existence. He was not an anarcho-primitivist (for a vibrant account of anarcho-primitivism see the writings of John Zerzan [1988, 1994] who interestingly hardly ever mentions Kropotkin. A short critique of Zerzan's "primitivism," from a social anarchist perspective, is to be found in Bookchin 1995, 39–42).

Contrary to the Hobbesian image, Kropotkin recognized that "savages" (hunter-gatherers) had complex social organizations and cultural forms and that their life was governed and sustained, not by a "war of all against all," but by an intricate web of customary norms and interpersonal relationships. Mutual aid and reciprocity were the guiding principles of such tribal or clan-based societies; the same could be said for the agricultural peoples whom the Romans called "barbarians." For Kropotkin this was a phase or era of human social evolution that was anterior to serfdom (feudalism) and to the rise of the state, as exemplified by the Roman Empire. "Barbarian" society thus constituted a phase between clan-based tribal communities (the savage "gentes" or foraging ethos) and the emergence of the state as an institutional form. It was represented in Europe in such peoples as the Celts, Teutons, and Slavs, who when they first came into contact with the Roman Empire, were undergoing, Kropotkin felt, a transitional phase of organization. For with the development and increasing concentration of wealth and power in tribal society, and a more settled existence, the patriarchal family steadily emerged as a separate unit, independent of the clans, and the village community became the central focus of social life. Although Kropotkin recognized that the village community was a form of social organization found throughout the world, he discussed in some detail three specific societies, the Buryats of Eastern Siberia, the Kabyles of Algeria (since made famous by the writings of Pierre Bourdieu), and the Mountain people of the Caucasia, relying specifically on the pioneer writings of Henry Maine and Maxim Kovalevsky. Kropotkin emphasized four aspects of their social life: that each of these people had their own complex and unique form of morality; that there was a strong emphasis among these people on reciprocity and sharing; that although they lacked state institutions, these people, through communal rituals and confederal relationships, had a sense of tribal solidarity or nationhood; and finally, that there were no institutions of "private property," land being held in common by the clans or village communities. Communism was thus a ruling principle among the "barbarian" people as it was for clan-based societies: "Common hunting, common fishing, and common culture of the . . . plantations of fruit trees was the rule with the old gentes (clans). Common agriculture became the rule in barbarian village communities" (MA, 110).

Land was thus under common control, hunting and cultivation were often communal activities, and the resolution of social conflict was achieved through clan institutions or village assemblies. With regard to the Kabyle, they "know of no authority whatever besides that of the *djemmaa*, or folkmoot of the village community. All men of age take part in it, in the open air . . . and the decisions of the *djemmaa* are evidently taken at unanimity: that is, the discussions continue until all present agree to accept, or to submit to, some decision. There being no authority in a village community to impose a decision, this system has been practised by mankind wherever there have been village communities" (MA, 121).

Although Kropotkin was an inveterate optimist when it came to the question of a social revolution, he was neither naive nor ill-informed when it came to understanding the realities of social life. He thus did not romanticize tribal society, and the suggestion that Kropotkin was an advocate of "post-industrial tribalism" (Keulartz 1998, 5) represents a total misunderstanding of Kropotkin's conception of a future anarchist communist society.

In stressing that humans did not live in a "state of perpetual warfare" and that mutual aid and reciprocity were the norm in tribal (or gentile) society—thus countering the "caricature" of tribal life put out by the acolytes of Hobbes—Kropotkin never sought to hide the limitations of the early forms of social life. He notes that among tribal people, infanticide and the abandonment of old people are often practiced; that raiding and feuds are common, with a blind commitment to the "rules of blood revenge"; that one finds secret societies and intitiations that give power to shamans and priests; that witchcraft beliefs are common; and that different ethical principles are often applied to those outside a particular tribal community—and that during conflict, "revolting cruelties" may thus be inflicted upon enemies, though such cruelties and punishments, he notes, hardly match the barbarities that are later recorded under Roman and Byzantium state rule (MA, 100–101, 116).

Kropotkin therefore never idealized tribal life and considered the views of both Rousseau and Hobbes to be thorough exaggeration, highly inaccurate. "The savage is not an ideal of virtue, nor is he an ideal of 'savagery'" (MA, 99). In fact, Kropotkin often put the term "savage" in inverted commas, and he stressed that tribal people, though not paragons of virtue, had highly developed forms of social life and morality. Kropotkin also emphasized the diversity of cultures within the "tribal stage" of human evolution and the fact that customary law, at the end of the nineteenth century, was still the law of daily life for the majority of human kind (MA, 128). Kropotkin also argued that conceptions of nationhood gradually developed in Europe long before the emergence of modern states (MA, 117).

But Kropotkin was not an advocate of anarcho-primitivism, nor did he suggest that the "tradition of authority" was to be replaced by the "authority of tradition," as Martin Miller contends (MK, 183). For Kropotkin stood firmly in the Enlightenment tradition, and unlike conservatives, he never advocated a reverence for, nor the restoration of, "traditional" social forms. He recognized only too well the hierarchical aspects of tribal life and the sometimes oppressive nature of public opinion: "There is no doubt that primitive society had temporary leaders. The sorcerer, the rainmaker—the learned man of that age—sought to profit from what they knew about nature in order to dominate their fellow beings. Similarly, he who could more easily memorise the proverbs and songs in which all traditions was embodied became influential."

Such individuals might attain a dominant role for themselves within the society, and Kropotkin notes that "All religions, and even the arts and all trades have begun with "mysteries" and modern research demonstrates the important role that secret societies of the initiates play to maintain some traditional practices in primitive clans. Already the germs of authority are present here" (FW, 163–64).

But he notes that while sociable customs were kept alive by usage and tradition, there was no authoritative power with which to "impose" it, and there was no alliance between the bearer of "law" (those who knew the traditions by heart), the military chief (the temporary leaders who engaged in tribal conflicts), and the sorcerer or shaman. Thus, there were no institutions that resembled the state and little in the way of coercive authority (FW, 164).

In a recent text, Jozef Keulartz seeks to discredit both radical ecology and anarchism by suggesting or insinuating that they imply a form of "totalitarian politics." He thus argues that a society without a state institution, as envisaged by anarchists such as Kropotkin, is a form of "disciplinary society" where customary rules entail "constant mutual surveillance" and permanent exposure to the "public eye"—such that public opinion and "popular assemblies" are viewed as oppressive and far inferior to the bourgeois liberal legal system with its abstract, universal rules (1998, 84–85). The emphasis Keulartz places on group-control discipline, biopower, and surveillance describes neither tribal society nor any society envisaged by anarchists—who have always stressed the autonomy of the individual and critiqued all forms of power, whether coercive, economic, or ideological. It rather describes social power under the modern bureaucratic state, as theorized by Foucault, whether this state be fascist, the Soviet state of the Bolsheviks, or the liberal-democratic state (Lotringer 1989, 130). Had Keulartz consulted the anthropological literature—as did Kropotkin—he would have recognized that his portrayal of tribal society (and the kind of society envisaged by Kropotkin and other anarchists) is something of a caricature. Following a long tradition of elitist scholars and conservative thinkers, Keulartz interprets customary rules and the social practices of ordinary people (in all cultures) in the most negative sense. The everyday life of ordinary people, tribal people especially, has long been interpreted in the most derogatory fashion, and not only in Hobbesian terms. Thus, the common people are described as the "masses," as being "herd"-like (Nietzsche) or as "Das Man" (Heidegger). Their social life as "tradition" is described as static and unchanging—and the people themselves are simply seen as conformists to this "tradition" or to "custom" or "public opinion," having no individuality or reflexivity (Giddens). However, having lived among tribal people—unlike the above-named scholars—Kropotkin recognized that their sociality and adherence to customary rules and social forms did not imply that they had no sense of individual autonomy or moral agency.

Although, as Purchase points out (1996, 114), Kropotkin often problematically stressed, in discussing the social insects, the subordination of the personal will of the individual to that of the common will, Kropotkin was equally concerned to stress—even for insects—individual initiative and conscious agency (MA, 30). In stressing the sociality of animal and human life, Kropotkin's emphasis is therefore on the "blending" or "co-ordination" of the individual will with that of the common (social) life, whether of animals or humans—not the complete subjection of the individual.

> Already in the animal world we see how the personal will of individuals blends with the common will. The social animals learn this from a very early age—in their play, where it is necessary to submit to certain rules of the game . . . the whole social life of bees, wasps, ants, termites, almost all the wading birds, parrots, beavers, monkeys etc.—all these facts are prominent examples of such subordination of the personal will. They clearly show the *co-ordination* of the individual will with the will and purpose of the whole, and this co-ordination has already become an hereditary habit—i.e. an instinct. (E, 65)

But Kropotkin recognized that in tribal societies the emphasis on sociality and sharing implied ethical principles that presupposed the autonomy and moral agency of the individual, and the various social institutions that handled disputes and antisocial behavior, like that of the Kabyle assembly, were a good deal more rational, efficient, and humane than the legal institutions of the modern state, focused as they are around coercive measures and the incarceration of so-called criminals (see Gulliver 1968 and Roberts 1979 for useful accounts of tribal legal systems).

In repudiating the radical dualism between the individual and society, as reflected in bourgeois social theory, Kropotkin did not view customary rules and common opinion as inherently antagonistic to individual autonomy and expression. Nor did he ever think of the human person as an asocial individual—the very idea of a human individual being "against" or outside of society he thought nonsense. The human person was neither in opposition to "society" nor simply an "effect" of language, culture, discourses, or social custom—as depicted by many cultural anthropologists and postmodernist theorists. And certainly Kropotkin never conflated subjectivity with subjection. "Society" for Kropotkin was not, however, some static, homogenous entity, nor, as Purchase graphically puts it, a "fire blanket of custom" (or tradition) that "descends upon innocent individuals in order to smother every last spark of originality," for human culture and customary practices "cannot be seen as diametrically opposed to the growth of individual expression and personality." This is because human subjectivity and social life are dialectically interrelated. Society and social responsibility cannot be equated with control and enforcement, still less with the state, although the ideology of laissez-faire capitalism—liberalism—"by equating individuality with individualism thereby endorsing egoism and individual license, actively supports these falsehoods" (Purchase 1996, 113).

Sociality and culture are not, therefore, for Kropotkin, the enemy of individual autonomy and expression but must be seen as "the structure without which no individuals can even begin to exercise their potentialities." Purchase notes that this is certainly true of one set of high-structured customary rules, namely, language, without which no person could fully express his or her needs and individuality. Purchase defends Kropotkin against his detractors: "The customary rules of language may certainly impose restrictions upon individual expression but nothing near the 'despotism of custom' which Mill thought was always and everywhere in 'unceasing antagonism' to individual advancement" (Purchase 1996, 112–13, cf. Mill 1972, 138–39, who falsely considered that outside of Europe people had no history, and trapped in the "yoke" of custom and public opinion, lacked any "spirit of liberty").

While some liberals take a Hobbesian view of tribal society, and human nature more generally, and see the individual as inherently aggressive, antisocial, and competitive, other liberals, like Mill, Giddens, and Keulartz, see the individual in tribal society as unreflective and as lacking any individuality, their lives completely determined by social norms and public opinion. Neither of these ideological portraits bears any resemblance to the nature of tribal life as described in many anthropological texts, studies that are singularly ignored by philosophers (see, for example, Barclay 1982; Morris 1982; Ingold 1987; Howell and Willis 1989). In his essay "Future Primitive," John Zerzan (1994) summarizes much of the anthropological material on hunter-gatherers and affirms that an ethic of generosity and sharing coexists with an equally strong emphasis on individual autonomy and independence.

Keulartz's attempt to foist upon Kropotkin and other anarchists a totalizing vision is utterly fallacious, for Kropotkin always stressed the need to develop social forms that not only respected but enhanced individual freedom and initiative. The most important condition that any modern ethical system is bound to satisfy "is that it must not fetter individual initiative, be it for so high a purpose as the welfare of the commonwealth or the species" (E, 27). Individual autonomy is of paramount importance to Kropotkin, and he neither romanticized tribal life, nor considered public opinion or tradition as some hallowed social form, but rather sought to develop a new form of society "in which the welfare of all would become the groundwork for the fullest development of the personality." Kropotkin was thus concerned to cherish and uphold the "development of individuality" and the creative power of the individual (E, 28).

Throughout his writings, Kropotkin made a clear distinction between two forms of individualism, the kind of bourgeois individualism associated with Hobbes and Nietzsche and the "true individualism" or "personalismus" of the anarchist communist tradition. The egoism—the "narrow and selfish" individualism—espoused by liberal theorists and by the anarchist followers of Nietzsche Kropotkin considered "spurious," for it was essentially asocial and implied the oppression of one's neighbors, or the elitist affirmation of a "superior type" of humanity. The egomaniac, or the narcissistic individual who was content to treat other people as objects, or as a means of their own empowerment, was not Kropotkin's idea of an anarchist. In a letter to the anarchist historian Max Nettlau in March 1902 (SW, 293–307), Kropotkin expressed his misgivings with regard to the "negativism" and "nihilism" of the "aesthetes" and of the individualist anarchists who followed Nietzsche (such aesthetes are still to be found within the anarchist movement) and affirmed his own conception of individualism—personalismus, or *pro sib communisticum*: "the individuality which attains the greatest individual development possible through practising the highest communist sociability in what concerns both its primordial needs and its relationships with others in general" (SW, 97).

Kropotkin acknowledged that next to Fourier, Nietzsche was unequaled in his critique of Christianity, and he was "great" as a theorist of "revolt," but nevertheless Kropotkin felt that Nietzsche always remained "a slave of bourgeois prejudice" (SW, 305). For Kropotkin, Nietzsche's philosophy was not so much a repudiation or "refusal" of modernity as its apotheosis.

In a recent study on the politics of individualism, L. Susan Brown (1993) essentially follows Kropotkin in making a distinction between two forms of individualism: the instrumental individualism of liberal political theory and the existentialist individualism that she argues is shared by both anarchist political philosophy and liberalism. Instrumental individualism implies an ontology that postulates not so much an "abstract" (asocial) individual as a possessive individual, an individual who *uses* others to further their own ends and self-interest. Instrumental individualism is thus based on the belief in freedom as a *means* to achieve individual interests and conceives the human person as a possessive, competitive individual, the owner of property, not only in terms of "self-ownership"—having property in oneself—but also as holding real, private property. For in liberal theory, having property is the essence of being free, or an autonomous agent (Gray 1986, 63; Brown 1993, 3).

Existential individualism, on the other hand—Kropotkin's "true" individualism—is "founded on the idea that freedom is an inherently valuable *end* in itself; self determination and individual autonomy are desirable for themselves, and need no other justification." Thus, freedom can have two very different meanings—that of instrumental freedom manifested through the market, and that of existential freedom, expressed in the individual's capacity to be autonomous and self-determining (Brown 1993, 32–33).

In an important critique of liberal feminism—as expressed in the writings of John Stuart Mill, Betty Friedan, and Janet Radcliffe Richards—Brown clearly demonstrated that liberal political theory contains an inherent contradiction in embracing both forms of individualism. For all three scholars, in their liberal commitment to an inherently unequal class system (capitalism) and in advocating state power, completely undermine the existential individualism that they also profess to espouse. Individualist anarchism, Brown suggests, is essentially a radical version of liberalism and not an alternative to it, and only social anarchism has political coherence in combining existential individualism with free communism (1993, 118). "Anarchism combines existential individualism with a free and voluntary communism that does not compromise individual freedom" (1993, 4).

In contrast, liberalism and individualist anarchism (or anarcho-capitalism), to the degree that they advocate private property and the free market economy, always compromise individual freedom and undermine existential individualism.

Brown also emphasizes the fact that social anarchism is not only opposed to governmental power (the state) but seeks to dissolve all forms of authority and power. She quotes from Rudolf Rocker: "Common to all anarchists is the desire to free society of all political and social coercive institutions which stand in the way of the development of free humanity" (1989, 20). She thus concludes that anarchists oppose any form of social organization that takes away or inhibits the self-determination of the individual (1993, 106–107).

The repudiation of instrumental individualism—as this is manifested in the upholding of private property and laissez-faire capitalism—is what distinguishes anarchist thought from liberal ideology. All this, of course, is consonant with Kropotkin's own theory of anarchist communism and his critique of instrumental (bourgeois) individualism, although Brown notes that Kropotkin never developed any explicit critique of sexism. In this he contrasts with his friend Emma Goldman, whose existential individualism Brown sympathetically outlines (1993, 113–47). What was crucial about Goldman's anarchism is that it embraced social relationships of cooperation and sympathy (free communism) without compromising its respect for individual freedom. Repudiating the ethics of "rugged individualism" and celebrating the "individuality" of the human person, Goldman stressed the importance of individual autonomy and the freedom to love. For anarchism, Brown concludes, "Cannot work without the capacity of human individuals to relate to one another in love and sympathy, while simultaneously maintaining a sense of self-determination" (1993, 139; cf. Goldman 1969, 1972).

Although Brown reaffirms the need to combine existential individualism with free voluntary communism—as did Kropotkin a century earlier—her analysis is strongly influenced by existentialist philosophy (Sartre, Beauvoir), which hardly provides a sound basis for social and political theory. In a rather strident critique, Bookchin has suggested that her study displays a rather "naive social myopia" (1995, 15), and certainly, in contrast to Kropotkin, her emphasis in the study is on individual autonomy rather than on social freedom. The idea that for Kropotkin anarchy is simply the "absence of the state" or that Kropotkin "naively points to the state as the root of all evil" (Brown 1993, 157) is, however, quite misleading, even though Kropotkin, like many other nineteenth-century anarchists, tended to ignore women and gender issues. But Kropotkin was not only critical of the state and all its manifestations and techniques of power (prisons, schools) but also of all institutions that limited or inhibited human freedom and the self-determination of the individual—Brown's existential individualism. Thus, Kropotkin was critical of private property, the wage system, capitalism, and all forms of religious authority—not just the state.

Kropotkin, as Purchase emphasized, never fantasized about a presocial state of nature, for he recognized that humans were intrinsically social beings—as well as being autonomous individuals. He thus repudiated entirely the philosophy of the individual as asocial, possessive, narcissistic, and competitive. He considered this narrow and selfish individualism to be both "misanthropic" and oppressive (SW, 296). But in stressing that humans were inherently social beings, this did not imply that human nature was "fixed" or "static," or that they had ontological "freedom." Kropotkin stressed social freedom and a communal individuality and advocated anarchist communism because he felt that this formed the best basis for individual development and freedom and allowed for the full expression of a person's faculties, capacities, and individuality (KRP, 141).

It is fashionable nowadays for academic philosophers, mostly in the process of writing dissertations, to dismiss Kropotkin and an earlier generation of anarchists as "essentialists" or "humanists" (both terms used pejoratively) and as having a romantic "benign" conception of human nature (May 1994). Kropotkin, of course, completely rejected the Platonic "two-world" theory and never conceived of the human person as having some unchanging, spiritual "essence" that sought expression or phenomenal manifestation. But equally, Kropotkin also critiqued—long before postmodernist philosophers and feminist theorists—the form of "essentialism" associated with Cartesian metaphysics, bourgeois political theory, or the Kantian "philosophy of the subject," which postulated either a transcendental ego who was the foundation of all knowledge and signification or an asocial individual divorced from phenomenal existence. If by "humanism" or "essentialism" one understands the notion of an abstract individual who transcends both history and society—a mode of understanding that disregards the role of social relationships in the very identity and constitution of humans—then all that one can say is that Kropotkin was anti-"humanist" and not an "essentialist." If suggesting that humans are intrinsically social beings implies that one is an "essentialist," then, pray, who is not an essentialist?

As for the notion that Kropotkin and the anarchists have a "benign" conception of human nature, thus making ethics redundant (May 1994, 63–64), this presents a complete travesty of anarchist thought. It has often been said that Kropotkin and anarchists more generally are too innocent, too naive, and they have too rosy a picture of human nature. It is said that, like Rousseau, they have a romantic view of human nature that they see as essentially good, cooperative, and peace-loving. But of course, real humans are not like this: they are cruel and aggressive and selfish, and so anarchy is just a pipe dream. It is an unrealistic vision of a past golden age that never existed. This being so, some form of coercive authority is always necessary—such is the familiar lament of liberal philosophers (Morland 1997 is a recent example). The truth is that Kropotkin and other anarchists do not follow Rousseau. Kropotkin, as we have seen, repudiated Rousseau's idealization of the "noble savage," while Bakunin was even more scathing in his criticisms of the eighteenth-century philosopher.

Kropotkin and most anarchists think of humans as having both positive and negative tendencies. If they did think humans all goodness and light, would they mind being ruled? It is because they have a realistic rather than a romantic view of human nature that they oppose all forms of authority that are coercive, or in any way inhibit the self-determination of the individual. In essence, anarchists oppose all power that the French describe as *puissance*—"power over" (rather than *pouvoir*, the power to do something), and they believe, like Lord Acton, that power corrupts, and absolute power corrupts absolutely (Morris 1998, 39).

In his study of nineteenth-century social anarchism, David Morland (1997) questions the assumptions of those political scientists who continue to suggest that anarchists like Kropotkin have a romantic, optimistic view of human nature, one entailing the belief in the "natural goodness" of humans. In an interesting and detailed scrutiny, Morland argues that Kropotkin (along with Proudhon and Bakunin) was not a starry-eyed visionary out of touch with the world but had a realistic attitude toward humans and human nature. These anarchists recognized that both an inherent sociability and an inherent egoism were rooted in human psychology. But because they acknowledged human "egoism," the classical anarchists like Kropotkin, Morland contends, could not logically and empirically advocate an anarchist society, a society without a state. Conflating politics and power with coercive government, and seemingly unaware that for most of human history people have in fact lived in societies without governments—on which Barclay (1982), Zerzan (1994), and Kropotkin have written at length—Morland argues that human "egoism" renders a stateless society "impossible." With "egoism" there inevitably arises conflicts and disputes, and these, for Morland, necessarily entail state institutions, although for most of human history such conflicts and disputes have been resolved—or not resolved—through social institutions that have no relationship to the state. To bolster his case, Morland highlights the inconsistencies and problematic nature of Proudhon's and Bakunin's anarchism—long recognized and critiqued by anarchists—and is continually engaged in the conflation of moral coercion and public opinion with state force. Anarchists, of course, have always recognized that public opinion and social norms (not state laws) can be problematic and oppressive.

Morland's essential argument is contained in the following: "Both humanity's egocentrism and the economic and political disputes that will ensue from this egocentrism have to be restrained. . . . Hence the need for the state. . . . The state's raison d'être is grounded in human nature and politics" (1997, 71).

Hobbes basically argued this three hundred years ago. But the state—centralized, coercive authority—is there not just to keep law and order or to settle disputes (stemming from our egoism) but to promote and uphold, and when necessary, defend, systems of social inequality and exploitation, that is, class interests. This has always been its raison d'être ever since the first state arose only a few thousand years ago. As the old liberal Adam Smith put it, government is for the security of property, and is, in reality, instituted for the defense of the rich against the poor, for those who have property against those who have none. Not severing politics from economics, the classical liberals had a much more historical sense of what the state is all about than it seems do contemporary liberals like Morland, who view the state simply as a neutral referee and as a guardian of public interest. Kropotkin, of course, was always to emphasize the intrinsic relationship between political (state) and economic (capitalism) power.

Some philosophers, however, seem to suggest that the very concept of human nature implies an "essentialist" perspective. But it is important to recognize that *all* scholars articulate some conception of human nature, if only implicitly; unlike Kropotkin, many however fail to theorize or make explicit their *own* conception of human subjectivity. Thus, when Foucault writes of the "individual" being the product of power, or of different "individuals" taking up "discursive subject positions" (what an earlier generation of sociologists referred to simply as social roles), he tended to underplay the fact that these individuals were persons with the capacity for autonomous experience and social agency. In his strident rejection of the "philosophy of the subject," Foucault tended to go to the extreme and to reject entirely the human subject—his work represents, as one scholar put it, "a bad piece of structuralist subject phobia" (Merquior 1985, 111). Thus Foucault neglects entirely to develop an alternative conception of human subjectivity. Kropotkin, in critiquing the "individualism" of Western metaphysics and political theory, at least attempted to outline an alternative conception of human nature (on Foucault's theory of the subject, see Foucault 1999, 158–81; McNay 1994, 102–103; Morris 1991, 438–42).

When Todd May writes that there is no natural human essence, and therefore one is "free" to create "oneself" (1994, 131), he completely fails to theorize, like Foucault, who or what does the creating. Kropotkin, in contrast, recognized that humans have certain inherent capacities and powers that are rooted in our biological inheritance: and that humans, like many other animals, are intrinsically social beings, constituted through social relationships. Thus, for Kropotkin, we are neither completely socially determined—a "docile body," or simply an "effect" of discourses, language, or power; nor are humans ontologically free of social constraints. But Kropotkin also, long before the poststructuralists, stressed the importance of social agency and "personalismus," a form of existential individualism that emphasized creative self-determination and autonomy—a "hermeneutics of the self" that did not entail submission or confession.

10
THE MODERN STATE
Its Historic Role

In March 1893, Kropotkin was invited by his friend Jean Grave to Paris to take part in a series of lectures to launch a new anarchist periodical. It was to be called *Les Temps Nouveaux*. But some ten years before Kropotkin had been imprisoned by the French authorities for belonging to an illegal socialist organization, the International Workingmen's Association, and thus when he arrived at Dieppe, he was detained by the police. The authorities feared that Kropotkin's presence in Paris might provoke demonstrations against the government, and he was therefore forced to return to Newhaven by the night ferry (WA, 272–73). Thus, he never came to give one of his intended lectures—on "The State: Its Historic Role." This was published in *Les Temps Nouveaux* in December 1896 and later, in an English translation, by Freedom Press as a pamphlet (1903).

This essay, which has been described as "brilliant, erudite and provocative" (Richards 1987, 6), is one of the most important that Kropotkin ever penned. It is certainly one of his most well-known and influential political essays. Aiming to give from an anarchist perspective a historical account of the rise of the modern state it covers much the same ground as the study *Mutual Aid*. Written around the same time, it is, however, focused on the concept of the state and on its "historic role."

The issue of the state was, of course, of paramount importance to Kropotkin and the anarchists, for it was on the question of state power that the socialists were divided, and which indeed gave rise to the famous split in the International in the early 1870s. This split focused around the leading figures of Marx and Bakunin, two men who had very contrasting personalities and political instincts. But the "schism" within the International was

191

much more than a clash of personalities; it reflected two very different political "currents"—state socialism and anarchism (WA, 111; Cole 1954, 2:174–212; Morris 1993, 58–64). Kropotkin noted that the two currents corresponded to different temperaments and ways of thinking, as well as to how the coming revolution was envisaged: "There are those, on the one hand, who hope to achieve the social revolution through the state by preserving or even extending most of its powers to be used for the revolution. And there are those like ourselves who see in the state, both in its present form, in its very essence, and whatever guise it might appear, an obstacle to the revolution, the greatest hindrance to the birth of [a] society based on equality and liberty. The [anarchists] work to abolish the state and not to reform it" (FW, 159).

This division, Kropotkin recognized, was a deep one and was reflected not only in political struggles among socialists but also more generally in philosophical thought and literature. It became imperative then for Kropotkin to explore the origins of the state and its social functions and to compare it with those social institutions that he felt it had in a sense replaced. As many German scholars had tended to conflate the state with society, Kropotkin was insistent that the state was an entity quite distinct from society, and the accusation that anarchists wanted to destroy "society"—still expressed by some Marxists—Kropotkin felt only indicated their own intellectual confusion. Kropotkin strongly emphasized that sociality was a phenomenon that existed prior to the appearance of *Homo sapiens* on earth (thus humans did not create society) and that humans had lived in societies for thousands of years before the emergence of the state. As far as Europe was concerned, the modern state, he contended, was of "recent origin"—as it barely goes back to the sixteenth century. The "most glorious periods" of human history were those in which civil liberties and communal life had not yet been destroyed by the state (FW, 160). Of course, when Kropotkin wrote that the state was of recent origin, he was referring to the origins of the centralized *modern* state that accompanied the rise of capitalism; the notion that he did not recognize the existence of earlier state forms or that he thought that the feudal state was benign is a wilful misreading of his work (cf. Draper 1990, 125; Black 1997, 77–78).

Kropotkin also made a distinction between the state and government. The state implied the concentration and centralization of power in the hands of an elite; the control of a specific territory; and the domination through an army of administrative and judicial functionaries of the majority of people, who neither controlled their own destiny nor participated fully in decision-making. With the modern state, "a whole mechanism of legislation and of policing has to be developed in order to subject some classes to the domination of others" (FW, 160).

Government, on the other hand, seemed to be a much more general concept for Kropotkin and signified the political apparatus involved in carrying out the will of the state. Thus, for Kropotkin, society, the social world of ordinary people living in communities, existed independently of the state. The state cannot exist without society, but society can and does exist without the state, and historically societies long existed without any state institutions (FW, 160; MK, 185). Thus, Kropotkin always maintained a clear distinction between what de Certeau (1984) was later to describe as the informal and local practices of everyday life and the "objective structures" or the "grid" of socio-economic constraints that manifested themselves through the bureaucratic state and through the capitalist economy. Habermas, likewise, was also later to make a clear distinction between a structured "life-world" (persons, society, culture) and the "system," the latter comprised of two main components—"exchange" (the market economy) and "power" (the bureaucratic state). Habermas also theorized the increasing "colonization" of the social life-world by the "system" (Outhwaite 1994, 82–88). Kropotkin, unlike Marx and Habermas, was not a systematic thinker, but he always maintained a clear distinction between society—as a structured social life-world—and both the state and capitalism.

Kropotkin recognized, of course, that states had existed prior to the emergence of the modern European state. He notes that the Roman Empire was a state "in the real sense of the word," and its imperial ethos came to have a deep influence on Western thought, especially legal theory. The whole life of the Empire was centered around the Caesar, as the all-powerful, omniscient god, and everything flowed toward Rome—wealth, education, economic and military life, even religion. A single law imposed by Rome dominated the Empire, although the Roman state never succeeded in stamping out the social life of local communities or the Roman municipia. But significantly, Kropotkin notes, people under the Roman Empire were "subjects" rather than citizens (FW, 160; MA, 137).

In order to discuss the origins of the modern state, and so attempt to capture its essence, Kropotkin decided to ignore both the city-states of antiquity and the "despotic monarchies," the theocratic states of Asia, and to concentrate on the European context. He took as a point of departure the breakup of the Roman Empire. He prefaces his discussions with a summary outline of the social life of foraging and agricultural peoples prior to the emergence of the state, aiming to counter the Hobbesian view that early human communities lived in isolated families and in a state of "perpetual warfare." Although, as we earlier noted, he did not see history an "uninterrupted natural development," he nevertheless saw it as following, throughout the world, a common pattern: "beginning with the phase of the primitive tribe, followed by the village commune, then by the free city, finally to [culminate] with the advent of the state" (FW, 200). This is a rather simplistic evolutionary schema, given contemporary knowledge, but it served Kropotkin well in ordering the ethnographic and historical data. It is, however, no more schematic than that of many contemporary scholars who also conceive of human history in terms of general evolutionary categories, whether as band/tribe/chiefdom/state, or as tribal, traditional, and modern societies (e.g., Habermas 1979; Lewellen 1992).

Among agricultural and pastoral peoples—Kropotkin cites the Kabyles, the Malays, the Mongols, the Hindus, and African people—the basic form of social organization consisted of federations of village communities that gave these communities a "sense of national unity." These communities consisted of individual families, all the families of the same village owning land in common. "They considered it as their common heritage and shared it out among themselves on the basis of the size of each family—their needs and their potential" (FW, 165–66).

Although the cultivation of the land in each village community was carried out by each household independently, the village community was sovereign in all its affairs. As local custom was the only "law," the plenary assembly of all heads of households, men and women, handled all disputes and complaints, and all the offenses against customary law or the moral code. Kropotkin emphasizes the importance of the local assembly, as well as the "fraternities" focused around trade or occupations, among such village communities, and the important role that "compensation" and "arbitration" played in the resolution of conflict and disputes. Such people as the Kabyles and Malays, he writes, do not appeal to government; they haven't one. "Being men of customary law and individual initiative, they have not been prevented from acting for themselves by the corrupting force of government and church" (FW, 167).

Thus, in response to the Hobbesian image, Kropotkin concludes that: "Far from being the bloodthirsty beast he was made out to be in order to justify a need to dominate, man has always preferred peace and quiet" (FW, 169). Kropotkin has little to say on the origin of chiefdoms, or on the emergence of the early states, whether the "barbarian kingdoms" in Europe and

Africa or the theocratic states of Asia (Mesopotamia, Assyria, Babylon, India, China). He focuses instead on the development of the modern state within Europe. But he recognized the important role that military chiefdoms played in the rise of the state and that the concentration of wealth and military force laid the foundations of the authority of kings and feudal lords in the later period, the accumulation of wealth through indebtiture, warrior bands, and the domestic slavery that focused around the chiefs' personal domain, eventually gave rise to petty states or chiefdoms, for, as Kropotkin notes, "power always follows wealth" (MA, 131). Unlike Foucault, Kropotkin was always to emphasize the materiality of power and that economic and political power were always intrinsically linked. He recognized that hegemonic structures, whether chiefdoms or modern states, always involve a combination of different forms of power: that religious ideas or culture are always utilized to construct and legitimize the political order, that no power is sustainable without a sufficient economic base, and finally, that coercive force is always an element in the exercise of hegemonic power (Gills 1993). Kropotkin emphasized that the judicial power of the chief was limited to his personal domain, and the ancient term for king (Latin, *rex*) originally meant only a temporary leader or chieftain of a band of men; it was only later, during the medieval period, that this role was sanctified through the church and Roman Law (MA, 134–35). But he stressed that the "concentration of powers"—particularly judicial and military (coercive) power—was a crucial element in the rise of chiefdoms and the early "barbarian" states (on the importance of chiefdoms in the rise of the state, see Carneiro 1981).

It was beyond the scope of his lecture, Kropotkin pleaded, to fully examine the history of Europe during the early medieval period—which involved the emergence of a feudal economy (serfdom), the rise of kingdoms and the power of the lords of the manor (both temporal and clerical), and the struggles and revolts of the peasants who resisted the growing domination of a landed aristocracy whose power was focused around the castle and the "men clad in iron" (FW, 170). By the tenth century, however, Kropotkin felt that the whole of Europe was moving toward the establishment of "barbarian" kingdoms or theocratic states such as were then to be found in Africa and throughout much of Asia. Yet he strongly argued that this development had been "arrested" in Europe by an urban revolution and by what he described as the "free communes" that arose within the medieval cities around the tenth century. He saw the emergence of the "free city" as a "natural" development that follows the tribe and village community, a "phase" in the evolution of human society, and in many regions he considered this to be a peaceful development. In essence, the commune of the middle ages, the free city "owes its origin on the one hand to the village community, and on the other, to those thousands of brotherhoods and guilds which were coming into life at that period independently of the territorial union" (FW, 171).

He saw this development as occurring all over Europe, and he noted that many of these free cities were later to become populated cities such as Amiens, Venice, Nuremberg, Bruges, Florence, and Cologne.

In his study *Mutual Aid*, Kropotkin outlined in great detail the economic and political life of these "free cities," citing a wealth of historical material, drawing especially on accounts of medieval guilds and the communes by such scholars as Thierry, Michelet, Sismondi, and Green (MA, 155). Kropotkin emphasized a number of key themes with regard to the social life of the medieval city, particularly the extent to which they were characterized by mutual aid and voluntary associations. These themes include the importance of guilds and fraternities in the organization of economic life, particularly as these were focused around trade and craft industry, for such guilds, Kropotkin felt, served as important checks on the oligarchic tendencies of the merchants; the role that the city played in the federation of both the small autonomous village communities and guilds; the importance of written charters and ordinances in regulating work and in curbing the powers of the landed aristocracy, Kropotkin describing these charters as "stepping stones" to freedom (MA, 163); the degree to which the city commune became an autonomous political unit, in being self-administering, political power being in democratic forums; and finally, the fact that although the city was a kind of "fortified oasis" in a country generally held in feudal submission, it was not a centralized state, for it consisted not only of independent guilds but also of autonomous sections or parishes, each with their own social life and communal rituals. Kropotkin therefore concluded that the medieval city was not only a political organization that aimed to protect certain political liberties, but "It was an attempt at organizing, on a much grander scale than in the village community, a close union for mutual aid and support, for consumption and production, and for social life altogether, without imposing upon men the fetters of the state" (MA, 152).

The rise of the "free" city—"independent city life"—between the tenth and fourteenth centuries was seen by Kropotkin as of crucial historical importance, for this was a time of the "greatest development of human intellect" during the whole Christian era, right down to the end of the eighteenth century (MA, 171). These cities transformed Europe, as "Oases amid the feudal forest" (MA, 138), giving rise to renaissance art and culture, allowing scope for the development of individual autonomy and initiative, and forming the cradle where all the great discoveries of modern science were first initiated. Compared to the social life in the industrial towns of his own time—where abject poverty, misery, and uncertainty were the lot of most working people—life in the medieval "free city" was described by Kropotkin in the most positive terms. He thus concluded that "never, either before or since, has mankind known a period of relative well-being for all as in the cities of the middle-ages. The poverty, insecurity and physical exploitation of labour that exist in our times were then unknown . . . for the first two centuries of their free existences [the cities] became centres of well-being for all inhabitants, centres of wealth and culture such as we have not seen since" (FW, 175).

Kropotkin has often been accused, like William Morris, of idealizing the medieval period—as well as being an advocate of "postindustrial tribalism" (Keulartz 1998, 5, 73), and even a sympathetic scholar like Paul Avrich describes Kropotkin as a more or less uncritical admirer of the local city-state (1988, 76). There is some truth in the contention that Kropotkin tended to play down or ignore the more negative aspects of medieval life—the fact that the great mass of the peasant population lived in poverty and bondage and that the medieval cities were largely under the political control of the rising bourgeoisie (merchants). Kropotkin may have been unduly influenced, as Purchase suggests, by his friend William Morris—that most "incurable of the 19th century romantics." Thus, Purchase concluded that "Kropotkin's intensely artistic nature, populist leanings, aristocratic upbringing and the relative backwardness of his mother Russia (from which he was exiled) irresistibly drew him to taking an overly romantic view" of the medieval period (1996, 64).

But it easy to misjudge Kropotkin. He was never an advocate of the "city-state," and the main emphasis in his writings on the medieval city are twofold: first, to stress the importance of voluntary associations and mutualism within the medieval city—of social life independent of the territorial state; and second, to affirm the importance of city institutions in resisting the growing powers of the feudal lords and the territorial dynasties, as well as of the burghers within the city itself.

Kropotkin was well aware that his contemporaries might accuse him of romanticizing the medieval city: "It will perhaps be pointed out that I am forgetting the internal conflicts, the domestic struggles, with which the history of the commune is filled, the street riots, the bitter wars waged against the lords . . . the blood spilled in those struggles and in the reprisals that followed."

And he responded: "No, in fact I forget nothing . . . I see that those struggles were the very guarantee of a free life in a free city" (FW, 177).

He was also clearly aware of the class nature of the medieval city, that the commune was largely a "citadel" of the rich merchants whose power the guilds and working people sought to arrest through "bitter struggles." He emphasized too the limitations of the medieval city, which tended to neglect agriculture, to be insular and parochial in seeking to enclose itself within the city walls, and it often came under the control of the bourgeoisie who wanted a "state" within a state. In many contexts, he noted, the "urban aristocrats" sought the support of the feudal lords and the imperial armies to subdue rebellions and revolts within the city (WR, 83). Kropotkin was probably better read and had a firmer understanding of the realities of the medieval city than many of his present-day liberal critics. Certainly Kropotkin never expressed a nostalgia nor advocated a return to the medieval city (still less to a "tribal" existence), for there is a "veritable abyss" between the commune of the medieval period and the kind of anarchist communist society that he envisaged and thought "might be established today" (WR, 82).

Struggles, conflicts, disputes, and debates within the commune—these Kropotkin always lauded, for he saw the state in creating a general political order as a "vast colourless and lifeless whole," which inhibited diversity and suppressed individual liberty and expression. He thus came to contrast the medieval commune with the state: "In the commune, the struggle was for the conquest and defense of the liberty of the individual, for the federative principle, for the right to unite and to act; whereas the states' wars had as their objective the destruction of these liberties, the submission of the individual, the annihilation of the free contract—and the uniting of men into a universal slavery to king, judge and priest—to the state" (FW, 177–78).

Kropotkin's writings on the medieval city and on the modern state are continually being misunderstood. Take Bob Black for example. An attorney-at-law who seemingly parades as an ultraradical primitivist, Black suggests that Kropotkin's free community implies a city-*state,* and that "no historian would regard as anything but ludicrous Kropotkin's claim that medieval cities were anarchist" (1994, 32). This shows a willful misrepresentation of Kropotkin's writings on both free communism and the medieval city. Failing also to understand that Kropotkin was attempting to explicate the rise of the *modern* state, Black continues to pour scorn on Kropotkin, accusing him of being an absolute ignoramus who wasn't aware that petty states existed in Europe prior to the sixteenth century (1997, 77–78). Such abusive commentary is more an indication of Black's poor scholarship than of Kropotkin's lack of knowledge. But then Black's avant garde reputation has been built less on his scholarship than on his slash-and-burn philosophy and his vituperative dismissal of social anarchism in favor of amoral terrorism, ludic revelries, and an uncritical affirmation of the Nietzschean free spirit. Black's use of the terms "workerism" and "leftism" as abusive epithets largely indicates his own elitism and his inability to distinguish Marxism from both anarcho-syndicalism and social anarchism. But to return to Kropotkin's discussion of the modern state.

During the sixteenth century, there emerged in many parts of Europe, Kropotkin contended, nascent states that undermined the independence of the free cities. The emergence of these states—focused around the dynasties that established themselves in such cities as London, Paris, and Moscow—constituted what Kropotkin described as a "new barbarism." It essentially involved a "triple alliance" of the military chief, the Roman judge, and the priest—"the three, united in one power, which will command in the name of the interest of society" (FW, 178). The "royal fortified cities" that were the capitals of these newly emerging states became a center for lawyers, who, versed in Roman Law, came to articulate a political ideology that Kropotkin describes as "Caesarism." It combined a fiction of popular consent, an emphasis on the "sanctity" of the ruler, with the force of arms (MA, 175; KRP, 148). Foucault in his essay on "Governmentality" was also later to stress the importance of the literature on the "arts of government" between the sixteenth and eighteenth centuries in Europe, which theorized a rational form of government and put an emphasis on the control of the populace rather that on territorial sovereignty (Burchell et al. 1991).

By degrees these European monarchies, Kropotkin argued, came to enforce control and to claim hegemony over both the feudal lords and the nascent urban bourgeoisie, as well as direct their growing power against the free cities. The Christian church, which had long attempted to establish a theocratic empire in Europe, came increasingly to bestow its approval and sanctity on these ruling dynasties, each personified by the king, who was crowned as god's representative on earth. The peasants themselves, in supporting the king or emperor against the feudal lords, tended to facilitate this growing trend toward absolutism and centralized power. The invasion of the Mongols and Turks, and wars against the Islamic States in Spain, tended,

Kropotkin argued, also to contribute toward the same end—the consolida-
tion of a number of powerful states in Europe (WA, 175; FW, 183).

Kropotkin strongly emphasized the role of legal theory and the church in
consolidating the power of these early modern states. In universities, Roman
Law was extolled and political doctrines widely disseminated, which suggested that peace and salvation could only be achieved through a "strongly-
centralized state, placed under a semi-divine authority" (WA, 178). Likewise,
the church worked relentlessly to reconstitute its authority through the inter-
mediary of the nascent monarchy. A symbiotic relationship was thus established between these ecclesiastical authorities and the state. In Paris,
Moscow, Madrid, and Prague, the church was "bending over the cradle of
royalty, a lighted torch in her hand, the executioner by her side" (FW, 180).

In the twelfth century, Europe was fundamentally a decentralized (federalist) polity, and the authority of the royal dynasty was somewhat limited.
The feudal state had feeble infrastructural powers, and as Michael Mann
was later to emphasize, it had little real power over or through society. The
power of the medieval king was indirect—through the church, through the
autonomous lords, or through corporate bodies—and thus limited (1993,
60). But from the sixteenth century onward, nascent states began asserting
centralized control throughout Europe—undermining the power of the city
communes, the local guilds, and the various regional federations (such as
those found in Tuscany, Lombardy, and Westphalia). Kropotkin wrote: "the
sixteenth century—a century of carnage and wars—can be summed up
quite simply by this struggle of the nascent state against the free towns and
their federations. The towns were besieged, stormed and sacked, their
inhabitants decimated or deported. . . . The role of the nascent state in the
sixteenth and seventeenth century in relation to the urban centres was to
destroy the independence of the cities; to pillage the rich guilds of merchants and artisans; to concentrate in its hands the external commerce of
the cities . . . as well as [to take over] the local militias and the whole
municipal administration" (FW, 186–87).

Once the state felt strong enough it also destroyed the village communes and plundered the common lands, which were taken over by the
nobility, clergy, or the rising bourgeoisie under the aegis of the state. Thus,
the absolutist state took control of the city, commercial activity, the terrain,
and emphasized the hegemony of Roman Law over that of customary practices. All this, for Kropotkin, implied an unholy alliance between the lord,
the priest, the judge, the merchant, the soldier, and the king (FW, 190; KRP,
131). It also implied that no separate associations of citizens could exist

within the state, and thus the state "systematically weeded out all institutions" that openly practiced mutual aid. The absorption of all social functions by the state, therefore, necessarily favoured the development of "an unbridled, narrow minded individualism" (MA, 182–83).

Individualism and state power therefore went hand-in-hand, and when Foucault was later to rhetorically declare that the "individual is the product of power" (1977, xiv), he was merely affirming what Kropotkin had intuited over half a century before him—if, that is, by "individual" one means not human subjectivity and agency per se, but the ego, the asocial subject of Cartesian metaphysics and liberal social theory.

Kropotkin continually stressed the close association between the church and the nascent power of royalty in establishing the dominion of centralized states and in undermining local associations: "It was the annihilation of all free unions: of village communities, guilds, trade unions, fraternities, and medieval cities. It was by confiscating the land of the communes and the riches of the guilds. It was by the absolute and ferocious prohibition of all kinds of free agreements between men. It was by massacre, the wheel, the gibbet, the sword, and the fire that church and state established their domination, and that they succeeded hence forth to reign over an incoherent agglomeration of 'subjects'" (KRP, 132).

But for Kropotkin, this power was never absolute or total, for people continued to struggle and resist the encroachments of the state and to maintain their own autonomous associations.

The victory of the state over the communes and "free cities" of the medieval period was not sudden but rather a gradual process that was resisted by many popular movements. Kropotkin notes the peasant uprisings in France and England, and the Anabaptist movement in Germany and Switzerland, which he described as a "complete revolt against the state and church, against Roman and common law, in the name of the primitive Christianity" (FW, 183). In stressing the absolute freedom of the individual, who must obey only the dictates of his or her own conscience, and in advocating a form of anarchist communism, Kropotkin felt that these religious movements had a radical thrust. Until, that is, they were usurped by the Lutheran Reformation. For the Reformation was supported by the state, and Luther encouraged the massacre of the peasant rebels with more virulence than the pope. The remnants of these popular movements were still to be found in the communities of the Moravian Brethren and the Mennonite community in Canada (FW, 184–85).

Kropotkin emphasized that the state involved a concentration of power,

and it was virtually "synonymous with war" (FW, 186), and the French
Revolution largely involved a shift of power from the landed aristocracy to
the bourgeoisie, who continued to divest the village communes of what
communal lands they still possessed. By the 1850s, throughout Europe, in
one way or another, the individual seizure of land that had once been communal was almost complete. In addition, Roman Law had come to replace
customary law, and the state through its schools, the church, the judiciary,
and the gendarme had come to penetrate and control all aspects of social
life. The state took over the export trade, seeing it as a source of profit; it
was the only judge in disputes; it introduced taxation, which was used as a
"formidable weapon" to favor its minions (the rich) and to suppress the
working people; through the school system and education, it sought to
induce a "spirit of voluntary servitude"—discipline; and finally, in the
industrial field, all the state was capable of doing, Kropotkin writes, "was
to tighten the screw for the worker, depopulate the countryside, spread
misery in the towns, reduce millions of human beings to a state of starvation and impose industrial serfdom" (FW, 194).

The Jacobin expression within the French Revolution Kropotkin saw
as the apotheosis of the centralist statist tendency—"the glorification of the
state"—that had become prevalent in the eighteenth and nineteenth centuries. And he bewailed the fact that many socialists and radicals had come
to embrace the Jacobin tendency, whose modern expression is graphically
detailed in James Scott's excellent study *Seeing Like a State* (1998).
Kropotkin was therefore to stridently conclude that the state, as an institution, tended always to prevent or curb voluntary associations (especially if
these curtailed the powers of the state), to shackle the development of local
and individual initiative, and to crush existing liberties—bringing in its
stead only wars and domestic power struggles (FW, 201).

Throughout European history, therefore, Kropotkin thought that two
political traditions had always confronted each other—the Roman tradition,
authoritarian, statist, and imperial, and the popular tradition, which was libertarian and federalist (FW, 200).

But while stressing in his essay on "The State" the intrinsic relationship between religious ideology and state power, Kropotkin in his other
writings continually affirmed also the close relationship that existed
between the modern state and capitalism. In fact, he wrote that the state and
capitalism were "inseparable concepts," and in history "these institutions
developed side-by-side, mutually supporting and re-enforcing each other."
It was therefore something of an illusion to hold as Marxists did that capi-

talism could be abolished while the state bureaucracy could be maintained (KRP, 181). State bureaucracy and centralization was "irreconcilable" with any form of real socialism, and an end to capitalism could only be achieved by popular forms of anarchy. The state, for Kropotkin, was essentially an institution that functioned through coercive power to establish economic monopolies and to uphold economic exploitation, whether in favor of slave or serf owners, a landed aristocracy, ruling dynasties, or, in the nineteenth century, the industrial capitalist (KRP, 166). Kropotkin therefore argued that a system of laissez-faire capitalism had never existed, that freedom to oppose exploitation had also never existed (at least in a legal sense), and that the rich know perfectly well that "if the machinery of the state ceased to protect them, their power over the labouring classes would be gone immediately" (KRP, 183).

The state was established precisely for imposing, and maintaining, systems of inequality and the continued hegemony of ruling elites or classes. The democratic state or representative government was for Kropotkin an expression of the "rule of capitalists," and the only form of political organization that was consonant with socialism was one that was "more popular, more decentralized, and nearer to the folk-moot self-government than representative government can ever be" (KRP, 184).

Kropotkin was thus keenly aware that nineteenth-century laissez-faire capitalism was a political project, a thesis echoed by the liberal scholar John Gray, who in a recent powerful critique of global capitalism, describes it as an artifact of state coercion: "The truth is that free markets are creatures of state power. . . . They are a product of artifice, design and political coercion. Laissez-faire must be centrally planned" (1998, 17).

Kropotkin always emphasized the instrinsic, dialectical relationship between state power and capitalism, which were mutually supportive, whether this implied laissez-faire, welfare, or state capitalism.

In his essay on the "The State," Kropotkin devotes little discussion to the issue of nationalism. Yet as with the Marxists, the "national question" was always of vital importance to Kropotkin, but unlike most anarchists, he never saw national sentiments and internationalism as irreconcilable opposites. He thought of the "nation" as a social concept that arose prior to the development of the modern state and entailed a kind of union between a people and a specific territory, the people sharing a common culture and historical traditions. His views are thus closer to those of Anthony Smith than of the "modernist" theorists of nationalism like Eric Hobsbawm and Ernest Gellner (see Gellner 1983; A. D. Smith 1991). Kropotkin even suggested that the more "internationalist" a person becomes, the greater will be his "regard for the local individualities which make up the international family, the more he will seek to develop local, individual characteristics" (*Les Temps Nouveux* [February 1899]; Cahm 1978, 53).

When, at his trial in Lyon in 1883, Kropotkin was accused, along with the other anarchists, of lacking patriotic feelings, he strongly protested, claiming that he had always held a strong attachment to Russia, as well as to France "because I consider this beautiful country as the home of revolutions" (Cahm 1978, 61). But Kropotkin was always hostile to the unification of the nation under a strong central government, and apart from his lapse at the outbreak of the First World War, when he fervently supported the Allies, he was always critical of "egoistic patriotism" or the kind of "chauvinism" that lent support to the state or imperial expansion. Unlike many Marxists (including Engels), Kropotkin always condemned colonialism and expressed sympathy and support for colonial peoples. Throughout his writings, there are critiques of the European exploitation of the peoples of Africa and Asia. Even though, like his contemporaries, he used terms like "primitive" or "savage," Kropotkin always expressed a certain respect for tribal peoples and their life-ways, without descending into a romantic ideology of primitivism. Although he thought it important to disseminate scientific knowledge to colonial peoples, he always acknowledged the integrity of their social life and culture, and indeed, he even suggested that in their moral life, tribal people were in some respects superior to many Christians.

Equally important, Kropotkin always supported the right of each nation to independence and argued that the international socialist movement should always "proclaim the complete liberty of each nation, however small it might be, and its absolute right to develop along the lines it wished" (Cahm 1978, 57). This meant that he always urged support for nationalist movements that sought to overthrow the yoke of a foreign oppressor or invader, whether this related to the oppressed nationalities in the Balkans under Turkish rule or within the Russian Empire. But he always felt that nationalist movements were inseparable from economic problems and the need for a social revolution, for he maintained that effective movements for national liberation must also be antigovernment and socialist (Cahm 1978, 55). According to Kropotkin, "the failure of all nationalist movements (Polish, Finnish, Irish, even I think, the Georgian . . .) lies in the curse of all nationalist movements—that the economic question (always agricultural) remains on the side. . . . In a word, it seems to me that in each national movement we have a major task: to set forth the question (of nationalism) on an economic basis and carry out agitation against serfdom etc. at one with the struggle against (oppression by) foreign nationality" (Letter to Marie Goldsmith, May 1897, MK, 230).

All struggles for national liberation therefore had both a political and an economic dimension. And Kropotkin clearly felt that true internationalism was not possible without the independence of each nationality. What he challenged was the inherent tendency of the modern state to control all aspects of social life within a given nation as well as to expand its dominion and the related issue—for he saw the state and capitalism as intrinsically linked—of the expansion of capitalism abroad, in its search for new markets. He thus always maintained that the problem of wars between European nations could only be solved by the destruction of both capitalism and bourgeois states.

In viewing France as the home of the revolutionary socialist tradition that needed to be defended, and critical of the collusion of the German social democrats with the German state, there was a certain logic in Kropotkin's support for the allies at the outbreak of the First World War—even if this seemed to completely contradict his own anarchist principles. Nettlau always accused Kropotkin of anti-German prejudices, and in his enthusiasm to support the French nation, Kropotkin, according to his daughter, was even eager to enlist in the French army—although he was then aged seventy-two (Avrich 1995, 12). But for all his limitations, Cahm concludes, Kropotkin made a "Much more serious attempt to grapple with the problems which the conflict of nationalities presented to the development of an international revolutionary socialist movement, than did those who criticised him" (1978, 65).

Kropotkin's essay on the rise of the modern state still has contemporary relevance, for Kropotkin theorized, if only in embryonic fashion, the three main features of the modern state: its symbiotic relationship with capitalism; its inherent tendency to penetrate, and thus influence, all aspects of contemporary social life; and its "individualizing" function. Such issues were later taken up and developed by Michel Foucault, whom I shall discuss in the next chapter.

11
THE
POSTSTRUCTURALIST
CRITIQUE of ANARCHISM

It is common these days, even among anarchists—usually those harking back to an ecoprimitivist existence—to dismiss an earlier generation of "leftist" anarchists, including Kropotkin, as being narrowly focused on the state, thus ignoring all other forms of power. Anarchists, we are told, were blind to the more subtle forms of power that emerged in the nineteenth century and tended to conceive of power only in a negative sense— as coercive and oppressive. Anarchists assumed that humans have a "benign essence" and are "naturally good" and that the nature of power (or "government") was therefore always to suppress and deny. Although acknowledging that anarchists like Kropotkin are suspicious of all power, and that as a political idea anarchism "expresses a negation of *all* power, sovereignty, domination and hierarchy" (Wieck 1979, 139), its critics nevertheless berate an earlier generation of anarchists for their "humanist naturalism" and for failing to recognize that "power" is creative and productive. As Todd May writes, some "power" relationships are positive and acceptable, and the task is to "construct power relationships that can be lived with, not to overthrow power as such" (May 1994, 45–66, 114; Keulartz 1998, 6).

Much of the inspiration for this critique comes from the writings of the French philosopher Michel Foucault (1926–1984), a kind of Nietzschean Marxist who tended to appropriate, with little or no acknowledgment, many of the essential ideas of anarchism. Foucault has in recent years become something of an academic "guru" and the subject of a veritable culture industry, although some scholars have dismissed him as an intellectual charlatan (Paglia 1992). But Foucault, though an elusive scholar, is an important figure and one of the most influential thinkers of the late twentieth century. A brief review of his writings on "power" may therefore be in order, before addressing the above critiques of Kropotkin and the classical anarchists.

According to Foucault, at the end of the eighteenth century a new mode of exercising power came into existence in Europe. This new "form" of power is seen as quite different from earlier conceptions of sovereignty (which focused on the rights of the monarch to exercise coercive power over a specific territory), for it implied techniques and mechanisms of power that would encompass and penetrate the "social body." This new type of power Foucault described as "one of the great inventions of bourgeois society," and as a "fundamental instrument in the constitution of industrial capitalism" (1980, 105). Foucault described this new economy of power, which essentially came to be deployed by the modern state, in terms of a number of different but related concepts—disciplinary power, biopower, pastoral power, governmentality. The essence of this form of power is that it was exercised "*within* the social body, rather than *from above* it" and that it had a capillary form of existence, reaching into the very grain of individuals, their bodies, discourses, and everyday activities. In his classic study *Discipline and Punish* (1977), which is subtitled "The Birth of the Prison"—although Foucault gives no indication of having read Kropotkin, who wrote extensively on the prison system—Foucault describes in detail the new "micro-physics" of power associated with the growth of the capitalist economy. He describes how the formulas and techniques of "disciplinary power" operated in the most diverse political circumstances and institutions—factories, schools, barracks, hospitals, all of which came to resemble prisons. This "disciplinary" form of power was invisible, and functioned through techniques of discipline, surveillance, and control, producing "docile bodies." Disciplinary methods, as Foucault recognized, had long been in existence, in monasteries and in the military, but now these same "tactics" were being exercised within the modern state for the control of bodies and individuals (1977, 136–39, 168). Foucault emphasizes that these techniques and power relations "go right into the depths of society," and they are not localized in the relations between the state and its citizens (1977, 27). He emphasized too that disciplinary power is fundamental to the development of capitalism—something forgotten by his admiring liberal devotees.

In his essay "Pastoral Power and Political Reason," Foucault clearly recognized that in European societies political power had evolved toward "more and more centralized forms" and that the various technologies and mechanisms of power were linked to the state. But Foucault was not interested in focusing explicitly on the state apparatuses (courts, police, the state bureaucracy, armies) but on the power techniques that are oriented toward individuals as subjects. He called the latter techniques—which focused on confession, guidance, security—pastoral power. Thus, Foucault sees the modern state from the beginning as both "totalitarian," the political form of a centralized and centralizing power, and "individualizing," the "pastoral modality of power" (1999, 135–52). To set up a radical dichotomy between state power and the various modalities of power that Foucault describes—surveillance, biopower, disciplinary power—as do many of his liberal acolytes, is therefore obfuscating.

In a later key lecture, and in a similar vein, Foucault writes of the emergence since the eighteenth century of a "governmental state" where "governmentality" consists of institutions and forms of knowledge that focus on the human population, on its control, welfare, and security. But as with disciplinary and pastoral power, a dialectical relationship exists between the state and "governmentality." Foucault thus writes: "if the state is what it is today, this is so precisely thanks to this governmentality, which is at once internal and external to the state, since it is the tactics of government which make possible the continual definition . . . of what is within the competence of the state and what is not" (Burchell et al. 1991, 103).

Disciplinary power, pastoral power, biopower, and governmentality all reflect different modalities of a new form of power that Foucault saw as emerging at the end of the eighteenth century. But Foucault was keen to emphasize that this form of power was productive: "it induces pleasure, forms of knowledge, produces discourse. It needs to be considered as a productive network which runs through the whole social body" (1980, 119). Yet this "productivity" is not be interpreted as something necessarily wholesome or conducive to human well-being. Far from it: essentially it refers to those techniques of social control and social regulation—discipline, normalization, biopower—that is achieved through noncoercive means. Power is a "positive mechanism" that "produces" disciplined subjects, prisons, docile bodies, and the science of penology; and though it does not work through overt coercion or repression, it nevertheless may result in misery (Foucault 1988, 113).

In stressing the importance of studying the new regimes of power, Foucault emphasizes the intrinsic relationship between power and knowledge. He thus writes, in an oft-quoted phrase: "that power and knowledge directly imply one another: . . . there is no power relation without the correlative constitution of a field of knowledge, nor any knowledge that does not presuppose and constitute at the same time power relations" (1977, 27).

For Foucault, it is not possible for power to be exercised without some form of knowledge, or "discourses of truth"; and knowledge, in turn, always engenders power relations (1980, 52).

Foucault defines power in two distinct ways. On the one hand, he conceives of power in terms of armed coercion, seeing politics as a means whereby a "military model" (war) is employed as a technique of internal peace and order (1977, 168). On the other hand, he defines power as distinct from force or "instrumental violence"—slavery is thus not a form of power—and sees power as therefore necessarily entailing a modicum of subjectivity. The characteristic feature of power is then that "Some men can more or less entirely determine other men's conduct" (1999, 52). Foucault distinguishes "power" relationships from other social relationships (economic, communicative, kinship) and like many generations of political theorists defines power as a more or less organized cluster of hierarchical relationships. Yet although he continually asserts that nobody has "power," Foucault also writes: "Let us not deceive ourselves; if we speak of the structures or mechanisms of power, it is only insofar as we suppose that certain persons exercise power over others." Fundamentally power is a hierarchical relationship, an "*unequal* and relatively stable relation of forces" (1980, 198–200; Dreyfus and Rabinow 1982, 217; see Lukes 1986 for a useful discussion of power by various scholars).

In placing a fundamental emphasis on "governmentality" and on the "mechanisms" and "instruments" of power, Foucault is critical of what he describes as the "juridical" or negative theory of power. This finds its expression both in classical liberal theory and in the "repressive hypothesis," associated with Marcuse and Reich. In this hypothesis, Foucault contends, the relationship between sexuality and power is defined entirely in terms of "repression." Sexual desire is seen as a natural energy, and power is that which controls, prohibits, condemns, and silences such desires. Although Foucault does not deny that power is repressive, he argues that the relationship between sex and power is far more complex and that it cannot be captured by such a simple hypothesis. There is no desire beyond the reach of power, for "where there is desire, the power relation is already present" (1979, 81). While critical of biological determinism many scholars have expressed an extreme disquiet over Foucault's extreme "constructivism," which appears to completely deny the role of biology in sexuality (Paglia 1992, 174–223; Assiter 1993, 94). But Foucault's main point is that "power would be a fragile thing if its only function were to repress, if it worked only through the mode of censorship, exclusion, blockage and repression" (1980, 59). No anarchist or political theorist has ever thought otherwise. Kropotkin, and indeed Reich, always recognized that power was economic and ideological (and thus psychological), as well as coercive (negative), and that religious ideology (with its "pastoral" power) has always formed a symbiotic relationship with state power. Biopower and "governmentality" have been around a long time and did not suddenly emerge, as Foucault contended, at the end of the eighteenth century, power before then being wholly coercive and negative.

Foucault, however, sees the "repressive hypothesis" as simply an expression of the juridical or liberal conception of power, which he felt was deeply rooted in the Western intellectual tradition. In this juridical model, power is seen as something one is able to possess—like a commodity: it is the idea that the constitution of power follows the model of a legal transaction, involving a contractual type of exchange. But with the emergence of "new mechanisms of power" during the modern era, the nature of state power cannot be understood, Foucault argues, simply in terms of this "juridical" model of power. We must therefore free ourselves of the "image" of "power sovereignty." First sketched by liberal theorists, this model gives theoretical privilege to law and sovereignty and to issues around the legitimacy of coercive state power. However, to understand power in contemporary society, Foucault insists, we must examine the "micro-physics" and "mechanisms" of power in specific historical and local contexts—although Foucault never denied the reality of state power. In political thought, he remarked, "we still have not cut off the head of the king" (1979, 89).

But as a disillusioned Marxist, Foucault is also critical of the Marxist theory of power, which, in being economistic, he saw as akin to liberal theory. This theory Foucault terms the "economic functionality of power," and in such a theory, "power is conceived primarily in terms of the role it plays in the maintenance simultaneously of the relations of production and of class domination. . . . On this view, the historical raison d'être of political power is to be found in the economy" (1980, 88–89).

Again, Foucault does not deny that there is an instrinsic link between the economy and power—in fact, his historical analyses demonstrate a close association between disciplinary power and the rise of capitalist hegemony, and he specifically suggests that power hardly makes sense if separated from economic processes (1980, 188). But he argues that to view the state as the only source or location of power, or to represent state power only in terms of class interests, leads one to miss the complexity of the mechanisms by which power is exercised in the modern world. Thus for

Foucault power is not simply a group of institutions or mechanisms that ensure the subservience of people to a given state (courts, bureaucracy, police, prisons); nor is it simply a general system of domination exerted by one group (or class) over another; nor, finally, is power something that can be seized, exchanged, or acquired, as if it were a commodity. He is therefore particularly critical of the Marxist conception of politics, which involves the revolutionary "capture of the state apparatus." To do this would mean that "the revolutionary movement must possess equivalent politico-military forces and hence must constitute itself as a party, organised internally in the same way as the state apparatus with the same mechanisms of hierarchies and organization of powers" (1980, 59).

In saying this, Foucault, of course, simply appropriates the anarchist critique of Marxism, without any hint of acknowledgment. Foucault thus stresses the need to avoid the soviet experience and suggests that as power isn't simply localized in the state apparatus, "Nothing in society will be changed if the mechanisms of power that function outside, below and alongside the state apparatuses, on a much more minute and everyday level, are not also changed" (1980, 60).

Important therefore for Foucault is not the sovereignty of the state, or the law, or the overall system of domination, but the "multiplicity of force relations" that are "immanent" in many social contexts, in the productive sphere, in families, in groups, in institutions, in discourses of truth. Such power relations form a "network" or "web" that passes through many social institutions, and they constitute strategies and mechanisms "whose general design and institutional crystallization is embodied in the state apparatus, in the formulation of the law, in various social hegemonies." So there is no radical dichotomy between the network of power relations—power is everywhere—and the state, for the state relies on "the institutional integration of power relations" (1979, 93–96). Foucault frequently writes of the "general mechanisms of state power" and lucidly expresses the relationship between the state and the network of "power relations" in the following: "I do not mean in any way to minimize the importance and effectiveness of state power. I simply feel that excessive insistence on its playing an exclusive role leads to the risk of overlooking all the mechanisms and effects of power which don't pass directly via the state apparatus, yet often sustain the state more effectively than its own institutions, enlarging and maximizing its effectiveness" (1980, 72–73).

The modern state is therefore, for Foucault, "superstructural" in relation to a whole series of power "networks" that invest the body, sexuality,

the family, kinship, and knowledge. And the state—this "metapower"—
"can only take hold and secure its footing where it is rooted in a whole
series of multiple and indefinite power relations." The state therefore consists in the "codification" of a number of power relations that render its
functioning possible (1980, 122). To some extent, this was equally true of
the premodern and colonial state. As many anarchists and political theorists
have long acknowledged—and which Foucault here affirms—no political
regime can sustain itself by force or repression alone: it must always seek
consent or legitimacy for its domination. Foucault continually emphasizes
that the power of the modern state—and one of its strengths—is that it is
"both an individualizing and a totalizing form of power" (Dreyfus and
Rabinow 1982, 213). In essence, it is because the modern state is so powerful and unitary that it is able to penetrate so deeply into the fabric of
social life, and the image of the "panopticon" expresses perfectly both this
concentration of power and its dispersive, individualizing, and surveillance
aspects. Foucault therefore concludes not that we should construct liveable
power relations (as May contends) but that we should seek ways to liberate
ourselves "both from the state and from the type of individualization which
is linked to the state." This means for Foucault (in Nietzschean fashion)
that we have to promote new forms of subjectivity (1982, 216). The relationship between the state and the power networks is for Foucault a dialectical one (although like Kropotkin he always tended to dissociate himself
from dialectics) in that "power" cannot be reduced to the state, but neither
is "governmentality" completely independent of state power.

There has been a common tendency among recent liberal scholars to
define "governmentality" so broadly that even a mother suckling a child, or
a person riding a bicycle, becomes a form of "government." (Liberals have
long reduced the body to a form of "property"—now they reduce human
agency to a mode of "self-government"!) But the power to direct or shape
the conduct of others, whether a ship's captain over the crew, the employer
—"boss"—over the workers, the psychiatrist over clients, the teacher over
pupils, or even parents over children in the modern world, only have substance because such "governmentality" has the sanction and is predicated
on the power of the modern state (cf. Dean 1999, 11; N. Rose 1999, 3).
When Todd May writes that capitalism and state institutions—as "structures" (and even the human subject!)—are simply "sedimentations" (whatever that may mean) of local practices, and even implies that "power is not
centralized" (1994, 78, 95), such reductionism oblates the complex
dialectic that exists between state power (and capitalism) and "governmen-

tality." In fact, it rather puts the cart before the horse: the state is not an effect or the sedimentation of local practices—whether therapeutic, penal, or pedagogic—but rather, as Foucault always implied, the latter practices are invisible "mechanisms" of state power.

Such in brief is Foucault's theory of power, which has, of course, been the subject of a plethora of critical commentary in recent years (see, for example, Dews 1987, 144–99; Merquior 1985; Hoy 1986; Habermas 1987, 238–93; McNay 1994).

Kropotkin's intellectual journeys at the end of the nineteenth century, and his reflections on the modern state, seem a long way from Foucault's "interpretive analytics." Yet the two men had much in common: both were humane persons critical of all forms of power and always prepared to defend human rights; both had a very ambivalent attitude toward the Enlightenment, although it is noteworthy that Foucault, unlike Kropotkin, expressed little interest in the French Revolution; both men had a fascination and love of empirical facts; and finally, both men made important contributions to a critical understanding of contemporary forms of social and political hegemony. But how may we respond to the critiques of Kropotkin and anarchism that have been put forward by the contemporary disciples of Nietzsche and Foucault? The first thing that must be said is that it is quite erroneous to dismiss Kropotkin as merely an "anti-statist," for like many other anarchists, Kropotkin was consistently "anti-political," in the sense of opposing all political relationships—that is, as Wieck expresses it, all "power-structural relationships." Kropotkin stood firmly in the anarchist tradition that expressed an opposition or negation of all power relations, and was thus critical of all forms of domination, sovereignty, representation, and hierarchy (Wieck 1979, 138–39).

The notion, however, that anarchists endorse unlimited freedom, as Andrew Heywood suggests (1994, 198), or that they dream of a society where "power" has ceased to exist, represents a serious misunderstanding of anarchism. For Kropotkin, order and power are intrinsic to social life. A human society has, by definition, both order and a normative structure and operates with regularized and relatively fixed modes of behavior. Humans without society (or some form of association) are not humans, for sociality, as Kropotkin continually insisted, is basic to the human condition. So is power. Power is a relationship and implies the ability "to get others to do what you want them to do." Power may mean influence or authority—convincing others by example, by economic rewards, by logical argument, or by the prestige of one's status. Or it may mean coercion—the implied or overt threat of physical injury. But power is intrinsic to any social group.

The question for Kropotkin therefore was not whether there should be order or structure, but rather, what kind of social order should there be, and what its sources ought to be. Equally, Kropotkin and the anarchists were not utopians who wished to abolish power, for they recognized that power is intrinsic to the human condition. As Bakunin expressed it: "All men have a natural instinct for power which has its origin in the basic law of life enjoining every individual to wage in ceaseless struggle in order to ensure his existence or to assert his rights" (quoted in Maximoff 1953, 248).

What anarchists like Kropotkin strove for is not the abolition of power but its diffusion, its balance, its decentering, so that ideally it is equally distributed, hierarchy and coercion being reduced to a minimum (Barclay 1982, 16–18).

Kropotkin, however, unlike Foucault, always maintained a clear distinction between sociality and power, and he never confused the coercive power of institutions to subjugate individuals, with social action, the following of rules and conventions within a particular social group (Said 1986, 151). In essence, Kropotkin confirmed the position of John Stuart Mill who, in his essay "On Liberty," argued that the only justification for interfering with the liberty of a person is to prevent physical harm either being done to oneself or others (Mill 1972, 78). Anarchism, for Kropotkin, did not imply license nor the repudiation of all forms of power and authority—but these had to be justified. As with Bakunin, Kropotkin recognized that social norms and public opinion often became a form of "social tyranny," but he also acknowledged, as Bakunin wrote, that "this power may be just as much beneficial as harmful. It is beneficial when it contributes to the development of knowledge, material prosperity, liberty, equality, solidarity, harmful when it has opposed tendencies" (Lehning 1973, 150).

Kropotkin and the anarchists thus did not conceive of all normative power as negative and repressive, but they did try to sketch the kind of society that was most conducive to human liberty and social solidarity—and thus were critical of all forms of power that hindered the free development of the individual. Kropotkin therefore not only opposed state power, but as we earlier noted, capitalism, the wage system, vanguard parties, all forms of knowledge that served to bolster the interests of power (such as religious ideology or the theory of political economy), as well as all modes of hierarchy, even within tribal society. But of course Kropotkin did not reject *all* forms of authority (power)—this would imply the repudiation of mother/child relationships and the authority of various specialists. He would have concurred with Bakunin, who wrote: "Does it follow that I reject all authority? Perish the thought. In the matter of boots I defer to the authority of the bootmaker" (Dolgoff 1973, 229). Or as Luigi Fabbri put it in his critique of the bourgeois influences on anarchism: "it would be crazy for a sick person to rebel against medical authority's methods of curing illness, for a bricklayer not to follow the architect's plans, or for a mariner not to follow the pilot's instructions on navigating a ship." But the important point is that in following their authority, they do so voluntarily (Fabbri 1987, 24).

The notion put out by poststructuralist philosophers that anarchists repudiate all forms of power simply indicates their woeful misunderstanding of anarchism.

What Kropotkin opposed was all forms of power that nullified or hindered existential individualism, the free development and enjoyment of every individual person.

Like Bakunin, Kropotkin postulated not only a negative conception of liberty—consisting of a rebellion against all forms of coercive authority—but also a positive conception of liberty. This was an eminently social matter and implied not only the "most complete development of individuality" and the full expansion of human faculties and intelligence, but also the highest development of voluntary association and mutualism (KRP, 123). Kropotkin thus advocated a kind of personal politics that expressed not only a negation of coercive power, but also a "struggle over agency"—an emphasis on autonomy, and the ability to freely choose whether to act, and what action to take in a given social context (Samuels 1993, 3).

Kropotkin seemed to be fully aware, even if he did not, like Foucault, theorize the issue, that the powers of the modern state were "totalizing" and were the destroyer both of "creative power" and free initiative, "penetrating," as he put it, into all aspects of social life.

Kropotkin was also acutely aware of what Foucault described as the "individualizing" modality of power and offered radical critiques of both the school system and the rampant "individualism" that was heralded by the neo-Darwinists and the political economists, as well as by Nietzschean anarchists. Like Foucault, Kropotkin was striving for a new form of subjectivity, but for Kropotkin, in contrast to both Nietzsche and Foucault, this subjectivity would be fundamentally social, an individuality *pro sibi communisticum*, made possible through practicing the highest communist sociability. The problem with Foucault is that in his radical anti-essentialism (biology), and his vehement dislike of the "subject," he completely failed to theorize any nonhegemonic theory of the human subject. He expressed an extreme nominalism (like the Buddha), and if he can be said to articulate a theory of human nature—a concept he consistently de-nounced—then the image we are given is a rather Hobbesian one, for Fou-cault suggests that within each person there is an inherent war of "all against all"—intrinsically we "all fight each other" (1980, 208).

In his obsession with power, Foucault completely lacked, unlike Kropotkin, any real social theory. As many have suggested, Foucault pres-ents a variant of Nietzsche's ontology of the "will-to-power" and thus pres-ents what Merquior describes as a consistent "Pancratism," the tendency to systematically reduce all social processes and relations to patterns of dom-ination (power). Power is seen by Foucault as coextensive with society and permeates all social relationships: but this does not mean that all social relationships bear the imprint of power as a defining feature (1985, 115).

Foucault writes that where there is power there is always "resistance," but as power is like God, everywhere and nowhere at once, and as Foucault has an aversion toward the human subject, it is difficult to see, as Zerzan writes, where such resistance might spring from, given that, for Foucault, "there is no resistance to power that is not a variant of power itself." Small wonder, Zerzan concludes, that Foucault was dismissive of anarchists as infantile in their hopes for a better future and faith in human potential (1994, 123–25). In fact, in contrast to Kropotkin, Foucault's political theory not only allows no agency of social change but also lacks any vision of non-alienated social relations. Foucault indeed, for all the libertarian impulse behind his work, seems to deny the possibility of social emancipation (Call-inicos 1982, 108–11; Merquior 1985, 143). Though he has indeed been described as a "Neo-anarchist," Foucault's perspective is closer to that of Stirner and Nietzsche rather than to the social anarchism of Kropotkin, who would, no doubt, have critiqued Foucault's asocial individualism in the same manner as he critiqued these two nineteenth-century scholars.

In his trenchant critique of Foucault's nihilism, Murray Bookchin acknowledges that power itself is not something whose elimination is actually possible. But he argues, "Hierarchy, domination, and classes can and should be eliminated, as should the use of power to force people to act against their will. But the liberatory use of power, the empowerment of the disempowered, is indispensable for creating a society based on self-management and the need for social responsibility—in short, free institutions" (1995, 183).

With Foucault's extreme individualism, Bookchin continues, no dis-tinction is made between state power and the power claimed by popular institutions, or between "institutions that lead to tyranny and those that lead to freedom" (1995, 183–84).

Bookchin thus reaffirms the kind of social anarchism that Kropotkin advocated.

Unlike Foucault, Kropotkin also affirmed, much more consistently, the coercive powers of the modern state and its close links with capitalism, which Foucault tended to deny or play down. Kropotkin emphasized the intrinsic links between prisons, schools, and political ideologies with state power. The development of subtle mechanisms and technologies of power and control—through schooling, discourses, the family, psychiatry—in no way undermines the power of the state institutions (police, bureaucracy), rather, as Foucault continually alluded, it strengthens the power of government. If the state is defined as a set of institutions through which public authority is exercised within a particular territory, and which claims a monopoly of coercive power, then the power of the nation-state is enhanced and not reduced by "governmentality" and "disciplinary power." This was the very nature of the modern state for Kropotkin—both "totalizing" (coercive) and "individualizing." But unlike Foucault, Kropotkin stressed that the modern state, including its ubiquitous "mechanisms" of power, played an essential role in supporting capitalist hegemony. This has been reiterated by many scholars, even in an age of capitalist globalization. For although there has been a structural shift in recent years from nation-states to global markets and multinational firms, with devastating results, the nation-state is far from disappearing. States still claim exclusive juridical sovereignty within a given territory—this didn't disappear at the end of the eighteenth century, as Foucault implied—and, as recent conflicts suggest, still contrive to assert the sovereign right to make war. As Robert Holton (1998) argues, the historical dynamic of the nation-state is very far from being played out, for the state still has instrumental value in securing political stability and infrastructural support for capitalism. Holton emphasizes the "complementarity" of interests between nation-states and multinational corporations (1998, 91), echoing what Kropotkin had written at the end of the nineteenth century.

Unlike Foucault, Kropotkin also emphasized the ideological nature of political and economic discourses—and even though, like many of his nineteenth-century contemporaries, Kropotkin tended to have a rather uncritical approach to science, he was fully aware that scientific discourses often served to bolster power. Like Bakunin, Kropotkin was critical of scientific "savants" and made trenchant criticisms of both political economy and neo-Darwinian theories. *Mutual Aid* was largely invoked by the need to offer critical reflections not only on Hobbesian political theory but of the evolutionary theories of Huxley and Spencer, and in his essay on modern science and anarchism, he questioned the theories and the "universal laws" propounded by the political economists. Kropotkin not only implied that these theories offered ideological support for capitalism but were essentially unscientific in postulating "inevitable economic laws." For Kropotkin, natural laws were based on empirical study and always had a "conditional character" (KRP, 177–79).

Although Kropotkin clearly recognized the instrinsic relationship between power and knowledge, what he never did was to conflate these two domains. In his rather monolithic account of power as domination, Foucault tends to emphasize that power and knowledge directly imply one another. This tends to yield, as Lois McNay suggests, an undialectical and functionalist account of power, with knowledge being seen as little more than the effect or instrument of power (1994, 64). This verily denies the ability of subjects to reflect critically on their social conditions and on the disjunction between their own social experiences and the categories and ideologies of power (Dews 1987, 191). Moreover, the concept of ideology, which Kropotkin implicitly employed in his analysis of individualism and neo-Darwinian theory, and which Foucault explicitly repudiates (given its association with Marxism) (1980, 117–18), can still be regarded as having theoretical utility. In fact, Foucault frequently used the concept of ideology, in, for example, writing that the discourses of state sovereignty often function to "efface" the domination intrinsic to state power (1980, 95). Kropotkin, in contrast, clearly recognized that forms of knowledge often had an ideological function, serving to maintain or bolster hierarchical relations. The concept of ideology thus does provide a means of understanding power "as a symbolic or non-material force," even though it also has a material dimension (McNay 1994, 109).

In his study of so-called poststructural anarchism, Todd May concludes that for the postructuralists (Deleuze, Foucault, Derrida, Lyotard) the activity of political reflection must have as its primary goal the freeing of the individual or group for new social practices, practices that undermine or abandon existing power relations (1994, 113). In this he was not saying anything new or original. Kropotkin was articulating such reflections a century before these academic mandarins.

Moreover, unlike these nihilistic philosophers, Kropotkin attempted to envisage an alternative future, whereas these academic scholars who "have spent their whole lives as members of the enviably privileged French mandarin caste," as Marshall Berman puts it (1992, 44), virtually alienated people, have no practical ideas about resistance, nor any alternative to capitalism to offer. As Karen Goaman (1999) writes, these poststructuralists and their adoring acolytes live like clerics in a safe world of abstract academic debate; unlike anarchists such as Kropotkin, who at least engages with history and with the rich vein of utopian thought and always remained in touch with an awareness of alternative realities and social forms that are now apparently taboo in academic circles (1999, 74).

In his discussions with Foucault on French capitalism—opposed by the "nomadic war-machine" (people!)—Gilles Deleuze suggests "Against this global policy of power, we initiate localized counter-responses, skirmishes, active and occasionally preventive defences. We have no need to totalize that which is invariably totalized on the side of power; if we were to move in this direction, it would mean restoring the representative forms of centralism and a hierarchical structure" (Foucault, 1977, 212).

Deleuze seems singularly unaware that this strategy had been advocated by Kropotkin and the anarchist tradition for more than a hundred years.

But although Kropotkin emphasized the growing and intrusive powers of the modern state and the equally intrusive nature of capitalism, at the same time he argued that there were large sectors of social life that were untouched by government (KRP, 64). He was also of the opinion, and this was fervently expressed in his early writings, that voluntary associations and "local actions"—the municipal control of schools, libraries, housing, and essential utilities (gas, water, electricity), as well as the emergence of cooperative and mutual aid societies, was inevitably undermining and beginning to replace both the state and capitalism. In fact, at the end of the nineteenth century, Kropotkin firmly believed that both the nation-state and capitalism were in crisis—and were in decline (WR, 24; AY, 93–94).

In this, however, he was unduly optimistic, and rather that experiencing the "coming revolution" that he envisaged, over the past century there has been an increasing concentration of political and economic power, reflected in a liberal "governmental state" that continues to "meddle," as Kropotkin put it, into all areas of social life, and a global capitalism that has engendered a "new world disorder"—growing social inequalities, an ecological crisis, the undermining of local communities, widespread poverty, the fragmentation of individual lives, and a "dialectic of violence" expressed in ethnic conflict, state repression, and religious fundamentalism. Kropotkin's vision of anarchist communism seems more in need of revitalization than ever before.

12
THE FRENCH
REVOLUTION

The French Revolution was truly a "world-historical" event, and along with the agrarian and industrial revolutions, constituted the "dual revolution" that radically transformed the modern world. All the major ideas and social movements of the nineteenth century—democracy, socialism, liberalism, as well as anarchism—had their roots in the French Revolution—the "great" French Revolution as Kropotkin always described it. The revolution was thus not some local event; it contained, as Eugene Kamenka suggests, a "universal soul" and thus shook Europe and the world (1988, 75).

Kropotkin had from boyhood days been fascinated with the French Revolution, ever since his French tutor, Monsieur Poulain, on afternoon walks through the woods, had regaled Peter with stories of French history and the French Revolution. One of the "debris" of Napoleon's grand army that stayed on in Russia after 1812, Poulain greatly stirred Kropotkin's imagination. Kropotkin long afterward recalled what his tutor had said about Count Mirabeau, who renounced his aristocratic title and put up a signboard with the inscription "Mirabeau tailor." Shortly afterward, still in his twelfth year, Kropotkin dropped the title "Prince" and thereafter signed himself "P. Kropotkin" (MR, 47). The title given to the well-known biography *The Anarchist Prince* is therefore somewhat disrespectful to his memory. But Kropotkin began his serious studies of the French Revolution when he was in London during the year 1877–1878, when he began researching at the British Museum. A decade later he resumed his studies, and in 1889 published several articles celebrating the centenary of the revolution, including "The Great French Revolution and Its Lessons," which was published in *The Nineteenth Century*. Given that Kropotkin had been imprisoned by the

French government, and in 1893 was refused entry to the country, he was never able to undertake any serious researches in the National Archives of France. His studies were therefore confined to the printed collections in the British Museum. It is nevertheless remarkable, as George Woodcock writes, that Kropotkin never held any bitterness toward the French people or the French nation, in spite of all that he had suffered from the reactionary regime that held power in France. In fact, Kropotkin was something of a Francophile and always took the side of France in its recurrent conflicts with Germany. This led him to support the Allied cause during the First World War, a stand that not only led Kropotkin to abandon his own anarchist principles, but to become estranged from the majority of his anarchist comrades, including Malatesta, Rocker, and Goldman (GFR, xiii).

Some twenty years after his first article on the French revolution, Kropotkin published his pioneering study, *The Great French Revolution 1789–1793*. He wrote it in French, and it was initially published in Paris to be translated into English by his friend Nannie Dryhurst, who was one of a number of associates grouped around the anarchist journal *Freedom*. The book, published in 1909, is one of the few studies of anarchist historiography, and though one of the less celebrated of Kropotkin's works, it is, as Woodcock rightly insists, an exceptionally good piece of historical writing, which stands comparison, both in terms of its style and its scholarship, with many of the more celebrated histories of that period (WA, 339).

The Great French Revolution is a popular work, and like all of Kropotkin's writings, it is written in a style that is lucid, readable, and engaging. It thus offers a marked contrast with the opaque, obscurantist, and rather pretentious writings of contemporary academic mandarins, particularly the French poststructuralist philosophers who so beguile and enamor many lifestyle anarchists and liberal scholars. This is because, unlike these mandarins, Kropotkin always aimed to reach the common reader and set great store by the clarity of presentation. But the study is, nevertheless, well researched and full of good scholarship and contains a wealth of authentic detail. The result, as Woodcock reflects, is a "very skilful and absorbing book" (WA, 340). But as it is essentially a popular narrative of the French Revolution, it has been singularly ignored by academic historians, and even anarchist scholars like Heiner Becker (1989) are hardly more than lukewarm toward Kropotkin as a historian.

Kropotkin regarded the French Revolution as the source and origin of all the present conceptions of communism, socialism, and anarchism, as well as a source of new vistas for humankind. He interpreted the revolution in terms of two broad currents—the combination of a current of "ideas" that arose among the Enlightenment philosophers of the eighteenth century and a current of "action" that stemmed from the peasants and urban workers who were concerned primarily with improving their economic conditions and expanding their freedoms. The idea of a state centralized and well ordered, governed by the classes that held property, had been forecast and described, Kropotkin suggests, in the writings of such men as Hobbes, Montesquieu, and Rousseau. During the revolution, people drew their inspiration and their logical force from these writings. But without the revolutionary actions and continual revolts of the peasants and urban workers, the emerging bourgeois radicals would not have accomplished anything. The revolution, for Kropotkin, had its origins in the revolutionary action coming from the people coinciding with the movement of revolutionary thought coming from the educated classes. There was, Kropotkin suggested, a "union of the two." As for the ideas of the peasants and working people, these were mainly negative: hatred of the clergy and the idle aristocracy, popular demands for land, and an end to exploitation and poverty (GFR, 1–15; cf. Rude 1975, 15, for a reaffirmation of Kropotkin's essential thesis).

Kropotkin's study was largely based on secondary sources, particularly the works of Jules Michelet and Alphonse Auland (1910), whose writings Kropotkin continually affirms and commends. But since that time historical scholarship has advanced considerably. Literature on the French Revolution is now extensive, with the writings of Jean Jaures (1922–24), Georges Lefebvre (1962, 1967), and Albert Soboul (1974) being of especial significance in formulating what has come to be known as the classical or orthodox interpretation of the revolution. But what is unique about Kropotkin's account is that Kropotkin not only highlighted the importance of the popular libertarian tradition emerging within the revolution, but he also saw it as an inspiration and as the beginning of a revolutionary process that would eventually lead to the demise of capitalism and the state. He thus ends his book, as Joll indicates (1964, 40), with a fervent invocation of the spirit of the French Revolution.

The orthodox interpretation of the French Revolution, over which there is now much academic debate, and which Kropotkin implicitly followed, is that it was essentially a bourgeois revolt. In essence it involved the overthrow of feudalism by the emerging and revolutionary bourgeoisie who, having won the commanding heights of economic power, seized political power from the monarchy and the landed aristocracy. Although the outcome of the revolution was indeed a strong, centralized state that gave the rising bourgeoisie power, thereby providing the conditions for the expansion of capitalism, the revolution was not in any meaningful sense led by an organized industrial bourgeoisie. The revolutionary transformation was altogether more complex, as the studies of Lefebvre and Soboul reveal. Indeed, Lefebvre's classic study indicates that all the major classes of the eighteenth century were involved in revolutionary action—the nobility, the bourgeoisie, the urban workers, and the peasants. Each independently, and for reasons of their own, initiated revolutionary action. As Soboul insightfully remarked: "The bourgeoisie did not make the French revolution. The French revolution made the bourgeoisie" (Kamenka 1988, 79).

In the myriad studies on the French Revolution, the tendency has been to ignore or play down popular libertarian attitudes of the time. A collection of essays on the French Revolution and its legacy, published to celebrate its bicentenary and written by a number of distinguished scholars, is an example of this trend. Although there is much discussion about the Thermidorians and the counterrevolution, there is hardly any mention of the *sans-culottes* (without breeches), the working people of Paris who played a crucial role in the revolution and articulated socialist and libertarian ideas that ran counter to the bourgeois nationalists (Best 1988). This is what is so crucial and important about Kropotkin's study: it gives an account of the French Revolution that emphasizes the fact that there were political movements within the revolution that expressed in embryonic form anarchist ideas. Kropotkin therefore outlines in some detail the activities and struggles of the popular movement, the sans-culottes, whose advocacy of direct democracy stood in opposition to the revolutionary movement of 1793–94.

As a narrative account, Kropotkin's book outlines some of the key events and political forces that went to make the French Revolution. At the end of the eighteenth century, social life in France was one of extremes, between the absurd luxury at the court of Versailles and among the landed aristocracy and the extreme misery of the great mass of French peasants, burdened by taxes to the state, tithes to the clergy, and feudal dues to the landed aristocracy (GFR, 16–17). As the absolutist state of Louis XVI was resistant to any reform, the years prior to the revolution were characterized by a "spirit of revolt"—food riots, revolts of the silk weavers in Lyons, and peasant insurrections throughout France. Moreover, the revolution in America, with the United States' War of Independence in 1776, had a far-reaching influence on the French bourgeoisie, its constitution, and declaration of human rights, serving as a model for the revolutionary intellectuals.

Throughout 1789 revolutionary pamphlets were published in Paris, which coincided with the urban insurrections, particularly over food prices. After the convocation of the Estates-General in May 1789—at which, Kropotkin highlights, there were no representatives of the people at all—the Third Estate (the bourgeoisie) declared itself a national assembly. But popular risings continued unabated throughout France. There were food riots in Paris, with cries of "Bread! Bread!" and in peasant insurrections throughout the countryside, abbeys and chateaux were destroyed, bonfires made of local records and land registers, demands made for the abolition of tithes, privileges, and feudal rights, and the peasants took possession of the lands that they felt had formerly belonged to the village communities. These insurrections and riots culminated in the fall of the Bastille, that "gloomy fortress," as Kropotkin described it, on July 14, 1789 (GFR, 78).

All this created a "great fear" among the nobility and middle classes, and the peasant insurrectionists were derided and attacked as "brigands" and "thieves." Kropotkin strongly emphasizes that the peasants were primarily concerned with the abolition of feudal ties and the recovery of communal lands and that the popular risings of the peasants from 1789, which lasted five years, were a crucial factor in enabling the revolutionary middle classes to accomplish their "immense work of demolition"—that is, putting an end to feudalism and the absolutist state. Thus, an important dimension of the French Revolution—and thus it contrasts with the English revolution, where the landed aristocracy retained their power and possession of the land—was, for Kropotkin, the fact that "It was above all a peasant insurrection, a movement of people to regain possession of the land and to free it from feudal obligations which burdened it" (GFR, 95–97).

But Kropotkin also emphasized the crucial role that was played by revolutionary ideas, particularly the influence that the United States' Declaration of Independence (signed in Philadelphia on July 4, 1776) had on the French intelligentsia. Kropotkin emphasized that all important events were the result of "many causes" (GFR, 22), and "It is always ideas that govern the world, and great ideas presented in a virile form have always taken hold of the minds of men" (GFR, 141). The democratic ideals of the new American state thus had an important impact on the French revolutionaries, and soon after the fall of the Bastille, the constitution committee of the National Assembly met to discuss the issue and to draft a "Declaration of the Rights of Man and of the Citizen." This was finally ratified by the king when he accepted the new constitution in September 1791. But Kropotkin emphasizes that these declarations failed to deal with economic relations between citizens—only affirming formal equality—and that the middle classes never questioned the rights of property (GFR, 142–43).

Although Kropotkin insisted that the abolition of feudal rights was one of the principal achievements of the French Revolution, and thus emphasized the importance of the peasant insurrections, he also put great stress on the popular risings in the towns, particularly in Paris. The revolution he felt had given rise within the urban context to a new form of social organization—the municipal commune. These communes, focused around the sans-culottes, were part of a popular movement that was quite distinct from the revolutionary government. Kropotkin saw them as a key factor in the revolution: "The soul of the revolution was therefore in the communes, and without these centres, scattered all over the land, the revolution never would have had the power to overthrow the old regime, to repel German invasion, and to regenerate France" (GFR, 181).

The principles of anarchism therefore, as expressed by William Godwin, had their origins not in theoretical speculations but in the social movements and actions of the French Revolution (GFR, 184). Kropotkin emphasized particularly the importance of the "sections" and "districts" within the Paris commune and the fact that these sections supervised the supply and the price of the bread, encouraged market gardening, and tended to be autonomous with their own local assemblies. The districts of Paris "laid the foundations of a new, free, social organization" (GFR, 186).

Kropotkin graphically outlines many of the key events of the revolution: the insurrection over food that broke out in Paris in October 1789, which led to a group of women marching upon Versailles, and escorting the king and his court back to Paris (GFR, 152–57); the reaction of 1790 and the struggles between the various political factions within the Assembly; and finally, the trial and execution of Louis XVI for the crime of treason in January 1793. With regard to the execution of the king, although Kropotkin suggests that Marat was quite right in protesting against it, he nevertheless seems to suggest that because the convention *was* sovereign, then, from a legal point of view, there was every justification for the charge of treason, and so for the king's execution. Why then so much lamentation, he asks, when high treason had clearly been committed by the king. By sending Louis XVI to the scaffold, Kropotkin avers, "the revolution succeeded in killing a principle"—the notion of the divine right of kings (GFR, 333–36). Kropotkin seems to have so identified himself with revolution that he tends to side with the revolutionary government itself, and, Woodcock writes, seems to express a "kind of gloating approval" over the death penalty. This sits uneasily with anarchist principles, for whom there can be no "legal point of view," and to employ the killing of a "principle" as a justification for killing a human being is highly questionable. Tom Paine, at considerable risk to himself, pleaded for the king's life and advocated banishment rather than the scaffold, even though Paine had long condemned the institution of monarchy. As Woodcock writes: "Kropotkin must have known Paine's arguments and his courageous stand, but he mentions neither" (GFR, xxvii; Powell 1985, 22–26; Morris 1995).

During the French Revolution, four major conceptions of politics were articulated, not counting the die-hard reaction that continued to support the old order. The first was that advocated by the liberal aristocrats, the followers of Montesquieu, whose ideal was a constitutional kingship along the lines of the English monarchy.

The second was a conservative form of bourgeois liberalism that tended to equate the bourgeoisie with the nation and advocated a representative system based on property. This kind of constitution was elaborated by Duquesnoy, a deputy to the Estates-General, who wrote: "Neither the magnates nor the brigands are the people: it is composed of the bourgeoisie, that throng of busy, virtuous men who are corrupted neither by opulence nor poverty; they truly are the nation, the people" (quoted in Comininel 1987, 109).

The third form of politics was that advocated by the Girondins and the Jacobins, namely, a constitutional democracy, a parliamentary system based on an elected assembly seen as representing the general will of the people. Kropotkin argues that the Girondins, which was a group centered around Brissot and Roland, were the "party of order" and the faithful representatives of the middle classes. The majority had royalist sympathies, advocated strong government to curb the revolution, and were vehemently against the revolutionary commune of Paris. The Jacobins, on the other hand, represented by Robespierre, wanted to abolish the last vestiges of feudalism and to destroy the great landed estates, and they wanted the revolution to accomplish such changes as would really modify the whole of the conditions prevailing in France: especially for the peasants, who represented more than two-thirds of population (GFR, 345). But like the Girondins, the Jacobins represented middle-class interests, and always defended the rights of property. But the more radical of the Jacobins, like Robespierre, often expressed socialist sentiments, and the Jacobin club took the name "friends of liberty and equality." Robespierre was a radical liberal and a disciple of Rousseau and could accept neither the British system of government—which he considered a fraud and a plot against the people—nor the representative assembly of a republic. For like Rousseau, he felt that elected assemblies or parliaments were in the same category as corporations or other vested interests and would lead to "representative despotism." Robespierre's sympathies with popular democracy and with the aspirations of the sans-culottes led to suspicions among his fellow Jacobins that he was colluding with the populace, suspicions that led to his eventual downfall. But for Robespierre, as well as for the man whom he described as the tutor of the human race, Rousseau, "the people" was a vague metaphysical idea. And as Robespierre clearly felt that democratic sovereignty could be expressed only by a single will, his politics have total-itarian implications. Who or what group is to express or represent this single general will? Yet although he expressed radical liberal ideas, Robe-spierre was certainly no socialist, and like his fellow Jacobins (Danton, Saint-Just), believed in the right of property as the basis of social order. His conception of revolutionary government was clearly intended to steer between two "rocks"—between, as he put it, reaction and extremism, between the "tyranny" of monarchy and the "anarchy" expressed by those sans-culottes who attacked property and the sovereignty of the national assembly. Kropotkin describes Robespierre as belonging to a group of "moderates" who for the revolution to triumph allied themselves with the popular movement, "leaving himself free to guillotine later the left wing, the Hebertists, and to crush the 'extremists'" (GFR, 345). It is all reminis-cent of Lenin during the Russian revolution, and many, besides Kropotkin, have suggested that the origins of Marxism can be traced to the Jacobin ten-dency in the French Revolution.

Robespierre, along with Saint-Just, occupies the extreme left of the con-stitutional-democratic spectrum: but despite the genuinely "social" aspects of his beliefs, Kropotkin thought a gulf separated his politics from those of the popular movements and the advocates of "anarchy" or direct democracy.

Direct democracy constitutes the fourth conception of politics that emerged during the French Revolution. It was the one articulated by the sans-culottes and the *enrages* (extremists) during the period 1793–95. It took seriously and concretely the notion that "sovereignty resides in the people" and stressed the importance of grassroots organization in political life. It was this conception of politics that Kropotkin sought to highlight in his account. He therefore quotes at length from two pamphlets published in October 1792 and May 1793 by the Girondin leader Jacques-Pierre Brissot. In these pamphlets, Brissot not only attacked the Jacobin leaders Robespierre, Danton, and Marat, but he also pleaded for action to be taken against the disrupters of the revolution, whom he termed the "anarchists." Three revolutions were necessary, he wrote, to save France: "the first to over-throw despotism; the second to destroy royalty; the third to beat down anarchy" (GFR, 346). This seems to have been exactly what happened. During each stage of the French Revolution, as Kropotkin outlines, the pol-itics of the revolution became more and more radical, until its final stage, when the Jacobin dictatorship and the later Thermidorians did what Brissot had advocated—they launched a savage coup d'état, a "third revolution," against the "levellers, the abettors of disorder, and the anarchists" (GFR, 358). They beat down anarchy. They suppressed the popular movement of the sans-culottes. In his pamphlets, Brissot demanded that those whom he termed anarchists be sent to the guillotine. He outlined the basic ideas of this group of revolutionary activists and explained what was meant by anarchy. "Laws that are not carried into effect, authorities without force and despised, crime unpunished, property attacked, the safety of individuals violated, the morality of people corrupted, no constitution, no government, no justice, these are the features of anarchy!" (GFR, 351).

The anarchists have usurped an influence in the convention, which, Brissot argued, "should belong to reason alone." Blaming anarchists for all the problems that beset France, he went on to say: "They are the men who have divided society into two classes, those who have and those who have not—the unbreeched ones (sans-culottes) and the property owners—and who have stirred up the one against the other" (GFR, 354).

The anarchists, he continued, are the disorganizers. They want to level everything—property, comfort, salaries, and the price of commodities. They denounce the property owners and merchants as "robbers" and "monopolists." They want an agrarian law, land for all. These brigands, as Brissot called the anarchists, with their attacks on property and on govern-ment officials in the name of equality, were disrupting the social order and the respect for law. Thus these anarchists, these insurrectionists, he said, are "the real enemies of the people," whose activities are undermining the republic. They must be dealt with, Brissot concluded, by "rigorous meas-ures." It was, however, the Jacobins who carried out this suppression on behalf of "order" and the bourgeoisie. It was they, not the Girondins, who launched the so-called third revolution and thus put an end to the French Revolution itself (GFR, 348–60).

The anarchists, Kropotkin suggests, did not form a party but were rev-olutionists, scattered throughout France, who had given themselves "body and soul" to the revolution. Many of them gathered around the Paris Commune; some were members of the Jacobin or Cordeliers Club. But their true domain was the sections and streets of Paris, and as Brissot admitted, it was the people of Paris and the commune who forced the hand of the convention "every time some revolutionary measure is taken" (GFR, 357).

For Kropotkin, the revolutionary year between May 1793 and July 1794 was the most important period of the whole revolution. During this period, the convention enacted many important decrees; there was the complete abolition of feudal rights without redemption; communal lands were restored to the village communes; and measures were made to fix the price of bread. Kropotkin emphasized the great difference between the abolition of feudalism in France, which was accomplished by popular revolution, and that accomplished by bureaucratic means in Prussia (1848) and Russia (1861), for in the latter two contexts the peasants lost a considerable amount of land through having to pay heavy indemnities (GFR, 413–31). In addition, with the execution of the king, and the establishment of a new, more radical constitution and a declaration of the "rights of man" in June 1794, the principle of "Royal Power" was finally eclipsed. But for Kropotkin, it was the revolutionary activities of the working people of Paris that were of crucial importance. During the upheavals of 1792—the storming of the palace and the formation of the revolutionary Paris Commune—the working people of Paris, the sans-culottes, had become a political force in their own right. For a time, during the period 1793–94, they shared the administration of France with the Jacobin dictatorship and became a recognizable political movement, operating through popular societies, section assemblies, and the revolutionary committees and armed citizens that Robespierre had initially encouraged. During those years, as Daniel Guerin suggests (1977, 45), the modern class struggle made its first appearance. Having eliminated absolutism, the bourgeoisie came into conflict with the people they exploited and enslaved—the working people.

Since Kropotkin wrote his classic text, there has been a wealth of research undertaken on the sans-culottes, the studies of Albert Soboul being especially significant (see, for example, Williams 1968; Soboul 1972; R. B. Rose 1983; Bookchin 1996, 1:312–28). What these more recent studies indicate is that the sans-culottes did not form an economic class but consisted essentially of a combination of socially disparate entities. The term sans-culottes refers to the type of clothing worn by the Parisian working man—trousers. The term had moral and economic as well as political significance. Soboul, like Kropotkin, stresses that the French Revolution was to a large extent the making of the working people of Paris. From the fall of the Bastille to the spring of 1795, they devoted their energies to the revolution: "They placed all their hopes in it. They lived and suffered for it." And it was largely through their support and political power that the bourgeois revolutionaries were able to bring down the ancient regime.

But "the sans-culottes, like the peasants, tended to look beyond the downfall of the aristocracy toward goals that were not precisely those of the revolutionary ruling class." In fact, Soboul suggests that the thinking of the sans-culottes was often identical to that of the peasants who, "faced with the advances made by capitalist agriculture and imbued with a spirit of agrarian individualism, were desperately eager to defend their rural communities and the collective rights that ensured their survival." The popular movement of the sans-culottes therefore tended toward decentralization and local autonomy. What emerged therefore in this period were two hostile groupings or "classes"—that of the artisan, journeyman, shopkeeper, and peasant smallholder on one hand, and that of the large farmers, powerful merchants, and leaders of industry on the other (Soboul 1972, xxix).

The majority of the sans-culottes, Soboul's studies reveal, included petty traders, shopkeepers, journeymen, craftsmen, and small masters as well as laborers, reflecting essentially the economic structure of Parisian industry at the time. What gave them their essential unity, in spite of this social heterogeneity, was their opposition to the "respectable people"—the rich, the "bourgeois aristocracy"—a label that, if sociologically imprecise, was a significant expression of the period. They had a deep-seated hostility toward the commercial bourgeoisie, toward those who had "grown fat off the sweat of the wage earners." As they were concerned primarily with the basic problems of living, of obtaining daily bread, the sans-culottes focused on the demand for equal incomes and the need to exercise restrictions on property rights. To the absolute right of property, the root of inequality, the sans-culottes counterposed the principle of "equal incomes," as Soboul shows. A basic egalitarianism was thus a central current in popular thinking. Jacques Roux put it this way in a petition of June 25, 1793: "Liberty is but a phantom when one class of man can starve another with impunity. Liberty is but a phantom when a rich man, through monopoly, possesses the power of life and death over his fellow man" (quoted in Soboul 1972, 48).

But Soboul stresses that the sans-culottes never questioned the principle of property as such; their idea, like that of the peasants, was a society of small independent producers whom the state would sustain by progressive taxation, public assistance, and curbs on the operation of the competitive market system and on large-scale capitalism. As small producers, the sans-culottes "based their ideas on personal work." This idea of a worker's private property based on his own labor corresponded to the artisan form of production still characteristic of the latter half of the eighteenth century. It was a method of production that could flourish only if the worker was a free proprietor, a peasant with his own land, or an artisan with his own premises and his own tools (Soboul 1972, 56).

The form of politics that the sans-culottes advocated was that of direct democracy, of popular participation. Sovereignty resided in the people. But they understood this not as an abstraction but rather as the concrete reality of people brought together in sectional assemblies and exercising all their rights (Paris at that time being administratively divided into forty-eight sections). This conception was quite different from that espoused by the Jacobins, who followed Rousseau in accepting a rather abstract conception of sovereignty, one that conformed to the interests of the bourgeoisie. One deputy complained to the committee of public safety about the indiscriminate use of the term "sovereign people." Sovereignty, he argued, "belongs to the people alone, taken collectively; hence, sovereignty is essentially one and indivisible, is but a pure metaphysical being, that is to say, the expression of the general will" (Soboul 1972, 105).

For the sans-culottes, however, sovereignty was made of flesh and blood; it was the people exerting their rights themselves, in the sectional assemblies. They thus took the principle of popular sovereignty to its logical conclusion—the dissolution of the body politic and the autonomy of the section. This denied the right of the National Assembly to enact laws; the only laws, one member of the sans-culotte declared, "will be those made by the people themselves on that particular day." No wonder the Girondin deputy Pierre Vergniaud declared that the anarchists were abusing the word sovereignty: "They have almost toppled the Republic by making each section believe that sovereignty was its own domain" (Soboul 1972, 133)

This emphasis on the political autonomy of the local sections was complemented by certain other social attitudes: that political life should be an open and public affair, that unity was necessary in the sections and in the popular societies, and that fraternization and mutual aid between sections and societies should be encouraged and supported. The sans-culottes attempted to give concrete expression to that great rallying cry of the revolution—liberty, equality, and fraternity.

It is important to stress that the sans-culottes, like the ruling class of the period, made frequent recourse to violence to achieve their aims and that the majority of the popular militants approved of it; they did not, however, exalt violence, especially against the bourgeoisie. To see this revolutionary violence as simply the action of brigands, mindless terrorists, and "drinkers of blood," as did moderates such as Brissot and the conservative reactionaries, is to accept a distorted picture of the period. In the class struggles at the end of the eighteenth century, popular revolutionaries were depicted by the bourgeois press in the most lurid and negative terms. To suggest that the sans-culottes believed in and practiced armed struggle is a valid assessment; but to suggest that they were "naturally violent" and gloried in the shedding of blood is to the demean these struggles and to adopt the rhetoric of the counterrevolution.

During the period 1792–93, a number of figures emerged who attempted to articulate the radical ideas of the sans-culottes, and this gave rise to what Kropotkin describes as the "communist movement." Known as the *enrages*, they were led by Jacques Roux and Jean Varlet. Roux was an ordained priest and taught philosophy in various seminaries. Kropotkin writes that he was extremely poor, lived alone with a dog in a gloomy house in the center of Paris, and preached communism in the working-class districts (GFR, 489). Practicing as a priest in Gravilliers, one of the slum districts of Paris, had turned Roux into a rebel, for he was appalled at the poverty and hardship endured by the common people. An influential orator and journalist, Roux was described by the disapproving historian James Joll as the most violent of the enrages—for he denounced the revolutionary bourgeoisie for their "indecent wealth" and profiteering during the revolution. As Roux wrote, freedom "is but an empty phantom if one class of men can starve another with impunity" (quoted in Joll 1964, 42–43). Robespierre quickly moved against Roux, who, as Kropotkin writes, he never ceased to slander. Roux committed suicide in prison in February 1794 (GFR, 503–505; Bookchin 1996, 1:354, who questions whether Roux's vision of social justice ever constituted a form of "socialism" in any real sense).

Another leading enragé, Jean Varlet, a postal clerk, also continually castigated the Jacobin dictatorship for its failure to meet the needs of the poor and for not controlling speculators and horders among the merchant class. He was a passionate egalitarian committed to the sans-culottes doctrine of absolute sovereignty of the sections. Unlike Roux, he managed to survive the terror.

Other enrages and supporters of the sans-culottes were silenced by the Jacobin government. One such supporter was Theophile Leclerc, whose love of justice made him many lifelong enemies; another was Claire Lacombe, an actress, whose society of revolutionary women was eliminated "because they wanted to sow too soon the seeds of a revolution that would liberate women" (Guerin 1977, 131; GFR, 489–90).

Kropotkin suggests that what the enrages understood was that it "was not enough to guarantee to each man the right to work, or even a right to the land; they saw that so long as commercial exploitation existed, nothing could be done; they maintained that to prevent this, commerce would have to be communalized" (GFR, 373).

Thus in the years 1793–94, through the sans-culottes and the enrages, a communist movement emerged that had three aspects—land, industrial, and commercial (GFR, 488). And the dominating idea of this movement was that land should be considered the common inheritance of the whole nation, that every citizen should have the right to land, that the means of existence should be guaranteed to each person, and thus that "No one could be forced to sell his or her work under the threat of starvation." It followed from this that people only had usufruct rights to land, in that land was communal property, and "every holder of land should get only the right of temporary possession of that land which he himself cultivated, and only for so long as he cultivated it" (GFR, 493–94).

By 1795, the tide of reaction had passed to the extreme right, with the wholesale purge of the commune, the disarming of the sans-culottes, and the regrouping of the Paris sections. Control over these sections was taken out of the hands of working people and shopkeepers and put under the jurisdiction of merchants and civil servants. Even the red caps that had been worn to symbolize liberty were banished from the streets. Popular demonstrations during the spring of 1795, in which the slogan "Bread and the Constitution of 1793" was brandished and in which large numbers of women participated, were ruthlessly put down by a force of twenty thousand soldiers. The popular movement was effectively suppressed by the troops and their cannon fire. Thus, as Gwyn Williams has put it, "The sans-culottes go out of history in 1795." The revolution was over, and the sans-culottes did not emerge again in France as political force until the insurrections of the 1830s (1968, 112).

Although it cannot be said that the sans-culottes and the enrages put forward a consistent program of opposition to the economic and political system of the revolutionary bourgeoisie, nevertheless during the French Revolution a "vein of anarchist thought" can be clearly discerned. Accusations by Brissot that the "anarchist" and the "brigands" wanted to dissolve the republic at the very moment of its birth point to the fact that, as Alfredo Bonanno writes in his introduction to Kropotkin's work, the sans-culottes did not want to end the revolution with the constitution and the death of the king, but they wanted to proceed further and in opposition to the Jacobins to achieve true equality and freedom. In their opposition to the Constitutional Assembly and to the centralized state of the Jacobins, the sans-culottes came to advocate the primary importance of direct action and popular democracy. Moreover, although the sans-culottes did not articulate a consistent socialist program—they emphasized petty trading and artisan production—they clearly saw that political and legal freedoms without economic freedom and independence were meaningless. A social revolution, not just a democratic revolution, was necessary.

Thus in the writings of the enrages and other populists, there is not only an overt critique of the state and authoritarian politics but also an implicit critique of the capitalist mode of production and its inherent inequalities and tendencies toward monopoly. Although Brissot used the word anarchism—derived from the Greek *anarchos*, meaning "without a ruler"—as a term of condemnation and abuse, he was in fact identifying key features of the social thought of the sans-culottes: its rejection of both state authority and economic inequality. And James Joll, for all his hostility toward anarchism, was essentially correct in accepting Kropotkin's thesis that the French Revolution was the source and origin of socialist and anarchist thought.

Neither the sans-culottes nor the enrages nor that much-neglected socialist Thomas Spence fully and explicitly articulated anarchism as a political doctrine. What they had in common was that they stressed local and popular democracy and were hostile toward big capital, whether of the merchant class or of the capitalist landlords. Their social ideal was that of an egalitarian society consisting of independent artisans and small peasant farmers. Even Spence, though he advocated communal property in land, parish democracy, and parish militias (people would be "lords of their own districts"), allowed for a structure of provincial and national assemblies. Even so, like the sans-culottes, he tended to see the parish of the local commune as the fundamental unit of society and sought any means to limit the power of the central government (Morris 1996, 112–22, discusses Spence's revolutionary socialism).

Kropotkin wrote that the principles of anarchism, as expressed by William Godwin in his famous work *Enquiry Concerning Political Justice* (1793), had their origin, not in theoretical speculation, but in "the deeds of the great French revolution" (GFR, 184). In fact, it could be argued that Godwin's *Political Justice*, written in the midst of the French Revolution, distilled and put into philosophical language the most radical aspects of the revolutionary tradition expressed by the sans-culottes—although this is not to deny the important influence of the English dissenting tradition on Godwin (Marshall 1984).

This tradition was a truly revolutionary one, going beyond the rationalism and democratic politics of the Jacobins and bourgeois radicals. The literary critic George Steiner writes that we find within the revolution "ultraradical and proto-socialist or, indeed, communist or communard critiques and embryonic movements of resistance for whom the French Revolution is an uncompleted, aborted act of emancipation whose inherent economic-social opportunism has brought gains only to the bourgeoisie" (1988, 129).

Steiner saw these embryonic movements as counterrevolutionary, whereas in reality they represented the true spirit of the revolution. Godwin's *Political Justice*, the first cogent statement of libertarian socialism, expresses this spirit and demonstrates that the real legacy of the revolution is the vision of a future society where liberty, equality, and fraternity can be fully and concretely expressed. The French Revolution is essentially not a permanent revolution but an unfinished one.

What the French Revolution was all about has long been a matter of dispute among historians. The orthodox interpretation is the one first suggested by the bourgeois revolutionaries themselves and later taken up by Marxist scholars, namely, that the revolution was essentially a bourgeois revolt. It constituted the ascendancy of the bourgeoisie as a class, the defeat of a more or less feudal aristocracy, and the eventual triumph of capitalism. Georges Lefebvre has summed up this transformation: "The Revolution is only the crown of a long economic and social evolution which has made the bourgeoisie the mistress of the world" (quoted in Cobban 1964, 8).

In broadest terms, this thesis is, I think, a valid one. But liberal historians in recent years, often using the empirical material provided by such Marxists as Lefebvre and Soboul, have questioned this thesis. They have argued that there was no great disjunction between the economic interests of the nobility and those referred to at the time as the "bourgeoisie"; that at the end of the eighteenth century in France, no industrial capitalism had developed, and so it is misleading to equate the bourgeoisie with the industrial capitalist; and that the revolution was more of a political upheaval than a socio-economic transformation. If anything, the revolution hampered the development of capitalism, preserving the essential social characteristics of the ancient regime. But, as Norman Hampson has argued, if the revolution was not primarily a class struggle, it is difficult to see what else the revolution could have been or why writers as diverse as Wordsworth and Goethe were so ecstatic about it (1969, 77–78).

However, it is evident, as Kropotkin suggests and the writings of Lefebvre and Soboul confirm, that the French Revolution was more than simply a political upheaval, for the class conflicts at the end of the ancient regime were concerned specifically with issues regarding the economic surplus. The bourgeoisie, though not industrial capitalists, were certainly a ruling class of property that even Robespierre, for all his advocacy of universal suffrage, defended. The bourgeoisie were simply those of the ruling class who lacked the privileges attached to noble status. George Comninel, in fact, has suggested that the French Revolution was essentially an intra-class conflict over basic political relations that at the same time touched directly on relations of surplus extraction. "It was a civil war within the ruling class over the essential issues of power and surplus extraction. The focus of the struggle was the nature of the State" (1987, 200).

Barrington Moore had earlier suggested that to deny that the predominant thrust and chief consequences of the revolution were bourgeois and capitalist is to engage in a trivial quibble. For although the bourgeois revolution was not initiated and achieved by a solid group of commercial and industrial interests, its ultimate outcome "was a victory of an economic system of private property and a political system based upon equality before the law," the latter being an essential feature of Western democracies (1966, 105–106).

Overall, the French Revolution had two important results. First, although it destroyed the power of the landed aristocracy, its consequences were ambiguous in that the revolution also entrenched small-scale peasant production. The same processes that destroyed the landed aristocracy created small-peasant property, an agrarian economy dominated by medium and small landowners with exclusive private rights to their lands. And it is ironic that the success of the revolution undermined the community and peasant solidarity that had made the revolution possible in the first place (Skocpol 1979, 127).

Second, the political struggles of the revolution led to the emergence of a highly centralized, bureaucratic state, one that was to guarantee private property and market relations. It was as much a "state-strengthening revolution" as it was a bourgeois revolution; and after the revolution, the people of France had to contend with a more powerful and intrusive state. It furthered the possibilities for authoritarian rule at the expense of civil liberties. (For important discussions of the French Revolution, see Rudé 1988; Greenlaw 1975; McGarr et al. 1989; as well as those cited earlier in text.)

In his own conclusions to his study, Kropotkin suggested that the French Revolution was notable for three important achievements: the return to peasant holdings led to a marked increase in agricultural productivity throughout France; it led to the complete abolition of serfdom (feudalism) and thus undermined the power of the landed aristocracy; and, finally, it led to an end of political absolutism in the divine authority of the monarchy (GFR, 573–79). But what was equally important for Kropotkin was that the French Revolution also bequeathed to humanity the principles of popular communism and modern socialism. He thus saw a "direct filiation" between the sans-culottes, the enrages, and the Babeuf conspiracy of 1795, and the socialist movements, like the International Workingmen's Association, at the end of the nineteenth century. He concluded that the French Revolution was the "source and origin of all the present communist, anarchist, and socialist conceptions" (GFR, 580–81).

It also provided lessons to be learned in the coming social revolution that he clearly felt was imminent around the turn of the twentieth century. Kropotkin thus ends his study with a fervent invocation of the spirit of the French Revolution.

> The one thing certain is, that whatsoever nation enters on the path of revolution in our own day, it will be heir to all our forefathers have done in France. The blood they shed was shed for humanity—the sufferings they endured were borne for the entire human race; their struggles, the ideas they gave to the world, the shock of those ideas, are all included in the heritage of mankind. All have borne fruit, and will bear more, still finer, as we advance towards those wide horizons opening out before us, where, like some great beacon to point the way, flame the words—Liberty, Equality, Fraternity. (GFR, 582)

PART FOUR
ANARCHISM

13
THE HISTORY
of ANARCHISM

Kropotkin makes two essential points about anarchism as a political tradition. The first is that anyone who sides with the oppressed, who critiques the present status quo, or who offers suggestions for a more viable future—one in which liberty, equality, and the well-being of all would have real, concrete expression—is more than likely to be dismissed by those in power (or their ideologies) as utopian, unpractical, or misguided (AY, 85). Second, Kropotkin emphasizes that anarchism is a social movement and thus was born among the working people and had little to do with the universities or intellectuals per se (KRP, 146).

Kropotkin firmly believed that capitalism had "served its time," along with the state structures that supported it, and a new form of social life— anarchist communism—was in the process of formation. Equally, this social revolution could and would only be initiated through local action by working people themselves, through the expropriation of land and property and by the organization of social life through local communities and voluntary associations.

But for Kropotkin forms of anarchism were inherent in social life itself and had coexisted with other social tendencies throughout human history. He therefore suggested that at all times two tendencies were copresent and continually in conflict: "On the one hand, the masses were developing in the form of customs a number of institutions which were necessary to make social life possible or all—to ensure peace amongst men, to settle any disputes that may arise, and to help one another in everything requiring cooperative effort" (KRP, 146).

This was not a context devoid of power; it was rather one of diffuse social power, an instituting "ground power," as Castoriadis describes it

(1991, 150), that was reflected in various institutions—the clan in tribal society, village communities, the guilds in medieval Europe. But at all times too there were explicit forms of power, represented by a minority—the "sorcerers, prophets, priests and heads of military organisations, who endeavoured to establish and to strengthen their authority over the people" (KRP, 71). In a sense, therefore, anarchism and "governmentalism" have coexisted throughout human history.

Anarchism is seen by Kropotkin as representative of the first social tendency, that is, "of the creative, constitutive power of the people themselves who aimed at developing institutions of common law in order to protect themselves from the 'power-seeking minority'" (KRP, 147).

Social life is therefore a creation of the human imagination and, as Clastres (1977) was later to stress, there developed in early human societies institutional means to curtail the concentration of power in individuals.

Like contemporary writers, Kropotkin implied that anarchism could be looked at in two ways. On the one hand, it can be seen as a kind of "river," as Peter Marshall (1992) describes it in his excellent history of anarchism. It can thus be seen as a "libertarian impulse" or as an "anarchist sensibility" that has existed throughout human history; an impulse that has expressed itself in various ways—in the writings of Lao Tzu and the Taoists, in classical Greek thought, in the mutuality of kin-based societies, in the ethos of various religious sects, in such agrarian movements as the Diggers in England and the early Zapatistas in Mexico, in the collectives that sprang up during the Spanish civil war, and—currently—in the ideas expressed in the ecology and feminist movements. Anarchist tendencies seem to have expressed themselves in all religious movements, even in Islam. One Islamic sect, the Najadat, believed that "power belongs only to God." They therefore felt that they did not really need an imam or caliph, but could organize themselves mutually to ensure justice.

On the other hand, anarchism may be seen as a historical movement and political theory that had its beginnings at the end of the eighteenth century. It was expressed in the writings of William Godwin, who wrote the classic anarchist text *An Enquiry Concerning Political Justice* (1793), as well as in the actions of the sans-culottes and the enrages during the French Revolution, and by radicals like Thomas Spence and William Blake in Britain. As a social movement, anarchism developed during the nineteenth century, and in its classical form, represented by Bakunin, Goldman, Reclus, and Malatesta, as well as by Kropotkin, it was a significant part of the socialist movement in the years before the First World War, but its socialism was libertarian, not Marxist. The tendency of writers like David

Pepper (1996) to create a dichotomy between socialism and anarchism is, I think, both conceptually and historically misleading.

Kropotkin seems to have acknowledged these two ways of looking at anarchism.

In his famous article on anarchism for the *Encyclopedia Britannica* (1910), Kropotkin defined anarchism as "A principle or theory of life and conduct under which society is conceived without government—harmony in such a society being obtained, not be submission to law, or by obedience to any authority, but by free agreements between the various groups, territorial and professional, freely constituted for the sake of production and consumption as also for the satisfaction of the infinite variety of needs and aspirations of a civilised being" (KRP, 289).

Society is thus envisaged as an interwoven network of an infinite variety of groups and associations at various levels of federation (local, regional, national, international) organized for a variety of different purposes and functions. Elsewhere, he gives another succinct definition of an anarchist society.

> The anarchists conceive a society in which all the mutual relations of its members are regulated, not by laws, nor by authorities, whether self-imposed or elected, but by mutual agreements between members of that society and by a sum of social customs and habits—not petrified by law, routine or superstition, but continually developing and continually re-adjusted in accordance with the ever-growing requirements of a free life stimulated by the progress of science, invention, and the steady growth of higher ideals. (KRP, 157)

(Kropotkin admitted that no society had ever existed that fully expressed these principles.)

Social life for Kropotkin was not therefore something immutable; there could be "no crystallization and immobility, but a continual evolution—such as we see in nature." Moreover, the advent of such a society would, Kropotkin believed, allow for the full development of the individual; "free play for the individual, for the full development of his individual gifts—*for his individualization*" (KRP, 157).

Anarchism was seen by Kropotkin as having a double origin: as the "constructive, creative activity of the people, by which all institutions of communal life were developed in the past," and as a form of protest against external forces, or as a mode of resistance against the development of all forms of authority whether coercive or ideological" (KRP, 149).

From the remotest antiquity, humans therefore have not only created anarcho-communist forms of association, but they have expressed what Kropotkin describes as the "no-government tendency," which has opposed the emergence of hierarchic forms of organization. The clan, the village community, the guild, the free medieval city were all institutions, Kropotkin argues, by means of which the common people resisted the encroachments of brigands, conquerors, and other power-seeking minorities (KRP, 287).

Such popular anarchist currents—which have occurred throughout history—often found expression in literature. Kropotkin mentions in particular the writings of Aristippus, Zeno of Citium, and Lao Tzu. The Stoic philosopher Zeno Kropotkin considered the best exponents of anarchist philosophy in ancient Greece, for Zeno's concept of a free society without government directly opposed the utopian statist politics of Plato. The Stoic "repudiated the omnipotence of the state, its intervention and regimentation, and proclaimed the sovereignty of the moral law of the individual—remarking already that, while the necessity of self-preservation leads man to egoism, nature has supplied a corrective to it by providing man with another instinct—that of sociability" (KRP, 288).

Kropotkin was always to emphasize the duality of human nature, that humans were intrinsically both egoistic and social, always striving to maintain the integrity of their own being while also motivated by social concerns. Both Lao Tzu and Zeno are thus seen by Kropotkin as expressing anarchist tendencies, as did the many religious movements that emerged throughout antiquity and the medieval period to challenge state and ecclesiastical authority. Christianity itself, as a movement against the Roman government, contained many elements, Kropotkin contends, that were "essentially anarchistic" (KRP, 149). Likewise with the Anabaptist movement. Drawing on the support of the peasantry, it initiated the Protestant reform movement until it was suppressed by the reformers under Martin Luther's leadership. But within the Anabaptist movement, there was a considerable element of anarchism, as was expressed by Hans Denk.

At the time of the Enlightenment, anarchist ideas were also expressed by the French philosophies, those of Rousseau and Diderot in particular, and such ideas, Kropotkin stressed, found their own expression later in the great French Revolution with the emergence of the independent "sections" in Paris and of many "communes" throughout the country.

But for Kropotkin, it was William Godwin (1756–1836) in his *Enquiry Concerning Political Justice* (1793) who first stated in definite form the basic principles of anarchism, even though he did not give that name to his own philosophy. Godwin advocated the abolition of the state, along with its laws and courts, believing that real justice could only be attained through free and independent social institutions. With regard to property, Godwin was openly a communist, stating that every person had the right "to every substance capable of contributing to the benefit of a human being." But Godwin, Kropotkin observed, had not the courage of his own convictions and was later to mitigate his communist views in the second edition of *Political Justice* (1796). Godwin was essentially an individualist anarchist—society, he declared, "is nothing more than an aggregation of individuals" (1971, 75)—and a utilitarian, and his vision of a free and equal society is ultimately based on the Greek notion of individual self-development, with its emphasis in reason and autonomy. (For important accounts of Godwin's philosophical anarchism, see Clark 1977; Marshall 1984, 93–117).

But the person who first described himself as an anarchist ("an-archy," no government, contrary to authority) was Pierre-Joseph Proudhon (1809–1865). As a critic of the society of his day—both capitalism and the state—Proudhon, Kropotkin thought, was both great and inspiring. As for his constructive suggestions regarding an alternative future society, these Kropotkin thought unpractical or problematic—even though he described Proudhon as "undoubtedly one of the greatest writers who have ever dealt with economic questions" (AY, 97). Being hostile to both communism and state socialism, Proudhon developed a system of mutualism that in essence retained the notion of private property, and following the ideas of Robert Owen, he advocated a system of labor checks, which represented the hours of labor required to produce a given commodity. The exchange of services and goods would be thus on the basis of strict equivalence, facilitated by a scheme of mutual exchange and mutual banking. Kropotkin considered Proudhon's scheme as something of a compromise with the interests of capitalism, its individualism incompatible with the common ownership of land and the instruments of production, its mutualism simply replicating the wages system, with all its problems and contradictions. But having experienced the reaction to the French Revolution and having lived through the revolution of 1848, Proudhon had seen with his own eyes, Kropotkin argued, the crimes perpetrated by the revolutionary republican government and the problematic nature of state socialism. This led Proudhon in such works as *General Idea of the Revolution in the Nineteenth Century* (1851) to advocate a society without government and to use the term anarchy to describe it.

(Proudhon's social and political thought is usefully discussed by Ritter

1969 and Hoffman 1972. Proudhon's horrific anti-Semitic outbursts and his consistent antifeminism, which separates him from Kropotkin and most other anarchists, is well aired in Marshall 1992, 256–57).

It was, however, with the founding of the International Workingmen's Association and in the aftermath of the Paris Commune of 1871 that anarchism came to be recognized in its modern form. The International Workingmen's Association was formally inaugurated in September 1864 in London—though its structure and constitution were not formally adopted until the first congress convened in Geneva in September 1866. It began primarily, as G. D. H. Cole notes, as a "trade union affair," though trade unions were then still illegal in France. Most of the French participants of the 1864 proceedings were not industrial workers but artisans and essentially followers of Proudhon's kind of socialism. Kropotkin describes them as "all mutualists" (KRP, 294; Cole 1954, 2:88). Hence the first International began as a joint affair between British and French trade unionists, with the participation of a number of exiles from other parts of Europe. Chief among these was Karl Marx (1818–1883), who quickly became one of its most important and active leaders. The first International, it is worth noting, was therefore not the creation of Marx, nor was it specifically Marxist at its inception (Morris 1993, 28).

What emerged in both the International and in the Paris Commune were two very different conceptions of socialism and the revolution. One, represented by the Blanquists and the Marxists, followed that of the Jacobin tradition in the French Revolution and advocated a revolution through the establishment of a "socialist republic"—the centralized state. The other conception suggested a free federation of independent communes and was advocated by workers mainly from the Latin countries, who came to be described as anarchists. The General Council of the International, led by Marx, Engels, and some French Blanquist refugees—whom Kropotkin describes as "all pure Jacobinists" (KRP, 165)—eventually used its position to make a coup d'état in the International, and this led to the famous "split" in the movement between the authoritarian socialists and the anarchists. It was in the personality of Michael Bakunin (1814–1876) that the anarchist tendency within the International "found a powerful, gifted and inspired exponent." And as Kropotkin writes, Bakunin soon became the leading spirit among those workers from Spain, France, Italy, and Switzerland (KRP, 294).

Bakunin had become a member of the Geneva section at the International Workingmen's Association in July 1868, for many of his associates were already members—and Kropotkin was to join the association four years later on his visit to Switzerland. The conflict between Marx and Bakunin came to a head at the sham conference of the International held in London in September 1871. This conference affirmed the authority of the General Council (under Marx), declared the necessity for workers in each country to form their own political party, and disparaged anarchism as a political heresy. The Swiss groups of the International, almost all followers of Bakunin, and thus hostile to Marx, immediately organized their own conference at Sonvilier in the Jura. It took place in November 1871 and produced the "Sonvilier Circular," which critiqued the idea of the "conquest of political power by the working class." The split in the International crystallized around the leading figures of Marx and Bakunin, but it was much more than a struggle of personalities. For, as Kropotkin's biographers write, "It was also a clash of two wholly different conceptions of social organisation, two mutually alien philosophies of life" (WA, 111).

These were, respectively: the state socialism of the Marxists, which put an emphasis on authority and acknowledged the need for a revolutionary government—"the dictatorship of the proletariat"—to secure the development of communism; and Bakunin's anarchism, which advocated the abolition of the state and its replacement by a federal society based on free communes and voluntary associations.

Although Kropotkin never actually met Bakunin personally, he saw Bakunin as a key figure in the development of modern anarchism. In countering the efforts of the General Council of the International and the Marxists to turn the entire labor movement into an "elective parliamentary and political movement," Bakunin and his associates were instrumental in the founding of anarchism. It was out of this "rebellion" that modern anarchism subsequently developed (KRP, 155). What was crucial about anarchism, Kropotkin argued, was that "It attacks not only capital, but also the main sources of the power of capitalism, law, authority, and the state" (KRP, 150).

Kropotkin thus felt that it was Bakunin, in a series of powerful pamphlets and letters, who first established the leading principles of modern anarchism, particularly in Bakunin's advocacy of the complete abolition of the state. This implied the repudiation not only of "revolutionary government" but also of the democratic state and all forms of representative government. "All legislation made within the state, even when it issues from the so-called universal suffrage, has to be repudiated because it always has been made with regard to the interests of the privileged classes" (KRP, 165).

Although Bakunin was at heart a communist, he described himself as a "collectivist" anarchist to express a state of affairs in which all the instruments of production are owned in common—collectively—by the working people, through either labor associations or free communes. The form of distribution, whether by labor checks or not, was to be left to the collectives themselves. The anarchists within the first International did not initially refer to themselves as anarchists but rather as "federalists" or as "anti-authoritarian" socialists. But in the aftermath of the Paris Commune, groups of workers by degrees adopted the label of their Marxist opponents and came to describe themselves as "anarchist communists." Among the workers of Spain, France, Italy, and Switzerland, there thus emerged what Kropotkin referred to as the "main current" of anarchism—anarchist communism that viewed anarchism and communism as necessarily complementary and mutually supporting. "The great bulk of anarchist workingmen prefer the anarchist communist ideas which gradually evolved out of the anarchist collectivism of the International Workingmen's Association" (KRP, 297).

Among the better known exponents of this tendency were Élisée Reclus, Jean Grave, Errico Malatesta, Emma Goldman, Sebastian Faure, Emile Pouget, and Johann Most—and, of course, Kropotkin himself, who spent a lifetime lucidly outlining, defending, and promoting the anarchist communist tendency. (For studies of Bakunin and the emergence of anarchist communism as a political movement, see Dolgoff 1973; Pyziur 1955; Morris 1993; and Cahm 1989, 36–75).

Besides anarchist communism, Kropotkin recognized and described three other currents within the anarchist movement as it developed toward the end of the nineteenth century in Europe and the United States—individualist, Christian, and literary anarchism. The first of these, the individualist anarchist, in turn, could be divided into two branches, the mutualists and the "pure" individualists.

The mutualists included, besides the many followers of Proudhon, the disciples of William Thompson in Britain and a contemporary of Proudhon, Josiah Warren (1798–1874). Having originally been a member of Robert Owen's socialist community "New Harmony," which was established in 1825 on the banks of the Wabash River in Indiana, Warren turned against communism, having felt that the failure of the New Harmony Community was due to its collectivism and to its suppression of individual initiative. In the following year, Warren established in Cincinnati a "store" in which goods were exchanged on the principle of time-value and labor-checks.

Such "equity-stores," Kropotkin noted, were still in existence in the 1860s
in the United States. In essence, as James Martin writes, Warren's radical
thought was a "forthright amalgamation of individualism, fear of the state
and economic mutualism" (1970, 4).

The ideas of both Proudhon and Warren, Kropotkin writes, had an
important influence in the United States, "creating quite a school." Of particular importance in the development of this school of economic thought
—individualist anarchism or mutualism (whose history has been lucidly
described by Martin 1970)—were William B. Greene, Stephen Pearl
Andrews, Ezra Heywood, and Lysander Spooner. At the end of the nineteenth century, its most prominent representative was Benjamin Tucker
(1854–1939), who had been a close friend of Warren. At the age of twenty-
one, Tucker had translated Proudhon's famous *What Is Property* (1840) and
in 1881 had founded the radical newspaper *Liberty*. Kropotkin described
Tucker's individualist anarchism as a "combination of [the conceptions], of
Proudhon with those of Herbert Spencer" (KRP, 296). For Tucker, "Anarchism means absolute liberty, nothing more, nothing less," and this meant
liberty in production and exchange, which he described as "the most important of all liberties." Like Proudhon, he was vehemently anticommunist and
described Proudhon as "perhaps the most vigourous hater of communism
that ever lived on this planet" (Tucker 1893, 389–91). Proudhon, of course,
had equated communism with state socialism and authoritarian religious
communities, and he thus came to declare that "communism is oppression
and slavery" a mode of organization that denied the liberty and sovereignty
of the individual and equality (251). Tucker therefore came to argue that
Kropotkin was not an anarchist but a revolutionary communist. Tucker had
the idea the communist anarchists would "force a communal property
system on everyone" and were thus not anarchists (Coughlin et al. 1986,
72). Kropotkin, however, always stressed the autonomy of the individual
and never denied the right of any person to cultivate their own plot of land:
"Of course, when we see a peasant who is in possession of just the amount
of land that he can cultivate, we do not think it reasonable to turn him off
his little farm. He exploits nobody, and nobody would have the right to
interfere with his work. But if he possessed under capitalist law more than
he can cultivate himself, we consider that we must not give him the right
of keeping that soil for himself . . . or of making others cultivate it for his
benefit" (AY, 104).

Kropotkin offered many criticisms of the individualist anarchism
(mutualism) of Proudhon, Warren, and Tucker—in its stress on egoism and

the right of individuals to oppress others if they have the power to do so, in its affirmation of private property, petty commodity production, and the wage system (the market economy) and in justifying the use of violence to enforce agreements and defend private property. Kropotkin acknowledged and applauded Tucker's admirable criticisms of capitalist monopolies and the state and of state socialism, as well as his "vigorous defence of the rights of the individual." But in defending the right to private property Tucker opens up the way "for reconstituting under the heading of 'defence' all the functions of the state" (KRP, 173–74, 296–97). Thus, Kropotkin concludes that the position of the mutualists is "the same as that of Spencer, and of all the so called 'Manchester school' of economists, who also began by a severe criticism of the state and end in its full recognition in order to maintain the property monopolies, of which the state is the necessary stronghold" (KRP, 162).

The debate between the defenders of private property (and so-called market socialists) and anarchist communists still reverberates in many contemporary anarchists journals. (For important studies of Warren, Tucker, and Mutualist forms of anarchism, see Schuster 1932; Martin 1970; Bailie 1971; Coughlin et al. 1986; Peacott 1991.)

Writing around the turn of the century, Kropotkin suggested that the individualist anarchism of the American Proudhonists found little support or sympathy amongst working people, that is, those who possessed no property: "Those who profess it—they are chiefly 'intellectuals'—soon realise that the individualisation they so highly praise is not attainable by individual efforts, and either abandon the ranks of anarchists, and are driven into the liberal individualism of the classical economists, or they retire into a sort of Epicurean a-moralism, or super-man theory, similar to that of Stirner and Nietzsche" (KRP, 297).

These last two writers represent a second form of individualist anarchism, which Kropotkin describes as "pure individualism." The fullest expression of this individualist anarchism was found, Kropotkin wrote, in the remarkable works of Max Stirner (1806–1856), whose book *The Ego and its Own* (1845) was brought into prominence by John Henry Mackay at the end of the century. Stirner was a left-Hegelian metaphysician who proposed a strident philosophy of egoism that repudiated all "abstractions"—freedom, god, truth, humanity—in its affirmation of the unique ego, the corporeal self. Along with Nietzsche, Stirner has been seen as a precursor of existentialism. Although (unlike Marx and Engels) Kropotkin acknowledged the importance of Stirner, and also the beautiful poetic writings of Nietzsche, he was never sympathetic to this form of strident egoism. Affirming Stirner's revolt against the state and all forms of authoritarian communism, Kropotkin wrote: "Reasoning on Hegelian metaphysical lines, Stirner preaches the rehabilitation of the 'I' and the supremacy of the individual; and he comes in this way to advocate complete 'amoralism' (no morality) and an 'association of egoists'" (KRP, 161).

But Kropotkin goes on: "how metaphysical and remote from real life is this 'self-assertion of the individual'; how it runs against the feelings of equality of most of us; and how it brings the would-be 'individualists' dangerously near to those who imagine themselves to represent a superior breed" (KRP, 172).

He points out too the impossibility of the individual to attain any authentic or meaningful development of the human personality in conditions of oppression and economic exploitation. In spite of its usefulness as a critique, and its importance in its advocacy of the full development of the individual person (ego), for Kropotkin, individualist, "life-style" anarchism was a limited expression of anarchism and one that mostly appealed to artistic and literary figures (KRP, 293). (For critical studies of Stirner, see Paterson 1971 and Clark 1976. In spite of calling the state a "cold monster" and having a great appeal to anarchists like Emma Goldman, Nietzsche was more a cultural elitist and nihilist than an anarchist; see Ansell-Pearson 1994.)

A second current of anarchism outlined by Kropotkin was in fact that which found its expression in literary and artistic circles. Kropotkin emphasized that not only had the best of contemporary literature deeply influenced anarchism itself, but hundreds of modern authors were expressing, in varying degrees, anarchist ideas at the end of the nineteenth century. He mentions Ibsen, Whitman, Thoreau, Marc Guyau, Spencer, Herzen, Nietzsche, and Edward Carpenter (KRP, 299).

The third current of anarchism described by Kropotkin was that of Christian anarchism, represented by Leo Tolstoy, although Tolstoy never described himself as an anarchist. Drawing on the teachings of the Christian gospels and following the dictates of reason, Tolstoy used all the powers of his imagination and rich talents to make powerful criticisms of the church, state power, and all the present property laws. Robbers, Tolstoy held, were far less dangerous than a well-organized government. Holding firm to the teachings of Christ, Tolstoy combined Christianity, anarchism, and pacifism; this led to important criticisms of patriotism and militarism as well as to Tolstoy being heralded as an apostle of nonviolent resistance, a political strategy later adopted by Gandhi, who always acknowledged his debt to Tolstoy (David Stephens in Tolstoy 1990, 18). Kropotkin concluded that Tolstoy's religious arguments are so well combined with arguments derived from a dispassionate scrutiny of present evils "that the anarchist portions of his works appeal to the religious and non-religious reader alike" (KRP, 299).

Although Kropotkin sympathetically deals with all forms of anarchism —his work is singularly free of the abusive epithets and rancor that mars much contemporary anarchist writing—Kropotkin makes clear his own allegiance to anarchist communism. This form of anarchism was advocated for the first time at the Jura congress in October 1880, and although Kropotkin was to play an important part in the development of anarchist communism and was later to become its chief exponent and advocate, he was not its originator. The linkage between anarchism and communism seems to have evolved spontaneously and independently among the many "collectivist" followers of Bakunin in Italy, Spain, and Switzerland. People important in the early development of anarchist communism, besides Kropotkin, include Élisée Reclus, Carlo Cafiero, Jean Grave, and Errico Malatesta (Cahm 1989, 51–64).

In his advocacy of anarchist communism, Kropotkin came, like other anarchists members of the first International, to draw a clear distinction between his own conception of socialism and that of the Marxists. We have noted Kropotkin's early critique of "revolutionary government" and the "workers state" of the Marxists, and throughout his life he made strident criticisms of state socialism. He was always hostile to the idea that for the sake of the future personal liberty could be sacrificed on the "altar of the state" (KRP, 130), and he felt that the plans of the state socialists were not only impractical—as it was impossible to foresee everything—but that state socialism would inevitably lead to party dictatorship (KRP, 76). On this issue, he and Bakunin were in close agreement, and with regard to the Russian Revolution, somewhat prescient. Emma Goldman, in fact, refused to describe the Bolshevik regime as "communist," considering it a form of "state capitalism." In Russia, there has never been any attempt "to apply communist principles in any shape or form" (1972, 363). Kropotkin always emphasized that state socialism, by giving the state control and management over the main sources of economic life, besides the powers that the state already possesses, would inevitably create a "new tyranny even more ter-rible than the old one." He therefore concluded that the state organization, "having been the force to which the minorities resorted for establishing and organising their power over the masses, cannot be a force which will serve to destroy these privileges" (KRP, 170–71). State socialism would lead to state capitalism and to new instruments of tyranny and "would only increase the powers of bureaucracy and capitalism" (KRP, 286).

When Kropotkin returned to Russia in 1917, his worst fears were confirmed. In a letter to the Danish art critic Georg Brandes, Kropotkin drew an analogy between the situation as it then existed in Russia (1918) and the Jacobin revolution in France from September 1792 to July 1794. The Bolsheviks "are striving to introduce the socialisation of land, industry, and commerce. Unfortunately, the method by which they seek to establish a communism like Babeuf's in a strongly centralised state makes success absolutely impossible and paralyses the constructive work of the people" (SW, 320).

In a message to the workers of Western Europe (April 1919), Kropotkin reiterated the same views, in acknowledging that the effort to introduce communism in Russia under a strongly centralized party dictatorship had been an abject failure: "This effort was made in the same way as the extremely centralised and Jacobin endeavour of Babeuf. I owe it to you to say frankly that, according to my view, this effort to build a communist republic on the basis of a strongly centralised state communism under the iron law of party dictatorship is bound to end in failure. We learn in Russia how communism cannot be introduced" (KRP, 254).

But though critical of the Bolsheviks, Kropotkin protested with all his strength against any type of armed intervention in Russia by the Allies, fearing this would only lead to reaction and "would bring us back to a chauvinistic monarchy" (SW, 321).

Kropotkin like other anarchists supported the revolution, but not the Bolshevik party, repudiating all forms of state socialism. (For important studies of anarchism see Woodcock 1963; Marshall 1992; Nettlau 1996; Skirda 2002.)

14
ANARCHIST TERRORISM
AND WAR

In the popular mind, wrote the liberal philosopher Bertrand Russell, "an anarchist is a person who throws bombs and commits other outrages, either because he is more or less insane, or because he uses the pretence of extreme political opinions as a cloak for criminal proclivities."

Russell was only too aware that this was a distorted and inadequate view of anarchism, that bomb-throwing and terrorism were far more evident among nationalists than among anarchists, and that for every person killed by an anarchist, "millions are killed by the violence of states" (1966, 38). It is thus of interest that while historians of anarchism highlight the terrorist actions of individual anarchists, historians of nationalist movements tend to ignore terrorist acts completely, though such acts are far more common among radical liberals and nationalists than among anarchists. But there has been a tendency among many historians, especially those focusing on what has been described as the "great age" of anarchism between 1880 and 1914 (Kedward 1971, 5), to portray the anarchist movement as consisting of only two kinds of people: gentle utopian thinkers who were completely out of touch with reality (Kropotkin, Reclus, Malatesta) and deluded and misguided men who, through desperation or insanity, committed senseless acts of violence. A number of scholars have offered such an interpretation of anarchism, and two may be briefly discussed, for they both seem to suggest, rather misleadingly, that Kropotkin was an advocate of individual terrorism.

An "ultra-radical" militant in his youth, Max Nomad (Nacht) was the son of a radical Jewish physician, and between 1902 and 1905, he edited and contributed to anarcho-syndicalist periodicals in Switzerland and Aus-

255

tria. He gave up his anarchism when he became an ardent apostle of the Polish revolutionary Waclaw Machajski (1866–1926) and by 1910 had withdrawn completely into a "sort of splendid isolation," repudiating all forms of radical thought, though during a long exile in the United States he always considered himself a despairing and pessimistic opponent of the status quo (1964, 237). Nomad was the author of numerous books on anarchism, socialism, and political heretics, and he knew personally many anarchists—such as Erich Mühsam, Luigi Bertoni, Errico Malatesta, and Alexander Berkman. His writings give the decided impression that all anarchists and political radicals are either idealist "cranks" and utopians completely out of touch with reality (such as Kropotkin and Malatesta), or terrorists bent on mindless destruction and assassination, or power-hungry apostles of revolution (such as Bakunin, Lenin, and Trotsky). Indeed, his book of reminiscences has the appropriate title *Dreamers, Dynamiters and Demagogues* (1964), and it is significant in hardly mentioning his brother Siegfried Nacht, who wrote many anarcho-syndicalist pamphlets in the early years of the twentieth century.

Although he did not know Kropotkin personally, Nomad in his youth had read Kropotkin's *Memoirs* and, urged by his brother Siegfried, had become a convert to anarchist communism. In 1908 he attended one of Kropotkin's lectures in Paris and was greatly disappointed not only by Kropotkin's relatively small stature—he expected some giant benevolent Santa Claus—but also by the content of Kropotkin's lecture, which seemed to Nomad extremely naïve in its optimism, in suggesting a kind of "romantic impossibilism." He clearly had a great admiration for the anarchist and wrote that Kropotkin "was unlike any revolutionary type found either in literature or in real life. He was not a lower middle-class déclassé motivated by hatred and envy; he was not a member of a minority group that had its legitimate grievances; he was not hungry for power, as were the famous rebels Blanqui, Marx, Bakunin, Lassalle, Lenin and Trotsky" (Nomad 1964, 71).

Nor was there any streak of vanity in Kropotkin's make-up or evidence of frustrations in his emotional life. Nomad even suggests that in moral stature, Kropotkin was superior to both St. Francis and Gandhi (1964, 71–73). But as with Malatesta, Berkman, Nettlau, and Elisée Reclus, Nomad suggests that while Kropotkin's personal life and character and his intellectual standing could only be admired, his politics had to be rejected as utterly naïve and utopian. Anarchism, for Nomad, was little more than a "childish utopia," and anarchists like Kropotkin were the "saints" or "knights errant" of a "cult of an unearthly, faraway ideal" (1964, 193). He thus concluded that Kropotkin was one of the finest examples of an "anarchist romantic"—a naïve, utopian thinker. But he also claimed that Kropotkin, while opposing various forms of revolutionary banditry, "was an ardent advocate of individual terrorism, which at that time was called "propaganda by the deed" (1961, 274–75).

Thus, Nomad made a clear distinction between anarchists who were utopian dreamers (Kropotkin, Reclus, Malatesta) and the "dynamiters," the bomb-throwers, and suggested that Kropotkin, for all his nobility of character and purpose, advocated terrorism.

This same distinction is made by a very different kind of historian, Barbara Tuchman, a liberal scholar who has written many best-selling historical texts. In her study *The Proud Tower* (1966), which is a portrait of the Western world between 1890 and 1914, Tuchman devotes a chapter to anarchism under the title "The Idea and the Deed." Following Nomad, she describes anarchism as "a daydream of desperate romantics" (Nomad 1932, 13) and argues that the anarchist movement consisted of two groups who had very little contact with each other. The first group consisted of the anarchist theorists, men of intellect, earnest and sincere, who loved humanity, men like Kropotkin, Malatesta, Jean Grave, and Reclus. All these men had suffered prison more than once for their anarchist beliefs, but Tuchman refuses to take their ideas seriously, or even to examine them. She dismisses them all as moral idealists who constructed "paper models" of an anarchist millennium, theories that indicated that they were completely out of touch with reality. The soothsayer of the anarchist movement, Élisée Reclus, with a face like that of a Byzantine Christ; the "firebrand," Errico Malatesta, with the look of a "romantic bandit"; the utopian Jean Grave; and the agreeable and saintly Kropotkin—all these men, Tuchman contends, with their childlike faith in humanity, went around with their heads in the clouds, or rather, in "ivory towers" (1966, 63–76).

On the other hand, the second group of anarchists consisted of estranged "little men." Anger, despair, misfortune, or poverty had led such men to be "susceptible" to the anarchist vision of a stateless society. Becoming obsessed with this "ideal," they were driven to acts of terrorism. Deluded and desperate, these men became regicides or assassins, and Tuchman follows the press of the late nineteenth century in depicting this group of anarchists as degenerates, crypto-lunatics, or common felons. Thus anarchism is seen by Tuchman as having a "dual nature," a group of utopian thinkers like Kropotkin who loved humanity and a group of assassins who hated society and indulged in senseless violence for its own sake.

Between the two groups of anarchists, she contended, there was very little real contact (1966, 108; see Joll 1964, 128 for a similar portrait of the two "levels" of anarchism).

Dismissing anarchist theorists like Kropotkin and Reclus as utopian dreamers and romantics, Tuchman's history of anarchism is largely devoted to outlining the lives and activities of a number of assassins or regicides who achieved notoriety at the end of the nineteenth century. These men were proponents of "propaganda by the deed." Among the more well-known of the incidents that occurred during this "era of violence," and which Tuchman graphically recounts, were the following: the Haymarket incident in May 1886, when during a labor demonstration in Chicago, a bomb killed seven policemen; the series of bomb explosions in Paris between 1892 and 1894, which were associated with such anarchist rebels as Ravachol and Vaillant; the assassination of President Carnot of France in June 1894 by the young Italian anarchist Santo Caserio, anxious to avenge the execution of Vaillant; the attempt by Alexander Berkman on the life of Henry Frick, manager of the Carnegie Steel Company, in July 1892, during a period of intense labor unrest at Homestead, Pennsylvania; the assassination in September 1898 of the Empress of Austria by the lonely Italian migrant worker Luigi Luchini; and, finally, the assassination of President McKinley of the United States in September 1901 by a young Polish worker Leon Czolgosz, who had only the most tenuous connections with anarchism. But this last incident led Theodore Roosevelt to famously declare that "Anarchism is a crime against the whole human race and all mankind should band against the anarchist" (Tuchman 1966, 107).

The important point of course is that at the end of the nineteenth century the majority of anarchists were neither intellectuals like Kropotkin and Reclus, nor "deluded" assassins, but rather ordinary working men and women (Quail 1978; Marsh 1981). But Tuchman follows Nomad in declaring that although Kropotkin was an agreeable person, who conventionally dressed like a Victorian gentleman, he was nevertheless "an uncompromising apostle of the necessity of violence" (1966, 71).

Although the idea of "propaganda by the deed" and acts of individual terrorism are an important part of anarchist history, they can in no way be identified with anarchism per se, either as a theory or in terms of anarchist practices. In his well-known but rather unsympathetic history of the anarchist movement, James Joll (1964) highlights a number of important issues relating to the terrorism that was invoked at the end of the nineteenth century. These include: the belief of many state authorities and the police of the existence of an international conspiracy to further social revolution; the use of agent provocateurs by the police to infiltrate and disenable anarchist groups; the fact that anarchist acts of violence were often acts of symbolic revenge against the state for its repressive measures; and that many leading anarchists like Kropotkin, Grave, Goldman, and Johann Most were often accused by the police of inspiring or instigating individual terrorist outrages of which they not only knew nothing but in many cases did not even approve. Johann Most, for example, was arrested after the assassination of McKinley, although he had long opposed all forms of terrorism, and his criticisms of Berkman in an earlier decade had, in fact, actually led to a serious breach with Emma Goldman within the New York anarchist community (Goldman 1931, 1:105). Equally important, it was these terrorist acts that led to the traditional picture of the anarchist as a shady delinquent with a bomb in his pocket and a dagger in his hand (Joll 1964, 124–38).

Although Kropotkin was undoubtedly associated with the development of the revolutionary tactic of "propaganda by the deed"—the idea of revolutionizing the masses by acts of individual terrorism—he never in fact liked the slogan, nor did he use it to describe his own idea of revolutionary action. For Kropotkin, the key idea was that of evoking the "spirit of revolt" among peasants and the working classes, not in engaging in propaganda by means of terrorist acts. Like other anarchists, Kropotkin was, from the very beginning of his revolutionary career, just as much preoccupied with the necessity of revolutionary action as he was with writing theoretical texts and propaganda pamphlets—which is why Tuchman can write of his continuing proclivity for writing "fiery paeans to violence" (Tuchman 1966, 71; Cahm 1989, 92). But such actions implied acts of insurrection and the expropriation of the land and all means of livelihood by the peasants and working people—"the seizing by the people of all social wealth" (WR, 175, 205–22)—not isolated acts of terrorism. He therefore clearly separated individual terrorism from the spontaneous mass action of the people, which he recognized might also involve violence. Kropotkin in fact, as many scholars have indicated, was extremely ambivalent, both toward violence generally and toward specific acts of terrorism. In general, he advocated revolts and insurrections in order to invoke a social revolution, and he hoped that such a revolution would involve as little violence as possible. As he wrote in his *Memoirs*: "The question is . . . not so much how to avoid revolutions, as to how to attain the greatest results with the most limited amount of civil war, the smallest number of victims, and a minimum of mutual embitterment" (MR, 291).

When Kropotkin was a member of the Chaikovsky Circle—several members of this circle (Sergei Kravchinsky [Stepniak] and Sophie Perovskaya) were later to commit acts of terrorism—he drafted a manifesto outlining the idea of a future socialist society and the political strategies he thought ought to be followed by the revolutionary circle. The manifesto was drafted in November 1873, only two months before Kropotkin's own arrest and imprisonment. Central to Kropotkin's vision was that populist agitators should live among and identify with the struggles of the peasants and urban workers and engage in propaganda and activities that were conducive to the radical social transformation of Russian society. The realization of the socialist ideal could only occur, he felt, by means of a *social* revolution, and though the revolutionary "populist" could engage in educational activities and in various forms of propaganda—in critiquing the existing state tyranny and in fostering insurrections—Kropotkin was convinced that no revolution was possible if the need for such a revolution was not experienced by the people themselves. Thus, the social transformation of Russian society, Kropotkin argued, could only come about by a widespread revolt of the peasants and urban workers themselves, and this would entail the "expropriation" of all lands, factories, houses, and capital by the working people and the establishment of various forms of self-management, such as the radicalizing of the village assembly, mir. Kropotkin recognized that such struggles and expropriations would inevitably involve violence, inflicted by the nobility and the Tsarist state, and "rivers of blood" might be spilled before the "social upheaval" that was necessary had been accomplished (SW, 80–114). But in this manifesto. Kropotkin did not advocate any form of individual terrorism, but rather he put his faith in the revolts of the peasantry and the urban workers.

The concept of "propaganda by the deed" has been traced back to the Italian revolutionary socialist Carlo Piscane (1818–1857), who perished in 1857 while engaged in an armed confrontation with the Bourbon state (Woodcock 1963, 308). But the person who was most closely associated with the slogan "propaganda by the deed" and its leading exponent was the French socialist Paul Brousse (1844–1912). Originally an anarchist and an ardent apostle of Bakunin, Brousse eventually abandoned anarchism and became a reformist socialist—under the brand of "possibilism" (for a useful study of Brousse, see Stafford 1971). In August 1877 Brousse wrote an article in *The Bulletin of the Jura Federation* titled "La Propaganda par le fait" ("propaganda by the deed"), in which he essentially identified the deed with individual acts of terrorism. The idea is on the march and "we must seek to inaugurate the propaganda by the deed. Through a royal breast is the way to open the road to revolution!" (quoted in Tuchman 1966, 71). At that period, Kropotkin was also fervent on the need for revolutionary violence, and in one of the most famous articles in the journal *Le Révolté* (December 1880), Kropotkin called for continual incitement and propaganda by "speech and written word, by dagger, gun and dynamite" (Graur 1997, 51). But Kropotkin always dissociated himself from Brousse's concept of "propaganda by the deed," and as Tuchman admits, he never actually recommended individual assassinations or terrorist acts. His biographer Martin Miller, emphasizing that the theory and practice of "propaganda by the deed" became an extremely sensitive issue for Kropotkin, suggests that it is doubtful if Kropotkin at this time understood by "deed" the kind of terrorist acts that were later associated with anarchists like Ravachol, and which Brousse clearly advocated. Kropotkin was uncompromisingly revolutionary, but the means for revolution were twofold: theoretical propaganda, and insurrectionary action and revolts. By "deed" Kropotkin therefore meant awakening the popular spirit of revolt for the expropriation of land and property, and revolutionary action was always conceived as collective. Kropotkin "urged the necessity of encouraging insurrectionary outbreaks rather than individual revolutionary acts, to build up the popular spirit of revolt for the revolution itself" (Cahn 1989, 113).

In his famous pamphlet *The Spirit of Revolt* (1881), Kropotkin had written—with the history of the French Revolution always in his mind—that the theoretical propaganda for the revolution would necessarily be translated into deeds—the acts of illegal protest and revolt, and such acts in a few days "does more than the propaganda of thousands of leaflets." Kropotkin writes of the "spirit of revolt"—of agitation, of insurrection, of songs of protest, of popular uprisings, and the need to keep this spirit alive "to propagate and formulate discontent, to excite hatred against the exploiters, to ridicule governments and expose their weakness, and above all and always to re-awaken audacity, the spirit of revolt" (WR, 186). Kropotkin was therefore advocating at this period not "propaganda by the deed" through isolated acts of terrorism, but the evocation of the "spirit of revolt" that would lead, as in the French Revolution, to popular uprisings and revolutionary actions. These, in turn, would eventually result in a social revolution and the transformation of social life. Equating the "acts of revolt" that Kropotkin emphasized with individual terrorist acts, Tuchman disdainfully notes that the acts Kropotkin so loftily called for on paper were not actually performed by him (1996, 72). But in fact, as Brousse had been jailed in 1879 and the only anarchist newspaper, *L'Avant Garde*, had been suppressed, even the publication of the new journal *Le Révolté* was itself, as Cahm writes, "an act of revolt" (1989, 118). She emphasizes that Kropotkin was therefore opposed to both the parliamentary road to socialism that came to be adopted by Brousse and Andrea Costa (1851–1910), both of whom were close friends of Bakunin and anarchists in their early days, and to propaganda by means of terrorism. Kropotkin was always insistent, as Cahm puts it, "in the need for a broad based and systematic work of propaganda and agitation for popular expropriation among the masses" (1989, 129).

In March 1881, the Russian tsar, Alexander II, was assassinated by a group of revolutionaries who went under the name of Narodnaya Volya, the People's Will. This had a dramatic effect on Kropotkin, and in a special issue of *Le Révolté*, he wrote that the assassination of the tsar had struck a mortal blow to the tsarist autocracy. The destruction of the tsarist system had begun, and "no one can say when and where this destruction will end." And he went on to suggest that the events of March "is an immense step towards the next revolution in Russia, and those who have done it will watch out to see that the blood of the martyrs is not to be shed in vain" ("Commune of Paris," 1881; Cahm 1889, 142).

Kropotkin defended the actions of the People's Will against the bourgeois press, who tended to depict the tsar as the benevolent liberator of the serfs, and the populists as evil assassins. He clearly expressed his sympathies with the Russian populists and expressed indignation at their executions, even though he was critical of their neglect of the revolutionary role of the masses and their narrow focus on political terrorism. Kropotkin held Alexander II responsible for numerous deaths and called him the "worst enemy" of the Russian people (Cahm 1989, 141–43; MK, 151–53).

Kropotkin's explicit support and defense of the Narodniks in Russia, and his wider revolutionary activities, led to his deportation from Switzerland at the end of August 1881.

Shortly after the assassination of the tsar, Kropotkin attended, in July 1881, the international anarchist congress in London. It was attended by forty-five delegates, including Louise Michel, Malatesta, Chaikovsky, and Joseph Lane, as well as by a sinister agent provocateur and spy of the French police, one Serreaux, who continually expressed a "near hysterical obsession with violence" (Cahm 1989, 152). The concept of "propaganda by the deed" figured prominently in the debates of the congress, and there were discussions relating to the making of bombs, and, with Malatesta, the advocacy of conspiratorial groups to further the revolution. A draft declaration, adopted by the congress, stressed the importance of revolutionary insurrections and propaganda by the deed and the need to utilize the technical and chemical sciences for revolutionary purposes. The congress was not a great success, and Kropotkin was somewhat perturbed at the narrow preoccupation with conspiratorial methods, bomb-throwing, and propaganda by the deed. Cahm suggests that Kropotkin's articles on the "spirit of revolt," written prior to the congress, were undoubtedly used to voice his opposition to this obsession with bombs (Cahm 1989, 153–60).

Nevertheless, as Miller emphasizes, Kropotkin's attitude to terrorism was always highly ambiguous. Although normally depicted as a person of high moral integrity who deplored assassinations and bombings, especially as a political strategy, Kropotkin, nonetheless, frequently accepted them, acknowledging that they were often the desperate acts of men reacting to tyranny, or to unbearable social conditions. Thus, he sympathized with the despair that drove workers like Luigi Lucheni to stab the hapless Empress of Austria in September 1898, simply because she was a member of the wealthy classes and cared little for the poor. As he wrote in a letter to his friend George Brandes, the Danish literary critic, "Individuals are not to blame; they are driven mad by horrible conditions" (SW, 23).

On the other hand, Kropotkin always repudiated indiscriminate violence, and unlike Reclus, never applauded the assassin Ravachol. In a speech in London in March 1893, Kropotkin stressed that he saw anarchism as the only political grouping which respected human life and loudly insisted upon the abolition of capital punishment and prisons, and therefore despaired at the recourse to terrorism over other forms of revolutionary tactics (Cahm 1989, 208).

Thus, Kropotkin always endeavored to make a clear distinction between individual acts of terrorism and the "spirit of revolt," the insurrections and uprising that were conducive to a social revolution. He therefore condemned those who interpreted the tactic "propaganda by the deed" as implying a licence to murder, and he wrote that "a structure based on centuries of history cannot be destroyed by a few kilos of explosives" (*La Révolte*, March 1894, quoted in MK, 174).

Despite his own dislike for violence, and his stress on the uselessness of individual terrorism in achieving a social revolution—for only people could make the social revolution—Kropotkin was able to justify certain acts of terrorism if he felt that these were provoked by state persecution or oppressive conditions. But like the Marxists, Kropotkin always repudiated terrorism as a political strategy, for such actions forced anarchism into conspiratorial channels, divorcing it from the people, as well as invoking state repression. Fundamentally, for Kropotkin, "Revolutions are not made by heroic acts. Revolution is above all a popular movement" (*La Révolte*, April 1892, quoted in Graur 1997, 54; WA, 357; MK, 174–75).

Kropotkin expressed the same ambivalence toward war as he did for individual acts of terrorism.

Although Kropotkin was never a pacifist, he was vehemently opposed to war, both emotionally and ideologically. His classic essay on war, *La Guerre* (1882), argues that the wars at the end of the nineteenth century were essentially concerned with economic domination—fought for the benefit of the barons of high finance and industry. They were instigated to impose customs and tariff on neighbors, to open up new markets, and to exploit people at the periphery of capitalism. War is seen as the logical extension of the violence and greed of capitalism, and, for Kropotkin, the state, war, and capitalism are intrinsically linked (WR, 64–66). Kropotkin was vigorously against the Franco-Russian alliance, fearing this would lead to the restoration of the French monarch, and he opposed both the Anglo-Boer war and the war between Japan and Russia. He was appalled at the "jingoism" that the Anglo-Boer war evoked and urged British workers to refuse to obey the government and to oppose colonialism. He equally refused to take sides in the Russo-Japanese war. This was not, he felt, a defensive war, but an imperialist war that was destructive to the people in both countries (MK, 221–22). But Kropotkin saw the First World War quite differently, and he strongly advocated supporting the Allies against Germany. His motives for this have been succinctly expressed by Avrich:

> His action was prompted mainly by the fear that German militarism and authoritarianism might prove fatal to social progress in France, the revered land of the great revolution and the Paris commune. Germany, with its political and economic centralisation and its Junker spirit of regimentation, epitomised everything Kropotkin detested. As the bulwark of Statism, it blocked Europe's path to the libertarian society of his dreams. He was unshakeably convinced that the Kaiser had launched the war with the aim of dominating the continent. (1988, 69)

Kropotkin, it seems, had long held such views. More than a decade before (in 1899), he had written a series of articles on "Caesarism"—provoked by the Dreyfus affair in Paris. In these articles, he expressed his extreme antipathy toward the German state, and he considered the defeat of

France in 1870–71 as "the triumph of militarism in Europe, of military and political despotism, and at the same time the worship of the state, of authority and state socialism, which is in reality nothing but state capitalism" (WA, 289). He seemed to equate both German culture and philosophy and Marxism with the German state. Like many Russian revolutionaries, Herzen and Bakunin included, Kropotkin detested all things German, for there had been a long and close association between the Romanov dynasty and Prussian militarism. Though Herzen had a Prussian mother and Bakunin was an eager disciple of Hegel in his early years, both were, in sentiment, anti-German. But Kropotkin disliked Hegelian metaphysics and had a fervent and passionate interest in the French Revolution and in the French socialist tradition—and a love of France that was akin to an "adoptive patriotism" (WA, 374). There was in fact a logic and a constancy in his anti-German sentiments and his lifelong admiration for France. Kropotkin sincerely believed that the German people posed a real threat to the progress of socialism in Europe, and thus he allowed himself to indulge in the "most reckless jingoism" (Purchase 1996, 33).

All this was most distressing for his anarchist friends and comrades. Although there is some truth in the notion that German imperialism and militarism were to some extent responsible for the war and the international debacle, Kropotkin's tendency to equate peoples with the state and to think in "nationalist" terms greatly upset his comrades. Many like Errico Malatesta and Emma Goldman were close friends and devotees. They could hardly believe that Kropotkin would abandon his internationalist outlook and his anarchist principles, especially as Kropotkin had long been advocating an antimilitarist position. But the anarchist historian Max Nettlau recorded that Kropotkin's attitude in 1914 did not surprise him, since Kropotkin "could not have acted otherwise." Both Nettlau and Gustav Landauer suggested that although Kropotkin in his scientific writings consulted and acknowledged German sources with interest and accuracy, he was in fact largely ignorant about German politics and cultural life (1992, 388).

Having then, at the outbreak of the war, declared himself an enthusiastic supporter of the Entente, Kropotkin wrote articles and letters urging his comrades and friends to take a stand against German militarism. In September 1914, he wrote a letter to Jean Grave in which he asked "what world of illusions do you inhabit to talk of peace" and in the most belligerent fashion wrote of the Germans as "savage hordes," an "army of Huns" who were about to trample humanity underfoot (MK, 225). Kropotkin urged the production of cannons, expressed his admiration for the worst Allied statesmen and generals, and treated as cowards those anarchists who refused to support the war effort. He regretted that his age and poor health prevented him from fighting the Germans. Kropotkin forgot completely that he was an anarchist and an internationalist, and he forgot too, that only a short time before (1913) he had written about the impending capitalist war. His close friend Malatesta thought Kropotkin a "truly pathological case" and described his estrangement from Kropotkin on this issue as "one of the saddest, most painful moments of my life" (Malatesta 1965, 260). Kropotkin could only think of defending his beloved France and the revolutionary tradition he identified with it—against German aggression, fearing that the German army would impose on Europe a century of militarism. Kropotkin was not alone in supporting the war, for Jean Grave, Varlaan Cherkezov, Charles Malato, as well as the veteran social democrat Georgi Plekhanov all sided with the Allies. But the majority of anarchists opposed the war and affirmed the principles of anarchism. Marxists lost no opportunity to deride Kropotkin for his chauvinism, Trotsky noting that Kropotkin "who had a weakness ever since youth for the Narodniks, made use of the war to disavow everything he had been teaching for almost half a century" (1980, 1:230).

Kropotkin's anti-German prejudices and prowar stand ran completely counter to his own anarchist principles, and it led to his estrangement from many of his closest comrades and friends and an end to his association with the journal *Freedom*. Malatesta urged Kropotkin to repudiate his prowar position and to reaffirm his own anarchist principles—both of these were something the Kropotkin was never able to do (WA, 382).

15
ANARCHISM AND
ANARCHO-SYNDICALISM

During what Kropotkin described as the "disturbed years" between 1890 and 1895, ferocious prosecutions were directed against anarchists throughout Europe. Middle-class sympathizers, frightened by the violence, left the anarchist ranks, and the libertarian journal *Commonweal* ceased publication. At the same time, the labor movement increasingly turned to what Kropotkin felt to be the "quagmire" of parliamentary politics. Yet as Kropotkin recalled when *Freedom* celebrated its twenty-first anniversary with a special issue (1907), it was during this period also that a new element was introduced—or rather developed—within the anarchist movement. This was the emergence of anarcho-syndicalism, the introduction of anarchist ideas and propaganda into the trade-union movement.

Kropotkin emphasized that anarcho-syndicalism was not a new phenomenon but had been a favorite mode of action among the "Bakunist" or federalist section of the International Workingmen's Association in the 1870s (AY, 119). Thus, revolutionary syndicalism did not begin in France at the turn of the century, as William Foster suggests (1990, 33), but much earlier—among the working class associates and followers of Bakunin in Switzerland, Italy, and Spain during an earlier decade. Indeed, there is a sense, as Rudolf Rocker suggested in his classic study of anarcho-syndicalism, that Bakunin is the "creator of the modern anarchist movement," as well as of its anarcho-syndicalist tendency (1989, 18). Kropotkin was always to insist that the revolutionary syndicalism that developed in France after the so-called terrorist phase of anarchism was not a separate movement but part of a wider revival of working-class protest, and it had its origins in the "Bakunist" faction within the First International: "syndicalism is nothing other than the rebirth of the International—federalist, worker, Latin" (letter to N. A. Rubakin, March 1913, quoted in MK, 176).

Anarcho-syndicalism is thus seen by Kropotkin as a direct continuation of those libertarian socialist aspirations that took shape within the bosom of the First International. Its leading advocates at the turn of the century were: Fernand Pelloutier, Tom Mann, Emile Pouget, James Guillaume, and Rudolf Rocker. The last named was later to emerge as one of the main theoreticians of anarcho-syndicalism. Many of these men were close associates or friends of Kropotkin, although Kropotkin, like Malatesta, was always to maintain a critical distance from revolutionary syndicalism.

The essential tenets of anarcho-syndicalism were the following:

It repudiated entirely the anarchist tactic of "propaganda by the deed," direct acts of violence against the bourgeois state by means of assassination or terrorism.

It also critiqued and rejected the parliamentary road to socialism, the reformist path that had come to be advocated in France by Jules Guesde and Paul Brousse. Participation in parliamentary politics was seen as a betrayal of socialist principles and a failure to recognize the true nature of the modern state—which was to defend social privilege and mass economic exploitation. As Rocker put it, "who fails to recognize this function of the state does not understand the real nature of the present social order at all" (1989, 30).

Finally, anarcho-syndicalism, like the earlier anarchist followers of Bakunin, repudiated entirely the Marxist concept of the "dictatorship of the proletariat" by means of a revolutionary party. A seizure of power by a revolutionary minority on behalf of the working class would only lead, as Bakunin had suggested, to the increasing concentration of power, and, eventually, to a form of bureaucratic state capitalism (Rocker 1989, 85; Morris 1993, 125–35).

All these tenets were consonant with Kropotkin's own anarchist communism. Indeed, many have seen Kropotkin as the "heir" to Bakunin's anarchism, and Kropotkin came to have an important influence on the development of anarcho-syndicalism. But more than Kropotkin, the anarcho-syndicalists put a fundamental emphasis on the class struggle and on the trade-union movement—the syndicates—as the means, or as the key factor, in the revolutionary transformation of society and as the foundation of the future socialist society. Trade unions were seen by the anarcho-syndicalists as having a dual purpose: defending the rights of workers in the present society with regard to safeguarding and enhancing living standards and general well-being, and providing the framework whereby in a future society, social life and production would be organized through industries under workers' control, and self-management. As Rocker put it: "According to the syndicalist view, the trade union, the syndicate, is the unified organization of labour and has for its purpose the defence of the interests of the producers within existing society and the preparing for and the practical carrying out of the reconstruction of social life after the pattern of socialism" (1989, 86; Maximoff 1985).

The trade union was therefore seen not as a mere transitory phenomenon but as the "germ" or "nuclei" of the future socialist economy. The anarcho-syndicalists thus had a thoroughly "working class conception" of socialism and were essentially "monistic" in their viewpoint, stressing the fundamental importance of trade-unions and emphasizing workers' control (Ostergaard 1997, 37–38). Their vision of the future society, however, was almost identical to that of Kropotkin, although socialists like Pelloutier were somewhat vague as to the exact structure of this society. But essentially the guiding principles were discernible: the control by the workers themselves of the productive process; the common ownership of land, raw materials, and the means of production; the rational organization of production for the common good; the organization of society on the basis of voluntary associations and federal principles; and the distribution of resources according to need. Rocker was explicit that anarcho-syndicalism should base its theoretical assumptions on the teaching of libertarian socialism (or anarchism) and administer itself according to the motto that Kropotkin constantly evoked: "From everyone according to his abilities, to everyone according to his needs" (Jennings 1990, 23; Graur 1997, 149).

The anarcho-syndicalists therefore closely followed the dictum of the First International—which Kropotkin continually emphasized—that the emancipation of the working class was the task of the working people themselves, that is, the emphasis was on self-emancipation, and the social revolution did not imply simply a political revolution but the socio-economic transformation of society. This did not mean, of course, that the anarcho-syndicalists saw themselves as having no interest in political struggles, for as Rocker wrote, "Every event that affects the life of a community is of a political nature" (1989, 115), but rather they repudiated the political strategies of both the Marxists and the parliamentary socialists.

The anarcho-syndicalists followed Kropotkin and other anarchist communists in vehemently attacking the capitalist economic order, both its monopoly of property and its associated wage-system, which they continually referred to as "wage slavery." In the classic pamphlet on syndicalism, William Z. Foster was to describe the wage system as "the most brazen and gigantic robbery ever perpetrated since this world began," and in emphasizing the class struggle, he likened the capitalists and the controllers of industry to arrant "thieves" (Ford and Foster 1990, 3). The anarcho-syndicalists therefore came to make a distinction between *political action*, which they identified with the strategies of the Marxists and the Socialist parties, who endeavored to seek control of the state in order to expropriate the capitalists, and *direct action*, which was unmediated. Revolutionary syndicalists like Foster tended, rather misleadingly, to equate socialism with state socialism and to think of anarchism as a purely individualist doctrine, one that proposed only an intellectual revolution, whereas, in contrast, "syndicalism is striving for an economic revolution" (Ford and Foster 1990, 30–31). This analysis tends to leave out the kind of libertarian socialism advocated not only by Kropotkin but also by many other anarchists, as well as by such antiparliamentarian socialists as William Morris. But importantly, Ford and Foster emphasize that the syndicalist is a "radical anti-patriot" repudiating both nationalism and militarism, as well as statism (1990, 28–29).

By direct action the anarcho-syndicalists want "every method of immediate warfare by the workers against their economic and political oppressors. Among these the outstanding are: the strike, in all its gradations from the simple wage struggle to the general strike; the boycott; sabotage in its countless forms; anti-militarist propaganda; and in peculiarly critical cases . . . armed resistance of the people for the protection of life and liberty" (Rocker 1989, 116).

The "general strike," involving all the key industries, was of particular importance to the anarcho-syndicalists, for it was seen as the key tactic in undermining capitalism and in thus initiating the radical transformation of the social order. It was conceived as the first stage in a social revolution and as fulfilling the same role as peasant uprisings in an earlier period (116).

These, in brief, are the main features of anarcho-syndicalism or revolutionary syndicalism as it emerged at the end of the nineteenth century, and which were expressed in such movements as Confederation Generale du Travail in France (founded in 1895), the Industrial Workers of the World in the United States (founded in 1905), and the Industrial Syndicalist Education League in Britain (founded by Guy Bowman and Tom Mann in 1910). (For useful studies of revolutionary syndicalism, see Dubofsky 1969; G. Brown 1977; Jennings 1990; Van Der Linden and Thorpe 1990.)

A revolution by the spontaneous actions of the peasants and working people was always a central feature, as Cahm suggests, of European anarchist communism. Kropotkin therefore was always somewhat ambivalent toward the trade-union movement. He clearly recognized its potential for mobilizing the working classes and defending their interests (on this score Tuchman woefully misunderstands Kropotkin's anarchism), but Kropotkin also recognized the tendency of trade unions to be reformist in their aims and authoritarian in their organization (1989, 213). As early as 1877, Kropotkin wrote a critical note on the British trade union movement, denouncing the tendency of these unions, prompted by the working-class MP Ramsay MacDonald, to compromise or collude with the capitalist system. Kropotkin noted how the trade unions "are now preaching worker's candidatures to remedy the evil (of capitalism). They are preaching conciliation with the employers, an alliance with the clergy; arbitration on questions of wages (always to reduce them, without useless strikes) . . . these are the salutary methods they recommend" (Cahm 1989, 238).

Kropotkin was therefore highly skeptical of the British trade-union movement and especially critical of its involvement in parliamentary politics. These trade unions, he wrote, tend to respect private property and are not concerned with the abolition of the employers or the capitalist mode of production, but rather they accept the order of things as they stand and concern themselves only with ameliorating existing working conditions. An organization "which is concerned with nothing but hours of work and wages without ever asking if it would not be better to abolish the wage system and individual property completely"—such an organization inevitably tends to follow the sterile path of parliamentary politics (*Bulletin of the Jura Federation* [July 1877], quoted in Cahm 1989, 240–41). Kropotkin, of course, was not opposed to workers fighting for better working conditions by direct action, but he was more concerned to radicalize the workers' struggles, and through a social revolution, to free labor completely from the yoke of capitalism. Kropotkin regarded strikes and various forms of labor protest positively, and he regarded them as a starting point for revolutionary organization. What he opposed was the linking of the trade union movement to Socialist parties and parliamentary politics. An article in Kropotkin's paper *Le Révolté* therefore repudiated all efforts to involve the worker's movement in parliamentary elections. "We are to organize the worker's forces—not to make them into a fourth party in parliament, but to turn them into a formidable machine for struggle against capitalism. We have to group all trades under the single aim 'War against capitalist exploitation!' And we have to pursue this war continually each day, by the strike, by agitation, and by all revolutionary methods" (Cahm 1989, 250).

If the trade union movement abandoned its revolutionary ethos and tactics and turned instead to parliamentary politics, it would inevitably end up, Kropotkin contended, simply as a bureaucratic organization, providing auxiliary support for bourgeois rule. Later that year (1881), Kropotkin wrote in another article on labor organization: "Since the enemy on whom we declare war is capital, it is against capital that we have to direct our efforts, without allowing ourselves to be distracted from our aim by the sham agitation of political parties. Since the great struggle for which we prepare ourselves, is an essentially *economic* struggle, it is on the economic ground that our agitation has to take place" (*Le Révolté* [December 1881], quoted in Cahm 1989, 255; Kropotkin's italics).

In placing a crucial emphasis on the "struggle against capital," that is, on the class struggle and on the abolition of the "wage system," and in conceiving the revolution as implying a "deep, thorough, economic transformation" (AY, 42), Kropotkin and the anarcho-syndicalists shared a common viewpoint. Equally important for Kropotkin was the fact that all strike action tends to involve direct and sometimes violent confrontation with the police; and thanks to such intervention "every rebel against the factory becomes a rebel against the state" (*Le Révolté* [December 1881], quoted in Cahm 1989, 256).

But whereas the anarcho-syndicalist placed a fundamental emphasis on the syndicalist organization and on workers' control in the future socialist society, Kropotkin always expressed a much broader vision. On his return from the United States in January 1898, Kropotkin thus wrote of three great movements or currents of ideas that, at a time of revolutionary crisis, would enable working people to carry through the complete transformation of the social economy. These were "the federation of *syndicates* which would take the factories and the task of production into their hands; the *co-operatives*, which would take care of distribution; and the *commune*, which would take the land, the houses and so on, for the needs of its members" (Rocker 1989, 105, my italics; Nettlau 1996, 277).

In contrast to the anarcho-syndicalists, Kropotkin thus put equal emphasis on the local commune. At the congress of the Jura Federation in Frubourg in August 1878, Kropotkin made therefore the following statement: "It is necessarily under the banner of the independence of the municipal and agricultural communes that the next revolutions will be made. It is also in the independent communes that socialist tendencies are inevitably going to appear. It is there that the first outlines of the new society will be sketched out, on the basis of collectivism" (*L'Avant Garde* [August 1878], quoted in Cahm 1989, 247).

The anarchist historian Max Nettlau has suggested that Kropotkin's syndicalist sympathies have tended to be overexaggerated, and Kropotkin was a "true anarchist." This implied a sympathetic attitude toward any progress "in the direction of liberty (voluntary association), solidarity (communist co-operation) and the creation of revolutionary forces (the proletariat organizing and rebelling)" (1996, 277).

But Kropotkin, as an anarchist communist, tended to envisage the local commune, not the trade union, as the key unit of organization, and he sought to replace the present bourgeois order with a system of decentralized, cooperative communes—the free commune (Hardy 1979, 166). The distinction between anarcho-syndicalism and anarchist communism is, however, more a matter of emphasis rather than a difference in kind, for both affirm the importance of class struggle and workers' control of the productive associations. All the anarcho-syndicalists of a later generation—Maximoff, Dolgoff, Meltzer—acknowledged the influence of both Bakunin and Kropotkin in their political struggles and in their conceptions of anarchism (Dolgoff 1986; Maximoff 1985; Christie and Meltzer 1970).

Not surprisingly, at the time of the London dock strike in 1889 Kropotkin threw his full support behind the striking dockers:

> The strike was a wonderful lesson in many respects. It demonstrated to us the practical possibility of a general strike. Once the life of the port of London had been paralysed, the strike spread wider and wider, bringing all sorts of industries to a standstill, and threatening to paralyse the whole life of the five millions of Londoners.
>
> Another lesson of this strike was—in showing the powers of the working men for organising the supply and distribution of food for a large population of strikers. The demonstration was quite conclusive. (AY, 116–17, WA, 232–33)

But for Kropotkin, the dock strike had another important lesson, namely, it demonstrated how too easily socialists and union officials become involved in parliamentary politics. For both John Burns and Ben Tillett, who were brought into prominence by the strike, were later to become members of the British parliament. This alliance between the trade unions and the political parties signaled, for Kropotkin, the beginning of the decay of the whole socialist movement in Britain (AY, 117).

Kropotkin always emphasized the importance of class struggle and of strike action, but he stressed also the need for the workers to "take possession" of the factories and the land and not to be lulled into simply opting for small reforms regarding wages or hours within the capitalist system, or to be sidetracked into parliamentary politics. In a letter to Luigi Bertoni (1872–1947), Kropotkin wrote that: "The syndicate is absolutely necessary. It is the only form of worker's association which allows the direct struggle against capital to be carried on without a plunge into parliamentarianism" (March 1914; Nettlau 1996, 280).

But all too often syndicalism—trade-union activity—was linked to political action and party politics, and thus for Kropotkin there was always the need for another element "which Malatesta speaks of and which Bakunin always professed"—namely, an anarchist alliance (Nettlau 1996, 280–81).

Syndicalism was therefore, for Kropotkin, only one aspect or tendency in the revolutionary struggle for a socialist society. Ultimately, as Martin Miller writes, Kropotkin tended to mistrust both the French syndicates and the British trade unions in that they tended to develop into bureaucratic institutions and to adopt reformist strategies within the present capitalist system rather than seeking a radical transformation of society (MK, 177).

Kropotkin did not attend the International Anarchist Congress of 1907 in Amsterdam, at which the famous debate took place between the syndicalist Pierre Monatte (1881–1960) and Kropotkin's close friend Errico Malatesta. Monatte, despairing of the parliamentary socialism of Guesde and Jaures and suggesting that "philosophy is not enough to make a revolution," made a strident and impassioned plea for revolutionary syndicalism. He stressed that the proletariat, organized into syndicates as "resistance societies," could be the agents of a social revolution, and syndicalism was "sufficient unto itself." By means of direct action—strikes, boycotts, and sabotage—the working classes would strike at the heart of capitalism and thus achieve their own emancipation by their own efforts. Monatte emphasized the importance of autonomy and federalism in the organizational structure of the Confederation Generale du Travail, and he called on anarchists to join forces with the syndicalists.

In his well-known reply, Malatesta repudiated the idea that syndicalism was sufficient unto itself. He affirmed that he was no "intellectual anarchist" who, since the collapse of the First International, had retreated into the "ivory tower" of theoretical speculation. On the contrary, he had always been involved in working-class politics. Malatesta therefore, like Kropotkin, fervently acclaimed the necessity of anarchists to actively participate in the working-class movement, to engage in anarchist propaganda, and to support the workers' struggles against capitalism and the state. But such struggles are a means to an end, he suggested, and while a general strike is important in initiating a social revolution, to see in the strike "a panacea for all ills" is "pure utopia." While in the past, Malatesta contended, he deplored the fact that his anarchist comrades had isolated themselves from the working-class movement, now they were going to the opposite extreme and becoming lost in a syndicalist movement that was easily prone to reformism and bureaucratic organization. Working-class organization, strikes, direct action, sabotage, armed insurrections, all these, Malatesta pleaded, are only a *means*. The end is anarchy (Woodcock 1977, 213–25).

Kropotkin would undoubtedly—as he indicated many times—have sided with Malatesta.

It would be rather naïve, as Nettlau wrote, to seek or create an image of Kropotkin as an anarcho-syndicalist (1996, 249), in that he did not conceive of trade unions as the "embryo" of a future society and always crucially emphasized the importance of agriculture and agrarian communes. And, as we have noted, he was skeptical of trade unions, given their tendency to become bureaucratic organizations and to be content with reformist aims. But this did not prevent Kropotkin when he was almost seventy years old from writing a warm preface to Emile Pataud and Emile Pouget's *How We Shall Bring About a Revolution*, first published in 1909. This classic utopian text was written by two leading revolutionary syndicalists—indeed, Pouget (1860–1931), along with Pelloutier and Rocker, was one of the leading figures in the development of anarcho-syndicalism. The book describes in semifictional form how working people might transform society through a social revolution in which a general strike figures prominently, and peasants take possession of the land through direct action. A central feature of the new society is the workers' control of production and the organization of social life through cooperative societies and communal services. It is a utopian text along the same lines as William Morris's *News from Nowhere* (1888).

In his preface, Kropotkin notes that all political theorists, and even men of action like Napoleon, have implicitly their own utopian ideals. In *The Conquest of Bread*, he had attempted to outline his own "communal utopia." Pataud and Pouget, in contrast, present a "syndicalist utopia":

> They show us how the trade unions, groups formed for combat against capital, could transform themselves, in a time of revolution, into groups for production. . . .
> They tell, in a very attractive way, how the groups, industrial, com-

munal and co-operative, could undertake the functions which up to the present have been appropriated by the state. (Pataud and Pouget 1990, xxxi–xxxvi)

Kropotkin also commends the spirit of the book—of its tolerance for diverse tendencies, even though different from those of the authors. He applauds the fundamental emphasis that is placed in the book on the "spirit of revolt" and on "propaganda by example"—not on parliamentary politics, nor on a reign of terror executed by revolutionary Jacobins (read: Marxists)—but on people creating a revolution that will cut down the "state and capitalist forest" (Pataud and Pouget 1990, xxxi–xxxvi).

Around the turn of the century, four distinct tendencies or types of anarchism were clearly evident. First, there were the individualist anarchists who adhered to the concept of private property or individual proprietorship and emphasized the supreme sovereignty of the individual. As followers of either Stirner's egoism or Proudhon's mutualism, they tended to repudiate all forms of communism and to equate socialism with state socialism. At extremes even "society"—social life—was deemed suspect, as it restricted the absolute sovereignty or autonomy of the individual. For the mutualist, private "property" was the focus of activity, whether in the form of a farm, trade or business; for the ultra-individualist the "affinity group" was important, a loosely structured assembly of like-minded individualists—a society of egoists (Horowitz 1964, 48; Jennings 1990, 25).

The second type of anarchism was anarcho-syndicalism, which we have discussed above. This form of anarchism put a focal emphasis on the *trade union* (or syndicate): it therefore considered, like the Marxists, the industrial proletariat to be the primary agent of social transformation, and it advocated various forms of direct action, of which the "general strike" was the most important.

The third type of anarchism was the kind of anarcho-pacifism that was associated with Leo Tolstoy (1828–1910), which led, around the turn of the century, to the formation of many Tolstoyan *communities*. Such communities sought to be entirely separate from any forms of involvement with capitalism or state power.

Finally, there was the anarchist communist tendency, which was espoused by many of the leading anarchists at the end of the nineteenth century—Reclus, Malatesta, Cafeiro, Goldman, Berkman. Kropotkin was not a collectivist anarchist, as Horowitz suggests (1964, 37) but the leading theorist and exponent of anarchist communism, and this tendency was not some "poor and despised relation" within the anarchist tradition, as Alain

Pengam also misleadingly suggests (1987, 60), but rather the dominant current between the years 1880 and 1920. Although not opposed to trade unions or the workers' control of industry, anarchist communism was more integrative and placed a primary emphasis on local and agrarian communes and on cooperative associations. Social revolution was conceived as involving local insurrections—in ways similar to that of the French Revolution—and the expropriation of land and property by the peasants and working people.

Kropotkin was always critical of the individualist anarchist tendency, both its advocacy of private property and its egoism—in fact, he tended to see both Stirner and Nietzsche as expressing a form of extreme bourgeois individualism. But Kropotkin was also critical of Tolstoyan experimental communities, divorced as these were from the wider society.

Given his background and his early involvement with Russian populism, it is hardly surprising that Kropotkin placed an important emphasis on the viability of the local community and the peasant commune. The local community or municipality and various forms of agrarian communes were a key feature of Kropotkin's vision of a future society. But he never envisaged the postrevolutionary society as consisting of purely autonomous agrarian communes, but rather one where autonomous agrarian communes or village communities were linked in a federal system with independent town and cities. In his study *Fields, Factories and Workshops* (1899), he describes a hypothetical agrarian-industrial village community consisting of around two hundred families. With a thousand acres of land under common tenancy with four hundred acres devoted to livestock, three hundred forty acres to cereal production, and around twenty acres to intensive market gardening, Kropotkin estimated that this would leave some one hundred forty acres for workshops, public gardens, and leisure activities. With every person involved to some degree in the production of food, there would be ample time, he felt, for other pursuits—artistic, scientific, or simply leisure. With decentralized industry, the combining of agriculture and manufacture, and a federal regional economy linking towns and cities with these village communities, Kropotkin did not envisage that these communities would be in any way isolated from the wider society (FFW, 237–43; Hardy 1979, 169).

Kropotkin was thus very skeptical of those anarchists who attempted to form experimental or autonomous colonies based on communistic principles. He recognized only too well that communism or close-knit communities could be oppressive and detrimental to human well-being. What he envisaged was a form of social life that would enhance "communal individuality." It was not simply a question of human nature, which was complex and contradictory, but of instituting the kind of society that would enable people to develop to the full their own sense of individuality and to achieve individual well-being. For Kropotkin this could only be achieved within a social context: "the only means of rendering men less rapacious and egoistic, less ambitious and less slavish at the same time, is to eliminate those conditions which favour the growth of egotism and rapacity, of slavishness and ambition" (AY, 83). For Kropotkin, this meant replacing competitive bourgeois society and all forms of coercive authority with a system of free communism. But he doubted whether this could ever be achieved through separate communist communities or colonies. He had visited several of these small communal experiments such as the Mennonite communities in Canada and the Clousden Hill Co-operative colony near Newcastle, England, and Kropotkin was clearly well read regarding the many religious communities and utopian socialist experiments that had been established during the nineteenth century. These include the short-lived New Harmony community associated with the socialist Robert Owen (to which the individualist anarchist Josiah Warren [1798–1874] belonged); the Oneida community established by John Humphrey Noyes (1811–1886) in 1848; and the various later communities associated with the Christian anarchist Leo Tolstoy, such as the Whiteway colony in Gloucestershire and the Purleigh colony near Chelmsford in Essex. Kropotkin, in fact, was a close friend of Vladimir Tchertkov, who was Tolstoy's foremost disciple (on early utopian communities, see Holloway 1951; Hardy 1979).

The Clousden Hill Free Communist and Cooperative colony on the outskirts of Newcastle was in fact established by a group of Newcastle communists in order to test experimentally the ideas of Kropotkin, as expounded in *The Conquest of Bread*, and to demonstrate the superiority of "free communism" over the competitive production of capitalism. The colony consisted only of a few families, who farmed twenty acres of inferior land on Clousden Hill. It only survived a few years (1894–1902), breaking up due to disagreements within the group (Hardy 1979, 181–83; Todd 1986).

Kropotkin's reservations regarding small communal experiments, and with utopian communes in general, were clearly expressed in his article "Communism and Anarchy" (*Freedom*, July/August 1901). Kropotkin begins the article by outlining the essence of communism, namely, the abolition of the wage system and individual property and the emancipation of the individual and social life from all forms of coercive authority. He notes that hundreds of communist communities were founded during the nineteenth century, and partial communism has come to be accepted by bourgeois society in many instances, such as in the municipal provision of gas, electricity, water, and public housing. Kropotkin reiterated the need to eradicate all forms of the wage system, even Robert Owen's system of "labour notes" within communist communities. But the failure of such communities and colonies had less to do with issues of labor, Kropotkin felt, than with practical difficulties and with restrictions they often placed on individual liberty. Such reflections, Kropotkin suggested, were not theoretical but based on the knowledge of actual life in communist communities that he had acquired from personal experiences and conversations and from wide reading. Kropotkin outlined many of the problems of such communities.

Nearly all these communities were founded by an almost religious wave of enthusiasm, and people were asked to become "pioneers of humanity." People had to "submit to the dictates of a punctilious morality, to become quite regenerated by communist life, to give all their time, hours of work and of leisure, to the community, to live entirely for the community" (1997, 8). This meant living under monastic or barrack room conditions and to demand of humans what they could not possibly give, for humans are neither angels nor slaves.

Such communities were also modeled on that of the patriarchal family and the desire expressed of managing it as one "great family": "They lived all in the same house and were thus forced to continuously meet the same 'brethren and sisters.' It is already difficult often for two real brothers to live together in the same house, and family life is not always harmonious; so it was a fundamental error to impose on all the 'great family' instead of trying, on the contrary, to guarantee as much freedom and home life for each individual" (1997, 9).

Besides, such a small community cannot last long, as the "brethren and sisters," forced to meet continuously, end by detesting each other. And if two people become rivals, or simply do not like each other, then inevitably they bring about the dissolution of the community. A prolonged life of such communities, Kropotkin concludes, "would be a strange thing, especially since all communities up to now have isolated themselves."

Thus, as it is a foregone conclusion that such communities are short-lived—without they come under the influence of a single person and lose their own individuality—then it is essential that there "ought to exist at least a dozen or more federated communities in order that those, for one reason or other, wish to leave the community, may enter another community, being replaced by new comers from other places" (1997, 9). In any case, Kropotkin suggests, communism should not be conceived in monastic fashion but rather as "the life of independent families united together by the desire of obtaining material and moral well-being by combining their efforts" (1997, 16). Kropotkin noted how many communities "fall into the hands of one individual," and in fact many communist communities, like that of the Oneida "Perfectionists," under the leadership of Father Noyes, were less a socialist utopia than a theocracy.

Kropotkin thus suggested that "all communities founded up till now isolated themselves from society; but struggle, a life of struggle, is far more urgently needed by an active man than a well-supplied table. This desire to see the world, to mix with its currents, to fight its battles is the imperative call of the younger generation" (1997, 9). In order to succeed, the communist experiment could not be an isolated venture or "refuge" but a part of a wider regional movement, and Kropotkin was persuaded that under present conditions a communist colony could only be viable if near a large city and engaged in intensive gardening.

Finally, recognizing that women, and the domestic work they undertake, are a constituent part of the working class, Kropotkin emphasized the importance of gender equality and the need to reduce household work. In most communist communities, this point was neglected. "The woman and the girl remained in the new society as they were in the old one—the slaves of the community. Arrangements to reduce as much as possible the incredible amount of work which our women uselessly spend in the rearing of children, as well as in household work, are, in my opinion, as essential to the success of a community as the proper arrangement of the fields, the greenhouses or agricultural machinery. Even more" (1997, 17).

Although Kropotkin's writings lack a gender perspective, and he seems to have held conventional views on marriage and family life, he nevertheless was committed, as an anarchist communist, to the abolition of the exploitation of women and sought their liberation from the burden of domestic work. In *The Conquest of Bread*, in discussing the "phalansteries" (agricultural communes) of the followers of Fourier, he not only critiqued their isolation from the wider society, but the gender inequality that they never questioned:

Servant or wife, man always reckons on woman to do the housework.
    But woman, too, at last claims her share in the emancipation of humanity. She no longer wants to be the burden of the house. . . .
    Why has woman's work never been of any account? Because those

who want to emancipate mankind have not included women in their dream of emancipation, and consider it beneath their superior masculine dignity to think of those kitchen arrangements. . . .

Liberty, equality, solidarity would not be a revolution if it maintained slavery at home. (CB, 141–44)

The communist colonies, Kropotkin argued, tended not to emancipate women, and in his advice to members of the Clousden Hill free communist colony, who had asked Kropotkin to be their treasurer (he declined), he emphasized the importance of reducing housework and upholding the equality of men and women (Todd 1986, 19–20).

Kropotkin thus concluded that communist colonies tended to fail because of their religious character and the fact that they were modeled on the "patriarchal family," that they were imbued with an authoritarian spirit, and that they were isolated from the wider society (1997, 14). Kropotkin therefore was by no means a supporter of isolated communal experiments, though he tried not to discourage the Newcastle communists in their efforts to form a "co-operative colony." He had a much broader vision of a regional federation of agro-industrial communes, linked organically with towns and cities, a federal system that allowed both social diversity and the maximum freedom and independence of individuals. In a later decade, Sam Dolgoff was to make similar criticisms of the Sunrise Farm community in Michigan, with its emphasis on "homogeneity" and the repudiation of the class struggle by many of its associates (1986, 66–67).

Liberal scholars still tend to misrepresent Kropotkin as having a vision of a society consisting only of peasant villages with medieval technology, or of advocating small communal experiments—nothing is further from the truth. Purchase ruefully remarks that it is a pity "that those who founded "hippy communes" in the 1960s (nearly all of which failed rather quickly) did not read Kropotkin more carefully" (1997, preface).

In his last years, isolated from his anarchist friends and increasingly hostile to the Bolshevik Party and its "dictatorship," Kropotkin nonetheless attempted to retain a buoyant spirit. When Emma Goldman visited him in 1920, he talked vividly to her of the need to combine anarcho-syndicalism with cooperatives in order to save the revolution from the fatal blunders and fearful suffering that Russia was then experiencing under the Bolsheviks (Goldman 1931, 2:863–64).

BIBLIOGRAPHY

F or important bibliographic references to Kropotkin's works, see M. Miller 1976, 313–30, and Cahm 1989, 350–65.

Kropotkin's Works in English

Books

1885. *Words of a Rebel*. Introd. G. Woodcock and Élisée Reclus. Repr. Montreal: Black Rose, 1992.

1887. *In Russian and French Prisons*. London: Ward and Downey.

1892. *The Conquest of Bread*. Introd. P. Avrich and Élisée Reclus. Repr. London: Penguin, 1972.

1899. *Fields, Factories and Workshops*. Repr. London: Nelson, 1919.

1899. *Memoirs of a Revolutionist*. Introd. G. Brandes. Repr. New York: Grove Press, 1968.

1901. *Modern Science and Anarchism*. London: Freedom Press, 1912.

1902. *Mutual Aid: A Factor of Evolution*. London: Heinemann.

1905. *Russian Literature: Ideals and Realities*. Introd. G. Woodcock. Repr. Montreal: Black Rose, 1991.

1909. *The Terror in Russia*. London: Methuen.

1909. *The Great French Revolution 1789–1793*. Trans. N. F. Dryhurst. Repr. Montreal: Black Rose, 1989.

1924. *Ethics: Origin and Development*. Ed. N. Lebedev. Dorchester: Prism Press.

1927. *Kropotkin's Revolutionary Pamphlet*. Ed. R. N. Baldwin. Repr. New York: Dover, 1970.

1942. *Kropotkin: Selections from His Writings*. Ed. H. Read. London: Freedom Press.

1970. *Selected Writings on Anarchism and Revolution*. Ed. and introd. M. A. Miller. Cambridge, Mass.: M.I.T. Press.

1975. *The Essential Kropotkin*. Ed. E. Capouya and K. Tomkins. New York: Liveright.

1987. *The State: Its Historic Role*. Trans. Vernon Richards. London: Freedom Press.

1988. *Act for Yourselves*. Ed. N. Walter and H. Becker. London: Freedom Press.

1993. *Fugitive Writings*. Ed. and introd. G. Woodcock. Montreal: Black Rose.

1993. *Anarchism and Anarchist Communism*. Ed. N. Walter. London: Freedom Press.

1995. *Evolution and Environment*. Ed. and introd. G. Woodcock. Montreal: Black Rose.

1995. *The Conquest of Bread and Other Writings*. Ed. M. S. Shatz. Cambridge: Cambridge University Press.

1997. *Small Communal Experiments and Why They Fail*. Ed. G. Purchase. Petersham, NSW: Jura Books.

Main Pamphlets and Articles

"Act for Yourselves." *Freedom* (January 1887).

"Advice to Those about to Emigrate." *Freedom* (March 1893).

"The Agrarian Question." *Le Révolté* (September 1880).

"Agriculture." *La Révolté* (December 1890).

"An Appeal to the Young." *Le Révolté* (August 1880) (pamphlet, Freedom Press, 1899).

"Anarchism." *Encyclopedia Britannica,* 11th ed., 1910.

Anarchism: Its Philosophy and Ideal. Freedom Press, 1897.

"Anarchist Communism: Its Basis and Principles." *The Nineteenth Century* (February–August 1887).

"The Anarchist Idea." *Report, Jura Federation*, 1879. In D. Guerin, 1998, 231–35.

"The Anarchist Ideal from the Viewpoint of its Practical Realization." *Le Révolté* (November 1879); *Freedom* (February 1967).

Anarchist Morality. Freedom Press, 1892.

"Anarchists in the French Revolution." *Freedom* (December 1903–January 1904).

"Anarchy in Socialist Revolution." *Le Révolté* (March–May 1886).

"Anti-Militarism: Was it Properly Understood?" *Freedom* (November 1914).

"Are We Good Enough?" *Freedom* (June 1888).

"Bakunin." *Freedom* (June–July 1905).

"Before the Storm." *Freedom* (December 1888).

"The Breakdown of Our Industrial System." *The Nineteenth Century* (April–June 1888).

"British Workers and the War." *Freedom* (March–April 1900).

"Caesarism." *Freedom* (April–June 1899).

"The Causes of So-Called Industrial Idleness." *Craftsman* (March 1908).

"The Collectivist Wage-System." *La Revolté* (August–September 1888).

"The Coming Reign of Plenty." *The Nineteenth Century* (June 1888).

"The Coming Revival of Socialism." *Freedom* (August 1903–March 1904).

"The Coming Revolution." *Freedom* (October 1886).

"The Commune." *Le Révolté* (May 1880).

"The Commune of Paris." *Le Révolté* (March 1880–1882) (pamphlet, Freedom Press, 1891).

"Communism and Anarchy." *Freedom* (July–August 1901).

"Communism and the Wage-System." *Freedom* (August–September 1888).

"Communist Anarchism." *Freedom* (March–April 1888).

"The Constitutional Agitation in Russia." *The Nineteenth Century and After* (January 1905).

"Conversations with Lenin 1919." In SW, 325–32.

"Co-Operation: A Reply to Herbert Spencer." *Freedom* (December–January 1896–97).

"The Czar's Manifesto." *Freedom* (April 1903).

"The Development of Trade Unionism." *Freedom* (March 1898).

"Direct Action of Environment and Evolution." *The Nineteenth Century and After* 85 (1919): 70–89.

"The Direct Action of Environment on Plants." *The Nineteenth Century and After* (July 1910).

"Domestic Slavery." *Freedom* (July 1891).

"Élisée Reclus." *Freedom* (August 1905).

"The End Set Before Us." *Freedom* (June 1887).

"The English Elections." *Freedom* (April 1910).

"Enough of Illusions." *Freedom* (August 1907).

"The Ethical Need of the Present Day." *The Nineteenth Century and After* (August 1904).

"Exile in Siberia." *The Nineteenth Century* (March 1884).

"Expropriation." *Le Révolté* (November–December 1882) (pamphlet, Freedom Press, 1895).

"A Few Thoughts about the Essence of Anarchism." *Freedom* (January 1914).

"Finland: A Rising Nationality." *The Nineteenth Century* (March 1885).

"The First Work of the Revolution." *Freedom* (August 1887).

"The Fortress Prison of St. Petersburg." *The Nineteenth Century* (June 1883).

"The Geneva Tragedy." *Freedom* (October 1898).

"Glimpses into the Labour Movement in This Country 1886–1907." *Freedom* (October 1907).

"The Great French Revolution and Its Lessons." *The Nineteenth Century* (June 1889).

"Herbert Spencer." *Freedom* (February–September 1904).

"The Industrial Village of the Future." *The Nineteenth Century* (October 1888).

"Inheritance of Acquired Characters: Theoretical Difficulties." *The Nineteenth Century and After* (March 1912).

"Inherited Variation in Plants/Animals." *The Nineteenth Century and After* (October 1914, 1915).

"In Memory of William Morris." *Freedom* (November 1896).

"Kropotkin's Farewell Letter." *Freedom* (July 1917).

"Law and Authority." *Le Révolté* (May–August 1882) (pamphlet, Freedom Press, 1892).

"Letter to George Brandes." *L'Humanite* (October 1919). In Guerin 1998, 278–80.

"A Letter to Francisco Ferrer." *Mother Earth* (August 1908).

"Letters to Lenin 1920." In SW, 335–39.

"Letter to Max Nettlau (on Individualism) 1902." In SW, 293–307.

"Letter to Workers of Western Europe 1919." In Shatz, ed., 1995, 249–53.

"Local Action." *Freedom* (May 1887).

"Massacre of Russian Workers at Lena Goldmine." *Freedom* (June 1912).

"The Modern State." *Freedom* (November 1913–September 1914).

"Modern Wars and Capitalism." *Freedom* (May–August 1913).

"The Morality of Nature." *The Nineteenth Century and After* (March 1905).

"Municipal Socialism." *Freedom* (December 1902).

"Must We Occupy Ourselves with an Examination of the Ideal of a Future System." Unpublished MS. November 1873. In SW, 47–116.

"Mutual Aid among Animals." *The Nineteenth Century* (September–November 1890).

"Mutual Aid among Ourselves." *The Nineteenth Century* (January–June 1896).

"Mutual Aid among Savages." *The Nineteenth Century* (April–December 1891).

"Mutual Aid among the Barbarians." *The Nineteenth Century* (January 1892).

"Mutual Aid in the Medieval City." *The Nineteenth Century* (August–September 1894).

"The Necessity of Communism." *Freedom* (September 1887).

"One War Over—When the Next." *Freedom* (June 1902).

"On the Teaching of Physiogeography." *Geography Journal*, 2 (1893): 350–59.

"Order." *Le Révolté* (October 1881).

"Organized Vengeance Called Justice." *Freedom* (October 1901).

"Outcast Russia." *The Nineteenth Century* (December 1883).

"Parliamentary Rule." *Freedom* (February 1887).

"Past and Future." *Freedom* (April 1889).

"The Permanence of Society after the Revolution." *Freedom* (October 1890).

"Peter Kropotkin's Speech to the Moscow National Conference 1917." In A. J. Sack, *The Birth of Russian Democracy*. New York: Russian Information Bureau, 1918.

"The Place of Anarchism in Socialist Evolution." *The Anarchist* (July 1887).

"Politics and Socialism." *Freedom* (February–May 1903). In Walter 1971, 34–43.

"Practical Questions." *Freedom* (July 1887).

"The Present Condition in Russia." *The Nineteenth Century* (September 1895).

"The Present Crisis in Russia." *The North American Review* (May 1901).

"Prisons and their Moral Influence on Prisoners." *Le Révolté* (August 1886).

"Proposed Communist Settlement: A New Colony for Tyneside or Wearside." *Newcastle Daily Chronicle* (February 1895).

"Recent Science." *The Nineteenth Century* (August 1892).

"The Reformed School." *Freedom* (June 1908).

"Representative Government." *Le Révolté* (March 1880).

"The Response of Animals to their Environment." *The Nineteenth Century and After* (November–December 1910).

"Revolution and Famine." *Freedom* (December 1887).

"The Revolution in Russia." *The Nineteenth Century and After* (December 1905).

"Revolutionary Government." *Le Révolté* (October 1882) (pamphlet, Freedom Press, 1892).

"Revolutionary Minorities." *Le Révolté* (November 1881).

"Revolutionary Studies." *The Commonweal* 7 (1891): 294–300.

"Rocks Ahead." *Freedom* (March 1888).

"Russian Prisons." *The Nineteenth Century* (January 1883).

"The Russian Revolutionary Party." *Newcastle Chronicle* (October 1881).

"Russian Schools and the Holy Synod." *The North American Review* (April 1902).

"The Situation Today." *Le Révolté* (March 1879).

"Some of the Resources of Canada." *The Nineteenth Century* (March 1898).

"The Spirit of Revolt." *Le Révolté* (May–July 1881).

"The State: Its Historic Role." *Les Temps Nouveaux* (December 1896) (pamphlet, Freedom Press, 1903).

"Syndicalism and Anarchism." *Freedom* (July–August 1912).

"Theory and Practice." *Le Révolté* (March 1882).

"The Theory of Evolution and Mutual Aid." *The Nineteenth Century and After* (January 1910).

"The Wage System." *Le Révolté* (September 1888) (pamphlet, Freedom Press, 1889).

"War." *The Anarchist* (1882).

"What Geography Ought to Be." *The Nineteenth Century* (December 1885).

"What Must We Do?" *Freedom* (December 1886).

"What Revolution Means." *Freedom* (November 1886).

Books and Articles on Kropotkin

Alexander, S. N.d. "Peter Kropotkin on Man and Society." In *Meeting Kropotkin*. Bombay: Libertarian Book House, pp. 17–22.

Avrich, P. 1988. *Anarchist Portraits*. Princeton, N.J.: Princeton University Press, pp. 53–106.

Barnard, A. 1993. "Primitive Communism and Mutual Aid: Kropotkin Visits the Bushmen." In C. M. Hann, ed., *Socialism*. London: Routledge, pp. 27–42.

Becker, H. 1989. "Kropotkin as Historian of the French Revolution." *The Raven* 7: 225–31.

Berkman, A. 1922. "Reminiscences of Kropotkin." *Freedom* (March).

Berneri, C. 1942. *Peter Kropotkin: His Federalist Ideas*. London: Freedom Press.

Bogardus, E. S. 1940. "Kropotkin and Co-operative Social Thought." In *The Development of Social Thought*. New York: Longmans, pp. 381–91.

Boyesen, B. 1927. "Peter Kropotkin." *The Road to Freedom* (February).

Breitbart, M. 1975. "Impressions of a Anarchist Landscape." *Antipode* 7, no. 2: 44–49.

———. 1981. "Peter Kropotkin: The Anarchist Geographer." In D. R. Stoddart, ed., *Geography, Ideology and Social Concern*. Oxford: Blackwell, pp. 134–53.

Cahm, T. C. 1978. "Kropotkin and the Anarchist Movement." In E. Cahm and V. Fisera, eds., *Socialism and Nationalism*. Vol. 2. Nottingham: Spokesman, pp. 50–68.

———. 1984. "Kropotkin and Law." In T. Holterman and H. Van Marseveen, eds., *Law and Anarchism*. Montreal: Black Rose, pp. 106–21.

———. 1989. *Kropotkin and the Rise of Revolutionary Anarchism 1872–1886*. Cambridge: Cambridge University Press.

Carr, E. H. 1980. "Kropotkin: Review of G. Woodcock and I. Anakumovic, *The Anarchist Prince*." In *From Napoleon to Stalin and Other Essays*. London: Macmillan, pp. 123–29.

Cleaver, H. 1994. "Kropotkin, Self-Valorization and the Crisis of Marxism." *Anarchist Studies* 2, no. 2: 119–35.

Cloete, S. 1947. "Kropotkin." In *Third Way*. New York: Houghton Mifflin, pp. 303–37.

Cook, I. 1991. "Kropotkin: Prince of Geographers." *Anarchism and Geography* 3, no. 2: 22–26.

DeHaan, R. 1965. "Kropotkin, Marx and Dewey." *Anarchy* 55: 271–86.

De Norcia, V. 1980. "Comparing Calvin and Kropotkin." In R. Fitzgerald, ed., *Comparing Political Thinkers*. Sydney: Pergamon Press, pp. 203–23.

DeVinne, T. W. 1899. "Diary of a Literary Wanderer: William Morris and Prince Peter Kropotkin." *New Century Review* 5: 261–68.

Dugger, V. M. 1984. "Veblen and Kropotkin on Human Evolution." *Journal of Economic Issues* 18, no. 4: 971–85.

Durant, W. 1923. "An Afternoon with Kropotkin." In J. Ishill, ed., *Peter Kropotkin*. Berkeley Heights, N.J.: Free Spirits Press, pp. 89–90.

Eltzbacher, P. 1908. "Peter Kropotkin." In *Anarchism: Exponents of the Anarchist Philosophy*. Trans. S. Bymington. New York: Chips Bookshop, pp. 94–121.

Ely, R. T. 1898. "Prince Kropotkin." *Atlantic Monthly* 82: 338–46.

Evers, W. M. 1978. "Kropotkin's Ethics and the Public Good." *Journal of Libertarian Studies* 2.

Galois, B. 1976. "Ideology and the Idea of Nature: The Case of Peter Kropotkin." *Antipode* 8: 1–16. In R. Peet, ed., 1977, *Radical Geography*. Chicago: Maarovfa Press, pp. 66–93.

Gibson, P. 1991. "Kropotkin, Mutual Aid and Selfish Genes." *The Raven* 4, no. 4: 364–70.

Goodman, P. 1968. "Kropotkin at This Moment." *Dissent* 15, no. 6.

Gould, S. J. 1992. "Kropotkin Was No Crackpot." In *Bully for Brontosaurus*. London: Penguin Books, pp. 325–39.

Harris, F. 1927. "Prince Peter Kropotkin." In *Latest Contemporary Portraits*. New York: Macauley, pp. 120–38.

Hecht, D. 1952. "Kropotkin and America." *Bulletin of the American Association of Teachers of Slavic and Eastern European Languages* 10: 5–8.

Horner, G. M. 1978. "Kropotkin and the City: The Socialist Ideal in Urbanism." *Antipode* 10, no. 3: 33–45.

Huston, S. 1997. "Kropotkin and Spatial Social Theory." *Anarchist Studies* 5: 109–30.

Ishill, J. 1923. *Peter Kropotkin: The Rebel, Thinker and Humanitarian.* Berkeley Heights, N.J.: Free Spirit Press.

Jourdain, M. 1920. "Peter Kropotkin." *Open Court* 34: 383–93.

Kandor, V. 1979. "Peter Kropotkin and Count Erwin Batthany." *Studia Slavica* 24, nos. 1–2: 121–35.

Kelly, A. 1976. "Lessons of Kropotkin." *New York Review of Books* 23, no. 17 (October 28).

Keltie, J. S. 1921. "Obituary: Peter Alexeivich Kropotkin." *Geographical Journal* 57: 316–19.

Kennan, G. 1912. "The Escape of Peter Kropotkin." *Century Magazine* 62: 246.

Kinna, R. 1996. "Revolution and Evolution. Review: *Words of a Rebel* and *Ethics*." *Anarchist Studies* 4, no. 1: 80–83.

Kropotkin, A. 1943. "My Father, Prince Kropotkin." *American Mercury* 57: 671–74.

Lancaster, L. W. 1959. "Peter A. Kropotkin." In *Masters of Political Thought*. Vol. 3. London: Harrap, pp. 244–64.

Lewis, P. M. 1908. "Kropotkin's Mutual Aid." In *Evolution, Social and Organic*. New York: Charles H. Kerr, pp. 97–114.

Libertarian Book House. N.d. *Meet Kropotkin*. Bombay: Libertarian Book House.

Macauley, D. 1998. "Evolution and Revolution: The Ecological Anarchism of Kropotkin and Bookchin." In A. Light, ed., *Social Ecology After Bookchin*. New York: Guilford Press, pp. 298–342.

Malatesta, E. 1965. "Peter Kropotkin: Recollections and Criticisms of an Old Friend." In V. Richards, ed., *Malatesta: His Life and Ideas*. London: Freedom Press, pp. 257–68.

Marshall, P. 1992. "Peter Kropotkin: The Revolutionary Evolutionist." In *Demanding the Impossible*. London: HarperCollins, pp. 309–38.

Mavor, J. 1923. "Prince Peter A. Kropotkin 1886–1921." In *My Windows on the Street of the World*. Vol. 2. London: Dent, pp. 91–106.

McCullough, C. 1984. "The Problems of Fellowship in Communitarian Theory: William Morris and Peter Kropotkin." *Political Studies* 32, no. 3 (September).

M. H. 1992. "Review of P. Kropotkin." In *Russian and French Prisons*, *Freedom* 53, no. 23: 6.

———. 1994. "Review of P. Kropotkin, *Fugitive Writings*." *Freedom* 53, no. 23: 6.

Miller, D. 1983. "The Neglected Kropotkin." *Government and Opposition* 18, no. 3: 319–38.

Miller, M. A. 1976. *Kropotkin*. Chicago: University of Chicago Press.

Morris, B. 1986. "Kropotkin: The Most Influential of Anarchists." *Green Anarchist* 13:14.

Nettlau, M. 1921. "Peter Kropotkin at Work." *Freedom* (February). In *The Raven* 5, no. 4 (1992): 379–88.

Nisbet, R. 1973. "Kropotkin and Mutual Aid." In *The Social Philosophers*. London: Heinemann, pp. 376–85.

Novomirsky, J. 1921. "P. A. Kropotkin: A Theorist of Anarchism." *Communist International* 16, no. 7: 90–97.

Osofsky, S. 1979. *Peter Kropotkin*. Boston: Twayne Publishers.

Padovan, D. 1999. "Social Morals and Ethics of Nature: From Peter Kropotkin to Murray Bookchin." *Democracy and Nature* 5, no. 3: 485–500.

Peet, R. 1975. "For Kropotkin." *Antipode* 7: 42–43.

Pipes, R. 1968. "Petr Kropotkin." *International Encyclopedia of Social Sciences* 8: 463–65.

Plaskacz, B. 1970. "M. Gonzalez Prada and Peter Kropotkin: Two Aristocrats Turned Anarchists." *Canadian, Slavic and Eastern European Studies* 15: 83–92.

Punzo, V. 1976. "The Modern State and the Search for Community: The Anarchist Critique of Kropotkin." *International Philosophical Quarterly* 16.

Purchase, G. 1996. *Evolution and Revolution: An Introduction to the Life and Thought of P. Kropotkin.* Petersham, NSW: Jura Books.

Read, H. 1992. "Peter Kropotkin 1842–1921." *The Raven* 5, no. 4: 311–22.

Reichert, W. O. 1967. "Proudhon and Kropotkin on Church and State." *Journal of Church and State* 9, no. 1.

Reszler, A. 1972. "Peter Kropotkin and His Vision of Anarchist Aesthetics." *Diogenes* 78.

Robinson, V. 1908. *Comrade Kropotkin.* New York: Altruians Press.

Rocker, R. 1942. "Kropotkin and the Jewish Labour Movement in England." In *Centennial Expression on P. Kropotkin 1842–1942.* Los Angeles: Rocker Publications Committee.

Rolland, R. N.d. "Kropotkin and Tolstoy." In *Meet Kropotkin.* Bombay: Libertarian Book House, p. 14.

Sargent, I. 1902. "Prince Kropotkin's Economic Arguments." *Craftsman* 2: 157–71.

Schnittkind, H. T., and D. A. Schnittkind. 1954. "Kropotkin's Progress from Riches to Rages." In *Living Adventures in Philosophy.* New York: Hanover House, pp. 278–90.

Sekelj, L. 1992. "Bakunin's and Kropotkin's Theories of Revolution in Comparative Perspectives." *The Raven* 5: 358–78.

Shpayer-Makov, H. 1987. "The Reception of Peter Kropotkin in Britain 1886–1917." *Albion* 19, no. 3: 373–90.

Shub, D. 1953. "Kropotkin and Lenin." *Russian Review* 12, no. 4: 227–53.

Slatter, J. 1981. "Kropotkin's Papers." *Geographical Magazine* 53: 917–21.

———. 1993. "The Peter Kropotkin Commemorative Conference." *Freedom* 54, no. 3: 6–7.

Smith, M. 1989. "Kropotkin and Technical Education: An Anarchist Voice." In D. Goodway, ed., *For Anarchism.* London: Routledge, pp. 217–34.

Stoddart, D. R. 1976. "Kropotkin, Reclus and 'Relevant' Geography." *Bulletin of Environmental Education* 58: 21.

Strypyansky, M. 1921. "Peter Kropotkin." *Soviet Russia* 4: 201–205.

Swan, T. 1907. "Modern Influences: Prince Kropotkin." *Millgate Monthly* 2: 21.

Tcherkesoff, F. 1931–32. "Peter Kropotkin as I Knew Him." *Freedom*, December 1931–March 1932.

Todes, D. P. 1993. "The Scientific Background of Kropotkin's Mutual Aid." *The Raven* 6, no. 4: 357–76.

Walter, N. 1971. *Fighting the Revolution.* Vol. 2. London: Freedom Press.

Ward, C. 1991. "Economics—Peter Kropotkin (1842–1921)." In *Influences: Voices of Creative Dissent.* Bideford: Green Books, pp. 65–78.

———. "Kropotkin's Federalism." *The Raven* 5, no. 4: 327–41.

Wells, D. 1988. "Evolution and a Free Society: Spencer, Kropotkin and Popper." *Australasian Journal of Politics* 23, no. 1: 48–55.

Wenzer, K. 1993. "In Remembrance of P. A. Kropotkin." *Social Anarchism* 18: 41–43.

Williams, L. H. 1921. "Prince Kropotkin's Philosophy in the Light of Today." *Hibbert Journal* 19: 441–48.

Woodcock, G. 1992. "Peter Kropotkin: A Libertarian Life." In *Anarchism and Anarchists.* Kingston, Ont.: Quarry Press, pp. 188–92.

Woodcock, G., and I. Avakumovic. 1950. *The Anarchist Prince.* New York: Schocken Books.

GENERAL REFERENCES

Amster, R. 1998. "Anarchism as Moral Theory." *Anarchist Studies* 6, no. 2: 97–112.

Ansell-Pearson, K. 1994. *An Introduction to Nietzsche as Political Thinker.* Cambridge: Cambridge University Press.

Assiter, A. 1993. "Essentially Sex: A New Look." In A. Assiter and A. Carol, eds., *Bad Girls and Dirty Pictures.* London: Pluto Press, pp. 88–104.

Aulard, A. 1910. *Political History of the French Revolution.* 4 vols. Trans. B. Miall. London: n.p.

Avrich, P. 1980. *The Modern School Movement.* Princeton, N.J.: Princeton University Press.

———. 1995. *Anarchist Voices.* Princeton, N.J.: Princeton University Press.

Axelrod, R. 1984. *The Evolution of Cooperation.* New York: Basic Books.

Bailie, W. 1971. *Josiah Warren: The First American Anarchist.* New York: H. C. Roseman. (Orig. pub. 1966.)

Barclay, H. 1982. *People without Government.* London: Kahn and Averill.

Barkow, J. H., L. Cosmides, and J. Tooby, eds. 1992. *The Adapted Mind.* Oxford: Oxford University Press.

Bauman, Z. 1999. *In Search of Politics.* Cambridge: Polity Press.

Beecher, J., and R. Bienvenu. 1972. *The Utopian Vision of Charles Fourier.* London: Cape.

Berman, M. 1992. "Why Modernism Still Matters." In S. Lash and J. Friedman, eds., *Modernity and Identity.* Oxford: Blackwell, pp. 33–58.

Berry, W. 1977. *The Unsettling of America.* San Francisco: Sierra Club Books.

Best, G., ed. 1988. *The Permanent Revolution: The French Revolution and Its Legacy 1789–1989.* London: Fontana.

Bey, H. 1985. *T.A.Z.: The Temporary Autonomous Zone, Ontological Anarchy, Poetic Terrorism.* New York: Autonomedia.

Biehl, J. 1998. *The Politics of Social Ecology.* Montreal: Black Rose Books.

Black, B. N.d. *The Abolition of Work and Other Essays.* Port Townsend, Wash.: Loompanics Unlimited.

———. 1994. *Beneath the Underground.* Portland, Ore.: Feral House.

———. 1997. *Anarchy after Leftism.* Colombia, Mo.: C.A.L. Press.

Blackburn, R., ed. 1991. *After the Fall.* London: Verso.

Blissett, L., and S. Home. 1999. *Green Apocalypse.* London: Unpopular Books.

Bohm, D. 1980. *Wholeness and the Implicate Order.* London: Routledge.

Bookchin, M. 1976. "Radical Agriculture." In R. Merrill, ed., *Radical Agriculture.* New York: Harper and Row, pp. 3–13.

———. 1991. *The Ecology of Freedom.* Repr. Palo Alto, Calif.: Cheshire Books.

———. 1995. *Social Anarchism or Life Style Anarchism.* Edinburgh: A. K. Press.

———. 1995. *Re-Enchanting Humanity.* London: Cassell.

———. 1996. "Anarchism: Past and Present." In H. J. Ehrlich, ed., *Re-Inventing Anarchy, Again.* Edinburgh: A. K. Press, pp. 19–30.

———. 1996/1998. *The Third Revolution: Popular Movements in the Revolutionary Era.* Vols. 1 and 2. London: Cassell.

———. 1999. *Anarchism, Marxism and the Future of the Left.* Edinburgh: A. K. Press.

Bourdieu, P. 1998. *Acts of Resistance.* Cambridge: Polity Press.

Bowler, P. J. 1992. *A Fontana History of the Environmental Sciences.* London: HarperCollins.

Brinton, M. 1970. *The Bolsheviks and Workers' Control.* London: Solidarity.

Brown, G. 1977. *Sabotage: A Study of Industrial Conflict.* Nottingham: Spokesman Books.

Brown, J. E. 1992. *Animals of the Soul*. Rockport, Mass.: Element.

Brown, L. S. 1993. *The Politics of Individualism*. Montreal: Black Rose Books.

Bufe, C. 1998. *Listen Anarchism!* Tucson: See Sharp Press.

Bunge, M. 1994. "Counter Enlightenment in Contemporary Social Studies." In P. Kurtz and T. J. Madigan, eds., *Challenges to the Enlightenment*. Amherst, N.Y.: Prometheus Books, pp. 25–42.

Bunin, I. 1951. *Memories and Portraits*. Garden City, N.Y.: Doubleday.

Burchell, G., C. Gordon, and P. Miller, eds. 1991. *The Foucault Effect: Studies in Governmentality*. London: Harvester Wheatsheaf.

Buss, D. M. 1999. *Evolutionary Psychology*. Boston: Allyn and Bacon.

Callinicos, A. 1982. *Is There a Future for Marxism?* London: Macmillan.

———. 1999. *Social Theory: A Historical Introduction*. Cambridge: Polity Press.

Cannadine, D. 1990. *The Decline and Fall of the British Aristocracy*. New Haven: Yale University Press.

Capra, F. 1997. *The Web of Life*. London: HarperCollins.

Carneiro, R. 1981. "The Chiefdom: Precursor of the State." In G. D. Jones and R. R. Kautz, eds., *The Transition to Statehood in the New World*. Cambridge: Cambridge University Press.

Castoriadis, C. 1975. *The Imaginary Institution of Society*. Cambridge: Polity Press.

———. 1991. *Philosophy, Politics, Autonomy*. Oxford: Oxford University Press.

Chamberlain, L. 1996. *Nietzsche in Turin*. London: Quartet Books.

Chomsky, N. 1988. *The Culture of Terrorism*. London: Pluto Press.

Christie, S., and A. Meltzer. 1970. *The Floodgates of Anarchy*. London: Sphere Books.

Clark, J. P. 1976. *Max Stirner's Egoism*. London: Freedom Press.

———. 1977. *The Philosophical Anarchism of William Godwin*. Princeton, N.J.: Princeton University Press.

———. 1984. *The Anarchist Moment*. Montreal: Black Rose Books.

Clastres, P. 1977. *Society against the State*. Oxford: Blackwell.

Cleaver, H. 1996. "Socialism." In W. Sachs, ed., *The Development Dictionary*. London: Zed Books.

Clunies-Ross, T., and N. Hildyard. 1992. *The Politics of Industrial Agriculture*. London: Earthscan.

Cobban, A. 1964. *The Social Interpretation of the French Revolution*. Cambridge: Cambridge University Press.

Cole, G. D. H. 1954. *A History of Socialist Thought*. Vol. 2, *Marxism and Anarchism 1850–1890*. London: Macmillan.

Comninel, G. C. 1987. *Rethinking the French Revolution*. London: Verso.

Coughlin, M. E., C. H. Hamilton, and M. Sullivan, eds. 1986. *Benjamin R. Tucker and the Champions of Liberty*. St. Paul, Minn.: Coughlin.

Crowder, G. 1992. "Freedom and Order in Nineteenth Century Anarchism." *The Raven* 5, no. 4: 342–57.

Darwin, C. 1909. *The Descent of Man*. London: J. Murray. (Orig. pub. 1871.)

———. 1951. *The Origin of Species*. 6th ed. Oxford: Oxford University Press. (Orig. pub. 1859.)

———. 1987. *Charles Darwin's Notebooks 1836–1844*. Ed. P. H. Barrett et al. Ithaca, N.Y.: Cornell University Press.

Dean, M. 1999. *Governmentality: Power and Rule in Modern Society*. London: Sage.

de Certeau, M. 1984. *The Practice of Everyday Life*. Berkeley: University of California Press.

Dennett, D. C. 1995. *Darwin's Dangerous Idea: Evolution and the Meanings of Life*. London: Penguin.

Dews, P. 1987. *Logics of Disintegration*. London: Verso.

Dolgoff, S., ed. 1973. *Bakunin on Anarchy*. New York: Knopf.

———. 1986. *Fragments: A Memoir*. London: Refract Publications.

Draper, H. 1990. *Karl Marx's Theory of Revolution*. Vol. 4, *Critique of Other Socialisms*. New York: Monthly Review Press.

Dreyfus, H. L., and P. Rabinow. 1982. *Michel Foucault: Beyond Structuralism and Hermeneutics*. Brighton: Harvester Press.

Dubofsky, M. 1969. *We Shall Be All: A History of the Industrial Workers of the World*. Chicago: Quadrangle Books.

Edwards, S. 1971. *The Paris Commune 1871*. London: Eyre and Spottiswoode.

———, ed. 1973. *The Communards of Paris, 1871*. London: Thames and Hudson.

Ehrlich, H. J., ed. 1996. *Reinventing Anarchy, Again*. Edinburgh: A. K. Press.

Ekins, P. 1992. *A New World Order*. London: Routledge.

Engels, F. 1940. *Dialectics of Nature*. Trans. C. Dutt. London: Lawrence and Wishart.

———. 1969. *Anti-Duhring*. Moscow: Progress Publishers. (Orig. pub. 1894.)

Fabbri, L. 1987. *Bourgeois Influences on Anarchism*. Trans. C. Bufe. San Francisco: Acrata Press. (Orig. pub. 1917.)

Fishman, W. J. 1975. *East End Jewish Radicals 1875–1914*. London: Duckworth.

Ford, E. C., and W. Z. Foster. 1990. *Syndicalism*. Chicago: C. H. Kerr. (Orig. pub. 1912.)

Foucault, M. 1970. *The Order of Things*. London: Tavistock.

———. 1977. *Discipline and Punish*. London: Allen Lane.

———. 1977. *Language, Counter-Memory, Practice*. Ed. D. F. Bouchard. Ithaca, N.Y.: Cornell University Press.

———. 1977. "Preface." In G. Deleuze and F. Guattari, *Anti-Oedipus*. New York: Viking Press.

———. 1979. *The History of Sexuality*. Vol. 1, *Introduction*. London: Penguin Books.

———. 1980. *Power/Knowledge* Ed. C. Gordon. New York: Pantheon Books.

———. 1988. *Politics, Philosophy, Culture*. Ed. L. Kritzman. New York: Routledge.

———. 1999. *Religion and Culture*. Ed. J. R. Carrette. Manchester: Manchester University Press.

Fromm, E. 1949. *Man for Himself*. London: Routledge and Kegan Paul.

Gay, P. 1969. *The Enlightenment: An Interpretation*. 2 vols. New York: Vintage.

Geddes, P. 1968. *Cities in Evolution*. London: E. Benn. (Orig. pub. 1915.)

Gellner, E. 1983. *Nations and Nationalism*. Oxford: Blackwell.

Giddens, A. 1994. *Beyond Left and Right*. Cambridge: Polity Press.

———. 1998. *The Third Way*. Cambridge: Polity Press.

Gills, B. K. 1993. "Hegemonic Transitions in the World System." In A. G. Frank and B. K. Gills, eds., *The World System*. London: Routledge, pp. 115–40.

Goaman, K. 1999. "Endless Deferral, Simulation, Surveillance, Social Postmodernism, Postsocialism." *Anarchist Studies* 7, no. 1: 69–74.

Godwin, W. 1971. *Enquiry Concerning Political Justice*. Ed. K. C. Carter Oxford: Clarendon Press. (Orig. pub. 1793.)

Goffman, E. 1961. *Asylums*. Harmondsworth: Penguin Books.

Goldman, E. 1931. *Living my Life*. 2 vols. New York: Knopf.

———. 1969. *Anarchism and Other Essays*. Introd. R. Drinnon. New York: Dover Publications. (Orig. pub. 1910.)

———. 1972. *Red Emma Speaks*. Ed. A. K. Shulman. London: Wildwood Press.

Goodall, J. 1986. *The Chimpanzees of Gombe*. Cambridge, Mass: Harvard University Press.

Goodman, P. 1948. "Fifty Years Have Passed." *Resistance* (New York) (March-April).

Goodwin, B. 1994. *How the Leopard Changed Its Spots*. London: Orion Books.

Gould, S. J. 1980. *Ever Since Darwin*. London: Penguin Books.

———. 1983. *The Panda's Thumb*. London: Penguin Books.

———. 1984. *Hen's Teeth and Horses' Toes*. London: Penguin Books.

Graur, M. 1997. *The Anarchist "Rabbi": The Life and Teachings of Rudolf Rocker*. New York: St. Martin's Press.

Gray, J. 1986. *Liberalism*. Milton Keynes, U.K.: Open University Press.

———. 1998. *False Dawn: The Delusions of Global Capitalism*. London: Granta Books.

Greenlaw, R. W., ed. 1975. *The Social Origins of the French Revolution*. Lexington, Mass.: D. C. Heath.

Guerin, D. 1977. *Class Struggle in the First Republic*. London: Pluto Press.

———. 1998. *No Gods, No Masters: An Anthology of Anarchism*. 2 vols. Edinburgh: A. K. Press.

Gulliver, P. H. 1963. *Social Control in an African Society*. London: Routledge and Kegan Paul.

Habermas, J. 1979. *Communication and the Evolution of Society*. Boston: Beacon Press.

———. 1987. *The Philosophical Discourse of Modernity*. Cambridge, U.K.: Polity Press.

Hampson, N. 1969. *The First European Revolution 1776–1815*. London: Thames and Hudson.

Hardy, D. 1979. *Alternative Communities in Nineteenth-Century England*. London: Longman.

Hare, R. M. 1952. *The Language of Morals*. Oxford: Clarendon Press.

Heller, C. 1999. *Ecology of Everyday Life*. Montreal: Black Rose Books.

Hewetson, J. 1965. "Mutual Aid and Social Evolution." *Anarchy* 55: 257–70.

Heywood, A. 1994. *Political Ideas and Concepts*. London: Macmillan.

Hobbes, T. 1651. *Leviathan*. 1962 ed. Ed. M. Oakeshott. London: Collier-Macmillan.

Hobsbawm, E. J. 1973. *Revolutionaries*. London: Quartet Books.

Hoffman, R. L. 1972. *Revolutionary Justice*. Urbana: University of Illinois Press.

Hofstadter, R. 1944. *Social Darwinism in American Thought*. Boston: Beacon Press.

Holloway, M. 1951. *Heavens on Earth*. New York: Library Publications.

Holton, R. J. 1998. *Globalization and the Nation-State*. London: Macmillan.

Horne, A. 1965. *The Fall of Paris*. London: Macmillan.

Horowitz, I. L. 1964. *The Anarchists*. New York: Dell.

Howard, E. 1965. *Garden Cities of Tomorrow*. Cambridge, Mass.: M.I.T. Press. (Orig. pub. 1898.)

Howell, S., and R. Willis, eds. 1989. *Societies at Peace*. London: Routledge.

Hoy, D. C., ed. 1986. *Foucault: A Critical Reader*. Oxford: Blackwell.

Huxley, T. H. 1888. "The Struggle for Existence in Human Society." *The Nineteenth Century* 23: 161–80.

Ingold, T. 1980. *Hunters, Pastoralists and Ranchers*. Cambridge: Cambridge University Press .

James, J., ed. 1998. *The Angela Y. Davis Reader*. Oxford: Blackwell.

Jaures, J. 1922–24. *Histoire Socialiste de la Revolution Française*. Ed. A. Mathiez. 8 vols. Paris: n.p.

Jellinek, F. 1937. *The Paris Commune of 1871*. London: Gollancz.

Jennings, J. 1990. *Syndicalism in France*. Oxford: Macmillan.

Joll, J. 1964. *The Anarchists*. London: Methuen.

Kamenka, E. 1988. "Revolutionary Ideology." In G. Best, ed., *The Permanent Revolution*. London: Fontana, pp. 75–100.

Kauffman, S. 1995. *At Home in the Universe*. London: Penguin Books.

Kedward, R. 1971. *The Anarchists*. London: MacDonald.

Keulartz, J. 1998. *The Struggle for Nature*. London: Routledge.

Landa, I. 1999. "Nietzsche, The Chinese Worker's Friend." *New Left Review* 236: 3–23.

Lefebvre, G. 1962. *The French Revolution: From Its Origins to 1793*. Trans. E. M. Evanson. London: Routledge and Kegan Paul.

———. 1967. *The Coming of the French Revolution*. Trans. R. Palmer. Princeton: Princeton University Press. (Orig. pub. 1939.)

Lehning, A. 1973. *Michael Bakunin: Selected Writings*. London: Cape.

Lewellen, T. C. 1992. *Political Anthropology: An Introduction*. Westport, Conn.: Bergin and Garvey.

Lewontin, R. C. 1991. *The Doctrine of D.N.A.* London: Penguin Books.

Lotringer, S., ed. 1989. *Foucault Live*. New York: Semiotext.

Lukes, S., ed. 1986. *Power*. Oxford, U.K.: Blackwell.

Lunn, E. 1973. *Prophet of Community: The Romantic Socialism of Gustav Landauer*. Berkeley: University of California Press.

MacIntyre, A. 1967. *A Short History of Ethics*. London: Routledge and Kegan Paul.

————. 1985. *After Virtue*. London: Duckworth.

MacPherson, C. B. 1962. *The Political Theory of Possessive Individualism*. London: Oxford University Press.

Magee, B. 1997. *Confessions of a Philosopher*. London: Weidenfeld and Nicolson.

Malik, K. 1996. *The Meaning of Race*. London: Macmillan.

Mann, M. 1993. *The Sources of Social Power*. Vol. 2, *The Rise of Classes and Nation-States 1760–1914*. Cambridge: Cambridge University Press.

Mannin, E. 1964. *Rebel's Ride*. London: Hutchinson.

Margulis, L. 1998. *The Symbiotic Planet*. London: Weidenfeld and Nicolson.

Margulis, L., and D. Sagan. 1986. *Microcosmos*. Berkeley: University of California Press.

————. 1997. *Slanted Truths*. New York: Springer-Verlag.

Marsh, M. S. 1981. *Anarchist Women 1870–1920*. Philadelphia: Temple University Press.

Marshall, P. 1984. *William Godwin*. New Haven: Yale University Press.

Martin, J. J. 1970. *Men against the State*. Colorado Springs: Ralph Myles.

Marx, K., and F. Engels. 1968. *Selected Works*. London: Lawrence and Wishart.

Marx, K., F. Engels, and V. Lenin. 1972. *Anarchism and Anarcho-Syndicalism*. Moscow: Progress Publishers.

Maximoff, G. P., ed. 1953. *The Political Philosophy of Bakunin*. New York: Free Press.

————. 1985. *Program of Anarcho-Syndicalism*. Sydney: Monty Miller Press. (Orig. pub. 1927.)

May, T. 1994. *The Political Philosophy of Poststructuralist Anarchism*. University Park: Pennsylvania State University Press.

Mayr, E. 1976. *Evolution and the Diversity of Life*. Cambridge, Mass.: Harvard University Press.

————. 1982. *The Growth of Biological Thought*. Cambridge, Mass.: Harvard University Press.

————. 1988. *Toward a New Philosophy of Biology*. Cambridge, Mass.: Harvard University Press.

————. 1991. *One Long Argument*. London: Penguin Books.

————. 1997. *This Is Biology*. Cambridge, Mass.: Harvard University Press.

McGarr, P. 1994. "Engels and Natural Science." In J. Rees, ed., "The Revolutionary Ideas of Frederick Engels." *Intern. Socialism* 65: 143–76.

McGarr, P., A. Callinicos, and J. Rees. 1989. "Marxism and the Great French Revolution." *Intern. Socialism* 43.

McKercher, W. R. 1989. *Freedom and Authority*. Montreal: Black Rose Books.

McNay, L. 1994. *Foucault: A Critical Introduction*. Cambridge, U.K.: Polity Press.

Merquior, J. G. 1985. *Foucault*. London: Fontana/Collins.

Midgley, M. 1985. *Evolution as a Religion*. London: Methuen.

Mies, M., and V. Bennholdt-Thomsen. 1999. *The Subsistence Perspective*. London: Zed Books.

Mill, J. S. 1972. *Utilitarianism, On Liberty, Representative Government*. Ed. H. B. Acton. London: Dent.

Miller, D. 1984. *Anarchism*. London: Bent.

Miller, D. L. 1989. *Lewis Mumford—A Life*. Pittsburgh: University of Pittsburgh Press.

Moore, B. 1966. *Social Origins of Dictatorship and Democracy*. Harmondsworth: Penguin Books.

Moore, J. 1997. "Anarchism and Poststructuralism, Review of Todd May (1994)." *Anarchist Studies* 5, no. 2: 157–61.

Morland, D. 1997. *Demanding the Impossible?* London: Cassell.

Morris, B. 1981. "Changing Views of Nature." *The Ecologist* 2: 130–37.

———. 1982. *Forest Traders*. London: Athlone Press.

———. 1987. *Anthropological Studies of Religion*. Cambridge: Cambridge University Press.

———. 1991. *Western Conceptions of the Individual*. Oxford: Berg.

———. 1993. *Bakunin: The Philosophy of Freedom*. Montreal: Black Rose.

———. 1993. "Tom Paine—The Radical Liberal." *Social Anarchism* 21: 65–81.

———. 1996. *Ecology and Anarchism*. Malvern Wells: Images.

———. 1998. "Anthropology and Anarchism." *Anarchy* 16, no. 1: 35–41.

Morton, A. L., ed. 1973. *Political Writings of William Morris*. London: Lawrence and Wishart.

Moss, C. 1988. *Elephant Memories*. London: Fontana/Collins.

Mumford, L. 1956. *The Human Prospect*. London: Secker and Warburg.

———. 1961. *The City in History*. Harmondsworth: Penguin Books.

———. 1970. *The Pentagon of Power*. London: Secker and Warburg.

Nelson, R. 1983. *Make Prayers to the Raven*. Chicago: Chicago University Press.

Nettlau, M. 1996. *A Short History of Anarchism*. Ed. H. Becker. London: Freedom Press.

Nietzsche, F. 1968. *The Twilight of the Idols and the Anti-Christ*. Introd. and trans. R. J. Hollingdale. Harmondsworth: Penguin Books.

———. 1972. *Beyond Good and Evil*. Trans. R. J. Hollingdale. Harmondsworth: Penguin Books.

Nomad, M. 1932. *Rebels and Renegades*. New York: Macmillan.

———. 1961. *Apostles of Revolution*. New York: Collier Books. (Orig. pub. 1939.)

———. 1963. *Political Heretics*. Ann Arbor: University of Michigan Press.

———. 1964. *Dreamers, Dynamiters and Demagogues*. New York: Waldon Press.

Noske, B. 1997. *Beyond Boundaries: Humans and Animals*. Montreal: Black Rose Books.

Nozick, R. 1974. *Anarchy, State and Utopia*. New York: Basic Books.

Ollman, B. 1993. *Dialectical Investigations*. London: Routledge.

Ostergaard, G. 1997. *The Tradition of Worker's Control*. Introd. B. Bamford. London: Freedom Press.

Outhwaite, W. 1994. *Habermas: A Critical Introduction*. Cambridge, U.K.: Polity Press.

Paglia, C. 1992. *Sex, Art and American Culture*. London: Penguin Books.

Pataud, E., and E. Pouget, 1990, *How We Shall Bring About the Revolution*. Introd. G. Brown. London: Pluto Press.

Paterson, R. W. K. 1971. *The Nihilistic Egoist: Max Stirner*. Oxford: Oxford University Press.

Peacott, J. 1991. *Individualism Reconsidered*. Boston: B. A. D. Press.

Pengam, A. 1987. "Anarcho-Communism." In M. Rubel and J. Crump, eds., *Non-Market Socialism in the Nineteenth and Twentieth Centuries*. London: Macmillan, pp. 60–82.

Pepper, D. 1996. *Modern Environmentalism*. London: Routledge.

Perlman, F. 1983. *Against His-Story, Against Leviathan*. Detroit: Black and Red.

Plant, S. 1996. "The Situationist International." In S. Home, ed., *What Is Situationism? A Reader*. Edinburgh: A. K. Press, pp. 153–72.

Porter, R. 1990. *The Enlightenment*. London: Macmillan.

Powell, D. 1985. *Tom Paine: The Greatest Exile*. London: Croom Helm.

Proudhon, P. J. 1898. *What Is Property?* Trans. B. R. Tucker. London: W. Reeves. (Orig. pub. 1840.)

Purchase, G. 1993. "Social Ecology, Anarchism and Trade Unionism." In

M. Bookchin et al., *Deep Ecology and Anarchism*. London: Freedom Press, pp. 23–35.

Pyziur, E. 1955. *The Doctrine of Anarchism of Michael Bakunin*. Milwaukee: Regnery.

Quail, J. 1978. *The Slow Burning Fuse*. London: Paladin Books.

Rachels, J. 1990. *Created from Animals*. Oxford: Oxford University Press.

Rand, A. 1964. *The Virtue of Selfishness*. New York: Signet Books.

Raphael, D. D. 1994. *Moral Philosophy*. Oxford: Oxford University Press.

Rawls, J. 1971. *A Theory of Justice*. Cambridge: Harvard University Press.

Reclus, E. 1995. *Man and Nature*. Petersham, NSW: Jura Books.

Rees, J. 1998. *The Algebra of Revolution*. London: Routledge.

Richards, V., ed. 1965. *Errico Malatesta: His Life and Ideas*. London: Freedom Press.

Ritter, A. 1969. *The Political Thought of Pierre-Joseph Proudhon*. Princeton, N.J.: Princeton University Press.

———. 1980. *Anarchism: A Theoretical Analysis*. Cambridge: Cambridge University Press.

Roberts, S. 1979. *Order and Dispute*. Harmondsworth: Penguin Books.

Rocker, R. 1989. *Anarcho-Syndicalism*. Introd. N. Walter. London: Pluto Press. (Orig. pub. 1938.)

Rorty, R. 1999. *Philosophy and Social Hope*. London: Penguin Books.

Rose, N. 1999. *Powers of Freedom*. Cambridge: Cambridge University Press.

Rose, R. B. 1983. *The Making of the Sans-Culottes*. Manchester, U.K.: Manchester University Press.

Rose, S. 1997. *Lifelines*. London: Penguin Books.

Rudé, G. E. 1975. "The Outbreak of the French Revolution." In R. W. Greenlaw, ed., *The Social Origins of the French Revolution*. Lexington: Heath, pp. 3–16.

———. 1988. *The French Revolution*. London: Weidenfield and Nicolson.

Russell, B. 1966. *Roads to Freedom*. London: Allen and Unwin. (Orig. pub. 1918.)

Said, E. W. 1986. "Foucault and the Imagination of Power." In D. C. Hoy, ed., *Foucault: A Critical Reader*. Oxford: Blackwell, pp. 149–55.

Sale, K. 1985. *Dwellers in the Land*. San Francisco: Sierra Club Books.

Samuels, A. 1993. *The Political Psyche*. London: Routledge.

Sapp, J. 1994. *Evolution by Association: A History of Symbiosis*. Oxford: Oxford University Press.

Sayers, S. 1996. "Engels and Materialism." In C. J. Arthur, ed., *Engels Today*. London: Macmillan.

Schumacher, E. F. 1974. *Small Is Beautiful*. London: Sphere Books.

Schuster, E. M. 1932. *Native American Anarchism*. Northampton, Mass: Smith College Studies in History.

Scott, J. C. 1998. *Seeing Like a State*. New Haven: Yale University Press.

Serge, V. 1963. *Memoirs of a Revolutionary*. Trans. P. Sedgwick. Oxford: Oxford University Press.

Seton, E. T. 1898. *Wild Animals I Have Known*. New York: Scribners.

Shiva, V. 1998. *Biopiracy*. Totnes: Green Books.

Shoard, M. 1997. *This Land Is Our Land*. London: Gaia Books. (Orig. pub. 1987.)

Simons, J. 1995. *Foucault and the Political*. London: Routledge.

Singer, P. 1993. *How Are We to Live*. Oxford: Oxford University Press.

———. *The Darwinian Left*. London: Weidenfeld and Nicolson.

Skirda, A. 2002. *Facing the Enemy*. Edinburgh: A. K. Press.

Skocpol, T. 1979. *State and Social Revolution*. Cambridge: Cambridge University Press.

Smith, A. D. 1991. *National Identity*. London: Penguin Books.

Smith, M. P. 1983. *The Libertarians and Education*. London: Allen and Unwin.

Soboul, A. 1972. *The Sans-Culottes*. Trans. R. I. Hall. Princeton, N.J.: Princeton University Press.

———. 1974. *The French Revolution 1787–89*. Trans. A. Forrest. London: Unwin Hyman.

Sokal, A., and J. Bricmont. 1999. *Intellectual Impostures*. London: Profile Books.

Spencer, H. 1885. *The Principles of Sociology*. 2 vols. London: Williams and Norgate.

Stafford, D. 1971. *From Anarchism to Reformism*. London: Weidenfeld and Nicolson.

Steiner, G. 1988. Aspects of Counter-Revolution. In G. Best, ed., *The Permanent Revolution*. London: Fontana, pp. 129–54.

Stepniak. 1883. *Underground Russia*. London: Smith, Elder.

Stirner, M. 1973. *The Ego and His Own*. Trans. S. T. Byington. New York: Dover Publications (Orig. pub. 1845.)

Taylor, M. 1982. *Community, Anarchy and Liberty*. Cambridge: Cambridge University Press.

Todd, N. 1986. *Roses and Revolutionists*. London: People's Publications.

Todes, D. P. 1988. "Darwin's Malthusian Metaphor and Russian Evolutionary Thought 1859–1917." *Isis* 78: 537–51.

———. 1989. *Darwin without Malthus.* New York: Oxford University Press.

Tolstoy, L. 1990. *Government Is Violence.* Ed. D. Stephens. London: Phoenix Press.

Trotsky, L. 1980. *The History of the Russian Revolution.* Trans. M. Eastman. New York: Pathfinder Press. (Orig. pub. 1932.)

Tuchman, B. 1966. *The Proud Tower.* London: Macmillan.

Tucker, B. R. 1893. *Instead of a Book.* Repr. New York: Apno Press.

Van der Linden, M., and W. Thorpe, eds. 1990. *Revolutionary Syndicalism.* Aldershot: Scholar Press.

Warnock, M. 1998. *The Intelligent Person's Guide to Ethics.* London: Duckworth.

Watson, D. 1999. *Against the Megamachine.* Brooklyn, N.Y.: Autonomedia.

Watson, G. 1998. *The Lost Literature of Socialism.* Cambridge, U.K.: Lutherworth Press.

Whitehead, A. N. 1920. *The Concept of Nature.* Cambridge: Cambridge University Press.

———. 1929. *Process and Reality.* London: Macmillan.

Wieck, D. 1979. "The Negativity of Anarchism." In H. Ehrlich, ed., *Reinventing Anarchy.* London: Routledge and Kegan Paul, pp. 138–55.

Williams, G. A. 1968. *Artisans and Sans-Culottes.* London: Arnold.

Wilson, E. O. 1998. *Consilience: The Unity of Knowledge.* London: Abacus.

Wood, E. M. 1986. *The Retreat from Class.* London: Verso.

Wood, E. M., and J. B. Foster, eds. 1997. *In Defence of History.* New York: Monthly Review Press.

Woodcock, G. 1963. *Anarchism.* Harmondsworth: Penguin Books.

———, ed. 1977. *The Anarchist Reader.* London: Fontana/Collins.

Wright, R. 1994. *The Moral Animal.* New York: Pantheon Books.

Zerzan, J. 1988. *Elements of Refusal.* Seattle: Left Bank Books.

———. 1994. *Future Primitive and Other Essays.* Brooklyn, N.Y.: Autonomedia.

INDEX

Ward, Colin, 91, 96–98
Warnock, Mary, 168
Warren, Josiah, 100, 248–49
weapons of mass destruction, 16
Weismann, August, 142–43
welfare state, 73
Whitehead, Alfred North, 119, 126,
    139, 145, 173
Wieck, David, 214

Williams, Gwyn, 234
Wilson, Edward, 146, 150, 170
Woodcock, George, 222
work, 82, 103–106
worker's state, 52

Zapatistas, 242
Zerzan, John, 180, 183, 188, 217

ABOUT PM PRESS

PM Press was founded at the end of 2007 by a small
collection of folks with decades of publishing, media, and
organizing experience. PM Press co-conspirators have
published and distributed hundreds of books, pamphlets,
CDs, and DVDs. Members of PM have founded enduring
book fairs, spearheaded victorious tenant organizing campaigns, and worked
closely with bookstores, academic conferences, and even rock bands to deliver
political and challenging ideas to all walks of life. We're old enough to know what
we're doing and young enough to know what's at stake.

We seek to create radical and stimulating fiction and non-fiction books, pamphlets,
T-shirts, visual and audio materials to entertain, educate, and inspire you. We
aim to distribute these through every available channel with every available
technology—whether that means you are seeing anarchist classics at our bookfair
stalls, reading our latest vegan cookbook at the café, downloading geeky fiction
e-books, or digging new music and timely videos from our website.

PM Press is always on the lookout for talented and skilled volunteers, artists,
activists, and writers to work with. If you have a great idea for a project or can
contribute in some way, please get in touch.

PM Press
PO Box 23912
Oakland, CA 94623
www.pmpress.org

FRIENDS OF PM PRESS

These are indisputably momentous times—the financial system is melting down globally and the Empire is stumbling. Now more than ever there is a vital need for radical ideas.

In the years since its founding—and on a mere shoestring—PM Press has risen to the formidable challenge of publishing and distributing knowledge and entertainment for the struggles ahead. With over 300 releases to date, we have published an impressive and stimulating array of literature, art, music, politics, and culture. Using every available medium, we've succeeded in connecting those hungry for ideas and information to those putting them into practice.

Friends of PM allows you to directly help impact, amplify, and revitalize the discourse and actions of radical writers, filmmakers, and artists. It provides us with a stable foundation from which we can build upon our early successes and provides a much-needed subsidy for the materials that can't necessarily pay their own way. You can help make that happen—and receive every new title automatically delivered to your door once a month—by joining as a Friend of PM Press. And, we'll throw in a free T-shirt when you sign up.

Here are your options:

- **$30 a month** Get all books and pamphlets plus 50% discount on all webstore purchases

- **$40 a month** Get all PM Press releases (including CDs and DVDs) plus 50% discount on all webstore purchases

- **$100 a month** Superstar—Everything plus PM merchandise, free downloads, and 50% discount on all webstore purchases

For those who can't afford $30 or more a month, we have **Sustainer Rates** at $15, $10 and $5. Sustainers get a free PM Press T-shirt and a 50% discount on all purchases from our website.

Your Visa or Mastercard will be billed once a month, until you tell us to stop. Or until our efforts succeed in bringing the revolution around. Or the financial meltdown of Capital makes plastic redundant. Whichever comes first.

Anthropology, Ecology, and Anarchism: A Brian Morris Reader

Introduction by Peter Marshall

ISBN: 978-1-60486-093-1
$24.95   288 pages

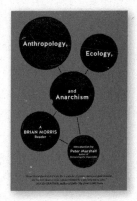

Over the course of a long career, Brian Morris has
created an impressive body of engaging and insightful
writings—from social anthropology and ethnography to
politics, history, and philosophy—that have made these subjects accessible to the
layperson without sacrificing analytical rigor. But until now, the essays collected
here, originally published in obscure journals and political magazines, have been
largely unavailable to the broad readership to which they are so naturally suited.
The opposite of arcane, specialized writing, Morris's work takes an interdisciplinary
approach that moves seamlessly among topics, offering up coherent and
practical connections between his various scholarly interests and his deeply held
commitment to anarchist politics and thought.

Approached in this way, anthropology and ecology are largely untapped veins
whose relevance for anarchism and other traditions of social thought have only
recently begun to be explored and debated. But there is a long history of anarchist
writers drawing upon works in those related fields. Morris's essays both explore
past connections and suggest ways that broad currents of anarchist thought will
have new and ever-emerging relevance for anthropology and many other ways of
understanding social relationships. His writings avoid the constraints of dogma and
reach across an impressive array of topics to give readers a lucid orientation within
these traditions and point to new ways to confront common challenges.

*"Brian Morris blazed a lot of trails. He is a scholar of genuine daring and great humanity,
and his work deserves to be read and debated for a very long time to come."*
—David Graeber, author of *Debt: The First 5,000 Years*

*"This is a marvelously original book bursting with new ideas. I have read it with
enormous interest and admiration. This collection of essays is an outstanding
contribution to anthropology, environmental thought, and anarchism."*
—Andrej Grubačić, professor and department chair in Anthropology and Social
Change, California Institute of Integral Studies

Anarchism, Anarchist Communism, and The State: Three Essays

Peter Kropotkin
with an Introduction by Brian Morris
and bibliographic notes by Iain McKay

ISBN: 978-1-62963-575-0
$14.95   160 pages

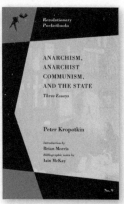

Amid the clashes, complexities, and political personalities of world politics in the late nineteenth and early twentieth centuries, Peter Kropotkin stands out. Born a prince in Tsarist Russia, sent to Siberia to learn his militaristic, aristocratic trade, he instead renounced his titles and took up the "beautiful idea" of anarchism. Across a continent he would become known as a passionate advocate of a world without borders, without kings and bosses.

From a Russian cell to France, to London and Brighton, he used his extraordinary mind to dissect the birth of State power and then present a different vision, one in which the human impulse to liberty can be found throughout history, undying even in times of defeat. In the three essays presented here, Kropotkin attempted to distill his many insights into brief but brilliant essays on the state, anarchism, and the ideology for which he became a founding name—anarchist communism.

With a detailed and rich introduction from Brian Morris, and accompanied by bibliographic notes from Iain McKay, this collection contextualises and contemporises three of Kropotkin's most influential essays.

"In this collection of essays, Kropotkin excels in his grasp of the state, its dynamics, and the social relations out of which it emerges, dovetailed with his radical vision for libertarian egalitarian social change. Including an informative foreword by Brian Morris on the great anarchist's colourful life, and Kropotkin's own extended analysis of the origins of anarchism, the book goes to the core of what makes Kropotkin's work so stimulating: he is peculiarly capable, through detailed historical accounts and discussions of his own times, of somehow speaking to our own contemporary dilemmas and challenges."
—Anthony Ince, coeditor of *Historical Geographies of Anarchism*

"This is one of the most excellent introductions to anarchism, putting paid to the usual objections to the system, synonymous as it has become, wrongly, with disorganisation and chaos."
—*Workers Solidarity*

Demanding the Impossible:
A History of Anarchism

Peter Marshall

ISBN: 978-1-60486-064-1
$28.95   840 pages

Navigating the broad 'river of anarchy', from Taoism to Situationism, from Ranters to Punk rockers, from individualists to communists, from anarcho-syndicalists to anarcha-feminists, *Demanding the Impossible* is an authoritative and lively study of a widely misunderstood subject. It explores the key anarchist concepts of society and the state, freedom and equality, authority and power and investigates the successes and failure of the anarchist movements throughout the world. While remaining sympathetic to anarchism, it presents a balanced and critical account. It covers not only the classic anarchist thinkers, such as Godwin, Proudhon, Bakunin, Kropotkin, Reclus and Emma Goldman, but also other libertarian figures, such as Nietzsche, Camus, Gandhi, Foucault and Chomsky. No other book on anarchism covers so much so incisively.

In this updated edition, a new epilogue examines the most recent developments, including 'post-anarchism' and 'anarcho-primitivism' as well as the anarchist contribution to the peace, green and 'Global Justice' movements.

Demanding the Impossible is essential reading for anyone wishing to understand what anarchists stand for and what they have achieved. It will also appeal to those who want to discover how anarchism offers an inspiring and original body of ideas and practices which is more relevant than ever in the twenty-first century.

"Demanding the Impossible *is the book I always recommend when asked—as I often am—for something on the history and ideas of anarchism.*"
—Noam Chomsky

"*Attractively written and fully referenced… bound to be the standard history.*"
—Colin Ward, *Times Educational Supplement*

"*Large, labyrinthine, tentative: for me these are all adjectives of praise when applied to works of history, and* Demanding the Impossible *meets all of them.*"
—George Woodcock, *Independent*

William Godwin: Philosopher, Novelist, Revolutionary

Peter Marshall
with a Foreword by John P. Clark

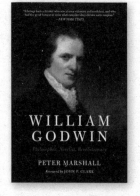

ISBN: 978-1-62963-386-2
$29.95   544 pages

William Godwin has long been known for his literary
connections as the husband of Mary Wollstonecraft, the
father of Mary Shelley, the friend of Coleridge, Lamb, and
Hazlitt, the mentor of the young Wordsworth, Southey,
and Shelley, and the opponent of Malthus. Godwin has been recently recognized,
however, as the most capable exponent of philosophical anarchism, an original
moral thinker, a pioneer in socialist economics and progressive education, and a
novelist of great skill.

His long life straddled two centuries. Not only did he live at the center of radical
and intellectual London during the French Revolution, he also commented on some
of the most significant changes in British history. Shaped by the Enlightenment, he
became a key figure in English Romanticism.

Basing his work on extensive published and unpublished materials, Peter Marshall
has written a comprehensive study of this flamboyant and fascinating figure.
Marshall places Godwin firmly in his social, political, and historical context; he
traces chronologically the origin and development of Godwin's ideas and themes;
and he offers a critical estimate of his works, recognizing the equal value of his
philosophy and literature and their mutual illumination.

The picture of Godwin that emerges is one of a complex man and a subtle and
revolutionary thinker, one whose influence was far greater than is usually assumed.
In the final analysis, Godwin stands forth not only as a rare example of a man who
excelled in both philosophy and literature but as one of the great humanists in the
Western tradition.

*"The most comprehensive and richly detailed work yet to appear on Godwin as thinker,
writer, and person."*
—John P. Clark, *The Tragedy of Common Sense*

*"An ambitious study that offers a thorough exploration of Godwin's life and complex
times."*
—*Library Journal*

*"Marshall steers his course . . . with unfailing sensitivity and skill. It is hard to see how the
task could have been better done."*
—Michael Foot, *The Observer*